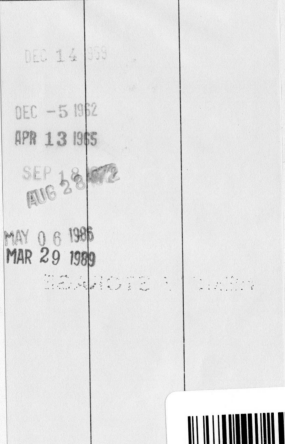

D1293097

THE LIFE AND WRITINGS
OF JEREMY TAYLOR

JEREMY TAYLOR

From the portrait in the possession of Gonville and Caius College, Cambridge.

THE
LIFE AND WRITINGS
OF JEREMY TAYLOR

by

C. J. STRANKS, M.A., M.Litt.

Canon of Blackburn, Examining Chaplain to the
Bishop of Blackburn, Warden of Whalley Abbey

(Published for the Church Historical Society)

LONDON

S · P · C · K

1952

First published in 1952
by S.P.C.K.
Northumberland Avenue, London, W.C.2

Printed in Great Britain by
The Camelot Press Ltd., London and Southampton

β
T243s
cap 2

CONTENTS

ILLUSTRATIONS

Engl. 1 Nov '52 Blackwell 12/6

NOTE: All references to Jeremy Taylor's Works in the body of this book are to *The Whole Works of The Right Rev. Jeremy Taylor, D.D., Lord Bishop of Down, Connor and Dromore*, edited by The Right Revd Reginald Heber, D.D., revised and corrected by The Revd Charles Page Eden, M.A., in ten volumes, London, 1847–52, an indispensable book for every student of Jeremy Taylor. The references in Appendix B are to *The Works of Jeremy Taylor*, 2 Vols. London 1862.

"This great prelate he had the good humour of a gentleman, the eloquence of an orator, the fancy of a poet, the acuteness of a school-man, the profoundness of a philosopher, the wisdom of a counsellor, the sagacity of a prophet, the reason of an angel, and the piety of a saint. He had devotion enough for a cloister, learning enough for a university, and wit enough for a college of virtuosi; and had his parts and endowments been parcelled out among his poor clergy that he had left behind him, it would perhaps have made one of the best dioceses in the world. . . . He is fixed in an orb of glory, and shines among his brethren-stars, that in their several ages gave light to the world, and turned many souls to righteousness; and we that are left behind, though we can never reach his perfections, must study to imitate his virtues, that we may come at last to sit at his feet in the mansions of glory; which God grant for his infinite mercies in Jesus Christ."

George Rust, A Funeral Sermon, preached at the obsequies of the Right Reverend Father in God, Jeremy Lord Bishop of Down, *Works*, Vol. i, p. cccxxvii.

PREFACE

IT is not often that a great divine is also a great man of letters, but when such a combination occurs as it does in Jeremy Taylor the interest is doubled. Students of pure literature have as much to do with research into his life and mind as theologians, and both are concerned with any additional details in relation to him which may be brought to light. A considerable amount of new material has been discovered since 1907, when Sir Edmund Gosse published his *Jeremy Taylor*. Some time ago, Canon Charles Smyth drew my attention to an article in the *Quarterly Review* for July 1871 in which an anonymous contributor referred to some letters of Jeremy Taylor "in the possession of Mr Murray", and not only referred to them, but printed one in its entirety and made short extracts of a line or two at a time from most of the others. Copies of these letters proved to be still in the library of Sir John Murray. Unfortunately, they are only copies and a note inside the cover states that "the originals were parted with to the Marquis of Bath some time in the eighties". These are no longer to be found at Longleat, where books and papers were disturbed when the house was used by the Government during two world wars, and are not always to be discovered again. The copies in Sir John Murray's library are written out in a neat, clear hand, on foolscap paper, and are strongly bound. The copying was obviously done with care, the spelling and punctuation and apparently the arrangement of the lines in the originals being strictly kept. Altogether there are twelve letters from Jeremy Taylor to Lord Conway, and one from Lord Conway to Jeremy Taylor. Their dates range from April 1658 to some time in 1666.

There is nothing in the papers themselves to show how they came into Mr. Murray's possession, but it is possible to make a likely guess. When the Conway family became extinct in 1683 their papers passed, with the estate, to Popham Seymour who joined the name of Conway to his own. Francis Seymour-Conway, a nephew of Sir Robert Walpole, was created Marquis of Hertford in 1793. Horace Walpole, who visited Ragley in August 1758, found that a careless steward had practically ruined the vast accumulation of papers which the Conways, who seem to have hoarded every scrap of writing addressed to them, had got together. Walpole salvaged as much as he could, and "brought away a chest near five feet long, three wide and two deep brim full".[1] From then on the papers were carefully preserved, and on the death of the third Marquis of Hertford in 1842 they passed into the possession of John Wilson Crocker. Thackeray, in *Vanity Fair*, drew a venomous picture of these two men and their relationship to each other, in his description of Lord Steyn and Mr Wenham. Disraeli was no kinder, when, in *Coningsby*, he used Croker as his model for Rigby. Croker wrote regularly for the *Quarterly Review* and was in close association with Mr Murray; obviously it was from him that the thirteen letters passed into Mr Murray's possession. The remainder of the Conway papers went to the British Museum and to the Public Record Office.

By the courtesy of Sir John Murray, the thirteen letters are used in this book for the first time in any biography of Jeremy Taylor. For convenience sake I have referred to them throughout as the Murray MSS. Their contents help to clarify the picture of Taylor in London just before he left for Ireland, and at a time when we have exceedingly little other information about him that can be relied upon. They tell us how it was that he came to go to Ireland and a little about his life there, both before, and after, he became a bishop. Through them all there are invaluable sidelights on Taylor's character, so impressionable, so apt to pour itself out in fervid speech, so lacking in wordly wisdom, as it was. Wherever I have used the letters I have modernized the spelling and punctuation. Throughout this book wherever there is a difference in the spelling of proper names—and the seventeenth century allowed a generous freedom in that respect—I have followed the usage of *The Dictionary of National Biography*.

Some other material is used in this book for the first time in any biography of Jeremy Taylor. Sir Edmund Gosse made some use of Adair's *True Narrative*, though he did not begin with it as early as he ought to have done, or borrow from it as extensively as he needed to do, if the bitter dispute between Taylor and the Ulster Presbyterians was to be properly elucidated. The State Papers offer some particularly valuable material. They throw new light on the circumstances of Taylor's death, which have always been obscure, the condition in which his family was left, and the scramble for his office which went on from the

[1] *Selected Letters of Horace Walpole* (Everyman), p. 123.

second that it was vacant, the details of which were all written
by his friend Major Rawdon within a few hours of the events
described. The late Dean Carmody in his *Lisburn Cathedral and
its Past Rectors*, and Marjorie Hope Nicholson in her fascinating
edition of the *Conway Letters*, printed this material but it is used
here for the first time in a biography of Taylor. The Irish portion
of his life is now better known than any other.

Two other little pieces of information add something to what
we know of his earlier years. A paper in the Tanner Collection
contains his signature to a written opinion of certain of the
Royal Chaplains, sent in answer to a question from the King
about the amount of toleration a Christian prince might allow
to differing religious opinions among his subjects. A letter from
Dr Hammond shows Taylor's influence at work among the London
clergy during the Commonwealth in a way which Hammond
considered would be harmful to the Prayer Book.

Further research is continually uncovering more and more
details of Taylor's work. Within the last few years the Revd
F. R. Bolton, who has been making an exhaustive study of the
Form of Consecration of Churches and Chapels in the Church
of Ireland, has decided that the Rite is almost certainly the work
of Jeremy Taylor. He hopes to publish his conclusions under
the title of *The Caroline Churchmanship of the Church of Ireland
with special reference to the Irish Form of Consecration of Churches
1666*.

It is some years now since I first began to study Jeremy
Taylor. I was then a missionary in Japan, and had with me one
or other of the ten volumes of Taylor's works on nearly all the
long journeys and frequent waits at wayside stations which a
missionary's life entails. Even now many pages bring back,
most vividly, the coloured crowds, the shouts of the food-sellers,
the smells, and all the clattering excitement of Japanese travel,
which were competing for attention when those passages were
first read. So many people have helped the work along since
then, that it is impossible to mention them all. The late Canon
Ollard saw it in its early stages and gave me most generous
encouragement. One instance of my indebtedness to Canon
Charles Smyth I have already mentioned, but he has been
unsparing with his interest and help. My wife has been a patient
auditor of all the enthusiasms and problems which this study
has produced in the mind of the writer, and a discerning critic
from the start. The late Dean Carmody of Down and Mr H. A.

Boyd of Ballycastle were among the many who answered letters and placed their special knowledge at my disposal.

No son of the English Church can read the Caroline Divines without pride in our inheritance, and yet a recent writer remarks, with some truth, that: "While a narrow local patriotism in theology would be disastrous, there is something strangely unreal in the prevalent neglect of the heritage of Anglicanism. Barthianism, Thomism, and even Counter-reformation thought possess a following in the English Church, and the study of the fathers of Anglicanism receives but a fraction of its rightful meed of attention."[1] In Taylor's case this may be partly due to the bulkiness of his work. Ten large volumes of close print, edited with all the wealth of scholarship which Heber and Eden lavished on their monumental edition, may well be frightening to those who do not know where to begin. For any who are hindered in this way, a book which tries to show the main outline of Taylor's thought, and to indicate where so much that is stimulating and delightful is found, may be of use.

[1] McAdoo, *The Structure of Caroline Moral Theology*, p. 1.

C. J. STRANKS.

WHALLEY ABBEY.
1952.

CHAPTER I

BACKGROUND

IN 1613, the year of Jeremy Taylor's birth, the seeds of the struggle which began in 1642 were already planted. James I had been King of England for ten years. During that time he had contrived to disappoint every important section of his subjects except the High Church party, and that solitary exception was able to stand him in no very good stead. It was obvious that unless the court and the people could be brought to a better understanding of each other the future was full of alarm.

The great dispute between Anglicanism and Puritanism was prominent in every institution in the land, and, from the nature of it, this was particularly so in the universities. In Oxford, where Laud was first President of a college and then Chancellor, Anglicanism was strong. Cambridge, which, from its position near the great trade routes, had early felt the influence of the Reformation, stayed predominantly Calvinistic in sympathy until near the end of the sixteenth century. Cartwright, Travers and Whitaker were all from that University and it was there that Sir Walter Mildmay founded Emmanuel College in 1584, to be a stronghold of Puritanism. Yet at that very time the challenge to it was growing stronger. Lancelot Andrewes who, in 1578, had lectured at Pembroke College, after some years of absence during which he held various posts in London, returned as Master in 1589. From 1596 he had the powerful support of Overall as Professor of Theology. Around them there grew up in Cambridge a vigorous school of High Church men who contributed a large number of outstanding figures to the Catholic Revival in the Church of England.[1] But although a few great teachers may form a party, and powerfully present a point of view, they do not necessarily decide the tone of the whole community in which they live, and so, in spite of them, Cambridge was still the most suitable place to which a Puritan could send his sons for their education. In 1613, when Jeremy Taylor was carried to the font in Holy Trinity Church, Cromwell was at Sidney Sussex College: St John, one of Hampden's counsel in the famous

[1] Besides Andrewes himself, Mountague, Wren, Cosin, Mountain all eventually became bishops.

ship-money trial, had his education at Queen's College. Milton
was at Christ's College, and Fairfax matriculated at St John's
College in 1626. Some of the strongest of those who thought and
acted for the Parliament in the Civil War had their training at
Cambridge.

It was a pleasant city then, as now. Harrison, describing it in
1577, wrote: "It standeth very well, saving that it is somewhat
near unto the fens, whereby the wholesomeness of the air is not
a little corrupted."[1] Provisions were cheap and plentiful. If the
fens tainted the air they compensated a little by supplying the
townsmen with wild-fowl and fish in abundance. The river
provided a convenient water-way by which coal and wood could
be brought from a distance to make good the local deficiency in
fuel. The fens were responsible for the fact that very little hay
could be grown in the neighbourhood, and that also had to be
borne by the Granta from villages on less marshy land. It was a
fresher if not a happier England into which the seventeenth-
century child was born. Local feeling was stronger, local self-
sufficiency was greater. Everything which a householder needed
could be made in his own home or his neighbour's, and made
to suit local and individual taste; rather than turned out by
mass production to appeal to that particular fancy in the public
which a strident advertising campaign has previously instilled.
Cambridge streets were as narrow and as filthy as those of other
towns, in an age when there was little to stop a man building as
he pleased and sanitation was no one's concern. But though
there was plenty of dirt, there was no drabness. The university
buildings were full of dignity and the ordinary ways and by-ways
of the town, with their multifarious signs, the timbered houses
overhanging and gabled, were at least more beautiful than our
modern streets.

It is a thankless task to guess where a genius receives his first
abiding impressions, but it may be more than a coincidence that
Jeremy Taylor was, in after life, fascinated by water in all its
states and that he was born near the fens. Water oozing out of
boggy soil, water dammed up, water in rivers, water winding in
slow streams, these were images which he used over and over
again in carefully worked passages—each one designed to point
a moral—and there is at least a likelihood that his memory was
recalling incidents observed in boyhood within a mile or two of
Cambridge.

[1] Harrison, *Elizabethan England* (ed. Furnivall), p. 249.

The universities were beginning to produce a different sort of clergy from the kind which had been all too common hitherto. Between the beginning of the Reformation and the inauguration of the Laudian régime the average of clerical attainment had not been very high. The account of himself which Greene put into the mouth of a "plain country Sir John or Vicar" was not an unfair characterization of many of the clergy under Elizabeth and James I. "For me, friend, I am indeed none of the best scholars; yet I can read an homily every Sunday and holy-day, and I keep company with my neighbours, and go to the alehouse with them, and if they be fallen out, spend my money to make them friends, and on Sundays sometimes, if good fellowship call me away I say both Morning and Evening Prayer at once, and so let them have the whole afternoon to play in. This is my life; I spend my living with my parishioners, I seek to do all good, and I offer no man harm."[1] It was not a high standard perhaps, yet there have been times in the Church's history when the average was lower still. Even the better part of the clergy were less inclined to make themselves conspicuous for their theological opinions than for useful lives, spent in devotion to some pursuit which might serve to augment the poverty of their livings. They were the schoolmasters and physicians of the countryside. Some of the schools which they began survived, through many hands, until they found their place in our modern educational system, others were but sporadic attempts to make a little money or meet a passing need. Jealousy on the part of the professional medical men curbed the activity of the clergy among the sick. Because of a complaint put forward by the College of Physicians, a convocation held at Westminster under Abbot in 1623 forbade the clergy to exercise physic except in their own parishes and for charity only.[2]

A good deal of the blame for the lack of energy in spiritual matters lay with the patrons of livings, who too often made simony of one sort or another the only means of preferment.[3] A man who had obtained his living either by discreet services

[1] Greene, " Quip for an Upstart Courtier", *Harl. Misc.*, Vol. V, pp. 417 ff.
[2] Cardwell, *Synodalia*, Vol. 2, p. 592.
[3] Burton, *Anatomy*, Vol. 1, p. 322. The wretched state of the clergy, which made them jump at any living they could get on any terms is emphasized often enough in the literature of the times:
"The pedant minister and serving clarke,
The ten-pound, base, frize-jerkin hireling,
The farmer's chaplain with his quarter-mark
The twenty-noble curate, and the thing called elder."
Storer speaks of in his *Wolsey*, p. 63. See also George Wither's *Presumption*.

while acting as somebody's chaplain, or by the actual transference of money, was not likely to hold opinions which might imperil his purchased property. It cannot be doubted that a servile clergy which was content to take its own small share of the pickings, and at the same time consent to the general robbery of the Church by those of the laity who had the power, greatly injured the prestige of the Establishment in its early days under Elizabeth. Here and there protests were made. The Puritan, Harrison, complains that "the Church were now become the ass whereon every market-man is to ride and cast his wallet".[1] But a resolute attempt to put an end to these scandals was soon to be begun.

Throughout the Reformation there had always been many who held a catholic conception of the Church of England, though they had not always been dominant. Toward the end of the sixteenth century, however, the catholic party began to gain strength. In 1596, Bilson became Bishop of Worcester, and nine years later Andrewes, the greatest figure in the catholic party before Laud, was given the See of Chichester. This tendency was continued when in 1608, Neile was made Bishop of Rochester, and on his translation to Lichfield, in 1611, was succeeded by Buckeridge, Laud's tutor and his predecessor as President of St John's College. With Laud's own appointment to the Deanery of Gloucester and his growing influence with the King, the principles for which he stood became the most powerful in the Church of England.

This position was not reached without setbacks. When Bancroft died in 1610, Andrewes, the great friend of James I, and a man whose learning and sanctity so obviously fitted him for the post, was passed over and the primacy given to the Puritan, Abbot. Whatever his office, Andrewes' character was the greatest asset his party could have. Everyone who is familiar with his *Private Devotions* knows something of the Bishop's learning and piety. His sermons, so much admired in their day, show the nimbleness of his wit, and some of the greatest of his contemporaries did honour to the charm of his character. It is conclusive testimony to the prevailing absenteeism of the time when even so exemplary a prelate as he spent only three months of each year in his diocese when Bishop of Ely.[2] There was very little difference between his theology and ritual and that of Laud. He was an Arminian

---

[1] Harrison, *Elizabethan England* (ed. Furnivall), p. 73.
[2] Pattison, *Casaubon*, p. 389.

before the days when Arminianism had become popular as a system, he was a ritualist before ritualism was considered necessarily an introduction to Romanism. It would be easy to draw parallels between Andrewes and Taylor, who was born in his diocese. In learning, in character, in the personal charm which all who met them had to acknowledge, each very much resembled the other. Taylor also seems to have studied the older bishop's works with care. In *The Real Presence of Christ in the Blessed Sacrament*, he speaks of Andrewes as a " wise prelate, a great and good man, whose memory is precious and had in honour".[1]

Andrewes' Arminianism came to be a leading characteristic of the High Church party. Loyalty to the Throne was as strong in him as in his successors, though he managed to be less provocative in his statements. For Andrewes the royal supremacy over the Church of England was only the external authority which must be in the hands of governors if they are to fulfil their function. It is an authority which the Scriptures approve, and such as kings and emperors have always exercised. Laud may have gone further than this and the bulk of the catholic-minded clergy in England may have followed him, but even then their Erastianism was not so thorough-going as that of their Presbyterian opponents. For the Laudians the State was the instrument of the Church, not its master.

However much the Presbyterian mind had broken loose from the past in other things, in matters of Church government it was as willing as any medievalist to use the secular arm. The Presbyterians and High Church men, as they worked side by side in the parishes of England in the days before the Civil War, offer interesting points of contrast in the performance of their ordinary duties, quite apart from whatever theory of the nature of the Church they might have held.

In the great towns, the Home Counties, and in sea-going districts where Puritanism was strong, the chief Sabbath Day exercise was a long sermon dealing with some controverted point in theology, or opening some text of the Scriptures. If the incumbent of the living was for any cause negligent of this work, then funds would very likely be produced by sympathizers, in order to

[1] *Works*, Vol. 6, p. 165. Taylor scarcely ever mentions Andrewes' name without adding some words of praise or admiration. In his *Works*, Vol. 4, p. 487, Taylor uses and expands in exactly the same manner as Andrewes an anecdote from Aeschylus. In *Works*, Vol. 10, p. 463, he borrows, and misapplies, the same line and a half of Homer which Andrewes had misapplied in his *Pattern of Catechistical Doctrine*, Pt. 11, Para. 2.

B

requite the services of some Puritan minister who would deliver his lecture after the authorized service had been read. Although the lectures did supply teaching where frequently no teaching at all would have been given, they were too often used as a means of increasing party rancour. On Laud's advice, the King directed that they should be delivered only after the minister who was to lecture had himself read the Prayer Book service, and that instead of the customary Genevan cloak the surplice should be worn. He hoped by these means to see that the incumbent was not overborne in his own church by an intruded lecturer.[1]

Lectures and sermons were the chief means which the Puritans used to achieve their objects of educating England in the Scriptures, and in what they considered to be the right view of the disputed points in theology. The Laudian parish priest conceived his chief duty to be the instruction of his people in the historic doctrines of the Church and he therefore paid great attention to teaching the Prayer Book Catechism.[2] But neither method was exclusively used by either party. There were great Anglican preachers and many of the Presbyterians valued catechetical instruction. There were good parish priests on both sides—men who knew their people intimately and served them to the full extent of their power. In the main, however, the Puritan's ideal of the ministry was most likely to be a prophetic one, while that of the Anglican was pastoral.

Between the High Church men and the Puritans there was a large number of beneficed clergy who sided habitually with the stronger party. They were not distinguished for any sort of piety. The highest aim they had was to hold as many livings as they could obtain by any means, doubtful or otherwise, while most of the pastoral work belonging to their office was done by a curate for eight or ten pounds a year. Bribery and powerful patronage were the two easiest means of advancement, without one or the other the inferior clergy stood a poor chance of ever becoming anything else.

There is an interesting pamphlet in the *Harleian Miscellany* dealing with the curate's lot. Two unbeneficed clergymen, Master Needham and Master Poorest, meet and begin to talk.

[1] "Instructions sent from the King to Archbishop Abbot in the year 1629", para. V (Laud's *Works*, Vol. 5, pp. 307-8). The same instructions are substantially repeated in "Instructions sent from the King to Archbishop Laud in the year 1634", para. V (Laud's *Works*, Vol. 5, p. 312).

[2] Herbert, *A Priest to the Temple*, p. 208. See also Taylor's own *Rules and Advices to the Clergy*, Vol. 1, p. 111.

After describing how, in spite of scholastic ability, he failed to get a scholarship at Oxford, being prevented, "once by half a buck and some good wine", once by "a great lady's letter", Master Poorest goes on to tell how he went into the country and became a curate "under a great prebend and a rich double beneficed man, where I found promises beyond performances, for my salary was inferior by much to his cook or his coachman, nay, his barber had double my stipend; for I was allowed but eight pounds per annum, and get my own victuals, clothes, and books as I could; and when I told him the means were too little, he said that 'if I would not he could have his cure supplied by another, rather for less than what I had' and so I was yoked to a small pittance, for the space of twelve years."

Master Needham had done very little better. His parson had a proud wife who robbed the curate of his fees to buy "lace, pins, fans, black bags, satin petticoats etc., and toward the maintenance of a boy servitor to go before her". This lady's husband had very changeable opinions about "where and how to place the Lord's Table; it stood in the Church, anon it must be advanced into the quire; then it must be East and West, and presently after North and South; covered, uncovered, railed, without rails, of this fashion, of that, of this wood, of another, nay he himself who was the first that altered it, hath now within this month or two, altered his opinion and placed it again in the body of the church. Oh fine weather cock!"

Master Poorest described how his rector, Dr Proud, "weareth cassocks of damask and plush, good beavers, and silk stockings, can play well at tables,[1] or gleek,[2] can hunt well and bowl very skilfully; is deeply experienced in racy canary, and can relish a cup of right claret; and so he passeth the time away". After discussing the idea of turning parish clerks, who are said to be very well paid, the two decide to better themselves; Master Poorest by going as chaplain to a ship, Master Needham by becoming preacher to a regiment of soldiers.[3]

Yet in spite of much neglect and rapacity of this sort there were places in England where the pastoral work was as thorough as anything the Church of England was to see again for nearly two hundred years. Sanderson at Boothby Pannel "did not think his duty finished when he had read prayers, catechized, preached and administered the Sacrament seasonably . . . besides

---

[1] Tables, i.e. backgammon.   [2] Gleek, i.e. a game of cards.
[3] *The Curate's Conference*, 4to, 13 pages; printed, 1641 (*Harl. Misc.*, Vol. 1, pp. 495 ff.).

this he practised what his conscience told him was his duty reconciling differences, preventing law-suits, visiting the sick and disconsolate and helping the poor with his alms".[1] George Herbert's life at Bemerton followed the same course. The influence of clergy like these touched every home in the parish. Their sermons and the Bible were the only means of enlightenment which the majority of the people possessed, for books were still few and dear. Bunyan must have been fortunate for, on his marriage, "though we came together as poor as poor might be, not having so much household stuff as a dish or a spoon between us", yet his wife brought with her *The Plain Man's Pathway to Heaven*, and *The Practice of Piety* which her father had left her when he died. A little later on he came across Luther on Galatians, "it was so old that it was ready to fall piece from piece if I did but turn it over". This was a considerable library for a small, country tradesman.[2]

We get glimpses now and then in the biographies of the period of a home life that was very simple and good. It depended to a great extent on the women of the family, and in households which were fairly well off they seem to have spent a large amount of time on their religion. Nicholas Ferrar's father was a merchant adventurer, and so his wife had no need to look after her seven children herself and consequently had time to call her own. It was her practice to read the Bible daily, to sing psalms and study the *Book of Martyrs*. On Wednesdays and Fridays she went to church prayers and "heard, as it was computed in her lifetime, twelve thousand sermons, for she was also addicted that way".[3] This was in addition to seeing that her daughters were properly taught singing, to perform on the "organ, viol, and lute" as well as needlework, ancient and modern languages, and other accomplishments of the time. All the children, of course, were expected to learn each day some part of the Bible and the *Book of Martyrs*. There were probably plenty of houses in England where the life was the same. It seems to have produced women of great character and charm. The boys were sent away to school too early to be very much under their mother's influence.

During the time between Elizabeth's reign and the beginning of the Civil War the attitude of a great part of the people toward Sunday was undergoing a profound change. The Christian

[1] Walton, *Life of Sanderson* (Wordsworth, *Eccles. Biog.*, Vol. 5, p. 473).

[2] Bunyan, *Grace Abounding*, p. 19.

[3] Skipton, *Life and Times of Nicholas Ferrar*, p. 25 (Oxford, 1907).

Church took over from the Jews the obligation to observe one
day in seven as a day of rest and worship, but felt no necessity
to observe the Jewish Sabbath, or all the ordinances concerning
it. Throughout the first seven or eight centuries of the Church's
life the majority of people did not observe the day with anything
like the strictness their teachers desired. "From the year nine-
hundred till the Reformation there was practically no limit set
to the amusements of the people on Sunday."[1] But with the
Reformation the troubles came.

The leaders of that movement could hardly admit that an
ecclesiastical rule was unchangeable, solely because it derived
from antiquity. To do so would have committed them to many
things they wished to destroy. They believed, of course, that
Genesis 2 and Exodus 20 were historical, but that did not enable
them to identify Sunday with the Jewish Sabbath.[2] They were
therefore compelled to rest the observance of Sunday on the
rational grounds of the universal need for a day of rest and joint
worship. Sunday was in their eyes, not a divine institution the
observance of which must be forced upon all, but a day which
after the obligation of worship had been discharged could be
used with godly discretion. Calvin accordingly played bowls on
a Sunday and John Knox was not inclined to be more repressive
on that day than on others. Under Queen Elizabeth necessary
work was actually encouraged. Merchants went to their businesses
to discharge urgent matters, carriers and pedlars did not remit
their journeys, and the Royal Council chose Sunday as its day
of meeting. But Puritan England in the sixteenth and seventeenth
centuries turned steadily toward Old Testament ideals, among
them a conception of Sunday approximating to the Jewish
Sabbath. In 1595, Nicholas Bounde, a Suffolk clergyman, published a book entitled *The True Doctrine of the Sabbath*, in which
he claimed with much boldness, if little reason, that the observance of the Christian Sunday as if it were the Jewish Sabbath
should be enforced by the State. Trivial as the argument of the
book was, it had a great influence both at home and abroad.
Fuller says, "it is incredible how taking this doctrine was",[3] and
Heylyn, though perhaps he is not the most impartial of witnesses
in this matter, mentions a Puritan preacher who declared that

---

[1] *Ency. Rel. and Eth.*, Art., "Sabbath".
[2] The use of the word "Sabbath" for the Christian Sunday began under Elizabeth
and became popular under James I and Charles I. Hallam, *Constitut. Hist.*, Vol. 1,
p. 368, note.
[3] Fuller, *Church History*, Bk. IX, Sec. VIII, para. 20.

"to do any work on the Lord's day was as great a sin as to kill a man or to commit adultery", and another who said "that to make a feast or to dress a wedding dinner on that day was as great a sin as for a father to kill his child".[1]

The Government was forced into the controversy. In 1618, the first *Book of Sports* insisted on the liberty of the people to keep Sunday in the way they had been accustomed, except for the savage sports of bull and bear-baiting. The Sunday Observance Act of 1625 forbade any to leave their own parishes on Sunday in search of amusement.[2] The second issue of the *Book of Sports*, in 1633, while it was strong in its admonition of the justices of peace to prevent any unruliness on Sunday, nevertheless allowed men to keep that day in "freedom with manlike and lawful exercises".[3] But the last traces of reasonableness in this controversy were fast disappearing as Puritanism became more and more Judaic in mind. In 1643, Parliament ordered the *Book of Sports* to be burnt by the common hangman, and imposed on all who accepted their authority a Sunday which differed little from the Jewish Sabbath. In 1648, with the formal adoption of Presbyterianism, the rigidities of the Puritan Sabbath were fixed upon England, to remain the ideal of the serious part of the nation for more than two hundred years.

Not all the High Church clergy were in favour of the policy recommended by the *Book of Sports*. The parson of Elstow, for instance, though apparently with High Church leanings, preached on the evils of breaking the Sabbath either with labour, sports, or otherwise. But that did not prevent Bunyan spending Sunday as he had always done, in playing cat, bell-ringing, and dancing.[4] The country people clung tenaciously to their ancient sports on Sunday. A parliamentary newspaper gives us an interesting glimpse of the way in which the Uppingham people kept that day in the July of 1643, nearly a year after Jeremy Taylor, lately their rector, had left them to go to the wars. "Some of Colonel Cromwell's forces coming by accident into Uppingham town in Rutland, on the Lord's day, found the bears playing there in the usual manner, and, in the height of their sport,

---

[1] Gee and Hardy, *Doc. Illust.*, Doc. 93.
[2] On a Bill "for the better observance of the Sabbath, usually called Sunday", introduced to Parliament in 1621, a Mr Shepherd remarked that "as Saturday was *dies Sabbati*, this might be entitled a Bill for the observance of Saturday, commonly called Sunday". For this, poor Mr Shepherd was reprimanded on his knees and expelled the House. Hallam, *Const. Hist.*, Vol. 1, p. 370.
[3] Gee and Hardy, *Doc. Illust.*, Doc. 93.
[4] Bunyan, *Grace Abounding*, p. 20.

caused them to be seized upon, tied to a tree and shot."[1] As the Uppingham men had not been taught the new rigidity in Sabbath-keeping, Cromwell's men, in this particular at least instructed them very forcibly.

Dr Piers, the Bishop of Bath and Wells, at the request of Charles I, enquired into the village feasts and found them nearly always innocent, and often performing a useful purpose. He divides them into four kinds. The first were the feasts of dedication and were held in honour of their churches, either on the patronal day or some Sunday near it. The second were the church ales. On these occasions the people went straight from afternoon prayers to sports on the village green or in the churchyard, or if the weather was against these places to a merrymaking in the alehouse. The proceeds of these meetings were often devoted to some good cause, such as beautifying the church, providing new bells, or helping the poor. The third kind of village feast was the clerk ale. At this the people sent provisions to the parish clerk and then gathered at his house for a festivity which they enlivened with the ale they purchased from him. In poor parishes this was almost the only means of recompensing the clerk. The fourth were the bid ales. These were held to set up some poor man by the liberal contributions of his friends at a Sunday joviality.[2] It is a pity that fanaticism should have stamped out gatherings which, though like all human institutions sometimes misused, were none the less a means of lightening the tedium of country life and often of forwarding worthy purposes.

The question of Sunday observance was but one of the problems current in those days, drawing men to one side or the other in the religious dispute. In the country districts the smaller squires, who were the backbone of the Puritan party in those places, were increasingly being alienated from the Laudians as the clergy grew more devoted to the Church and more inclined to claim her rights. Laud's clergy could not, like so many of their predecessors, be bullied and treated with contempt. At least while Laud was free they had the power to make themselves felt. It may be objected against them, as a body, that they had no desire to adapt their teaching to the capacity of ordinary people at a time when it would have been of supreme service to their cause had they done so. "Jewel and Bull, Hall and Donne,

---

[1] *A Perfect Diurnal of Some Passages of Parliament*, 24 July to 31 July 1643. These bears were brought over from Holland by the Queen.

[2] Hutton, *Church of England from Charles I to Anne*, p. 108.

Hooker and Taylor, lived and wrote for their peers and for future ages but not for the commonalty of their own."[1] It was just to this commonalty that the Puritan addressed himself. Yet it was these men who gave the Church of England a reputation for learning that many years of sloth and ignorance were not afterwards able to destroy. Nor were they learned only, they were filled with a piety which it is the glory of the Church of England to claim as peculiarly her own. Priests like George Herbert, laymen like Isaac Walton; holy, erudite in their degree, endowed with a true simplicity of mind and life, they did not attempt to escape from the troubles of this world by absorption in the idea of the next, but illuminated their daily path with heavenly splendour. Nicholas Ferrar sought to reclaim something of the monastic ideal for Anglicanism by an adaptation of it which, in happier times, might well have survived.

In the ennobling of the material fabric of the Church these men were as conspicuous as they were in its spiritual enrichment. When the Laudian movement began to make itself effective in the parishes every church in the land was eloquent of Reformation vandalism, and nearly a hundred years of subsequent neglect. In most places the images, shrines and tabernacles, rood lofts and "monuments of idolatry had been removed taken down and defaced".[2] Where the painted windows were left it was mostly because it would be an expensive business to replace them with plain glass. Drabness had settled down even where there was no conspicuous neglect. The glory of worship had departed. Instead of the Mass with its splendour of lights, vestments and ritual, the minister clad in a black gown, read Mattins or Evensong "in the body of the Church with his face toward the people in a little tabernacle of wainscot provided for the purpose".[3] Placed in the nave, the altar served any end to which it might be put by casual irreverence or deliberate profanation. In at least one case, that of the Abbey Dore, there was no place to worship in save the ruins of the ancient church, and there, kneeling beneath an arch which still remained intact to shield his book from the weather, the curate read prayers. In this instance a truly appalling condition was soon to be remedied by the generosity of Viscount Scudamore, who rebuilt the Abbey and retrieved the ancient altar "one entire stone twelve foot

[1] Sir James Stephen, *Essays in Eccles. Biog.*, Vol. II, p. 4.
[2] Harrison, *Elizabethan England* (ed. Furnivall), p. 77.
[3] Ibid.

long four foot broad and three inches thick, from its desecrators who had used it to salt meat and make cheese upon".[1]

Laud and Juxon were both energetic church builders, Archbishop Neile reported in 1636, that six thousand five-hundred and sixty-two pounds, fifteen shillings and sevenpence had been spent in restoring and beautifying churches in the Archdeaconry of York, the West Riding, and Nottingham. The cavalier John Harrison built St John's, Briggate, the most lovely of all the older churches in the city of Leeds. Herbert rebuilt the church at Leighton Bromswold and repaired that at Bemerton. Many other less-known people, up and down England, were doing similar things. A fair amount of decency, and in some cases even beauty, began to come back to the people's worship. One of the tasks of Laud's Vicar-General was to see that all altars were restored to the east end again.[2] Lights, and here and there incense, found their way into use once more, while in some cathedrals and parish churches the ministrant once again arrayed himself in a cope. The old custom of decorating the church at the great festivals with holly, ivy, rosemary, and green boughs had never died out in some places, and was now revived in others.[3]

The services differed in frequency and type. In the parish church Holy Communion was usually celebrated once a month. Nearly always it followed Mattins, and both services were over before noon. The direction of the Prayer Book that those intending to present themselves at the altar should notify the clerk some time during the preceding week was widely kept. Evensong was generally said at about three o'clock in the afternoon and this was the recognized time for the priest to catechize his people. Saints' days and their eves were widely observed and the Litany was said, in most places, on Wednesday and Friday. In the cathedrals Holy Communion was celebrated more often, usually on every Sunday and saint's day. The music was good and there were frequent sermons. In the early years of the seventeenth century the Church of England had one of her greatest preachers, and perhaps her greatest musician, both at the height of their powers. From 1621, John Donne, as Dean of St. Paul's, preached to vast congregations and held them enthralled as much by the depth of his devotion as by the magnificence of his oratory.

---

[1] Hutton, *The Church of England from Charles I to Anne*, p. 103.
[2] Articles to be inquired of in the Metropoliticall Visitation, etc., in and for the Diocese of Winchester (Laud's *Works*, Vol. 5, p. 421).
[3] Hutton, *The Church of England from Charles I to Anne*, p. 99.

Orlando Gibbons, first at the Chapel Royal and then at Westminster Abbey, gave to English music a grace and dignity it had
not known before. Donne had no connection with Cambridge,
but Gibbons was born there and took his degree of Bachelor of
Music from that University in 1606; his fame would, in all
probability, be well known to the aspiring youth of the city.

While Jeremy Taylor was a boy in Cambridge, already wrapped
up in his books and well on the way to the vast learning of his
later days, there were everywhere signs of greater hopefulness
for Anglicanism than any which had appeared for a century; if
only the Puritans could be rapidly overcome, or a serious struggle
with them avoided. But there was to be a war of extermination.

CHAPTER II

BIRTH AND EDUCATION

NATHANIEL TAYLOR, the father of Jeremy, was a barber in Cambridge. On 13 October 1605 he married Mary Dean, and their family, six sons and one daughter, was born between the years 1606 and 1619. Edmond, presumably the eldest, was baptized on 13 August 1606; Mary was baptized on 11 June 1609, Nathaniel on 8 December 1611, and Jeremy on 15 August 1613; to be followed by Thomas and John, baptized in July 1616 and April 1619. The order of the Taylor children is important, for, since we have no authentic information of the actual year of Jeremy's birth, conjecture has been at work. Sir James Ware, whose learned works on Irish history were published in the eighteenth century, in order to overcome a chronological difficulty in Taylor's later life, suggested that he was born in 1611.[1] If such a thing did happen, then either Nathaniel and Jeremy were born, but not baptized, in the same year, or all the members of the Taylor family after the eldest were not baptized until they were two years old, neither of which suppositions seems over-likely.

Nathaniel Taylor was at that time living in a house that stood opposite Holy Trinity Church, but which was afterward converted into an inn and named The Black Bull. But, so uncertain is everything to do with Jeremy Taylor's early years, even this has been disputed and the idea put forward that he was born in Petty Cury, in a house which also became an inn called The Wrestler's. This is improbable, for that particular hostelry is outside the bounds of Holy Trinity parish, where beyond doubt the Taylor family was baptized, and the father held office as churchwarden. Possibly a move was made to Petty Cury at a later period. There is likewise no evidence to support the contention that Nathaniel Taylor belonged to the higher rank of barber-surgeon, which is only one of the slightest of the attempts that have been made to elevate the stock of the Taylors. Heber did the best he could to help forward this philanthropic work,[2]

---

[1] Ware, *Works* (ed. Harris), Vol. I, Irish Bishops: Art. "Taylor".
[2] Heber, "Life", *Works*, Vol. 1, p. 10 ff.

drawing the materials for the ancestry, with which he presented
Taylor, from some alleged manuscripts generally referred to as
the Jones MSS., from their reputed owner William Todd Jones
of Homra in County Down.

Jones was a politician and pamphleteer, but there was a story
that at one time he intended to write a life of Jeremy Taylor,
with whom he was remotely connected. The material which he
got together for his work included a family book, which gave in
the Bishop's own handwriting an account of his life and ancestry.
Besides this there were some autographed letters which he had
written and received; a letter from Lady Wray, Jeremy Taylor's
granddaughter, to William Todd of Castle Martin dated 31 May
1732; and many other interesting documents. Jones died in 1818
as a result of a carriage accident, and these particular manuscripts
disappeared. Jones' other papers had been placed under the
care of the Earl of Moira and Montalto and were afterwards
said to have been transferred to Donnington, but no trace of
anything referring to Taylor was ever found there. The best
explanation Heber could find for their absence was that they had
possibly been in the London Custom House with some things
of the Marquis of Hastings and were destroyed there by fire.
A few extracts which Jones had made with a view to his intended
work, together with some traditions about the bishop and his
descendants, and the marriage settlement of his youngest daughter,
were "liberally communicated" to Heber by Jones' sisters, Mrs
Wray and Mrs Mary Jones.[1]

With this as his authority, Heber included in his biography
the following statements as matters of fact: That the Taylor
family had originally belonged to the smaller gentry of Gloucester-
shire, where they had long held an estate at Frampton-on-
Severn. That Nathaniel, Jeremy's father, was descended from
Dr Rowland Taylor of Hadleigh, who was burned at the stake
for his Protestantism in the Marian persecutions. Both these
pieces of information had been taken from the extracts which
Todd Jones had made from Lady Wray's letter. Apparently the
rest of the notes offered little of importance. Apart from this
alleged statement of Lady Wray the only support for these two
stories of more than plebeian ancestry lies in the fact that Taylor
once applied to Dugdale the antiquary for information about a

[1] Heber, ibid. From what has been said above, it will be seen that they were only
extracts, which may or may not have been accurate, taken from papers which had
unaccountably disappeared and which cannot be proved to have existed.

coat of arms "borne by the Taylors of Cumberland and Northumberland".[1] Dr Rowland Taylor had come from Rothbury in Northumberland. What Dugdale's answer was we do not know, but the coat of arms enquired about was granted in 1604 to "Roger Taylor, son of Thomas Taylor, son of Roger Taylor, Esq., of London", between whose family and that of the bishop there is no traceable connexion.

Heber, seeking for more support for the story of descent from Rowland Taylor, refers to a passage in Jeremy's "Apology for Set Forms" in which the martyr is spoken of with "something like filial fondness".[2] Rowland Taylor had been chaplain to Archbishop Cranmer and was burned to death on Aldham Common in Suffolk, in 1555, fifty-eight years before Jeremy Taylor's baptism. If there was any connexion, it is extraordinary that the first hint we have of it should come from Lady Wray, sixty-five years after Jeremy Taylor's death.[3] Edmond Taylor, Nathaniel's predecessor as churchwarden, must then have been the son of the martyr, and if that were so there should have been plenty of people in Cambridge who knew of the fact. The world had not forgotten Rowland Taylor. Fox's *Book of Martyrs*, the author's final edition of which appeared in 1583, had lifted him up as the ideal minister of a parish, a scholar, and a man of great general ability. If he had died a normal death he would have been a man with whom it would have been an honour to claim kinship; but, in Protestant Cambridge, one who had sealed his devotion to reformed principles with his blood would have been an even more desirable ancestor. Yet Jeremy Taylor never makes any such claim, and George Rust, who was brought up in Cambridge and was probably only a little junior to his bishop, never mentions it; neither does Anthony Wood, who knew personally many of Taylor's friends. If Edmond Taylor, churchwarden of Holy Trinity Church, Cambridge, in 1589, was a relative of Nathaniel Taylor, and even that is uncertain, he must be taken as the first of Jeremy Taylor's ancestors to emerge into the light of history. If his claim is

[1] Hamper, *Life of Dugdale*, letter numbered 65, dated 1 April 1651; mutilated portion only.
[2] Heber, "Life", *Works*, Vol. 1, p. 12. Taylor's remarks occur in *Works*, Vol. 5, p. 237.
[3] Rowland Taylor at his trial twice mentioned that he had "nine children and all in lawful matrimony". In his will he gives the names of five who were dead (Susan, George, Ellen, Robert, and Zachary). Of the four remaining, Fox mentions the names of two only, Thomas, the eldest living son, who was a child at his father's death, and Mary. While it is possible that one of the two unnamed children was the Edmond Taylor who, thirty-four years later, became churchwarden of Holy Trinity, Cambridge, it does not seem likely.

disallowed, we must fall back on the only certainty, Nathaniel Taylor, churchwarden and barber.

But that is not the last problem connected with Jeremy Taylor's early years. We may suppose him being brought up at home, in a godly family, taught to say his prayers, and learning his letters; a little later on getting by heart stories from the Bible and Fox's *Book of Martyrs*. But the time comes when he must go to school and the actual date of his going offers another difficulty.

Dr Stephen Perse, Fellow of Caius College, Cambridge, when he died in 1615, left his money to found a free school. He already owned some land on what had been the site of the Augustinian Monastery of Grey Friars, and here a building was erected with a room each for the master and the usher. By the terms of the will one hundred boys were to be admitted, chosen from Cambridge, Barnwell, Chesterton, and Trumpington.[1] The first headmaster was Thomas Lovering, a man of considerable reputation who taught his pupils so well that they are said to have become "Minerva's darlings". In 1618, the foundation stone of the new school was laid, and in 1619 the first boys were admitted. Jeremy Taylor was then six years old.

On 18 August 1626 Jeremy Taylor was admitted a sizar of Gonville and Caius College, and it is the admission book there which makes the difficulty, for it states that he was then in his fifteenth year and that he had been for some ten years (*per decennium*) the pupil of Thomas Lovering "*in schola publica*". If we accept 1613 as the most probable year of his birth, the first statement is wrong, for he would then be only thirteen years old. The last half of the entry is more puzzling, but not necessarily incorrect. To overcome a little of the difficulty, Sir James Ware suggested that Taylor was born as early as 1611. Heber seems to have been ignorant of the date when the Perse School was founded.[2] He first takes 1613 as the proven year of Taylor's birth and then doubts the truth of the admission book entry, on the grounds that no one would send a child of three to a public school. Sir Edmund Gosse considers the whole entry incorrect, remarking that "the book proves itself of slight authority in the matter of dates by saying that Jeremy had attended the Perse School for some ten years",[3] but this the book does not say. As it stands, the entry may only mean that Taylor had

[1] Cooper, *Annals of Cambridge*, Vol. 3, pp. 95–101. Also Cooper, *Memorials of Cambridge*, Vol. 3, pp. 154–60.
[2] Heber, "Life", *Works*, Vol. 1, pp. 13–14, and Eden's note.
[3] Gosse, *Jeremy Taylor*, pp. 4–5.

completed more than nine years under Lovering; that they could not all have been spent at the Perse School is clear when we remember that the school was not open until 1619. Lovering, however, before he went as Headmaster to the new Perse foundation, had kept a school in St Edward's Church, Cambridge, after which he had gone as a master to King's College School. It is quite possible that Jeremy Taylor began under Lovering there and moved with his master to the Perse School.

Children began their education early in those days. It was the continual endeavour of the founders of the new grammar schools, which were being opened in so many places at that time, to prevent children being forced into school by their parents before they were old enough to gain any advantage by attendance. The statutes of Christ's Hospital demanded that candidates for admittance should be "above four years of age", and although the rules of most other schools insisted that they should be older, there is no reason to suppose that a private teacher would make the same demands if the parents of a precocious child could pay the small dues required for him. The phrase "*in schola publica*" would more accurately describe earlier tuition of this sort, for Dr Perse's foundation was a free rather than a public school. Rust says that Jeremy Taylor "was ripe for the university before custom would allow of his admittance; but by the time he was thirteen years old he was entering into Caius College",[1] a testimony which fits in with 1613 as the year of his birth, and does not contradict the supposition that he had been at school longer than most children if he was so forward in his studies.[2] What would be more natural, under the circumstances, than that the parents should put the age of their child at a little more than it really was in order to get him into college while a vacancy existed, especially in days when birth certificates were unknown and their word was all there was to go upon? If this is so, the only mistake in the admission book is that of his age, and that was made in good faith.

Scholarship in the seventeenth century was no easy pursuit, even for small boys. Lessons began at six o'clock in the morning at the Perse School and went on until five in the evening, with a break of only two hours. There were no fees to be paid except twelvepence to the usher, who wrote the boys names down in

---

[1] George Rust, "A Funeral Sermon", *Works*, Vol. 1, p. cccxxii.
[2] Isaac Barrow was entered at Peterhouse when he was only thirteen. Hammond went up to Oxford at the same age. Hooker entered Corpus Christi, Oxford, as a chorister at fourteen. Nicholas Ferrar entered Clare Hall, Cambridge, at thirteen.

two books, one kept in the school, the other handed over to the executors of the doctor's will, who chose the scholars. Most masters enforced discipline by savage beatings. Burton complained that many made "children endure a martyrdom all the while they are at school; with bad diet, if they board in their houses, too much severity and ill-usage, . . . still chiding, railing, frowning, lashing, tasking, keeping, that they are . . . weary of their lives".[1] School founders of that period, from Colet onwards, generally set down the chief aims which they wished to be pursued in their schools, and the executors of Dr Perse, doubtless stating in writing what had been his expressed wish, set down in the ordinances that the scholars were to be "carefully and diligently taught as well in good manners as in all other instruction and learning fit to be learned in a grammar school". What such "instruction and learning" was we know from contemporary sources, and so can form an accurate picture of the curriculum through which Jeremy Taylor passed. In what is often considered his greatest work, Taylor remarked that "education is so great and invincible a prejudice that he who masters the inconvenience of it is more to be commended than he can justly be blamed that complies with it".[2] He was thinking of the education of Dissenters and evil-disposed persons, but he would probably have agreed that the good effects of his own training were as permanent. Certainly no one could think of an education more likely to turn out the sort of man he became than that through which he passed.

In his time religion lay at the base of all learning. Every schoolmaster aimed at making his pupils, first of all, well-instructed Christians; then as good Latinists and as capable orators as might be. The day began with prayers. For a text-book a Life of Christ, or some other religious compilation, might be used, in which the purity of the Latin was safeguarded by writing it entirely in words and phrases from Virgil. If a sermon was being preached that day the whole school would be taken to hear it. Prayers closed the school day.

On Sunday all the classes went to hear the sermon in their parish church, and not merely to let it flow over their heads in a string of unheeded words, but to make of it another school exercise, and one as severe as any other. The boys were expected to take notes of what they heard, keeping the headings and divisions which the preacher had made and jotting down in the

---

[1] Burton, *Anatomy of Melancholy*, Vol. 1, p. 333.   [2] *Works*, Vol. 5, p. 503.

margin a word or two of brief analysis, and any Scripture references which might occur. After church the whole was to be revised and the analysis expanded. On Monday the revised copy was to be taken to school and turned into Latin, and on the Monday week some forward boy was to stand up before the class and recite the whole without a book.[1] Sermons in the seventeenth century were long and learned. How the boys in the congregation must have felt their hearts faint within them as they listened to Sunday's hour-long discourse on predestination, knowing that they themselves were destined to stew over it for eight days, and then perhaps to stand up and repeat it to a master whose theological principles had made him critical of it from the preacher's lips and intolerant of it from his pupils.

From Latin the boys were never free; they were expected to speak it even at games. They learned their Latin grammar by question and answer in that language. They translated into it, composed in it, and read text-books drawn from a very wide area of its literature. Beginners generally started with *Pueriles Confabulatiunculae*, went on to Corderius *Dialogues* and Aesop's *Fables*, then to Cicero, Ovid and Virgil, Pliny, Seneca, and recognized Latin authors nearer to their own times. Behind this intensive training in one subject lay the desire to send students up to the universities with such a mastery of Latin that they should be competent to pursue all their studies in it, without further trouble, and to converse freely in any country in Europe in the medium common to all educated persons.

Greek was little taught, though it had found its way into some grammar schools by 1600. There the boys were instructed in grammar, and read a little of Isocrates, Hesiod, and Homer.

A strictly practical purpose, similar to that which underlay the study of Latin, also prescribed the careful attention paid to oratory in both school and university. It was an age in which the pulpit and public assembly exerted a tremendous influence. A good proportion of the boys in any school would, in after life, become divines, lawyers, or schoolmasters, and they would need a knowledge of oratory either for their own use or to teach to their pupils. Many of the others, either as merchants or tradesmen, would be called upon to express their views in their parish vestry or possibly even in the national Parliament. Just as boys were taught Latin as the indispensable necessity for study and

[1] Mitchell, *English Pulpit Oratory*, p. 74.

C

communication with foreigners, so they practised oratory as a
requisite for success in after-life.

Rhetoric was studied in Latin like everything else, the chief
text-books in use being those produced by famous teachers of
oratory in the early days of Christianity. A favourite one was the
Progymnasmata of Aphthonius, a sophist of Antioch and a fellow
pupil with St Chrysostom of Libanius, the greatest orator of his
day.[1] "So trial subjects set to Chrysostom and Aphthonius by
Libanius became the trial subjects prescribed by Brinsley and
attempted by Jeremy Taylor."[2] The *Progymnasmata* was severely
technical in its method. It was divided into fourteen heads, the
rules of each being given and their working illustrated by
examples. As soon as this was mastered, the boys were set to
writing themes of twelve or thirteen lines each in imitation of
their models; these must be handed in to the master, and then
the whole learned by heart and repeated aloud. In order to
enrich these compositions, the boys were to search every author
they read for suitable illustrations and comparisons, which were
to be written down in commonplace-books to be ready when
needed. It is not mere accident which makes the illustrations of
seventeenth-century sermons seem so remote from life, for the
preachers were obeying the instructions of their early years and
taking experience at second hand. In addition to these embellish-
ments, portions from standard authors might be woven into the
young orator's work in order to give it strength, and an air of
learning. So the long passages of Latin or Greek which the
modern reader is apt to find such a wearisome feature of the
seventeenth-century sermon also had a partly schoolboy origin.
A favourite manual on how to make these excerpts was that of
the Jesuit Drexilius, an author with whose works Jeremy Taylor
shows a greater acquaintance than any other preacher of his
day, a fact which is not without interest when we remember
the masses of quotation in Taylor's writings.[3]

Orators, who had spent years in seeking out and memorizing
striking passages in classical authors, would naturally be quick
to use their accumulated stores when they came to make speeches
in English. Foster Watson remarks that "unless the school and
university training in rhetoric are borne in mind, an important
factor in accounting for the wealth of imagery and expression

[1] Mitchell, *English Pulpit Oratory*, p. 56.
[2] Ibid, p. 56. John Brinsley was the Puritan schoolmaster of Ashby-de-la-Zouch.
His *Ludus Literarius*, published in 1612, was an important educational handbook.
[3] Ibid., p. 82.

in the English Literature of the sixteenth and seventeenth centuries is overlooked".[1] Letter-writing was almost the only other subject in the school curriculum, and that also was included from practical considerations, since up to the time of the Civil War the only method of conveying information other than by word of mouth was by long letters from one to another.

With nine or ten years of this training at his back, Jeremy Taylor, in 1626, entered Gonville and Caius College. Originally founded in 1348 by Edmund Gonville, the Dominican Vicar-General of Ely, and named by him the Hall of the Annunciation, it had by the time of the Reformation fallen into decay, but was re-founded in 1557 by Dr Caius, one of its own graduates. A successful physician who had done well academically at Cambridge and Padua, Dr Caius devoted the large fortune, which his practice in London had brought him, to restoring what he called "that poor house Gonville Hall". He built lavishly and beautifully, three famous gates being a conspicuous feature of his work. Freshmen entered the college from Trinity Street through the gate of Humility, a simple archway with entablature inscribed with the one word "*Humilitatis*". From this a broad walk bordered by trees led to the gate of Virtue, a gateway tower on the east side of Caius Court adorned by the word "*Virtutis*". To the south, fronting on Schools Street, stands the gate of Honour bearing the word "*Honoris*". Beautiful as it is now, it must have been still more lovely in its first state, painted white with carved roses and coats of arms picked out in crimson and gold.[2]

Possibly because he was a medical man, Dr Caius had ideas on sanitation which were not shared by many in his time. He ordered that no dirt or filth of any kind was to be thrown into the courtyard, neither were beds or linen to be aired there, and a man was to be permanently employed in keeping the pavements clean.

Though at the time of his graduation in the reign of Henry VIII the college had a reputation for being a hotbed of reformed opinion, Caius himself was credited with a strong leaning toward the old religion. It may have been nothing more than a hatred of vandalism, for he always regularly attended the college chapel and never spoke of Protestantism without respect. He certainly had a collection of Mass vestments, books, and

---

[1] Foster Watson, *The English Grammar School to 1660*, p. 82.
[2] Stubbs, *Cambridge*, art. on Caius College, *passim*.

ornaments in his room, and he was forced to submit to a visitation from the Vice-Chancellor and Heads of Colleges, who burnt the Doctor's treasures in his own courtyard.[1] Harvey, the discoverer of the circulation of the blood, graduated from the College in 1597, and Dr Cosin was a Fellow there. Though a number of years intervened between them, Caius' love of vestments and symbolism may have had some effect upon Cosin, whose ritualism at Durham afterwards caused the Revd Peter Smart so much anxiety.[2]

Taylor was put under the tutelage of Thomas Batchcroft, a conscientious if not very brilliant person, who soon after that date was elected Master of the College. From this office he was later ejected by the Puritans. A sizar's life such as that which Jeremy Taylor was now living was by no means enviable, though it offered to poor men's sons the means of getting the education which would otherwise have been beyond them. Burton quotes with approval Howson's description of a poor scholar's lot. "When we come to the university if we live of the college allowance we are needy of all things but hunger and fear."[3] On the other hand the best education of his day was open to a sizar, and at this period at least, there was no rigid class distinction which cut him off from other students. It was an age in which servitude did not necessarily carry with it contempt, since it was not, primarily, something sold for money, but a duty attached to rank. Some of the greatest churchmen of the age received their training in this manner, and it was rarely made a cause of reproach to them in after-life.[4]

A student who could afford to pay his own way had a pleasant enough time. Harrison complained that such "study little other than histories, tables, dice and trifles".[5] Mrs Hutchinson, a little less prejudiced author, mentions that her husband when at

---

[1] Bass Mullinger, *History of the University of Cambridge*, p. 127.

[2] See, Peter Smart, *The Vanitie and Downe-Fall of Superstitious Popish Ceremonies: A Sermon preached in the Cathedrall Church of Durham, 27 July 1628*, Edenborough, 1628, 4to. Smart was a prebendary and master of Durham School. The introduction to his unintentionally amusing diatribe against Cosin contained the gist of the sermon and is reprinted in More and Cross, *Anglicanism*, No. 254.

[3] Burton, *Anatomy of Melancholy*, Vol. 1, p. 311.

[4] John Howe, chaplain to both Oliver and Richard Cromwell, a moderate as well as famous Nonconformist divine, was a sizar at Cambridge in the first half of the seventeenth century. So also was the great Isaac Barrow, mathematician and theologian, and in Tillotson's eyes "as near St James' perfect man as might be". Pepys the diarist and great naval administrator; Sir Robert Sawyer, first Attorney-General and then senior counsel for the Seven Bishops, were sizars and so were Newton and Bentley.

[5] Harrison, *Elizabethan England* (ed. Furnivall), p. 253.

Cambridge "for his exercise practised tennis and played admirably well at it; for his diversion he chose music, and got a very good hand which he afterwards improved to a great mastery of the viol. There were masters who taught to dance and vault whom he practised with."[1] Townsmen and gownsmen fought out their quarrels with their fists, then and for a couple of centuries after. A long list of contemporary observers wailed over the vicious life which privileged undergraduates lived, and yet in spite of all, these were the men who served their country in a great crisis of her history with complete devotion on the one side or the other.

Certainly so far as numbers were concerned the universities were not so prosperous again until nearly two hundred years had passed.[2] The subjects studied were very limited. Arithmetic, music, geometry, and astronomy were attracting less and less attention. Taylor himself is said to have been taught mathematics and grammar at home by his father, a statement which Gosse accepts as true;[3] rather strangely, since the authority for it is a reputed letter of Jeremy Taylor to Batchcroft in the Jones MSS. which Gosse has previously dismissed as "a mystification or hoax".[4] Those students who did not intend to take holy orders read law or physic, which offered them the entrance to a career in one or other of those professions. But by far the greater number of those who went to the University as poor scholars had no future before them but to "teach a school, turn lecturer or curate, and for that he shall have falconer's wages, ten pounds *per annum* and his diet, or some small stipend so long as he can please his patron or his parish".[5]

Gradually learning was widening out, but every new direction in which her activities spread was suggested to her by the prevailing, all-absorbing interest in religion. Some Greek authors were read at the University, and a little Hebrew. Oriental languages were beginning to attract attention, and researches were being undertaken into heathen cults contemporary with the Old Testament to see what contribution they could make to the understanding of sacred history. The foundations were being laid of those studies which afterwards produced marvels of patient learning, such as the Polyglot Bible, which Brian Walton edited, and those minutely particularizing commentaries on Scripture which Puritan scholarship delighted to produce and

---

[1] Hutchinson, *Memoirs of Colonel Hutchinson*, p. 51.
[2] Bass Mullinger, *History of the University of Cambridge*, p. 212.
[3] Gosse, *Jeremy Taylor*, p. 4.
[4] Ibid., p. 1. [5] Burton, *Anatomy of Melancholy*, Vol. 1, p. 306.

Puritan zeal to ponder. Controversial divinity was, however, the main learned pursuit and in that men spent incredibly laborious lives.

Cambridge had listened to a presage of the coming Arminianism from the lips of Peter Baro, the Lady Margaret professor in 1595, before the Calvinists, in their zeal for unqualified predestination, had deprived him of his office. The movement which was beginning to bring something like dignity into the worship in parish churches established itself in the Cambridge colleges also. At Peterhouse, where Cosin was Master from 1635 to 1644, the ritual caused deep anxiety to those who, like Hutchinson, then an undergraduate, belonged to the Puritan side.[1]

In this atmosphere Jeremy Taylor spent his youth. We do not know who were his friends or what special predilections he had in his studies. Dr Samuel Ward, the Master of Sidney Sussex College, was at that time Lady Margaret professor and engaged in a magnificent feat of theological endurance—the delivery of a course of lectures lasting "nine years or thereabouts" on original sin. Taylor attended them sometimes and thought them very futile.[2] This is the only opinion we have of his on either his teachers or their teaching. There is no hint in his later life that he came into contact, while at Cambridge, with any of his famous literary contemporaries. Milton, then at Christ's College, is said to have had a great respect for him, but it is only a rumour. George Herbert is so near akin to Taylor in character that had they ever met, one or the other of them might have recorded the fact. But with all his future dependent on academic success, and that in turn to be decided, so far as he could do it, by unremitting labour, Taylor would have no time to spare for cultivating the literary cliques; so it is not very strange that he seems to have been without acquaintances among the band of authors who passed through Cambridge at that time, and afterward made a name for themselves. Nor does he seem to have been intimate with many of the theologians either, though in later days he knew Henry More well and that particular friendship may have had its beginning when he was an undergraduate. It is possible that he was also acquainted with George Rust.

Dr Perse's benefaction remained Taylor's means of subsistence throughout his life at Cambridge, for the Doctor, in addition to founding a school, had established six bursaries and six fellowships

---

[1] Hutchinson, *Memoirs of Colonel Hutchinson*, p. 51.   [2] *Works*, Vol. 7, p. 542.

at Caius College, preference for these posts being given to suitable candidates from the Perse School. It was on this foundation that Taylor entered the College, but so many students were hoping for assistance that it was not until 1629 that he received any money. At Michaelmas 1628 he was granted a bursary and held it for five years. In 1630/1 he took his B.A. degree and in 1633 was rewarded with a junior Fellowship, again on the Perse foundation. At the same time he relinquished his bursary.[1]

He was now of a standing in the University, which allowed him to take pupils, and naturally, being a poor man, he began to earn a little money by teaching. Two of those who came under him at this time are specially interesting: Martin Perse because it would seem that Taylor had some slight opportunity to show his gratitude to Dr Perse by attention to one who bore his name, and the other, Edward Langsdale, because he was almost certainly the brother of Taylor's future wife.

The exact date of Taylor's ordination, like many other dates in his life, is unknown. Dean Comber in his *Discourses on the Offices of Ordination* published in 1699, mentions "the most famously learned Bishop Ussher ordained before he was twenty-one; and the pious and eloquent Bishop, Jeremy Taylor, who entered into Orders younger than he". That is the only light we get upon an incident the details of which are now past recovery. In the following year Batchcroft appointed Taylor a Reader in Rhetoric and he took his degree of Master of Arts.

So far his career had been such as might have been foretold for a brilliant, and industrious young scholar who had been given a fair chance. Speaking of the impression which he made at this time, Rust remarks, "had he lived amongst the ancient pagans he had been ushered into the world by a miracle, and swans must have danced and sung at his birth; and he must have been a great hero, and no less than the son of Apollo, the god of wisdom and eloquence. He was a man long before he was of age and knew little more of the state of childhood than its innocency and pleasantness."[2] This last sentence sounds a little melancholy. It hints at so many long days spent grinding ceaselessly at books, with no time to spare for a boy's natural pursuits.

[1] Heber ("Life", *Works*, Vol. 1, p. xvi) disagrees with the statement that Taylor received a Fellowship. Rust (Funeral Sermon, *Works*, Vol. 1, p. cccxxii) says "as soon as he was graduate he was chosen fellow" and Rust was in a good position to know. The Absence Book of the College offers proof. His name first occurs there as a Fellow on 8 November 1633. These facts are discussed in the *Gentleman's Magazine* of April 1855.

[2] Rust, "A Funeral Sermon", *Works*, Vol. 1, p. cccxii.

However, Rust no doubt meant it for praise. But now the opportunity which shaped the whole of his future life came to him by mere chance.

In college two graduates generally shared rooms together, having two scholars also in their apartments and under their care. Taylor's room-mate had been a certain Thomas Risden, a man his senior by three years and now engaged in London as a lecturer at St Paul's Cathedral. Something made it impossible for Risden to fulfil his duties and he asked his room-mate to go in his place. Taylor accepted the invitation, and in London, preaching at St Paul's, met the patron without whom his brilliant gifts would have found little scope.

CHAPTER III

PATRONIZED BY LAUD

TAYLOR was now about twenty-one years old, and if Rust's evidence is true, he had grown into an exceedingly handsome young man.[1] His personal attraction combined with an oratorical gift which was already apparent, made such an impression on the congregation of St Paul's that the news of the brilliant young preacher just come to town was brought to the ears of Archbishop Laud. There was very little that was of any importance to the Church he loved which did not come to his notice sooner or later. For good men, if of the right principles, Laud had a patronage as ready as his interest was keen. Taylor received a command to appear at Lambeth and preach before the Archbishop.

Laud was a very shrewd judge, a hard man to sweep away by one dazzling exhibition, no matter how powerful the abilities displayed might be; nevertheless, Taylor seems to have come near to performing this feat. The Archbishop listened with "wonder and satisfaction"[2] to a discourse that was "beyond exception and beyond imitation".[3] When it was all over the only adverse remark he made was that the preacher was too young. This was a fault for which Taylor humbly begged his pardon and promised that if he lived he would mend it.[4] Laud knew very well that if Taylor was to develop as he ought to do he must not stay in London; too much popularity and too much preaching are both bad for a young priest. So it was with a promise that he would do something for the young man that he sent him away from the interview. Rust and Lloyd are eloquent about the impression which Taylor had made and their words are sometimes quoted as if they were the Archbishop's own, but probably they do nothing more than give as vivid an account of the meeting as possible.

So far as we can tell, Taylor never resumed the academic life

[1] Rust, "A Funeral Sermon", *Works*, Vol. 1, p. cccxxii. Rust says that all this happened soon after Taylor had taken his M.A., which was in 1633.
[2] Ibid.
[3] Ibid.
[4] Rust, ibid., Lloyd, *Memoirs*, p. 702. This retort is credited to a number of people in similar circumstances, but there is no reason why it should not have been made by Taylor. It is a piece of wit which is likely to occur to a good many.

at Cambridge which this visit to London had broken. There was little present inducement for him to remain in Caius College. His Fellowship, being only on Dr Perse's foundation, carried with it neither the same standing nor emolument as a Fellowship on the College would have done, and in Cambridge Taylor seems to have had few friends powerful enough to push him into anything better. It has been said that after leaving London Taylor retired into the country to a place called Maidley Hall, near Tamworth in Staffordshire.[1] This has been contested on the sufficient grounds that no such place exists, and either Madely in the northern part of the county should be substituted, or Tamworth in Warwickshire for Tamworth in Staffordshire.[2] The next clear light that we get on Taylor's movements comes from the Absence Book of Caius College, which shows that he returned to the College for one day in October 1635, arriving on the 13th and leaving on the 14th, probably to make arrangements for going away from Cambridge for good. He vacated his Fellowship on Lady Day 1636.

Laud was making definite efforts to obtain preferment for the young man whose preaching had so impressed him. Taylor almost certainly knew what was being done on his behalf when he paid his last visit to his old University in October 1635. On the 20th of the same month, some part of the intervening six days being probably spent in riding through the pleasant autumn landscape from one seat of learning to the other, Taylor was incorporated M.A. at University College, Oxford, as the indispensable preliminary to his receiving some settlement there. On 23 October Laud addressed the following letter:

To Dr Richard Astley, Warden of All Souls.

Salutem in Christo.

SIR,

These are on behalf of an honest man, and a good scholar. Mr Osborn, being to give over his Fellowship, was with me at Lambeth, and, I thank him, freely proffered me the nomination of a scholar to succeed him in that place. Now, having seriously deliberated with myself touching this business, and being willing to recommend such a one as you might thank me for, I am resolved to pitch upon Mr Jeremy Taylor, of whose abilities and sufficiencies everyways I

[1] Heber, "Life", *Works*, Vol. 1, p. xviii. Heber based his statement on a letter in the *Gentleman's Magazine* for 1783, p. 144.

[2] Willmott, *Bishop Jeremy Taylor*, p. 95. Also *Gentleman's Magazine* for 1792, p. 109. This last writer says that he searched for and did not find *Maidley Hill*, but the correspondent in 1783 wrote *Maidley Hall*.

have received very good assurance. And I do hereby heartily pray you to give him all furtherance by yourself and the Fellows at your next election, not doubting, but that he will approve himself a worthy and learned member of that society. And though he hath had his breeding, for the most part in the other University, yet I hope that shall be no prejudice to him, in regard he is incorporated into Oxford, *ut sit eodem gradu et ordine, etc.*, and admitted into University College. Neither can I learn that there is anything in your local statutes against it. I doubt not but you will use him with so fair respects, as befits a man of his rank and learning, for which I shall give you thanks. So I leave him to your kindness, and rest

Your very loving Friend,

LAMBETH HOUSE,   W. CANT.[1]
  October 23, 1635.

Mr Osborn had done something he had no right to do. The nomination to the Fellowship was not his to offer, but Laud who seems also to have been ignorant of other provisions in the statutes of All Souls, took Osborn at his word and expected his nominee to be elected without question. The Archbishop was not disappointed so far as the majority of the Fellows were concerned, they were willing to elect Taylor; but one of their number, Gilbert Sheldon, himself to become Primate later, was against the whole proceeding and opposed the election.[2] There the matter rested, for time was on the side of Laud so long as the majority refused to change their minds. The Archbishop was Visitor of the College and, if no valid election was made, the right of appointment accrued to him by virtue of his office. Sheldon does not seem to have been in any way bitter about the matter, but this was the first of one or two unfortunate disagreements between the two men which were to have a deeper influence than Taylor himself was aware. Yet for the time all went well, for although Taylor found it hard to forget how nearly his hopes had been wrecked there was no open breach; on 3 November 1635 he received a probationary Fellowship, and on the 14th of

[1] Tanner MSS., Vol. CCCXL, fol. 116 *a*, Printed Laud's *Works*, Vol. 6, p. 437. A copy with some alterations and omissions was printed by Wood, *Ath. Ox.*, Vol. 3, col. 782, and copied by Heber into the notes of his *Life* ("Life", *Works*, Vol. 1, p. ccliii). A note written in Sancroft's hand on the Tanner MSS. copy records the initial opposition and Taylor's election on Laud's mandate of 21 November 1635. The mandate itself is given in the Archbishop's Register, fol. 234b.

[2] Heber, "Life", *Works*, Vol. 1, p. xviii, speaks of Sheldon as the Warden of All Souls; this is incorrect. Richard Astley, elected 1618, died 23 February 1636, held office at the time. A letter of Laud's dated 18 December 1635 (*Works*, Vol. 6, p. 445) speaks of Astley's weakness still continuing, so probably Sheldon, who succeeded him, did the work. Heber's mistake has often been repeated.

the next January, Laud, this time in the unquestionable exercise of his right, appointed him a Fellow of All Souls.[1]

Anthony Wood's comment on the situation is in the main correct: "He came in merely by the paramount interest of the said Archbishop; yet it was done against the statutes of the college in these two respects. First because he had exceeded the age, within which the said statutes make candidates capable of being elected, and secondly that he had not been of three years standing in the University of Oxon, only a week or two before he was put in. However he being a person of most wonderful parts and like to be an ornament thereunto he was dispensed with."[2] Wood was wrong in one respect. The statutes did not exactly forbid a person of Taylor's age being elected, and, so far as his standing in the University was concerned, Laud probably thought that he carried his standing at Cambridge with him.

Taylor was now definitely started upon a career, having for patron the greatest man in the Church of England of that day. But his allegiance was no doubt decided before he met Laud. To one who loved beauty and kindness as much as Taylor did the aridities of Puritan worship and theology must inevitably prove distasteful. Yet there was something in his temperament which prevented him from ever becoming the complete party man. Taylor made some lasting friends at Oxford, yet we know little more of his life there than we do at Cambridge. Wood says it was during this time that he obtained the knowledge of casuistry for which he was afterwards famous.

It was at Oxford that Taylor got to know William Chillingworth, another protégé of Laud. What Chillingworth thought of Taylor is fairly clear from a letter which he wrote to a correspondent whom he calls his "Dear Harry", a person who was, in all probability, Sir Henry Coventry. "Mr Taylor", runs Chillingworth's letter, "did much confirm my opinion of his sufficience; but let me tell you in your ear—methinks he wants much of the ethical part of a discourser and slights too much many times the arguments of those he discourses with; but this is a fault he would quickly leave, if he had a friend who would discreetly tell him of it."[3]

[1] Wood, *Ath. Ox.*, Art. "Jeremy Taylor", note, prints the Archbishop's mandate. It was dated 21 November 1635, but the College did not act until the next year.
[2] Ibid.
[3] Des Maiseaux, *Life of Chillingworth*, p. 50. It is a fact to be remembered in view of Taylor's later interest in toleration that Chillingworth was at work during this period on his great book, *The Religion of Protestants a Safe Way of Salvation*, 1637; one of the most damaging attacks on the Roman position that has ever been written, and an unequivocal demand for liberty of conscience.

The "Mr Taylor" has not been absolutely identified with Jeremy, but the circumstances make it almost certain. Each of these two great men has his character illuminated to some extent by the letter. Chillingworth's respect for mere dialectics was the greatest weakness in his magnificent mental equipment. Truth is not always with the victor in an argument. To Taylor, Chillingworth's logic-chopping must often have seemed a wearisome business when it was employed in defence of or attack upon things which Taylor's intuition had already convinced him were true. But however inattentive he may have seemed at the time, the companionship bore great and lasting fruits.

The other known acquaintance of Taylor's at this time affords a curious reversal of much that has just been said about Chillingworth. Francis a Santa Clara was the name in religion of Christopher Davenport.[1] Born about 1598, he was educated at Merton College, Oxford, but afterwards went abroad to Douay, Ypres, and Salamanca. While on the Continent he became a Franciscan and returned as a missionary to England. He was a great deal thought of by both Roman Catholics and Protestants. Queen Henrietta made him her chaplain. Writing, proselytizing, raising money for Roman Catholic work overseas, and ministering to Romanists in England, these were the occupations of Santa Clara's long life and were carried on under many aliases. Oxford was the scene of a great deal of his activity, and it was there that he and Jeremy Taylor came into contact. Similarity of tastes no doubt drew them together, Santa Clara being "excellently well versed in school divinity, the Fathers and Councils in the philosophers and in ecclesiastical and profane historians".[2] Taylor himself was reading a good deal of school divinity at this period. The acquaintanceship gave rise to a rumour that Taylor was on the verge of going over to Rome, and in later times the Romanists themselves declared that he had entertained some such idea. There is only slight indication apart from his connexion with Santa Clara that it was ever likely, though so far as the missionaries were concerned, the wish to obtain such a convert was no doubt father to the thought that they had already almost obtained him.[3] In the first of the three "Letters to a Gentleman

[1] Wood, *Ath. Ox.*, Vol. 3, Col. 1,221.
[2] Ibid.
[3] Rust says: "In his younger years he met with some assaults from Popery and the high pretensions of their religious orders were very accommodate to his devotional temper; but he was always so much master of himself that he would never be governed by anything but reason, and the evidences of truth, which engaged him in the study of those controversies." "A Funeral Sermon", *Works*, Vol. 1, p. cccxxvi.

tempted to the communion of the Romish Church", Taylor
remarks about a subsequent rumour that he was on the point
of going over: "Sir be confident, they dare not tempt me to do
so and it is not the first time they have endeavoured to serve
their ends by saying such things of me. But I bless God for it;
it is perfectly a slander."[1]

The intimacy between Taylor and Santa Clara only lasted
during the time of Taylor's residence at Oxford. Santa Clara
wrote books; one of them, *Deus, Natura, Gratia*, was so concilia-
tory in tone toward the Protestants that it was put on the *Index
Expurgatorius* in Spain and only just escaped being publicly
burned in Italy.[2] An intimacy with him was one of the charges
against Laud at his trial. Santa Clara found times hard under
the Commonwealth, but continued his comings and goings in
various disguises until Charles II returned, when he was once
more made a Queen's chaplain, this time to Catherine of
Braganza. He was elected Provincial of his Order on several
occasions. In May 1680 he died and his body was buried in the
Church of the Savoy Hospital, London.

Jeremy Taylor's academic life came to an end in 1638. In
March of that year Juxon, Bishop of London, presented him to
the living of Uppingham in Rutlandshire. Rust states that he
was given the living by the Archbishop, but it was not Laud's
to give, though he may have brought Taylor to Juxon's notice.
The former incumbent of the living was Dr Edward Martin,
President of Queen's College, Cambridge. He was a Loyalist and
a definite Laudian, since he was one of the Archbishop's chaplains, and he had preached vigorously against Presbyterianism
at Paul's Cross.[3] This fact does not seem to have made him a
better parish priest than his neighbours. His other preferments
took him away from home a good deal and so the care of the
Uppingham people devolved upon his curate, Peter Hausted, a
man whose theological and political views were similar to his
rector's. Hausted himself does not appear to have been out-
standingly zealous in the parish. He was a dramatic author of
some talent both in Latin and English, and died among the
King's supporters at the siege of Banbury Castle.[4]

Taylor can scarcely have done more than go to Uppingham

[1] *Works*, Vol. 6, p. 667.
[2] It is important to distinguish between the *Index Librorum Prohibitorum*, which
contains a list of books forbidden to Roman Catholics, and the *Index Expurgatorius*,
which names those not to be read without revision.
[3] *D.N.B.*, Art. "Edward Martin".   [4] *D.N.B.*, Art. "Peter Hausted".

and instal himself in his new preferment before he was back at
Oxford again, this time to preach the annual Gunpowder
Treason sermon on 5 November. This is the first of Taylor's
productions to survive. The London sermons and his college
addresses may have supplied some of the material which was
woven into his later work, but they are not extant in recognizable
form. This first sermon of his to be made public has come in for
a good deal of adverse criticism. Heber on the whole speaks
highly of it, though he finds fault with the scholastic arrangement,
and condemns some of the language as, "the mere cant of travelled
foppery".[1] Gosse thinks it dull, and overloaded with authorities,
though he points to one passage which he considers a presage of
coming greatness.[2] No one would deny that the sermon is the
work of a young man who has not yet broken away from the
usual style of his times.

The sermon is dedicated to Laud by his "Grace's most observant
and obliged chaplain, Jeremy Taylor". This is the first indication
we have that he had ever received such preferment. When it was
given to him we do not know, though if he had held it throughout
his residence at All Souls it may explain a number of those
absences of his which are recorded in the College books. The text
of the sermon is taken from Luke 9.54, where the two disciples
James and John ask for fire from heaven to consume the inhospit-
able Samaritans. The subject matter is rigidly arranged under
headings: "1. The persons who asked the question. 2. The cause
that moved them. 3. The person to whom they propounded it.
4. The question itself and 5. The precedent they urged to move
the grant, drawn from a very fallible topic, a singular example,
in a special and different case."[3] Following the first division,
each head is briefly expanded, then gone over again and fully
treated. Under the first division a little is said about the sinfulness
of the Apostles in wishing to call down fire from heaven, and it is
suggested that their fault was due to over-hasty characters and a
defective education under the law. By a none too clear transition,
the preacher passes on to Romanists generally and Jesuits in
particular, whose sinfulness was of the same kind as the apostles',
since they wished for violent means to destroy their enemies.
Taylor's reading must already have been extraordinarily wide or
he must have spent a great deal of time preparing for his sermon,

[1] Heber, "Life", *Works*, Vol. 1, p. cxlviii.
[2] Gosse, *Jeremy Taylor*, p. 20. The passage referred to is in *Works*, Vol. 8, p. 495,
concluding paragraph. Heber had previously noticed the same passage.
[3] *Works*, Vol. 8, p. 458.

because his illustrations range from "Sanders our countryman", Emanuel Sa, and Mariana to the "damned act of Jacques Clement the monk upon the life of Henry the third of France, of Jean Chastel and Ravaillac upon Henry the fourth".[1] He sums up with references to a series of Roman casuists representing almost every European country of importance, in order to show that the trend of Roman teaching on the duties of a subject was to encourage treason if the ruler was not in obedience to the Pope.

The preacher returns to his text for a time in the second section and then begins a long passage dealing with the papal bull in Queen Elizabeth's time. This brings him to a statement that under Elizabeth "none were put to death for being a Roman Catholic, nor any of them persecuted for his religion".[2] The bull urged people to disobedience, therefore laws of increasing severity had to be made to put a stop to the disobedience. It was not a religious matter at all. Their religion allowed the Romanists to associate with the Anglican Church before the publication of the bull, so why not after. Taylor seems to overlook the fact that the authority of the Pope in such matters was a part of the Romanists' religion. In the third section Taylor devotes most of his time to proving that "He that conceals an intended murder or treason makes himself as much as a party for concealing as is the principal for contriving".[3] This, of course, opens up the whole question of the inviolability of the confessional; though he insists that the plotters did not confess something they had already done, but only put a question as to the righteousness of what they intended to do, a fact which, in Taylor's opinion, released that particular matter from the seal of confession. But, he goes on, even supposing that their confession had been "formal and direct, there is no such consent of the present Church nor any universal traditional of the ancient Church for the inviolable seal but plainly the contrary".[4] For the present Church, meaning by that the Church of England, he refers to the Canons of 1604, "they forbid not disclosure in case of murder or treason". Even in the Roman Church there

[1] *Works*, Vol. 8, p. 465.

[2] *Works*, Vol. 8, p. 469. It is interesting to compare with this the opinion of a modern historian: "The foundation of Elizabeth's persecutions was that *opinions* as such were of no consequence but that people who would not conform their *conduct* to her regulations must either be potential traitors politically or anarchists socially". Innes, *England under the Tudors*, pp. 417–18.

[3] *Works*, Vol. 8, p. 487.

[4] Ibid., p. 489. Modern casuists hold the seal utterly inviolable.

had been casuists who held that a confession might be revealed
to prevent an incestuous marriage, and it was universally held
that heresy was outside the seal. In the ancient Church both
Sozomen[1] and Origen[2] indicate that a priest might use his
discretion in revealing what he had heard in confession. St Leo
seems to assume that the practice of the Church went to the other
extreme, for he says, "some sins are inconvenient to be published"
and he derives it not from any simple necessity of the thing or a
divine right, but lest men out of inordinate love to themselves,
"should rather refuse to be washed than buy their purity with
so much shame".[3]

Sections 4 and 5 are quite short, dealing with the heinous-
ness of the sin which, in Taylor's opinion, was aggravated by the
use of gunpowder, which would have caused such devastation
to the surrounding districts if the Houses of Parliament had
indeed been blown up. There are a few passages here and there
which give promise of the orator who was later to develop. It is
odd that there are not more, because the eloquence of later
times was of that exuberant kind which generally goes with
youth. It was in that style apparently that Taylor had preached
in London and ravished all who heard him. Possibly in the case
of the Gunpowder Treason sermon the academic audience
checked him a little. In the presence of his teachers he dare not
let himself go. One thing is certain: the sermon, no matter how
much its subject matter interested an audience of good Protestants, could have ravished none by its literary charms.

Neither is it the type of sermon which anyone who intended
to join the Church of Rome could preach without a good deal
more duplicity in his character than Taylor ever possessed.
There is a story told by Anthony Wood, that the sharpest expressions in the sermon were not Taylor's own but were inserted by
the Vice-Chancellor.[4] This, as most critics have been quick to
point out, can scarcely be possible, because the whole sermon
is so much of a piece, the anti-Roman attitude so consistent
throughout, that no one could have influenced the tone to any
extent without writing the entire thing himself. Yet according
to this account the Romanists were so disgusted at Taylor's
weakness or duplicity that they refused to have any more to do
with him. There is some question whether it was at the request
of Laud or the Vice-Chancellor that Taylor undertook to preach.

---

[1] *Hist. Eccles.*, lib. vii, cap. 16. [2] *Homil. ii in psal. xxxvii.*
[3] *Works*, Vol. 8, p. 493. [4] Wood, *Ath. Ox.*, Art. "Taylor".

D

His own words are, "it was obedience to my superior tha
engaged me"[1] and, as the phrase occurs at the beginning of th
dedication of the sermon itself to Laud, it may be an indicatio
that it was another person who set him to work. As Hebe
points out, among all the reasons which the author alleges fo
dedicating his publication to the Archbishop, the fact that i
was undertaken at the Archbishop's command is never men
tioned, though that would have been the strongest of all had i
occurred.[2] If it was the Vice-Chancellor then it is easy to se
why the Romanists saw his hand in the sermon.

Some time, soon after Taylor's induction to his living,, anc
possibly as a return favour for the dedication, Laud was instru
mental in getting Taylor appointed one of Charles 1st chaplains.
This occurred as he was settling down at Uppingham to begir
his parish duties. He was still very young, only twenty-five, bu
a good scholar and already possessed of a reputation both as ε
preacher and a casuist. We are given an interesting glimpse o
his new parish by the diarist Evelyn who, under the heading
7 August 1654, notes: "Went to Uppingham the Shire town o
Rutland, pretty and well built of stone which is a rarity in tha
part of England, where most of the rural parishes are but o
mud, and the people living so wretchedly as in the most impover
ished parts of France, which they much resemble, being idle anc
sluttish. The country (especially Leicestershire) much in common
the gentry free drinkers." So on that evidence it would seem tha
in Uppingham, Taylor, like his brethren elsewhere, had tc
wrestle with two of the most deeply rooted vices of the seven
teenth century.

One of Taylor's first acts as rector of Uppingham was to builc
an organ for the church. In his *Ductor Dubitantium*, published ir
1660, he expressed the opinion that "the use of musical instru
ments may also add some little advantage to singing but the
are more apt to change religion into airs and fancies, and take
off some of its simplicity". In 1638 he was probably of a differen
mind. On 21 March of that year, the Bishop of Peterborougł
granted a faculty to build an organ in the parish church o

---

[1] *Works*, Vol. 8, p. 454.
[2] Heber, "Life", *Works*, Vol. 1, p. xxii.
[3] Rust, Funeral Sermon, *Works*, Vol. 1, p. cccxxii. One of the charges against
Laud at his trial was that he "hath taken upon him the nomination [Prynne and
Rushworth read 'commendation'] of Chaplains to the King". To which Laud
replied that it was an office belonging by ancient custom "in great part to the Lord
Chamberlain" and "I never named any to His Majesty, but I did fairly acquaint
the Lord Chamberlain with it and desired his favour". *Works*, Vol. 3, pp. 408, 410.

Uppingham and added a recommendation that the organist should be paid a salary of twelve pounds a year.[1] This was a large salary for a country congregation to find for one church functionary. The grant was made two days before Taylor's induction to the living by Bishop Dee, and so the movement to obtain an organ may have been begun by Taylor's predecessor. It was the first of a number of additions made to Uppingham Church in Taylor's time, most of them indicative of Laudian principles. On 10 May Bishop John Towers of Peterborough dedicated in his Cathedral a number of other ornaments for Uppingham.[2]

Seventeen days later the register records that "Mr Jeremiah Taylor, Rector, and Mrs Phoebe Landisdale married May 27th".[3] There is a possibility that this Phoebe Landisdale, or Langsdale, was a sister of the Edward Langsdale whom Taylor had coached in his Cambridge days; certainly she had a brother of the same name who became a physician of some reputation. If Taylor's former pupil and the lady who became his wife were brother and sister, then she came of a good family, for when Edward Langsdale entered Caius College in 1633 his father was described as Gervase Langsdale of Holborn, London, gentleman. The place of residence would lend some colour to the suggestion that Taylor met his bride during that, for him, eventful time when he was preaching at St Paul's.[4] On the other hand, it has been possible to argue from the fact that the marriage took place at Uppingham that Phoebe Langsdale was a resident of the town.[5] Both these pieces of guess-work may really have hit the mark. At a later date Taylor mentions his wife's mother, but not her father; there is therefore a possibility that he had died some time before the marriage took place. Under those circumstances, it would be very reasonable for the widow to remove her residence into her future son-in-law's parish, and the plan would be all the more attractive since her son Edward was now settled as a physician at Gainsborough, some seventy miles North of Uppingham, on the Lincolnshire border. If she did so she probably

[1] Uppingham Vestry Book for the years 1638–42.
[2] Ibid. "1 Chalice with a cover silver and gilt. 2 Patins silver and gilt. 2 pewter flaggons. 1 Diaper napkin for a Corporall. 1 Bible. 1 Book of common prayer. 1 Altar cloth of greene Silke Damaske. 2 Altar Cloths of Diaper. 1 long cussion of crimson velvit lin'd with crimson searge, with 4 great tassells of crimson silke. 1 Short cussion of the same. 1 Tippit of taffety sarcenit. 1 Surplice. 2 Black hoods of Searge lin'd with taffety sarcenit."
[3] Uppingham Marriage Register, page bearing date from 1632 to 1638.
[4] Brown, *Jeremy Taylor*, p. 19.
[5] Heber, "Life", *Works*, Vol. 1, p. xxiii.

moved back to London again when Taylor left his parish, for it would seem that she had a house in London 1653.

Of what happened during Jeremy Taylor's years at Uppingham we know very little. He only mentions his family affairs now and then in his books, and has indeed there given his opinion that an author should keep his domestic life in the background. The parish register of burials under the year 1642 gives us one small glimpse of sorrow visiting him, for it records that "William the son of Jeremy Taylor and Phoebe was buried May 23rd". In the *Autobiography of Henry Newcome*[1] we see Taylor again, this time in his capacity as a confessor. A certain Mrs Turner, whose husband was the incumbent of Little Dalby in Leicestershire, had her doubts about the position of the English Church, and was strongly inclined to join that of Rome. Naturally, this was a grief to her family, and someone persuaded her to consult the rector of Uppingham before she made up her mind. She did so and Taylor "enjoined her penance". This does not inevitably mean that she made a sacramental confession, but, knowing how much importance Taylor attached to the confessional in later days, it is probable that he would urge her to make use of it on this occasion. Mrs Turner afterwards told her son that during this visit to Taylor she saw in his study a little altar, with a crucifix upon it. This story is interesting, not only for the glimpse of the ecclesiastical atmosphere in which he worked, but also for the proof it gives that his reputation as a casuist was as great in the country as at Oxford. His learning, however, was not of much use on this occasion: the lady went over to Rome after all.

Taylor was now definitely placed by the world among the highest of High Church men. Barlow in 1641 reckoned him with Heylyn, Thorndike, and Pocklington among those who were forcing the Church of England into extremes of doctrine and practice not allowed by the law. It was no doubt only his obscurity as a young country parson, with no important published work to his credit, which saved him from that torrent of scurrilous abuse, embellished with the foulest epithets of brothel and tavern, which the Puritan pamphleteers poured over High Church men.[2]

The remainder of Taylor's life at Uppingham lies outside our

---

[1] Published by the Cheetham Society, 1852, Vol. 2, p. 312.
[2] Anyone who wishes for a sample of this propaganda, which even in these days is unprintable, should see two pamphlets in the *Harleian Miscellany: A Nest of Perfidious Vipers, Har. Misc.*, Vol. 5, p. 590, and *The Character of an Oxford Incendiary*, ibid., p. 497.

knowledge. It probably lasted about three years. In August 1641 he signed his name at the bottom of the page in his parish register. By the time the next August came round the King had set up his standard at Nottingham, and called all loyal subjects to his side to join in the now inevitable struggle. Taylor most probably considered that his chaplaincy to the King necessitated his answering the call. The next page in the parish register was not signed, and it was full by December 1642. Taylor's action in joining the royal forces would at once render him obnoxious to the committee which the Parliament had set up to remove all scandalous ministers.[1] If they then declared the living vacant, the Committee of Plundered Ministers which had been set up in 1642 to provide for those Puritan ministers who had been ousted by the Royalists would find a substitute. When Taylor left home, never to return as unchallenged rector again, he carried with him the manuscript of his first important book, *Episcopacy Asserted*. Where he left his wife and family, or whether they went wandering with him, we do not know. In November 1642 Taylor was with the King at Oxford, having, in all likelihood, accompanied him in his passage through the Midlands.

[1] On 19 December. This was a sub-committee of the Grand Committee for Religion which was set up on 6 November 1640.

CHAPTER IV

EPISCOPACY ASSERTED

TAYLOR was young, he was ambitious, he was well read, and he had a gift for writing; it was inevitable that sooner or later he would take his part in the theological battle of books which was raging at the time. Of all the subjects which were being debated there was every reason why episcopacy should seem the most urgent in its claims. So it was during that last year or two at Uppingham, when the system was being violently attacked, that his thought and reading upon it shaped themselves into a book. Probably he did not hope to do more than strengthen the known weak adherence to episcopacy of some of the King's friends. It is likely that eventually the book succeeded in this, for Charles was so pleased with it that on 1 November 1642, possibly before the work was actually made public, the degree of D.D. was conferred on Taylor by royal command. As the King had then only been in Oxford eight days, it may indicate that Taylor had been with the King during the Edgehill campaign, and that at some time during the march Charles had seen and approved the manuscript of *Episcopacy Asserted*.

Those who are acquainted with the episcopal controversy from the Reformation onward will have already met most of the arguments to be found in Taylor's book. It is prefaced by a dedication to the "Truly Worthy and most accomplished Sir Christopher Hatton". When, in 1657, it was republished bound up in one volume with the *Apology for Liturgy*, and *The Liberty of Prophesying*, Taylor was conscious that unkind critics might consider his use of the Fathers in *Episcopacy Asserted* contradicted what he declared to be his opinion of their value in *The Liberty of Prophesying*, and so he added a second dedication to Lord Hatton in which he made an attempt to reconcile this apparent difference. As we now have the book this second dedication comes first, but consideration of it will be better delayed until after we have made a study of *The Liberty of Prophesying*.

Although the King was pleased with Taylor's book, he was not prepared to add to his unpopularity by defending the author, should need arise. Taylor was under no illusions about that, as he very clearly shows at the beginning of his dedication to Hatton.

SIR:

I am engaged in the defence of a great truth, and I would willingly find a shroud to cover myself from danger and calumny; and although the cause both is and ought to be defended by Kings, yet my person must not go thither to sanctuary unless it be to pay my devotion, and I have now no other left for my defence; I am robbed of that which once did bless me, and indeed still does (but in another manner), and I hope will do more; but those distillations of celestial dews are conveyed in channels not pervious to an eye of sense, and now-a-days we seldom look with other, be the object never so beautious or alluring. You may then think, sir, I am forced upon you; may that beg my pardon and excuse.[1]

The reference to Laud is touching, for the Archbishop was then in the Tower and had only his prayers to give to his protégé. The new patron to whom Taylor offered his book seemed as good a choice as could be made. Whether they had met before they were both with the King at Oxford we have no means of knowing. It is just possible that they had, for Hatton was at Jesus College, Cambridge, when Taylor was at Caius, and Hatton's country house, Kirby Hall in Northamptonshire, was only a few miles from Uppingham. In 1643, Hatton became a Privy Councillor and was, in Clarendon's words "a person of great reputation". It was, however, a reputation which he was soon to lose.

There was no doubt in Taylor's mind that bishops and kings stand or fall together, and he makes his opinion clear in the dedication of his book. Bishops, he says, look to the King both for their livelihood and their promotion; in return they keep men firm in their duty to the King, assist him with their counsel and pay him taxes greater in proportion than those of the laity. This first important dedication of Taylor's is quite short, but written with the same skill in this type of composition which he showed all his life.

He begins his book by remarking that by far the most severe persecutions of the Church in former times were those that aimed at extirpating the bishops, whom the old persecutors always considered fundamental to the Church's life. Taylor concurs with St Cyprian in the opinion that the abolition of episcopacy is the forerunner of the great apostasy. It has been

[1] *Works*, Vol. 5, p. 9.

the catholic practice of Christendom for fifteen hundred years and he demands that those who would overthrow it "bring admirable evidence of Scripture, or a clear revelation proved by miracles, or a contrary undoubted tradition apostolical for themselves, or else hope for no belief against the prescribed possession of so many ages".[1] Episcopacy is built upon three bases, "Divine Institution, Apostolic Tradition, and Catholic Practice". Taking them in that order, Taylor was able to proceed with his study upon historical lines, and so give a unity to his book which he was not always able to achieve in his other works. He is confident that he can prove his case from the Bible, for Scripture, which legislates so carefully for personal behaviour, could not "make default in assignation of the public government, insomuch as all laws intend the public and general directly, the private and the particular by consequence only and comprehension within the general".[2] For the time being Taylor must have forgotten his Hooker, for this was an argument which had been dealt with very faithfully in the *Ecclesiastical Polity*.[3]

Does episcopacy derive from Christ? This is the most necessary part of Taylor's thesis, for if he establishes that he establishes everything. He thinks it must have done, otherwise its origin would be in human prudence which could change what it had begun and thus produce schism almost without end. But in fact Taylor finds the apostolic commission quite clearly given in the power of binding and loosing which our Lord bestowed upon the apostles and this was reinforced and amplified by the teaching of Jesus about "the faithful and wise steward".[4] A steward, says Taylor, is a pastor; a pastor and a ruler the same thing. "This is a known truth to all who understand either laws or languages".[5] Receiving these powers in their own persons, the apostles had authority to hand on to their successors, not their miraculous gifts, but the ordinary office of apostolate. "Now in clear evidence of sense these offices and powers are preaching, baptizing, consecrating, ordaining and governing."[6] That these successors were bishops is clear from Scripture, particularly in the cases of Titus and Epaphroditus, for "their Apostolate was a fixed residence and superintendence of their several churches".[7] This is still more apparent in the case of the angels of the seven churches who were commended for trying "those who say they are apostles and are not". This last reference Taylor considers

---

[1] *Works*, Vol. 5, p. 16.   [2] Ibid.   [3] Hooker, *Ecclesiastical Polity*, Bk. 3, Sec. 2.
[4] Luke 12.42.   [5] *Works*, Vol. 5, p. 18.   [6] Ibid., p. 20.   [7] Ibid., p. 23.

proof that the apostolate was an office episcopal in its nature. The impostors did not counterfeit a person but an office; this office, of course, being that of pastor and governor of Christ's Church—in fact, the episcopal office. The point which Taylor is concerned to make is, that from the time of the apostles to his own day there had been an unbroken transmission of certain powers from bishop to bishop by the laying on of hands; but he is careful to refrain from any illustration or elaboration of the succession which would tend to represent it as mechanical.[1]

Having proved the divine origin of bishops, Taylor goes on to seek the origin of the presbyterate. He finds it, as others did before him, in Christ's commission to the seventy who, although they are only heard of once in the Gospels, according to Taylor, soon began to exercise a function in the Church. He instances Ananias, who baptized St Paul; and Philip the deacon. This brings him to one of the most hotly debated points in the controversy. Were bishops and presbyters equal? Taylor says they were not, because only the apostles ordained and confirmed. An obvious case was that of Philip, who had to obtain apostolic confirmation for his converts at Samaria. The apostles were also the rulers of the Church, for Christ said to them, "*as* the Father hath sent me so send I you"—that is, with plenitude of power. This seems to be putting a greater burden on one small word than it can bear. To these arguments from Scripture Taylor adds the belief of the primitive Church which held that "Bishops are the ordinary successors of the Apostles, and Presbyters of the seventy-two; and therefore did believe that episcopacy is as truly of divine institution as the apostolate, for the ordinary office both of one and the other is the same thing. For this there is abundant testimony."[2]

Taylor now goes on to prove the apostolic tradition of episcopacy, which he has stated is the second basis of the system. The apostles, he contends, ordained bishops to several churches; he supports this statement with an enormous range of patristic quotation. Ordinations mentioned are those of St Simeon to be the successor of St James at Jerusalem, Timothy at Ephesus, Titus in Crete, Mark at Alexandria, Linus and Clement at Rome, and Polycarp at Smyrna. He argues from the Epistles

[1] Such, for instance, as Mason's illustration of orders passing through the bishops as through "conduit pipes". Mason, *Vindication of the Church of England*, p. 165.

[2] *Works*, Vol. 5, p. 40. St Thomas Aquinas and most of the great schoolmen except Scotus (*Sent.*, iv, xxv, 1) held that episcopacy is not a distinct order. Throughout his works Taylor's leaning toward the Scotists is apparent.

to Timothy and Titus that there is a clear transference of episcopal power in each case. In dealing with the passage from St Jerome, with which the Presbyterians made such play, Taylor insists that Jerome's only claim is for the bishops and presbyters to rule the Church in common; Jerome's own words prove that each had not the same office, for he clearly states that presbyters could not ordain.[1]

The third basis of episcopacy is catholic practice. Although at first titles were used indiscriminately, the early Church soon began to appropriate special names to special offices. In this process the word "bishop" came to be applied exclusively to the supreme officer of the Church, but not as his sole name. "Pastor" was also used, and this brings a protest from Taylor against the Genevan practice of calling presbyters "pastors", since in the early Church that designation was restricted to bishops, for whom also there were other special titles such as *doctor*, *pontifex*, and *sacerdos*. The subordination of presbyters to bishops was proved by the fact that when a priest was elevated to the episcopate he had to be specially ordained to his new office, and in this new ordination the presbyters were not allowed to join in the laying on of hands.

Some of the Presbyterians had ingeniously argued that if the consecration of the sacred elements in the Eucharist is the highest work to which man can aspire, and a presbyter undoubtedly had the power to consecrate, how could he be inferior to a bishop? Taylor retorts that it is presumptuous to compare the sacraments, but in any case, those who could exercise a double right of consecration—that is to say, those who could both consecrate the Holy Eucharist and bestow Holy Orders—were undoubtedly greater than those who could exercise only one. Not that the point needs serious argument for "these men that make this objection do not make it because they think it true, but because it will serve a present turn. For all the world sees that to them that deny the real presence this can be no objection, and most certainly the anti-episcopal men do so in all senses."[2]

Taylor on the reformed Churches is particularly interesting. They and their opinions had been bandied about so much in theological controversy that Taylor was obviously getting tired of them:

What think we of the reformed Churches? For my part I know not what to think; the question hath been so often asked, with so much

---

[1] Jerome's words are: "*Quid facit episcopus excepta ordinatione quod presbyter non faciat?*" *Ad Evangelum*, Tom. iv, Pt. 2, Col. 803.
[2] *Works*, Vol. 5, p. 109.

violence and prejudice, and we are so bound by public interest to
approve all that they do, that we disabled ourselves to justify our own.
For we were glad at first of abettors against the Roman church; we
found these men zealous in it; we thanked God for it, as we had
cause; and we were willing to make them recompense by endeavouring
to justify their ordinations, not thinking what would follow upon
ourselves; but now it is come to that issue that our own episcopacy
is thought not necessary because we did not condemn the ordinations
of their presbytery. Why is not the question rather what we think of
the primitive church than what we think of the reformed churches?[1]

It was the duty of these Churches, if they thought their own
bishops corrupt, to seek ordination from pure sources. But he
will not condemn them. They must stand or fall to their own
master. Taylor was obviously more sceptical of the necessity
which the reformed churches were under than some other writers
of his time, and the history has shown that his feeling was right.
In Scotland especially the break with episcopacy was deliberate
and unforced by circumstances.

As bishops had always had the sole right of ordaining, so had
they always had the sole right of confirming.

The next section, which comprises nearly half the book, bears
out the suggestion that it was the lukewarm friends of episcopacy
in the King's party whom he specially wished to influence, for it
is addressed to those who "by all means would be thought to be
quite thorough on behalf of the bishops' order and power, such
as it is, but call for a reduction to the primitive state, and would
have all bishops like the primitive".[2] In this part Taylor's
arguments are an expansion of those already used by John
Davenant. The primitive Church "expressing the calling and
office of a bishop did so in terms of presidency and authority".
Again many quotations from the Fathers are brought in to show
that they used the highest terms possible when they referred to
the dignity of a bishop. They had complete spiritual authority
over clergy and laity, they were appointed the judges of all
spiritual causes by the canons; the bishops' powers were universal,
but they did not trespass on those of royalty; the Church had its
sphere and the King his. Taylor ends this section with a description of the Church's disciplinary powers:

As no human power can disrobe the church of the power of excommunication, so no human power can invest the church with a lay-
compulsory. For if the church be not capable of a *jus gladii*, as most

[1] *Works*, Vol. 5, p. 118.   [2] Ibid., p. 129.

certainly she is not, the church cannot receive power to put men to death, or to inflict lesser pains in order to it, or anything above a salutary penance, I mean in the formality of a church tribunal, then they give the church what she must not, cannot take.[1]

After going over a little of the old ground about the difference between presbyters and bishops he suddenly brings the question into his own age. "We have seen what episcopacy is in itself, now from the same principles let us see what it is to us".[2] It was, and is, necessary to the very being of a Church and both Ignatius and Cyprian are brought in to support his statement. Without bishops there can be no unity. To those who respect episcopacy but object to the outward honour which had come to be associated with it, he replies that they can love a thing little who grudge it good words, and did not St Paul say that bishops were worthy of double honour? Some people objected to bishops having secular employment in the State. Why should they object? The councils of the Church had never forbidden it and the practice was reasonable in itself. Bishops were often the fittest persons that could be found for certain offices, and when they were away from their dioceses they could delegate their power to a proper person.[3] Taylor ends with a request for his reader's prayers, both for the King and for episcopacy.

Without adding much to the arguments already in circulation, Taylor had produced a notable book. Heber very justly calls it "a specimen of manly and moderate disputation", though his theological opinions did not entirely coincide with the author's and he was not impressed by the evidence which Taylor had offered for the divine institution of episcopacy. Taylor was handicapped in a similar way to most of his contemporaries who wrote on this subject. They went to antiquity to find one, precise model of Church government and they were often put to a good many shifts when they found something which was not quite one thing or the other. A more critical method of dealing with their sources would have been a great help to them. If a statement was plain, it was generally, for controversial purposes,

---

[1] *Works*, Vol. 5, p. 147.
[2] Ibid., p. 192.
[3] Ibid., p. 207. Taylor's handling of this part of his subject met with Laud's particular approval. In his *Answer to Lord Say's Speech against the Bishops*, he refers to "a book entitled, *Episcopacy Asserted*, made by a Chaplain of mine, Mr Jer. Taylor, who hath learnedly looked into and answered such Canons of Councils as are most quick upon bishops or other clergymen for meddling much in temporal affairs. And therefore thither I refer the reader, being not willing to trouble him with saying over another man's lesson". *Works*, Vol. 6, pp. 199–200.

taken at its face value; if it was obscure it could be argued over. The endeavour to estimate the respective values of ancient authors, what opportunities they had for knowing the subject they wrote about, or their freedom from prejudice, was only just beginning. Taylor's reading was immense and he uses the material it offered him liberally. We may feel sometimes that the quotations he brings out so confidently in a number of cases prove very little, and even to do that they are strained more than they ought to be; but even then we must admit that they are not the mere ostentation of pedantry, they are there because Taylor thought them relevant. The language is very temperate for a theological disputant of those days. Taylor was too gentle-minded to pad out his book with abuse, or to whip up the spirits of his party by calling the other side names. There are none of the gorgeous passages which decorate a great part of his later work. The prose is plain, and apart from the lavish quotations and a few obsolete words here and there it is very readable. Once or twice he even drops into colloquialisms.

Since he had lost Uppingham, Taylor had now no means of livelihood except what little his chaplaincy to the King and his writing might produce; so early in 1643 the King appointed him to the living of Overstone, in the district between Northampton and Wellingborough, where the royal authority was still respected.[1] Gosse conjectures that this was given to Taylor through the influence of the Earl of Northampton, who was to some extent Taylor's friend.[2] After the Earl's death at the Battle of Hopton Heath on 19 March 1643, his widow still continued to befriend Taylor; so it is possible, though there is no proof of it, that the gift of Overstone was made at their request. It is doubtful if Taylor ever went to his new charge, just as it is doubtful how long he stayed at Oxford. Wood says that he was a frequent preacher before the Court and that he was attached to the royal army as chaplain until the decline of the King's cause made him seek refuge in Wales.[3] That is probably, like many more of Wood's statements, true enough in the main, but not to be pressed in detail. Taylor, as a royal chaplain, a popular preacher, and in favour at Court because of his book, would be almost certain to preach before the King. There is reason also to suppose that, for a time at least, he was acting as chaplain with a part of the King's forces; but it is almost certain that

[1] The Overstone registers for the period of Taylor's incumbency are no longer in existence.
[2] Gosse, *Jeremy Taylor*, p. 27.   [3] Wood, *Ath. Ox.*, Art. "Jeremy Taylor".

Taylor was not in unbroken attendance on the King and the army from the time he left Uppingham until settling in Wales.

During the spring of 1644 he may have paid a visit to Uppingham, for in that year the issue of the Cavalier news-sheet, *Mercurius Aulicus*, for one of the early weeks in May contained a piece of information about that parish which had probably been conveyed to Sir John Birkenhead, the writer of the publication, by Taylor himself. Birkenhead would jump at the story, for it came very handy to his purpose that week, which was to illustrate the character of the ministers whom Parliament was forcing on the parishes of England in place of the royalist clergy:

Monday, May 6.—Now, if you would see what heavenly men these lecturers are, be pleased to take notice, that at Uppingham, in Rutlandshire, the Members have placed one Issac Massey to teach the People, (for the true pastor, Dr Jeremy Taylor, for his learning and loyalty is driven thence, his house plundered, his estate seized, and his family driven out of doors.[1]). This Massey, at a communion this last Easter, having consecrated the bread after his manner, laid one hand upon the Chalice, and smiting his breast with the other, said to the parishioners—"Neighbours, here's to ye all!" and so drank off the whole cupfull, which is none of the least. Many of the parish were hereby scandalized, and therefore departed without receiving the Sacrament. Among which, one old man, seeing Massey drink after this manner, said aloud, "Sir, much good do it you". Whereupon Massey replied, "Thou blessest with thy tongue, and cursedest with thy heart; but 'tis no matter, for God will bless whom thou cursedest". This Massey coming lately into a house of the town, used these words, "This town of Uppingham loves Popery, and we would reform it, but they will not," (and without further coherence, said,) "but I say, whoever says there is any king in England besides the Parliament at Westminster, I'll make him for ever speaking more." The master of the house replied, "I say there is a King in England besides the Parliament in Westminster," whereupon Massey, with his cudgel, broke the gentleman's head. Whoever doubts that Mr Massey is injured by these relations, may satisfy themselves in inquiring of the inhabitants of Uppingham parish."

Written with a purpose though the story is, there is no need to reckon it untrue. *Mercurius Aulicus* is trustworthy, on the whole, until the decline of the King's cause.[2] We have no means of

[1] This does not necessarily mean that Taylor's sequestration had only just taken place, as the *D.N.B.* would imply.
[2] *Camb. Hist. Eng. Lit.*, Vol. 7, p. 343. But S. R. Gardiner (*Civil War*, Vol. 1, p. vi) is of the opposite opinion, remarking that it is "untrustworthy to the end" being written with the sole object of making Puritans and Parliamentarians ridiculous.

determining what happened to Taylor between the spring of
1644, when he was probably in Uppingham and heard the story
that has just been recounted, and the early part of 1645 when he
appeared in Wales, this time bearing out Wood's statement that
he served as an army chaplain.

His name occurs during the struggle which centred round
Cardigan Castle. At Christmas-time 1644, Rowland Laugharne
had captured the castle for the Parliament, though the Royalists,
recognizing it as a strategic point of great importance, had
garrisoned it very strongly. As soon as the news that it had fallen
came to Colonel Gerard, he set out from Newcastle Emlyn, one
of Lord Cardigan's residences in South Wales, to retake Cardigan
for the King. He attacked on 22 January 1645, and was repulsed,
but tried again, and this time managed to get into the town and
cut the bridge, thereby blocking the entry of provisions into the
castle. Gerard then ordered Colonel Poole, the Parliamentary
commander, to surrender. But Poole did no such thing. By some
means or other, he managed to get news of his plight through
to Laugharne, who doubled back and attacked the besiegers
from the rear while Poole sallied out and went at them in front.
Caught between these two forces, Gerard was very badly beaten,
losing "two hundred slain upon the place, four brass pieces of
ordnance, six hundred arms, and one hundred and fifty prisoners
taken, whereof Major Slaughter, divers inferior officers, and
Dr Taylor".[1] No specific statement is made that this is Jeremy,
but there is no reason to suppose that it was anybody else. It is
difficult to decide what had brought him to Wales. Several
reasons might be given, but none with absolute certainty. Possibly
he had gone with Gerard, as Fuller went with Hopton, to escape
from the noise and unruly life of Oxford. Wood's statement that
he was a chaplain with the King's forces bears this out to some
extent, there are also a number of passages in his works which
seem to show that he had some first-hand acquaintance with
army life.[2] But on the other hand, it may not have been the
army which took him into Wales at all; the need to earn a living
for himself and his family may have already settled him there,
and he may only have visualized a temporary absence from the
school he was keeping when he set out with Gerard's ill-fated
expedition. Yet again, how he was earning his living, whether
the chaplaincy to Lord Carbery (which we know he afterwards
held) was his chief support and the school only a subsidiary

[1] Whitelocke, *Memoirs*, p. 130.   [2] *Works*, Vol. 4, p. 245.

venture; or whether, as seems more likely, the school came first and the chaplaincy afterwards is by no means clear. Neither do we know how he escaped out of the hands of his captors. Laugharne, after his success at Cardigan, advanced to Newcastle Emlyn, but there the Royalist forces defeated him and Taylor may have been recaptured or he may have been left behind at Cardigan and afterwards exchanged.

Taylor himself did once refer to the events which brought him into Wales, but in so obscure a fashion that we get very little help. He says:

In this great storm which hath dashed the vessel of the church all in pieces, I have been cast upon the coast of Wales, and in a little boat thought to have enjoyed that rest and quiet which in England in a greater I could not hope for. Here I cast anchor, and thinking to ride safely, the storm followed me with so impetuous violence, that it broke a cable, and I lost my anchor; and here again I was exposed to the mercy of the sea, and the gentleness of an element that could neither distinguish things nor persons. And but that He who stilleth the raging of the sea, and the noise of His waves, and the madness of His people, had provided a plank for me, I had been lost to all opportunities of content or study. But I know not whether I have been more preserved by the courtesies of my friends, or the gentleness and mercies of a noble enemy: "And the barbarous people shewed us no little kindness: for they kindled a fire, and received us every one, because of the present rain, and because of the cold."[1]

A good deal of ingenuity has been spent upon this passage, it must be confessed with no very certain results. Heber's suggestion that Taylor's first wife was dead by this time and that the "little boat" represented his marriage to his second wife Joanna Bridges of Mandinam, can hardly be accepted. All the evidence points to Phoebe Taylor's death having taken place in 1651. But the second part of Heber's conjecture—that the "storm" which followed him was Gerard's attack on Cardigan Castle and that the noble enemy "was Laugharne" seems more likely.[2]

Gosse thinks that the "little boat" represents clerical work of some kind in Wales and that the "greater" represents Oxford. He objects to the identification of Laugharne as the "noble enemy" on the ground that "noble" points to one who was technically a nobleman. He adds that "it would greatly simplify our enquiry if we could persuade ourselves that the noble enemy was Richard Vaughan, the Second Earl of Carbery".[3] Gosse

[1] *Works*, Vol. 5, p. 341. Taylor gives the quotation from Acts (28.2) in Greek.
[2] Heber, "Life", *Works*, Vol. 1, p. xxvii.   [3] Gosse, *Jeremy Taylor*, p. 33.

admits that Carbery was not at this time actually an enemy, but his standing was so doubtful that diffidence about giving offence, either to the King, to whom the *Liberty of Prophesying*, the book which contained the passage, was to be presented, or to Carbery, his patron, may have been the very cause of the ambiguity. It is an interesting suggestion but there are arguments against it.

In the first place, "noble" was undoubtedly applied in the seventeenth century to many who were not technically of noble birth.[1] It signified moral characteristics as much as rank and could undoubtedly be applied to Laugharne, who, if he released Taylor, had acted nobly.[2] There is another point in this connexion worth noticing. Rust, when he preached Taylor's funeral sermon in 1667, used very similar language about this incident to that which Taylor had used himself though there was no longer any need to spare the feelings of Charles I or Carbery, since both were dead. It might be argued that Rust knew no more than we do about what actually happened, and in this case it is hard to see why he mentioned the incident at all since he was not writing a biography. It is more likely that the same reasons for discretion existed then as existed in 1647. If Taylor's leaving Oxford was something which the hotheads were liable to misunderstand, then it was probably as well to speak about it as vaguely as possible.

We may perhaps reconstruct what happened in some such fashion as this: Taylor is in Oxford, feeling as both Chillingworth and Fuller and no doubt a host of other decent-minded people felt, grieved and angry at the sin and bigotry of the place as well as finding the need to seek a settled livelihood for himself and his family. He comes across an old acquaintance, one William Nicholson, who is Archdeacon of Brecon, but has lost his living on account of his refusal to sit in the Assembly of Divines to which he had been nominated.[3] Like Taylor, Nicholson has nothing to do and therefore, since he was a schoolmaster in early life, he is considering setting up a school again; in Wales, since his connexions are there and it is a place where Royalist

[1] Cp. "this was the noblest Roman of them all". Shakespeare, *Julius Caesar*, Act V, Sc. v, line 68.
[2] It may not be irrelevant to note that Laugharne deserted to the King in 1648.
[3] William Nicholson, 1591–1672. Chorister and Bible-Clerk of Magdalen College, Oxford. Master of the Free School, Croydon, 1616–29. Rector of Llandilo-Vawr, Archdeacon of Brecon. Partner with Taylor in his school and, at the Restoration, Bishop of Gloucester. Patron and friend of George Bull and author of a well-known exposition of the Catechism and other works.

E

sympathies are strong. Taylor agrees to join him in the venture and suggests that they should take another Oxford friend of his with them, William Wyatt, to act as usher.[1] But Taylor is already a well-known man, and leaving Oxford is not so easy for him. The hotheads look upon his going as, to some extent, a defection from their cause. It is this which makes him refer to it in veiled terms when he comes to write the dedication to *The Liberty of Prophesying* a year or two later. The school has just been started when the trouble at Cardigan Castle breaks out, and Colonel Gerard gets together his force to retake it for the King. Taylor, smarting a little perhaps at the things which have been said about his leaving Oxford, decides to go with the expedition; he has some experience of a chaplain's work, gained when he was with the King at Edgehill, and is therefore as fit a person as anybody in the neighbourhood for the post. He is taken prisoner, and it is not until Nicholson and possibly some of the more influential supporters of the school can get into touch with Laugharne that he is released and allowed to go back to his pupils, whose numbers have suffered both through his absence and his connexion with the weaker party. All this is admittedly conjecture, but it fits the facts. One thing we do know for certain: that Taylor went to Wales in search of peace and quiet and that, ultimately, he found it there.

[1] William Wyatt, 1616–1685. Entered St John's College, Oxford, but took no degree, owing to the Civil War, until 1661. Taught in Wales under Taylor, at Evesham, and at Twickenham under William Fuller: who, on becoming Bishop of Lincoln, made Wyatt first Prebendary, then Precentor.

CHAPTER V

FIRST YEARS AT GOLDEN GROVE

ALL over England there were Royalist clergy, dispossessed of their churches, seeking refuge and a means of livelihood. Taylor was more fortunate than many. He was able to spend the best years of his life in peace, away from persecution; straightened for money at times, but not depressed by hopeless poverty, in a congenial occupation which left him time enough to develop the literary gift of which he was now fully conscious. In Wales he was to learn how that gift could best be employed. The three friends had considerable success with their school. Several youths were "educated there most loyally and afterward sent to the university".[1] It produced at least one distinguished man, Sir John Powel, who was dismissed from his place on the King's Bench for stating at the trial of the seven bishops that the Declaration of Indulgence was a nullity. At his death it was recorded on his tombstone that he was educated under Jeremy Taylor.

The school was kept at Llanfihangel-Aberbythych, Carmarthenshire, in a house called Newton Hall, which suggests that the masters had a fair number of boys under their charge. At the start Hatton was the patron of the venture, although he was displaced by Carbery later on. His name is connected with two out of the three publications with which Taylor was concerned during the first years of his life in Wales. The first of these was an edition of the Psalms called *Hatton's Psalter*, which is sometimes classed as Taylor's sole work, but on insufficient grounds. The next, *A Discourse concerning Prayer Extemporary*, appeared anonymously in 1646, but because of the favourable reception it met with from Charles I, Taylor afterwards expanded the work and republished it under his own name with a dedication to the King, then nearing his end. The third, *A New Institution of Grammar*, was an ordinary piece of schoolmaster's writing. Wood says that Wyatt wrote it, and apparently he always claimed it as his,[2] though it has been credited to Taylor, whose part was probably

[1] Wood, *Ath. Ox.*, Art. "Taylor".
[2] Wood, *Ath. Ox.*, Art. "Taylor". See also Wood, *Fasti Oxoniensis*, Art. "Wyatt".

nothing greater than looking over the MS., making a few suggestions and contributing an English dedication to the "Most Hopeful Christopher Hatton, Esquire", one of their pupils and a son of Lord Hatton of Kirby, their patron. Wyatt supplied a Latin dedication in which he rather pompously refers to the school as "*Collegium Newtoniense*". Taylor's name had a greater value with the public than Wyatt's. The latter was merely an unknown usher in a Welsh academy, so the work was put out as Taylor's.

Nearby was Golden Grove, the seat of the Vaughan family, with whom Taylor was becoming more and more intimate as the years went by. Richard Vaughan, the Second Earl of Carbery, was at this time a man nearly fifty years of age. He had lived the ordinary life of an influential country gentleman before the Civil War. He had travelled, represented a constituency (Carmarthen) in the Parliament of 1624, and succeeded to his earldom in 1634. When the war began, energetic action on one side or the other was looked for from him. He disappointed the expectation. As he had raised some troops, he received command of the King's forces in Wales and an English peerage in 1643, but did little to justify his appointment, for when Rowland Laugharne defeated him in the following year, Carbery was glad to pay his fine as a delinquent and, in 1647, receive a pardon from Parliament. It did not increase his popularity with the Royalists when he escaped the sequestrations with which their enemies were so liberal in that neighbourhood. It was whispered that Essex procured him his pardon "for service done by him to Parliament while he was General and proved by a certificate from the General to Parliament".[1] This however did not entirely allay Carbery's fears. When, in 1648, Cromwell's campaign in Wales brought him into the neighbourhood of Golden Grove, the owner thought it wiser to be out of the way, and accordingly withdrew to one of his outlying farms and left his wife to do the best she could with the victorious general should he chance to call. He did call, but whatever his intentions were before he paid the visit, the charm and courtesy of his hostess so disarmed him that when he went on his way he had done no hurt to her or her family. Later on he must have felt some friendliness toward Lord Carbery, since, when he became Protector, "Cromwell sent from the parks he then possessed near London several stags unto him to furnish his park at Golden Grove in Wales".[2] He

---

[1] MS., *circa* 1660, printed in the *Cambrian Register*, Vol. 1, p. 164.   [2] Ibid.

was "in a word a fit person for the highest public employment, if integrity and courage were not suspected to be often failing in him".[1]

It was a time when those who were not strong for one side or the other could scarcely hope to be understood. Carbery was a man of some refinement, home-loving, but without that nobility of mind which is willing to suffer death for a cause. He was weak and drank more than was normal even in those heavy-drinking days. Men of his type do not serve their fellows in heroic ways, but they have their uses. If their interest with those in power is great enough, they may furnish an asylum to those arts which war is apt to destroy. Though Carbery was lukewarm both to King and Parliament, he afforded a refuge to Jeremy Taylor. The Parliamentary leaders were not eager to harry a man whose opinions might be different from theirs if he was willing to go quietly about his business and keep the laws. Evelyn, for instance, lived at Deptford as a known Royalist and even kept up a correspondence with his father-in-law, the King's Ambassador in Paris, but no one interfered.[2] Carbery, whatever people may have said about his doubtful loyalty in parliamentary times, managed to retain enough interest with the Royalists to be made Lord President of the Welsh Marches at the Restoration, in which capacity he found a place in his household for another famous literary man—Samuel Butler, the author of *Hudibras*, who was his secretary.

Golden Grove is a lovely name for a very lovely place. The original house where Taylor was entertained was burned down in 1729 and a new dwelling was built afterwards on the site. An engraving published as a frontispiece to Taylor's *Polemical Discourses* in 1657 shows what the house was like when the author lived there. It was a large building surrounded by parkland. About a mile away the River Towy flowed past it on the north. There were the ruins of two old castles, Dynevor and Dryslwyn, well in view. The countryside was thick with trees of differing foliage and sheltered by hills. Grongar Hill, a place which Dyer's poem has made famous, is a little to the west. All this had its influence on Taylor. Although it was a time when natural scenery was not given the place in literature which it has since received, Taylor's writings at Golden Grove show

---

[1] M.S., *circa* 1660. See also Phillips, *Memoirs of the Civil War in Wales and the Marches* (1874), Vol. 2, p. 157.

[2] Evelyn, *Diary*, 21 March 1649. The Diary for this and the following years records a continual series of open visits to his father-in-law in Paris.

that he was not entirely indifferent to the beauty with which he was surrounded.[1]

But he had not yet escaped from the neighbourhood of wars. On 14 June 1645 the King's army was defeated at Naseby by the parliamentary forces which outnumbered the royal troops by nearly two to one. By 1 July the King was at Abergavenny, not much more than forty miles from Golden Grove, seeking help from the gentlemen of Herefordshire and South Wales.[2] It was near enough for Taylor and his friends to have ridden over and paid their respects to the defeated monarch had they wished. On 3 July the King moved on to Raglan, still hoping for, and striving to obtain, help from the Welsh, but none was forthcoming. The gentry offered promises which they could not fulfil. Volunteers came in very slowly and pressed men ran away, for the people of those parts were not eager to serve the King outside their own borders.[3] All the while bad news came in fast. Pontefract had surrendered, Scarborough Castle had fallen, Hereford was besieged and had little chance of effective resistance; all hope of real succour for the royal cause was dwindling away. Monmouthshire had offered a few men, Glamorganshire a few more men and a little money, but disaffection was growing and every day the King's personal safety grew less. Yet out of this darkness a light began to arise. Scotland showed an unexpected disposition to come to terms. Hopeless of doing any good in Wales, on 5 August the King marched northwards. Before another year was over he had surrendered himself to the Scots.

In 1647 Taylor published his *Liberty of Prophesying*, a work which is important, not only in his own development, but in relation to English life and literature as a whole. This was the first of his books to be printed in London. Richard Royston was now his publisher, and had bought up the copies which remained of *Episcopacy Asserted* and reissued them with a new title page in 1647. It was on the whole a fortunate relationship, though there were some misunderstandings during its course. Royston was at the head of his profession in his day. He was Bookseller to Charles I and the two kings who succeeded him. During the parliamentary days his royalist publications got him into some trouble with the authorities, but the printing of the *Eikon Basilike*, and the

[1] See *Works*, Vol. 3, p. 330, for a simile drawn from the effect of a high wind on scenery similar to that of Golden Grove.

[2] Clarendon, *History of the Rebellion*, Vol. 9, p. 68.   [3] Ibid.

consequent monopoly of printing Charles I's works which he
received at the Restoration, must have made full amends.

Taylor's own writings, especially his devotional books, were
extremely popular and likely to be profitable to any publisher.
But it is to be doubted whether the inducement to make money
had any effect in setting him to work on the *Liberty of Prophesying*.
The sum he would be likely to gain by it would hardly compensate
him for the necessary expenses. Authors then and for some time
after looked to the dedication as the most remunerative part of
their work, but Hatton, to whom the book was to be offered,
was not in the circumstances likely to be very liberal. Taylor
wrote because he could not help writing. He confesses this in the
dedication:

Since I have come ashore, I have been gathering a few sticks to
warm me, a few books to entertain my thoughts, and divert them
from the perpetual meditation of my private troubles and the public
dyscrasy,[1] but those which I could obtain were so few, and so impertinent and unuseful to any great purposes, that I began to be sad upon
a new stock, and full of apprehension that I should live unprofitably,
and die obscurely, and be forgotten, and my bones thrown to some
common charnel-house, without any name or note to distinguish me
from those who only served their generation by filling the number
of citizens.[2]

Taylor had the scholar's mentality. In the midst of distress
he turned to books to find an anodyne, and reading led on
naturally to writing without any thought for the result than that
it may bring him fame. He wanted a subject which would not
need continual reference to a library, for he had few books of
his own. In later years no doubt Royston would lend him a good
many of the books he wanted, for booksellers were generally
willing to help their authors out by lending them the works of
reference they needed, but at this time that source of supply was
not open. Oxford and Cambridge were far away, and apparently
he was not yet sufficiently intimate with Lord Carbery's household to have the run of the collection which would almost certainly
be found at Golden Grove. The great difference in the number
of quotations to be found in this book and those in the works
which were published in later years shows that somehow, in the
meantime, Taylor had obtained access to a larger collection of

---

[1] Dyscrasy, i.e. δυσκρασία =a bad condition of the air, or the body. Taylor
occasionally anglicized a Greek word like this.
[2] *Works*, Vol. 5, p. 341.

books than probably he was ever able to buy. He found the subject he wanted. It was a subject on which he had thought for a number of years, which he had often discussed with Hatton, and which the struggle, going on all around him and inflicting suffering on so many, made more important every day.[1] Where should the bounds of religious toleration be set? It was plainly contrary to the Gospel that men should fight over religion. Could not some way be found to settle the differences between Christians without resort to the sword? Would it not show a greater zeal for the cause of Christ if his followers tolerated some differences among themselves in obedience to the spirit of his teaching rather than forcibly establish the letter of it?

Once Taylor had made up his mind he wrote eagerly. "As if I had thought it possible to have persuaded the rough and hard-handed soldiers to have disbanded presently."[2] The arguments were already in his head, what he himself had suffered had only made their truth more apparent. We know that he was friendly with Chillingworth in the days when they were both living in Oxford, and we know how much Chillingworth's experience, as well as an inherent dislike of dogmatism, had made him willing to tolerate religious differences. No doubt in his wanderings, captivity, and poverty Taylor recalled some of those discussions in the old University days to which Chillingworth had at the time thought him inattentive.

As a chaplain to the King, Taylor had some personal experience of the perplexities which assailed the King when political expediency seemed to suggest toleration. In August 1647 he was himself in London, in close contact with the King and no doubt aware of much that was being done. On the 28th, Charles who was in doubt this time about how far he ought to tolerate the Independents, once more consulted the clergy, and Jeremy Taylor was among those whose opinion was asked. There are copies of the question and answer still surviving, one of them written out in Dr Hammond's own beautiful, clear hand.

Que:

Whether upon any necessity or exigence of state it bee lawfull for a Christian Prince, beside the religion established, so to tolerate the exercise of other religions in his Kingdom as to oblige himself not to punish any subject for the exercise of any of them.

---

[1] "I remembered the result of some of those excellent discourses I had heard your Lordship make." *Works*, Vol. 5, p. 343.

[2] Ibid., p. 342.

Answe:

That although every Christian Prince bee obliged by all just and Christian wayes to maintain and promote to his power the Christian religion in the truth and purity of it, yet in case of such exigence and concernment of Church and State, as that they cannot in human reason probably bee preserved otherwise, We cannot say that in conscience it is unlawfull, but that a Christian Prince hath in such exigents a latitude alowed him, the bounding whereof is by God left to him.[1]

This opinion was signed by twelve leading clergy, among them Jeremy Taylor. *The Liberty of Prophesying* had been published in the previous June, and no doubt Taylor's ostensible purpose in London was to see his book through the press. Neither the King, who is thought to have disapproved of the wide bounds of the toleration which Taylor had proposed in his work, nor Hammond who objected to the teaching on baptism which Taylor included, can have been seriously displeased with him, since they were willing to listen to his opinion on so important a matter.

Toleration, like episcopacy, Taylor's earlier subject, was a living topic; one upon which men all around him were thinking, writing, and in some cases acting. It is a mistake to consider him a lonely thinker in a country place cut off from all that might shape his thought or influence his book. He is likely to have been familiar from past reading with all that the Fathers or the Anglican writers on toleration had produced, and the various political negotiations in which toleration had been a feature would, for the most part be known to him. He would be certain to be well acquainted with the opinion of the Oxford clergy which had been used as the basis of the Uxbridge proposals, for he had many friends in that city. The lines on which Hales and Chillingworth had been thinking would be familiar to him; Castellio's book, and possibly the *Racovian Catechism*, would be handy.[2] Daillè's *Du Vrai Usage des Pères*[3] we know Taylor used,

[1] Bodleian, Tanner MSS., 58. There are two copies of this document, both in the Tanner MSS. and numbered 58. That in Hammond's writing has only nine signatures, the other has twelve, though in both cases the signatures are original and Taylor is the last to sign.

[2] Taylor makes no reference to Socinianism in this book, but in his other writings he shows himself well acquainted with it. *Works*, Vol. 1, pp. lxvii, lxxi, Vol. 7, pp. 551, 563. The book attributed to Castellio was a reply to Calvin's defence of the execution of Servetus. It was signed "Martin Bellius" and was issued at Basle, 1554. It is a collection of extracts from the Fathers and modern authors in favour of toleration, prefaced by a cautious letter on toleration addressed to the Duke of Württemberg. There is a good modern edition by R. Bainton, *Concerning Heretics*, London, 1936.

[3] Geneva, 1632.

because he refers his readers to it.[1] It was a book of which the Great Tew group thought highly and which Falkland himself had partly translated. Here was all the material he needed. To say that he took his thoughts from other sources no more detracts from the greatness of his work in a literary sense than it detracts from Shakespeare's plays to say that he borrowed his plots elsewhere.

Taylor's dedications are always important and the one to Lord Hatton prefixed to *The Liberty of Prophesying* is particularly so. After describing the conditions under which he set to work, he quotes fifteen texts as the basis of all that he has to say in the book which is to follow. He makes an effort to clear the air; to get members of one body to look at those of another without letting theological prejudice colour their vision too much. It is the essentials which ought to be stressed. "If persons be Christians in their lives and Christians in their profession if they acknowledge the eternal Son of God for their Master and their Lord, and live in all relations as becomes persons making such professions, why then should I hate such persons whom God loves and who love God?"[2] But lest this attitude should make people think that he is indifferent to all distinctions he defines those views which he is not prepared to include within the scope of his treatise.

Whatsoever is against the foundation of faith, or contrary to good life and the laws of obedience, or destruction to human society and the public and just interests of bodies politic, is out of the limits of my question, and does not pretend to compliance or toleration; so that I allow no indifferency, nor any countenance to those religions whose principles destroy government, nor to those religions (if there be any such) which teach ill life.[3]

But he pleads "that men would not make more necessities than God made which indeed are not many".[4] In the difficult points of religion God alone can be judge. It is no part of his purpose to encourage singularity of opinion, for no part of his discourse "teaches or encourages variety of sects and contradiction of opinions, but supposes them in being".[5] Instead it is his aim to promote honesty rather than dissimulation, and to plead against the use of too severe remedies in cases of theological disease.

Taylor goes on to show the origin of intolerance in the Church. It came in he says, "with the retinue and train of Antichrist",

[1] *Works*, Vol. 5, p. 488.   [2] Ibid., p. 346.
[3] Ibid, p. 346   [4] Ibid.   [5] Ibid., p. 347.

by which he means the increasing worldly prosperity of Christian-
ty. "When the Church's future grew better, and her sons grew
worse and some of her fathers worst of all".[1] The first three
hundred years were the golden age of the Church. There was no
persecution at all then. This appeal to the witness of the early
Church is thoroughly Anglican. He mentions fifteen of the
Fathers whose testimony he intends to refer to in his book as
condemning persecution. To be able to do this he must have
had some compendium of the relevant passages similar to
Castellio's to which he could refer. If the works of all the Fathers
from which he quotes had been accessible he could hardly have
complained of a shortage of books. As the ages grew worse so
men grew more cruel. Arius behaved himself so badly that a
temporary decree for his relegation had to be obtained, but it
was soon taken off and then God punished the heretic, but
Atticus and Nestorius and some others persecuted relentlessly.
The wisdom of toleration is proved by the prosperity of merciful
princes. In the Church of Rome the Popes, from Innocent the
first onward, became increasingly fond of persecution, but they
stopped short of inflicting death until Dominic preached his
crusade against the Albigenses.

Taylor is very careful to impress upon the reader what his
attitude to error really is, as if he feared some misunderstanding:

Let all errors be as much and as zealously suppressed as may be
(the doctrine of the following discourse contradicts not that); but let
it be done by such means as are proper instruments of their suppression,
by preaching and disputation (so that neither of them breed disturbance), by charity and sweetness, by holiness of life, assiduity of
exhortation, by the word of God and prayer.[2]

A man who believes the Apostles' Creed and lives a good life
is secure. There is no need for men to argue about the smaller
points on which the sects are so severe. "In five hundred sects
which are in the world (and for all I know there may be five
thousand) it is five hundred to one that every man is damned;
for every sect damns all but itself, and that is damned of four
hundred and ninety nine".[3] The only hope for a Christian
distracted by mutually condemnatory sects is "to cling to the
creed of the Apostles; and in all other things an honest endeavour
to find out what truths we can, and a charitable and mutual
permission to others that disagree from us and our opinions".[4]

[1] *Works*, Vol. 5, p. 349.   [2] Ibid., p. 354.   [3] Ibid., p. 355.   [4] Ibid., p. 357.

Christian controversialists ought not to falsify their opponents' case either by suppressing or altering their books or fathering upon them arguments which they themselves repudiate; truth and modesty are the best as well as the strongest weapons. All his life Taylor's chief concern was with practical religion rather than speculative theology and he draws his dedication to a close on that note. Personal holiness was a thing everybody could understand. "I am certain that a drunkard is as contrary to God, and lives as contrary to the laws of Christianity, as a heretic; and I am also sure that I know what drunkenness is; but I am not sure that such an opinion is heresy."[1] So much time and energy is wasted in inessentials.

How many volumes have been writ about angels, about immaculate conception, about original sin, when all that is solid reason or clear revelation in all these three articles may be reasonably enough comprised in forty lines? And in these trifles and impertinences men are curiously busy, while they neglect those glorious precepts of Christianity and holy life which are the glories of our religion, and would enable us to a happy eternity.[2]

In the last paragraph of his dedication Taylor admits that he owes a good deal of what he is about to say to Hatton himself. "Your lordship knowes your own; but out of your mines I have digged the mineral, only I have stamped it with my own image, as you may perceive by the deformities which are in it."[3] He then ends with a well-turned compliment on the estimation in which Hatton is held by both the learned and the pious.

The book which follows is divided into twenty-two subsections, but it really falls under three main heads. First, that while the essentials of our duty are clear, there is no infallible guide to truth; secondly, that the enlightened reason is the best guide we have; thirdly, an enquiry how far people of a good life who seem to err in speculative matters are to be tolerated. Taylor begins with an enquiry into the nature of faith, meaning by that word what is objectively to be believed rather than a psychological function. This is in reality quite simple, the only thing which is indispensable is that men should believe Christ to be the Son of God, for:

All that Christ when he preached taught us to believe, and all that the apostles in their sermons propound, all aim at this, that we should acknowledge Christ as our Lawgiver and our Saviour; so that nothing

---

[1] *Works*, Vol. 5, p. 359.   [2] Ibid., p. 361.   [3] Ibid., p. 364.

can be necessary by a prime necessity to be believed explicitly, but such things which are therefore parts of the great article.[1]

If it is argued that what is deducible from this ought to be believed also, Taylor is willing to agree if the person who is to believe it really does see it to be deducible; but there will certainly be many who cannot, and on them the obligation is not binding. The Apostles' Creed describes all the essential functions of Christ as "lawgiver and saviour", therefore it is the only indispensable standard of faith. If it is insufficient, why was it accepted in the early days as the badge of Christianity? Everyone is at liberty to add to this for himself such things as he may be honestly persuaded of, but he must not attempt to force these additions upon others. The only foundation necessary for religion is that simple one which Christ and his apostles laid.

Having thus defined what he means by "faith", Taylor now explains what he means by "heresy". In apostolic days, he declares, heresy was always the denial of the simple, fundamental, doctrines of Christianity mentioned in the Apostles' Creed, or such teaching as resulted in evil life. As time went on, heresy was given a wider connotation, and so the word was more frequently used, but still everybody who was classed as a heretic was not condemned. He tries to show that as time went on the Church's treatment of heretics became less wise and less certain and "even when general assembles of prelates have been, some controversies that have been very vexatious have been pretermitted, and others of less consequence have been determined".[2] Even the Council of Nicea was unsuccessful in its aim to produce a creed which would provide a final settlement of the Church's faith.

Taylor next goes on to see if it is possible to find some sufficient authority which will be able to settle all the vexed questions which lie outside the Apostles' Creed. The Bible, he decides, is not capable of providing this authority, since it contains in itself too many causes of uncertainty. In the first place there are many different versions and many different readings. There are also different ways of expounding the Scriptures; some may do it in a literal, some in a spiritual, manner. Often the sense of two different passages taken plainly and literally may seem contradictory. For instance, anyone arguing that there are differences in degrees of reward hereafter might well quote the parable of

[1] *Works*, Vol. 5, p. 370.   [2] Ibid., p. 402.

the talents; his adversary, arguing that all are rewarded to the same extent might equally well quote the parable of the labourers in the vineyard. There are also many places where the mysteries spoken of are so deep that only "very holy and spiritual people" can understand them. Some passages, if they were pressed, would overthrow the practice of a good part of Christendom. The text that says, "Except a man be born of water and of the spirit he cannot enter into the kingdom of God",[1] is used as an argument for infant baptism; but it is not common to use the other text, "Except ye eat the flesh of the Son of man, and drink his blood, ye have no life in you",[2] as an argument that infants ought to be communicated. So from its own nature Scripture is difficult to understand, and this difficulty is added to by the absence of any certain means of exegesis, and here again no certainty is to be found except in those things upon which all Christians are said to be agreed—namely, the contents of the Apostles' Creed.

Tradition is the next source of enlightenment to be examined. There are those who claim that it can expound Scripture satisfactorily and bring clear light to bear upon difficult questions. But these claims are ill founded, for traditions are both contradictory and uncertain, and the churches which value traditions most highly spoil their effect by picking and choosing among them. But,

since we are all this while in uncertainty, it is necessary that we should address ourselves somewhere where we may rest the sole of our foot; and nature, scripture, and experience, teach the world in matters of question to submit to some final sentence. For it is not reason that controversies should continue till the erring person shall be willing to condemn himself; and the Spirit of God has directed us by that great precedent at Jerusalem, to address ourselves to the church, that in a plenary council and assembly she may synodically determine controversies. So that if a general council have determined a question or expounded scripture, we may no more disbelieve the decree than the Spirit of God himself who speaks in them.[3]

Yet here again there is no absolute certainty to be found, for councils have been so often corrupt and unworthy and there is no promise that God will reveal the truth by them in all circumstances and "there are so many questions concerning the efficient, the form, the matter of general councils, and their manner of proceeding, and their final sanction, that after a question is

[1] John 3.5.   [2] John 6.53.   [3] *Works*, Vol. 5, p. 442.

determined by a conciliary assembly, there are perhaps twenty more questions to be disputed before we can with confidence either believe the council upon its mere authority or obtrude it upon others".[1] This section of Taylor's argument is reinforced by such a wide range of historical allusion in illustration of the discrepancies and contradictions of councils, that either he had one of the most amazing memories for theological history that England has ever known, or else he had some compendium of the relevant passages at hand. All the authorities themselves he could not have had, if his earlier statement about lack of books is true, for the number of references is enormous.

In the next section the unavailing search for competent authority goes further. As neither Scripture nor councils are infallible, neither is the Pope. Taylor examines a mass of Biblical passages which have constantly been used, and misused, in the cause of papal infallibility. He dismisses the Roman interpretation of most of them as fanciful and strained. To take one example. It has been argued that because our Lord prayed for St Peter that his faith might not fail, it followed that the prayer included the Popes also, since they are St Peter's successors. That argument is of little use:

For it must be remembered that for all this prayer of Christ for St. Peter, the good man fell foully, and denied his Master shamefully; and shall Christ's prayer be of greater efficacy for his successors for whom it was made but indirectly and by consequence than for himself for whom it was directly and in the first intention?[2]

Even if it should be granted that St Peter was head of the apostles it does not follow that the privileges and mission conferred upon St Peter descended to the Popes. The Fathers give very little aid to the upholders of papal infallibility, for a good many of them opposed Rome, and a good many more were very equivocal in their support. In addition, the dealings of the Popes with false doctrine have often been so uncertain and wavering that they can by no means be relied upon. The Fathers are of little more use than the Pope in the determination of vexed questions. In the past many people have dissented from their conclusions with good cause, and there is no reason why we should not do the same. Those who quote the Fathers most undermine their authority by picking and choosing, refusing to follow those

[1] *Works*, Vol. 5, p. 452. Compare Hales "On Scism", *Works* (ed. 1765), Vol. I, p. 60.
[2] Ibid., p. 464.

authorities that are against them. One other possible source of enlightenment, "the Church in her diffusive capacity", by which is meant "the Church diffused in all her parts and members", cannot by its own nature afford any help, for if the whole Church be agreed, then there is no problem to be decided; if it disagrees, there can be no united witness.

So then all the authorities upon which man is inclined to lean proving of no real help to him in his search for truth, he must learn to fall back upon his own reason and not give himself over wholly to any other director for:

He that follows his guide so far as his reason goes along with him, or, which is all one, he that follows his own reason (not guided only by natural arguments but by divine revelation and all other good means) hath great advantages over him that gives himself wholly to follow any human guide whatsoever, because he follows all their reasons and his own too; he follows them till reason leaves them, or till it seems so to him, which is all one to his particular; for by the confession of all sides an erroneous conscience binds him when a right guide does not bind him. But he that gives himself up wholly to a guide is oftentimes (I mean if he be a discerning person) forced to do violence to his own understanding, and to lose all the benefit of his own discretion, that he may reconcile his reason to his guide.[1]

Reason itself often errs but in ways that are not culpable, for understandings are different and in their differing bound to err; therefore everyone should be modest in his opinion, and the less a man knows the more modest he should be. Often men are misled by prejudice or the apparent success of wrong opinions, or by a faulty education. Sometimes the impostures of adversaries confirm men in their own wrong opinions, or they are overcome by the testimony of false miracles, or some small thing like a proverb, or the mere reputation of a learned man will fix wrong opinions in the heads of many people. But none of this in itself is punishable. Only the wrong teaching which leads to bad action deserves to suffer. In words which really sum up the whole of what he has set himself to persuade the world by his book, Taylor declares that:

No Christian is to be put to death, dismembered or otherwise directly persecuted for his opinion, which does not teach impiety or blasphemy. If it plainly or apparently brings in a crime, and himself does act it or encourage it, then the matter of fact is punishable according to its proportion or malignity.[2]

[1] Works, Vol. 5, p. 495.   [2] Ibid., p. 514.

But it must be wrong to give a punishment which cannot help but be certain for a fault which is clearly uncertain. If a man is killed "he is certainly killed; but if he be called heretic, it is not so certain that he is a heretic".[1] In the parable of the wheat and the tares the right way to treat error is shown, for both are to grow together until harvest.

Persecution is not only wrong, it is unwise. When times change the persecuted may themselves persecute. No man can be compelled by force to make any real alteration in his opinion. Taylor rapidly reviews Church history to show that persecution came into the Christian family with the growth of self-interest and temporal designs. But because persecution is not to be allowed, it does not follow that the governors of the Church are to be neglectful of their charge. Those who are in error "must be convinced by sound doctrine, and put to silence by spiritual evidence, and restrained by authority ecclesiastical, that is by spiritual censures".[2] So far as the attitude of princes toward faulty doctrine among their subjects is concerned it is clearly their duty to tolerate all differences of opinion which do not lead to evil deeds. To do otherwise would be to usurp the function of God. Nevertheless, the laws must be maintained and those who plead weakness of conscience as a ground for exemption from their working are by no means to be encouraged. Taylor had had personal experience of what sometimes lay behind the plea of tender conscience:

I have known in some churches that this pretence hath been nothing but a design to discredit the law to dismantle the authority that made it, to raise their own credit and a trophy of their zeal, to make it a characteristic note of a sect and the cognisance of holy persons; and yet the men that claimed exemption from the laws upon pretence of having weak consciences, if in hearty expression you had told them so to their heads, they would have spit in your face, and were so far from confessing themselves weak, that they thought themselves able to give laws to christendom, to instruct the greatest clerks, and to catechize the church herself.[3]

The Anabaptists were the class of Dissenters to whom the orthodox Presbyterians and Anglicans were least willing to extend toleration. Taylor now takes up their case. The two main tenets which distinguished them in spite of a number of changing beliefs were the repudiation of infant baptism and the refusal to recognize certain functions of the civil power. Taylor

[1] *Works*, Vol. 5, p. 517.   [2] Ibid., p. 531.   [3] Ibid., p. 538.

F

first states the case for infant baptism, then against it to show that there is something to be said for the Anabaptists. It was felt, after the issue of the book, that he had put their case too strongly, so in the second edition[1] he developed his refutation of it more fully. The other opinion of the Anabaptists, that "it is not lawful for princes to put malefactors to death, nor to take up defensive arms, nor to minister an oath, nor to contend in judgement",[2] is answered very simply. There must be law and order in the world, and if notions such as these were tolerated it could not exist.

There remained only the Roman Catholics to be considered and here Taylor was on particularly difficult ground. The Roman Catholics hold all the articles of the Apostles' Creed. They hold a good deal more, but Taylor had previously stated that so long as a man's opinions were harmless, and he made no attempt to force them on others, he could believe what he liked. He held to that opinion still though his doing so would infallibly damn his book in the eyes of the party with whom the decision to tolerate, or not to tolerate, would come to rest more and more. If he had merely intended to write an eloquent appeal for Anglicanism to be let alone, Taylor ought to have avoided Romanism. That he mentions it may perhaps show his desire for complete toleration to be genuine. Taylor is willing to allow to Romanists the liberty he allows to others, freedom to hold any speculative doctrines which do not endanger either good morals or the State. This was a great advance on all the schemes for toleration which had preceded Taylor's, for the Protestant dissenters, while vigorously demanding freedom of worship for themselves, were equally vigorous in refusing it to Roman Catholics.

The last question to be touched upon is how far communion—that is, fellowship—between different Churches is to be allowed. He decides that churches are "bound to allow communion to all those who profess the same faith upon which the apostles did give communion".[3] Individuals must follow the rules of their Churches. There the original book ended, but in the edition of 1657 Taylor added the beautiful story of Abraham which he had found, he says, in "the Jews' books". In fact he quoted it from Gentius, who in turn borrowed the story from the Persian poet Saadi and inserted it in the dedication he prefixed to his translation of Rabbi Solomon ben Virga's *Shebet Jehuda* (Rod of

---

[1] That of 1657.   [2] *Works*, Vol. 5, p. 589.   [3] Ibid., p. 604.

Judah).[1] The fact that he found it in a book of Jewish history probably led Taylor to make the mistake about its origin:

When Abraham sat at his tent door, according to his custom, waiting to entertain strangers; he espied an old man stooping and leaning on his staff, weary with age and travel, coming towards him, who was a hundred years of age. He received him kindly, washed his feet, provided supper, caused him to sit down; but observing that the old man eat and prayed not, nor begged for a blessing on his meat, he asked him why he did not worship the God of heaven: the old man told him that he worshipped the fire only, and acknowledged no other god; at which Abraham grew so zealously angry that he thrust the old man out of his tent, and exposed him to all the evils of the night and an unguarded condition. When the old man was gone, God called to Abraham, and asked him where the stranger was; he replied, "I thrust him away because he did not worship Thee". God answered him, "I have suffered him these hundred years, although he dishonoured Me, and couldst thou not endure him one night when he gave thee no trouble?" Upon this saith the story "Abraham fetched him back again and gave him hospitable entertainment and wise instruction".[2]

This story has had an interesting history since Taylor brought it to light. Benjamin Franklin sent it in a letter to Lord Kaimes and, as he had not mentioned the author's name, it was assumed that it was written by Franklin himself. That misconception has, however, long since been put right and the passage finds its way into a good many anthologies as an example of Taylor's style.

The Liberty of Prophesying is a remarkable book. Many people may be inclined to class it as Taylor's greatest work, though to do so is to undervalue higher achievements of his elsewhere. There are, it must be admitted, points in which it falls short of what it might have been. Not much in *The Liberty of Prophesying* was completely new. It did not lay down and develop any far reaching philosophical principles, and here Taylor seems to have missed his chance; for there was a germ of freedom in Arminianism which, had he possessed gifts of mind equal to those with which he was endowed in heart and imagination, might well have been made the basis of his thesis. But the most that he claims is that no one should persecute since there is not enough certainty in religious matters for its justification. It would be hard to prove that the book had any great influence

---

[1] 4to, Amsterdam, 1651. Taylor was therefore not acquainted with the story when he published the first edition of *The Liberty of Prophesying*.
[2] *Works*, Vol. 5, p. 604.

at the time of its publication or afterwards. Lovers of intellectual freedom have never saturated their minds with it as they have done with Milton's *Areopagitica*. Certainly it was not that sudden flame of liberty breaking out in the universal darkness of persecution which it is sometimes said to be. Most of the arguments in favour of that toleration for which he pleads he had borrowed from others, notably from Chillingworth,[1] Hales, and Daillè, and it has been objected that to some extent he spoiled the arguments he borrowed by carrying them far beyond the limits to which their originators intended them to go. There are, unquestionably, many different versions and readings of the Bible, but they invalidate the Scriptures to a far less extent than Taylor would have us believe. Neither is it outside the bounds of possibility to decide what is, in the main, the opinion of the more important Fathers, in spite of some errors and contradictions inevitable in the works of all men. Taylor repudiated papal infallibility, but, as Coleridge remarked, the position he had taken up led either to that or agnosticism.[2] If all the guides whom Taylor examines one after another are as untrustworthy as he pretends, then we have no real grounds for the principles upon which all Christians are agreed. It depends only upon a consensus of opinion which might any day be broken.

But when so much has been said by way of criticism, the book still remains undeniably great. Those who respect and admire *The Liberty of Prophesying* do so for the character revealed in it; for the earnestness, the boldness, the sincerity of its intellectual propositions, rather than for their originality. A hatred of dogmatism, and a widespreading lovingkindness broods over the whole. Taylor presents his appeal with the greatest skill. Chillingworth's controversial purpose had deflected attention from his plea for toleration; Hales in his short tract *On Scism* had been content to leave his "hardy paradoxes" without proof. Taylor greatly widened the influence of the ideas of both these men by making them the subject of a whole work, by reinforcing their statements with arguments and proof, by making explicit what they had left implied, and by writing his work in such a way that it would certainly be read. His own kindness of heart made him stress, further than his predecessors had done, toleration by agreement to differ, rather than by mutual concession. How far he would

[1] "Three fourths of his arguments were written under the influence of Chillingworth's great work", Gardiner, *Civil War*, Vol. 3, p. 311.

[2] Coleridge, *Table Talk*, 4 June 1830.

have been willing to carry this is hard to say. He may have intended his arguments to have a wider implication than he cared to state. On his own showing there was really no undoubted source of truth which could be used to support even the Apostles' Creed, therefore those who dissent from that—Jews, Mohammedans, heathen or atheists—ought not to be persecuted so long as they are willing to conform to that standard of morality which the State expects of all citizens. But Taylor never said anything like that and the omission has been charged against him as a fault.[1] As he was writing for England and Englishmen, he may have thought the problem of these others too remote for him to hamper his case with it. For his purpose he had done enough. He had given to the world a noble and generous-hearted outburst which was to convince men of the folly of persecution, and to take them at least one step nearer to that toleration which the spread of sectarianism and changing concepts of religious truth had made so desirable. In style *The Liberty of Prophesying* is comparatively simple. There are none of those exuberant flights which enrich the *Sermons* and *Holy Living* and *Holy Dying*, but there is plenty of point and strength.

Taylor's subjects always carried him away. In this case when he began to write, he probably intended only to produce such arguments as would induce the dominant Presbyterians to allow the Anglican Church organization to remain side by side with their own. This is what he himself says in the dedication to Lord Hatton of the collected edition of his controversial writings, published in 1657:

When a persecution did arise against the Church of England, and that I intended to make a defensative for my brethren and myself by pleading for a liberty to our consciences to persevere in that profession which was warranted by all the laws of God and our superiors, some men were angry and would not be safe that way, because I had made the roof of the sanctuary so wide that more might be sheltered under it than they had a mind should be saved harmless.[2]

Anthony Wood says much the same thing.[3] But it is obvious that as the book now stands, it is far wider in scope. It is more charitable, and possibly wiser, to suppose that, instead of Taylor being in 1657 a little ashamed of what he had written in 1647, he recalled then the original design rather than the mature

---

[1] Heber, "Life", *Works*, Vol. 1, p. clxxxiv.   [2] *Works*, Vol. 5, p. 3.
[3] Wood, *Ath. Ox.*, Art. "Jeremy Taylor".

execution of his book. His complete absorption in the argument in hand did more than widen its scope, it led him sometimes into condemning an authority which the course of a previous discussion had encouraged him to rely upon. His critics were quick to see this, especially in the markedly different weight which he allows to the Fathers, the councils and the apostolic canons in *Episcopacy Asserted* and in *The Liberty of Prophesying*. In an effort to explain the discrepancy he included a lengthy defence of his apparent inconsistency in the 1657 dedication to Lord Hatton. He had been accused, he said, of seeming "to pull down with one hand what I build up with another".[1] His defence takes the form of asserting that the Fathers and the councils may afford an excellent corroborative to arguments which can be proved true on other grounds, but have no absolute authority in themselves. He had appealed to them in *Episcopacy Asserted* because some who read that book might value their testimony. "But Episcopacy relies not upon the authority of the Fathers and councils, but upon Scripture, upon the institution of Christ, upon an universal tradition and an universal practice not upon the words and opinions of doctors." This type of argument does very little to mend the situation. Taylor had attacked the final authority of Scripture as strongly as he had that of the Fathers and the councils, and if the testimony of the Fathers was actually ignored it would be a harder task to prove that universal tradition and practice upon which Taylor now professed to rely. Possibly, though he does not admit it, some of the difference in treatment was due to the fact that in the interval he had been reading Daillè.

The immediate reception of *The Liberty of Prophesying* was not enthusiastic. Far as the theories of toleration were advanced among thinkers, the times were not yet ripe for so sweeping a measure as that which Taylor proposed. A rumour got about that *The Liberty of Prophesying* had the King's support behind it, and Charles was not pleased. It was the section in which Taylor presented the Anabaptist's case against infant baptism which seems to have given his Oxford friends most cause for dislike. Hammond, at the King's request, set himself to answer it, and in a *Letter of Resolution to Six Queries of Present Use with the Church of England*, devoted his attention especially to the question of infant baptism. It was rather an amicable disagreement than a controversy, for Hammond wrote with courtesy and respect for his

[1] *Works*, Vol. 5, p. 4.

opponent. The result of it was that Taylor himself produced a refutation of the position he had outlined, more satisfactory than his earlier one, and inserted it in the second edition of his book.

Taylor's desire for toleration, however, came in for a particularly virulent attack from Samuel Rutherford, the Professor of Divinity at St Andrew's, who published in 1649 *A Free Disputation against Pretended Liberty of Conscience*, directed against Taylor by name. It is as thorough-going a defence of religious persecution as could be imagined. Rutherford knew no weakness. Persecution in his eyes is not a regrettable necessity, but a holy duty. All the most bloodthirsty passages in the Old Testament are marshalled to prove his case. The Mosaic Law, the practice of the ancient Jewish heroes, the denunciations poured out upon the Babylonian harlot by the prophets, even St John's command that no true believer shall say "God-speed" to a false prophet, are all used in the worthy cause of promoting persecution. "He seems in one place to have some compunctious doubts as to the propriety of fire as an instrument of conversion and, on the whole, to give the preference to hanging", yet he elsewhere seems to think "that burning hath something in it marvellously suited to the occasion and to the necessities of Christendom".[1] Taylor took no notice of Rutherford's crude savageries, but this effusion is said to be the reason why Milton inserted Rutherford's name, among some others, in his sonnet on the new forcers of conscience. There is a rumour that Milton always had a great respect for Taylor, which adds some support for the story.

We have already seen how Taylor's rhetoric obscured the details of his arrival in Wales. A long letter to Dr Bayly, dated on the "Vigils of Christmas, 1648" offers another instance of Taylor's deliberate use of picturesque language in order to veil his meaning, and in this case also he used it so successfully that it is impossible to discover his secret. All that is clear is that Taylor had received a letter from Bayly, who was an old friend of his, and that the two men had recently met, and on this occasion there had been some misunderstanding between them. The letter had contained "severities" as well as "just and religious kindnesses". Then Taylor refers to the conversation which had taken place at their meeting:

What I delivered *in transitu*, when I had the happiness last to meet you, I knew I poured into a breast locked up as religiously as the

[1] Heber, "Life", *Works*, Vol. 1, p. ccixi.

priests of Cybele, and, but that I was certain you permit all your friends and servants to speak to you with a freedom as great as that of the sun or the air, I should not have delivered to you so displeasing a truth lest by an unnecessary discourse I should have discomposed the state of that friendship, from which I have received so many effluxes and profitable emanations.

However, Sir, I shall most religiously observe your cautions (and had done so by my own proper purposes), not to dispute *in triviis* that point which is of so secret consideration and is too apt to be mistaken and misconstrued by avaricious and prejudicate spirits. I know it is easy to encourage crime by a neighbouring truth, but nothing is sufficient to secure the church's just interests if any colour may be pretended for an injury.[1]

All that it is possible to make of this is that Bayly had misunderstood Taylor in some way and considered himself aggrieved, and that Taylor had explained himself, but that the affair was so secret that it had to be referred to with the greatest caution. Although he had given him his confidence Taylor had remonstrated with his friend a little sharply. So far as we know Taylor had done nothing remarkable since he published *The Liberty of Prophesying* in 1647. It is therefore tempting to suppose that the secret had to do with that book. The last sentence quoted indicated that Taylor had been trying to do some good to the Church, but that his action had been wilfully misconstrued. It is possible that the rumour which connected Charles I with *The Liberty of Prophesying* had some justification, in spite of the King's denial.[2] If so, that might have been the secret which Taylor entrusted to the bosom of his friend in justification of having exceeded, what Bayly thought, the bounds of toleration. After these cryptic paragraphs the letter goes on to fulfil its ostensible purpose of answering a question which Bayly had put as to the lawfulness or otherwise of the King alienating church lands. Taylor's opinion is that it is impossible for lands to be given to God in the sense that they become entirely and forever sacred, therefore with reasonable cause the King may alienate them.

On 12 June 1643, Parliament, partly to provide a system of Church government to replace the episcopacy which they had

---

[1] Bodleian, Tanner MSS., 468; printed, *Works*, Vol. 1, p. cclxiii.

[2] "At Causham [Caversham] I had the honour to come into his [the King's] presence tho' I stayed not there; but, by all I could perceive either from himself or any other, he was very apprehensive in what hands he was, but was not to let it be discerned. Nor had he given that countenance to Dr. Taylor's Liberty of Prophesying which some believed he had but that really and truly it was refreshment to his spirit to be used with some civility and to serve God as he was wont, and to see some old faces about him". Warwick, *Memoirs*, p. 301.

abolished, partly to curry favour with the Scots, called together an assembly of "godly and learned divines" to settle the government and liturgy of the Church of England and to revise her doctrines. Of the one hundred and thirty-one divines who were summoned only sixty-nine appeared at Westminster, Taylor's friend Nicholson being one of the absentees. The proceedings began with a fast and a long debate on the Thirty-nine Articles which was intended to wile away the time until the Scots commissioners arrived. When they came, the price of any assistance which their country might give to the Parliament was soon made clear. They were to demand that England took the Solemn League and Covenant. Parliament was not eager to do so and some of the divines greatly disliked it, but there was nothing else to be done. Both bodies accepted the oath for themselves and the government ordered that on 2 February everybody in England over eighteen years of age should take it also. Though the oath was not imposed as rigidly as it might have been, it pressed very hardly on the loyal Anglican clergy, many of whom were forced to vacate the preferment which they had managed to retain until then.

For nearly a year no effort was made to fill up the vacancies thus caused, which were accordingly seized upon by the sectaries with influence, and these intruders the Presbyterians later found it exceedingly difficult to dislodge. At length, on 22 September 1644, the Assembly, in reply to a petition of the London ministers, put out a temporary plan for ordinations, which set up committees in London and the chief towns to examine candidates, and ordain those who were suitable, by imposition of hands.[1] One month later they attempted to remedy the equally chaotic state of worship by agreeing to a *Directory of Public Worship*, to take the place of the Prayer Book, so much disliked by the Scots and their imitators. In effect the new book followed the old proposals of Cartwright and Travers. It did not, however, receive its final authorization until 3 January 1645. In the meantime it had been submitted to and approved by the General Assembly of the Church of Scotland. The order enjoining the use of the *Directory* was followed in August by another, imposing a penalty of forty shillings for each offence on all ministers who refused to use it; and a fine of ten pounds for the first offence, ten pounds

[1] For a full description of a seventeenth-century Presbyterian ordination (1657), see "An Account of the Life and Death of Mr. Philip Henry", Wordsworth, *Ecclesiastical Biography*, Vol. 6, pp. 156 ff.

for the second, and a year's imprisonment for the third on all ministers who used the Book of Common Prayer. The King retorted by a proclamation from Oxford (13 November 1645) eulogizing the Prayer Book and condemning the *Directory*. Nor was this the only opposition offered.

In 1646 Taylor published, probably hurriedly and certainly without his name, a short booklet which was both a defence of the Prayer Book and a criticism of the *Directory*.[1] This he reissued in 1649, considerably expanded and with the title changed from *A Discourse of Prayer Extempore*, to *An Apology for Authorized and Set Forms of Liturgy*. The Prayer Book, says Taylor, has always had a peculiar hold upon the affections of Englishmen. It was compiled by men whom everyone who professed to love the Reformation was bound to honour. Nothing that Taylor could say on behalf of the Church of England would be listened to more readily than a defence of the Prayer Book. High Church men revered it because of the catholic teaching it conveyed, and because of the ancient sources from which it was drawn. Ordinary church-going people of no special religious party liked it because it was what they were used to. Only the most rigid of the Presbyterians and Independents objected to it utterly. Consequently, Taylor could appeal not only to his own party, but to those also who were technically outside its bounds.

As Taylor's *Apology* now stands it is not so much one book as a collection of tracts written at various times upon cognate subjects. First comes the dedication to the King, written probably toward the end of 1648; this is followed by the author's preface, which first appeared in 1658, when it formed an introduction to the *Collection of Offices* which Taylor published in that year. These Offices were intended for the use of episcopalian congregations who, as the Prayer Book was suppressed, found themselves in need of some regular guide for their worship. At the Restoration all necessity for such a collection of devotions disappeared with the renewed freedom of use for the Prayer Book. So when a third edition of *An Apology for Liturgy* was printed in the 1673 issue of *Sumbolon Theologikon*, this preface was transferred from the Offices, where it might have been overlooked, to its present position in the *Apology*. In the position which it now occupies it is followed by a letter to Bishop Leslie, which was originally

---

[1] This was one of a number of criticisms of the *Directory*. Hammond published *A View of the New Directory*, and David Jenkins, a Welsh judge and a strong Royalist, published a biting *Scourge for the New Directory*.

included in Leslie's *Discourse of Praying with the Spirit*. It was on the title page of this book published in 1659 that Leslie defied his enemies and claimed to be still "maugre all antichristian opposition, Bishop of Down and Connor". *The Apology* itself follows as it was issued in 1649.

In the preface Taylor enumerates fifteen advantages which a liturgy has over extempore prayer, or over forms hastily devised to suit the necessity of the moment. They are practically the same as the arguments in favour of liturgy in the *Apology* itself. He passes on to praise the conservative spirit which the Reformers showed so clearly in the compilation of the Prayer Book. Although the Protestant refugees who afterward fled to Frankfort had some scruples of conscience about the book, Calvin, to whom they went for advice, did not give them much encouragement. Those on the other side—namely, the Roman emissaries who came to England about the same time—could never charge the book either with heresy or impiety. Indeed, so well had the Edwardian divines compiled the book that "it was accounted the work of God". When it was suppressed Protestants sealed their devotion to its principles by their death. Archbishop Cranmer, in his purgation, offered, if the Queen would give him leave, to prove the Prayer Book to be both Scriptural and catholic. In the next page or two Taylor sets out to perform what Cranmer had offered to do, and his demonstration shows how widely he had read in ancient liturgies before he began it. Later on he emphasizes once more the great love which the original reformers had for the Prayer Book. He probably felt that this was the line of argument most likely to be successful with that very large number of people who reverenced the Reformation but belonged to no particular Church party. It is in this connexion that he mentions again, as he had done earlier, Dr Rowland Taylor, but says nothing which might show special knowledge of him or any close relationship with him. Finally he enumerates thirty-one detailed objections to the *Directory* and closes his preface with a burst of affection and praise for the Book of Common Prayer.

The letter to Bishop Leslie sets out some of the usual arguments against extempore prayer. Then the *Apology* begins with a criticism of the *Directory* in general. So great is the "public disrelish" of it which he finds "amongst people of great piety of all qualities" that he is forced to believe that the compilers of it hoped to prevail "more by the success of their armies than the strength of reason and the proper grounds of persuasion".[1] In order to satisfy the many people who have asked him to consider it Taylor proposes to make an examination of the work. He will do so without bitterness, knowing that he differs as much from those of the other persuasion as they from him. Two different schools of thought compiled the *Directory*, those who objected to all set forms of prayer and those who refused all forms but their own. So in order to begin at the beginning, Taylor starts with a discussion of extemporary prayer. The questions he is about to consider are, briefly, "whether it is better to pray to God with consideration or without? Whether is the wiser man of the two, he who thinks and deliberates what to say, or he that utters his mind as fast as it comes."[2]

That reverence towards God demands set forms of prayer is a thing not only evident in itself but confirmed by excellent examples, for "the wisest nations have always prepared their verses and prayers with set forms".[3] So at the very first considera-tion extempore prayer has the worst of it. But it is contended by some that there is a gift of prayer. Undoubtedly God gives his Spirit to the Church, but that Spirit always chooses to work through the best human means. As an example the writers of the Bible may be instanced, for they undoubtedly were moved by the Spirit; but that did not release them from the obligation to use whatever of this world's skill they had in the presentation of their message. The next question is more difficult. Some men do not object to set forms, but only to those imposed by authority. But although the Church insists on a liturgy for public worship she does not prevent any man developing in private whatever gift of prayer he may possess. To the argument that the same set form may not always fit the mood of the worshippers Taylor replies:

Public forms, it is true, cannot be fitted to every man's fancy and affections, especially in an age wherein all public constitutions are protested against, but yet they may be fitted to all necessities, and to every man's duty; and for the pleasing the affections and fancies of men, that may be sometimes convenient, but it is never necessary.[4]

The Church has been given a stewardship in prayer and so her ministers must not only pray for the people but teach the people themselves how to pray, and for this there is no method so convenient as the use of a set form.

[1] *Works*, Vol. 5, p. 259.   [2] Ibid., p. 261.   [3] Ibid., p. 262.   [4] Ibid., p. 282.

Taylor now examines both Scripture and catholic tradition to show how consistent their witness is to the necessity of a liturgy. He gives us an interesting glimpse of worship in a family below the rank of those who kept a chaplain; for such a family, says Taylor, a liturgy is most convenient so that the "children and servants may be enabled to remember, and tacitly recite the prayer together with the Major-domo".[1] But a set form of public prayer has many more uses than this. It is a bond of union for all who worship by its means, it affords an assured standard of doctrine, it teaches the faith at a time and in a way that is most easily received, it preserves the authority of the Church and is a great security for the religion of the whole people.

In the place of the set form of prayer which Taylor was defending, a good many of those on the other side would substitute what they called "conceived forms", by which they meant forms invented by the minister to suit the occasion; it was argued that while set forms confined the Spirit conceived forms set it free. To this Taylor replies that, so far as he can see, the Spirit may be free in either; but supposing the argument to be correct, the minister by the self-invented form which sets free the Spirit in him binds the Spirit in his people. Besides, the *Directory* had appointed everything to do with prayer except the actual words, and therefore imprisoned the Spirit. There is a difference between prayer and preaching, the same liberty cannot be applied to both. In one case the minister addresses his words to the people, in the other he speaks to God on their behalf, and it is clearly right that they should know what it is he intends to say. Some latitude may be allowed in language which is addressed to men, but no care can be too great in that which is to be offered to God. To those who argue that the encouragement of conceived forms will make a learned ministry, Taylor points out that it is a mistake "to offer that as a means of getting learning which cannot be done at all as it ought but after learning is already gotten".[2] He concludes with the telling remark that in the public prayers of a whole national Church "an unlearned man is not to be trusted and a wise man dare not trust himself".[3]

This is the best piece of controversial writing Taylor ever did. He was pleading in defence of something which he loved very dearly, and he was helped by the knowledge that the sympathies of many in all parties were with him before he began. He had reasonableness and antiquity on his side and he loved both.

[1] *Works*, Vol. 5, p. 299. [2] Ibid., p. 313. [3] Ibid., p. 314.

Though he is prone even in so short a work as the *Apology* to repeat himself, and the repetition is emphasized by different tracts written at different times being printed together as we have said, yet he does not here, as he does in so many other places, spoil the effect of a good argument by trying to reinforce it with an obviously doubtful one.

When Taylor's criticism of the *Directory* appeared in its final form, the Assembly which produced the *Directory* had melted away. Its constituent elements had never been such as to guarantee it a smooth or a long career. From the beginning, the greater part of its Anglican representatives had refused to sit, and time only brought out more clearly the differences between Presbyterian and Independent members. During the long discussion on a scheme of ordination, to replace the temporary one of September 1644, the division grew wider still. At length a form was completed, but only London and a few Presbyterian strongholds elsewhere, made any attempt to put it into practice. Neither could the rigid system of Presbyterian government which had been hoped for by some be carried out. The sectaries and an Erastian Parliament were too strong for its supporters. The Assembly was happier in the acceptance it gained for its doctrinal statements. Its two catechisms—the Longer and the Shorter—with its Confession of Faith, have served ever since as the standard exposition of Calvinism in this country. The fate of the Assembly showed how little chance there was of Presbyterianism displacing Anglicanism in England.

None the less, it was a bold thing to issue an attack on the *Directory* together with a panegyric of the Prayer Book in 1649, and Taylor added to his risk by the dedication to Charles I. Before the book was in many people's hands the King was dead. The Scots to whom he had surrendered in May 1646 had given him up to the Parliament, and from the Parliament the army had taken him. After nearly two years more of unsuccessful shifts, he had been sentenced to death by a court whose authority he refused to recognize, and he was beheaded in Whitehall before a multitude which was filled with amazement and pity at the deed. The Prayer Book had been cut to pieces and burned at the hands of the common hangman. Charles had probably been beheaded by the same man, though his executioner wore a mask.[1] Taylor's book, then, came to his readers as a protest on behalf of royalty and the Church of England, two institutions

[1] Gardiner, *Civil War*, Vol. 4, p. 322, note.

which, though many might wish to reform them, few would wish to abolish. There is a story that Jeremy Taylor, in an interview with the King just before his execution, received from him as a parting gift his watch, a ring set with two diamonds and a ruby, and some pearls and rubies which were taken from the ebony case in which the King kept his Bible.[1] In August 1648 Taylor was again in London, but it is not very likely that on that occasion he saw the King. According to this account, which comes from Dr William Webster, a friend of Warburton, when Lord Herbert of Cherbury was on his death-bed in London in August 1648,[2] he sent for Jeremy Taylor and asked that he might receive the Blessed Sacrament from him. Taylor refused unless the dying man would first recant the heretical opinions which he had published in his books, and this he would not do. It was this incident, so the story runs,[3] which set Taylor to work thinking out the Moral Demonstration, which he afterwards included in *Ductor Dubitantium*.[4] But in August 1648 the King was in Carisbrooke Castle and it is most unlikely that Taylor would visit the Isle of Wight, or be allowed to see the King if he did. On 1 December Charles was removed to Hurst Castle, and from then until the King's death, there seems no occasion when an interview with Taylor could be supposed likely, even if he had prolonged his absence from Wales to so late a date, or had made another visit to the neighbourhood of London so soon. There is no proof that the ring, the watch, and the jewels were ever given to Taylor by the King.

The Great Exemplar, Taylor's next work, published in 1649, must have taken some time to prepare, since it is a very large book, indeed second only in bulk to the enormous *Ductor Dubitantium*. If it had not been so unwieldy it would have received far more attention than it has done, since it stands definitely among the best of Taylor's writings. It is the first clear indication that he had arrived at that stage of his literary development when he could write at will those glowing passages, saturated with beauty both of thought and sound, with which his name is inseparably connected. It is a book of practical piety, and an

---

[1] See Appendix D.

[2] Aubrey, *Brief Lives* (ed. Clark), Oxford, 1898. His tombstone says that he died "Vicesimo Die Augusti 1648".

[3] Nichols, *Literary Anecdotes*, Vol. 2, p. 36. London, 1812.

[4] *Works*, Vol. 9, p. 157. Archbishop Ussher is also said to have refused the Sacrament to Lord Herbert of Cherbury when on his death-bed because of the sick man's remark that "if there was good in anything it was in that; or if it did no good it could do no harm".

innovation in religious literature, for it is the first life of Christ ever to be written in English. There had been works of a similar character in Latin; but devotion, like everything else, was coming more and more to be recorded in the vernacular.

One of the most famous of Latin lives was written by a German monk, Ludolf of Saxony, in the fourteenth century. John Sergeant, an indefatigable Roman controversialist, asserted that *The Great Exemplar* was nothing more than a translation of Ludolf's *Vita*.[1] As soon as the two books are examined Sergeant's accusation is refuted. There are similarities, but they are only slight, while the differences are many and obvious. The *Vita Christi* not only gives a history of our Lord upon earth, but illustrates and enforces its lessons with copious extracts from the Fathers, and gives also meditations, and prayers, and instructions concerning the spiritual life. It was extremely popular, both for its own qualities and because of the great reputation of its author. There are a good many MS. copies of it in existence and the printed editions are very numerous, the earliest being issued at Strasbourg, and there was another at Cologne in 1474. So far as is known, no English translation was ever made, but a very famous French one by Guillaume Lernenand was published in folio at Lyons in 1487 and was often reprinted, the latest edition being issued at Paris in 1878. It was in a Spanish translation that Ignatius of Loyala, very near death's door with the wounds which he had received at the defence of Pampeluna, read the book and experienced that change of heart which led to his conversion and ultimately to the founding of the Jesuit Order. Taylor, whose reading was omnivorous, had probably seen the book, and it is possible that it interested him sufficiently to be kept in mind when he began arranging his materials for *The Great Exemplar*. If it had some slight effect on the plan of Taylor's work, that is the full extent of its influence.

The few years before and after 1642 seem to have been the germinative period of Taylor's life, but it was not until he had settled down into the quietness of life at Golden Grove that these early seeds could be brought to harvest. It was then that the line of thought which produced *The Liberty of Prophesying* was apparently developed, and Taylor definitely says that *The Great Exemplar* had its origin at that time. In the dedication of the second part of the book to Lady Mary, Countess Dowager of

---

[1] Sergeant, *Literary Life of John Sergeant*, written by himself in Paris at the request of the Duke of Perth (ed. Kirk), London, 1816.

Northampton, Taylor gives all the credit for the general idea of his work to her late husband, the Earl of Northampton, killed at the Battle of Hopton Heath,[1] who had first conceived the work which became *The Great Exemplar*. He says of his book, "your Honour best knows in what soil the first design of these papers grew", and later on he speaks of being left "to the pains and danger of bringing forth" what "that rare person [the Earl of Northampton] had conceived".[2] This may mean one of two things. Either the Earl suggested to Taylor that the subject was a fit one for him to undertake; or else he intended to write a book of that sort himself and consulted his friend about what he had in mind, but afterwards, on account of more pressing business, had to leave the execution of it to him. This is as good a suggestion as any. It was a time when quite a number of the nobility wrote books and some of them were not averse to having their produc- tions worked over by a clever chaplain or some other dependent. Taylor performed a service of that sort for Hatton when he produced his *Psalms*, and probably would have been glad to do something similar for Northampton. As it is, we have no reason to regret that the collaboration was never undertaken.

Taylor was not writing a critical life. He makes no attempt to fit events into their chronological sequence or to discuss time and place. He takes the most glaringly improbable stories from the apocryphal gospels without scruple if they add any dramatic interest to his narrative. His concern was not so much with instruction as devotion; he wished to make men love God and one another more, and so everything which served that end was utilized. All Taylor's gifts are dedicated in *The Great Exemplar* to the main purpose of his life—making men and women holy. So he directs all the affection and attention of those who will be taught to the contemplation of the divine life of Jesus Christ upon earth.

The Great Exemplar is divided into three parts. The first ends with the baptism and temptation of Jesus. The second ends with the miracles, which are not taken in any chronological order but are considered together. The third closes with the Resurrection and Ascension. Each of these parts is subdivided into sections containing a portion of narrative, one or more discourses, considerations, and prayers.

[1] He was leading a charge when his horse was killed under him, and his helmet knocked from his head. He was offered quarter. "I scorn to take quarter from such base rogues as you are," he replied, and was immediately slain with a halbert.
[2] *Works*, Vol. 2, p. 283.

G

The first part is dedicated to Taylor's old patron, Lord Hatton, who in 1648 had retired to Paris, where, for a time, he did what he could to help the royalist exiles until poverty and the loss of his great reputation overtook him. Controversial theology had left Taylor mentally tired and hopeless of any result from disputation. He admits this:

I am weary and toiled with rowing up and down in the seas of questions, which the interests of christendom have commenced; and in any propositions of which I am heartily persuaded, I am not certain that I am not deceived; and I find that men are most confident of those articles which they can so little prove that they never made questions of them; but I am most certain, that by living in the religion and fear of God, in obedience to the King, in the charities and duties of communion with my spiritual guides, in justice and love with all the world in their several proportions, I shall not fail of that end which is perfective of human nature, and which will never be obtained by disputing.[1]

The hope which he has set before himself is to help forward the salvation of all men. Three words at the end of this dedication have caused more trouble than they should. Taylor says, politely, that the best reward he can think of for his labours is to be counted among Lord Hatton's "relatives and servants", so the possibility that he was united in some way by ties of blood with his patron's family has been debated. It is not easy to see where the difficulty lies. If Taylor was connected already by blood or by marriage with the Hatton family, it is hard to understand how such a relationship could be a reward for his labours in writing *The Great Exemplar*; but he uses the word "relative" in other places without any implication of kinship, and here also he probably means nothing more than that he hopes the connexion between himself and Hatton will be made still closer. The dedication of the second part is the one already mentioned—to the Dowager Lady Northampton. The third part was originally dedicated to the second Lady Carbery, and is full of gratitude for the kindness shown by her and her household to Taylor in his distress. When, after this lady's death, *The Great Exemplar* came to a second edition, Taylor added another dedication to the third part, this time to Alice, the third Lady Carbery. A compliment was no doubt intended, but the dedication is too full of the praises of her predecessor for the recipient to be very grateful.

Those who go through Taylor's works in the order in which

[1] *Works*, Vol. 2, p. 3.

they were written will read *The Great Exemplar* with the feeling
that they have come at last to the Jeremy Taylor they have been
led to expect. The preface is an eloquent meditation upon the
whole family of man, a part of creation which wants nothing but
Christianity for its perfection. When we come to the first of the
considerations, that on the Nativity, we realize that here is
devotion written in a spirit new to English religious literature.
Not even Bishop Andrewes in the most rapt of his sermons on
the Nativity had come near to the warmth and elevation which
suffuses all Taylor's thought. He had now become a great artist
in words, and here he uses his gift for the first time to express
the tenderest piety illuminated by the imagination of a poet.
The whole scene of the Nativity, as Taylor sets it out, is bathed
in a soft glow, like those old paintings of the birth of Christ, in
which the only light which illuminates the stable is that which
radiates from the Son of God. There can be few more winning
pictures in any book of devotion than Taylor's presentment of
the Blessed Virgin as she broods lovingly, one by one, over the
limbs of her new born child, when "she kissed him and worshipped him, and thanked him that he would be born of her, and
she suckled him and bound him in her arms and swadling bands".[1]

This section is followed by a quaint, and perhaps at that time
necessary, discourse, "Of the Duty of Nursing Children". It
was meant to encourage mothers to feed their children themselves
and not to follow the usual custom of handing them over to
foster-mothers.[2] This is only one of the twenty discourses scattered
throughout the book. They represent, in all probability, sermons
preached by Taylor in the period immediately before the Civil
War. It is possible that it was from discussion of some points in
them that Northampton went on to consider the idea of writing
a life of Christ himself or of encouraging Taylor to do so. The
discourses were obviously intended to be preached. They could
very well be taken out of their present setting and published
separately. Indeed, two of them were issued in that way in 1672.
In that year a publisher put out a couple of sermons, one entitled
Christ's Yoke an Easy Yoke, the other *The Gate to Heaven a Strait
Gate*. They were supposedly unpublished and were said to be
printed from a manuscript "supplied by a person of honour yet
living". This person was most likely the third Earl of Northampton, but the publisher made a mistake in supposing that the

---

[1] *Works*, Vol. 2, p. 66.
[2] There is a tract on the same subject in the *Harleian Miscellany* (Vol. 2, pp. 27–33)
entitled "The Countess of Lincoln's Nurserie", Oxford, 1622.

sermons were new. Taylor had utilized them both in the composition of *The Great Exemplar*.[1] As neither of them contains any of
those elaborately decorated passages which are so characteristic
a feature of what we know of Taylor's preaching at Golden
Grove, they were probably preached in the days before he had
settled in Wales. It would be easy for several manuscript copies
of an admired sermon to exist, and for one of them to get into
the hands of the Northampton family. None of the sermons in
The Great Exemplar are closely linked with the preceding narrative,
though being upon cognate subjects they fit in very well where
they are. Certainly no one who does not object on principle to a
long book will find fault with them, for they add greatly to the
beauty of the work even though they are not essential to it.

At every pause in the story, and at the end of the discourses,
suitable prayers are interspersed. This was another of Taylor's
splendid gifts. He wrote prayers as few divines since the Reformation have been able to do. Compared with the great models of
antiquity, and with the Prayer Book, Taylor's devotions may
perhaps seem to lack conciseness and balance; but they are
eclipsed only by these, the superlative expressions of man's
religious instincts throughout all ages.

Following upon the account of Christ's baptism and temptation
a section upon the baptism of infants is introduced. It was
probably inserted to make quite clear to those who were still
troubled by the arguments advanced for the Anabaptists in
The Liberty of Prophesying that Taylor held orthodox views on
the subject. There are other doctrinal sections inserted later on,
one on faith, another on repentance, another on the Blessed
Sacrament, but as they differ very little from the teaching contained in Taylor's definitely doctrinal works, the consideration
of his opinions on these matters can best be undertaken when
his more theological books are under review. But it is in these
places that by far the greatest portion of the direct Latin and
Greek quotations are to be found. It was the fashion of the
Anglican divines in Taylor's day to fill their works with masses
of learned references to, and quotations from, great numbers of
other theological authors, most of whom had written in Latin.
The Puritans were not so given to this practice, and it was
possibly because of this fact that Taylor found it necessary to

[1] The first appears partly in "Considerations upon the Death of the Innocents",
Works, Vol. 2, p. 148; and partly in "The Discourse of the Excellency of the Christian
Religion", ibid., p. 515. Much of the second appears in "Considerations upon the
Circumcision", ibid., p. 99.

apologize for the fewness of his own citations from the authorities. The strait-laced might consider that *The Liberty of Prophesying* had shown a regrettable taste for the unorthodox, and though Taylor was certainly not going to defeat his purpose by overloading *The Great Exemplar* with learning, he did not wish to be misunderstood. His object, he says, is to attract men to religion and therefore he intends to use anything which is in itself attractive. Nothing could serve this purpose better than the classics, and it is to them therefore that he continually appeals, laying aside "the triflings" of those authors who "added nothing to Christianity but trouble, scruple, and vexation". To Greece and Rome he turns continually and always skilfully. Now it is a phrase or two that he borrows from the poets, now a recollection of some story from the histories, now a wise saying from the philosophers, now a few instances gathered together from various places to prove a point. In speaking of miracles he recalls that:

One Caius was cured of his blindness by Aesculapius, and so was Valerius Aper; and at Alexandria, Vespasian cured a man of the gout by treading upon his toes, and a blind man with spittle.[1]

The Great Exemplar undoubtedly suffers in these days from its length. It might also have been injured by want of unity, with the different portions tending to fall into isolation, if the figure of Jesus Christ upon earth had not been made as prominent as it is in all. For our Lord, Taylor is very fond of two special titles—the Holy Jesus, and the Prince of the Catholic Church. The first of these is the most commonly used name throughout the book. Mystical interpretations which startle the more literal minded reader of to-day occur with frequency. When Christ cleansed the Temple we are told that "the Holy Jesus made a whip of cords, to represent and to chastise the implications and the enfoldings of sin, and the cords of vanity".[2] There is another exegesis of the pierced side which, from the minuteness with which every detail is interpreted, would be more likely to shock than to help the devotional piety of the present day. But the vivid imagination which, to a more reticent age seems sometimes misused, fills the whole book with life and movement.

Taylor's imagination was pictorial, and throughout *The Great Exemplar* he is specially fond of using it to evoke scenes which resemble victorious processions in the increasing triumph of their progress. One of these describes Jesus entering Hades after his death. The righteous men of old catch the first glimpse of their

[1] *Works*, Vol. 2, p. 312.   [2] *Ibid.*, p. 495.

coming enlightenment and rejoice to see it. The accursed spirits shrink backward in anger and dread, amazed that a man durst come among them or a God should die. These elaborately beautiful passages are generally found in the "considerations". In the narrative portions Taylor is content to tell the story simply, in the discourses it is turned to some practical use, in the "considerations" its appeal to the soul is heightened by every art of language which the author could compass.

One of the loveliest passages in the book occurs in the meditation upon the Passion, and is built up round the figure of the mourning Virgin:

By the cross of Christ stood the holy Virgin-mother, upon whom old Simeon's prophesy was now verified; for now she felt a sword passing through her very soul: she stood without clamour and womanish noises; and silent, and with a modest grief, deep as the waters of the abyss, but smooth as the face of a pool; full of love, and patience, and sorrow and hope. Now she was put to it to make use of all those excellent discourses her holy Son had used to build up her spirit, and fortify it against this day. Now she felt the blessings and strengths of faith; and she passed from the griefs of the Passion to the expectation of the Resurrection; and she rested in this death, as in a sad remedy; for she knew it reconciled God with all the world. But her hope drew a veil before her sorrow; and though her grief was great enough to swallow her up, yet her love was greater, and did swallow up her grief.[1]

The Great Exemplar has often been reprinted apart from Taylor's other works, but it has never found the great popularity of *Holy Living* and *Holy Dying*, or the *Sermons*. Its length is a considerable drawback to many people; it also suffers from being neither a life of Christ simply and solely, nor a book of instructions, nor a collection of sermons. The three different types following on one another make continual demands for readjustment on the mind, which are rather disconcerting. The reader has no sooner got the flavour of one than he must pass to another. Taylor meant the book to be used, rather than read, in which case the variety would be stimulating, but to fulfil the author's intention demands both leisure and perseverance. This is not so much criticism as an attempt to suggest possible reasons why *The Great Exemplar* has not found the wide and continuous popularity which it deserves. For it is a beautiful book. To Taylor it came as a splendid discovery. It taught him the magnificence of his strength and where that strength most truly lay.

[1] *Works*, Vol. 2, p. 710.

CHAPTER VI

QUIETNESS AND SUCCESS

NOT every author receives due recognition in his lifetime. His work may be so far in advance of his age that only a few forward-looking individuals recognize its value, or he may be so constitutionally opposed to the general tenor of his times that his contemporaries will have nothing to do with him. Taylor was fortunate. He belonged enough to his age to understand its needs and to offer something in satisfaction of them; but he had roots enough in the past, and appeal enough to the future, to lift him out of the ranks of those who achieve only a contemporary fame.

In 1649, while Taylor was living quietly in Wales developing the gift that was in him, Parliament, which had executed Charles I and sent Charles II into exile, transformed England from a monarchy into a republic. Everyone hoped that a new election would give the country a form of government which had, at least, the full support of all those who had opposed the King. But what remained of the Long Parliament still clung resolutely to power. Their ideal was to establish in England an aristocratic oligarchy of a form already familiar in Holland and Venice. All legislative power they proposed to retain in their own hands, the executive authority was to reside in a Council of State composed of forty-one persons; between them these two bodies hoped to settle the country, and provide liberty of worship for such forms of religion as they considered truly Protestant. But the Army was the real master of the situation, and the soldiers were among those who were most bitterly disappointed that a new Parliament had not been called. For the present they were too busy to intervene. Levellers within their own ranks threatened the overthrow of all discipline; wars both in Ireland and Scotland needed their presence; the Rump was the government in being, and for the time England must submit to its rule.

Taylor must have set to work upon *Holy Living* as soon as *The Great Exemplar* had been launched upon the public, and he was convinced not only that he wrote devotional books better than any other, but that the world was more eager to welcome them. In 1650 the book was published. It is so famous that it hardly needs any description; whoever has heard of Jeremy Taylor has heard of *Holy Living* and *Holy Dying*.[1] The two are now generally bound up together and regarded as one work. Actually there was a year between them in publication and there is a considerable difference in their tone. But the two are quite properly linked, since both were undoubtedly the outcome of the same design. Taylor could hardly have written a book dealing as fully with the Christian life as he intended to and treat sickness and death so very briefly, unless he had planned subsequently to write a special work for that purpose. The very title itself, *The Rule and Exercises of Holy Living*, suggests that it needs the parallel, *Rule and Exercises of Holy Dying*, to bring it to a completion.

The plan of *Holy Living* is worked out on a method similar to that of *The Great Exemplar*. There are four chapters, each divided into sections and these again subdivided. In the first portion the particular virtue under review is treated generally, in the succeeding portion it is reduced to rule, with prayers and meditations suitable for it. Positive teaching occupies the author throughout. He does not care to waste more time than is absolutely necessary by inveighing against evil. He assumes that in the main his readers want to be holy, and only require from him such help as may enable them to bring their desires to good effect. Taylor had trained himself in an orderly school. He believed that the visible, divinely appointed order of the Church had its counterpart in the disciplined life of the soul. Neither was left to the sway of its own emotions.

God will go out of His way to meet His saints, when themselves are forced out of their way of order by a sad necessity; but else God's usual way is to be present in those places where His servants are appointed ordinarily to meet. But His presence there signifies nothing but a readiness to hear their prayers, to bless their persons, to accept their offices, and to like even the circumstance of orderly and public meeting.[2]

The Christian Religion could be divided into three parts, "sobriety, justice, religion. The first contains all our deportment

---

[1] *Holy Living* was not the first manual of popular devotion to be published after the Reformation, though it is the most attractive of all the early books. A widely used work, *The Practice of Piety*, was "printed about forty times in 8vo, and 12mo, the eleventh edition of which was printed in London 1619. It was also printed once or more in the Welsh tongue, and once or more in French, A.D. 1633, written by Dr Lewis Bayley, consecrated December eighth 1616. Bishop of Bangor" (Kennet's *Register*, p. 350). It aimed at being a complete manual of Christian teaching and practice. Besides the numerous printed sermons, there were also books of pious thoughts similar to Henshaw's *Daily Thoughts* (1637) and Hall's *Meditations and Vows* (1606) in existence to provide religious reading.

[2] *Works*, Vol. 3, p. 24.

in our personal and private capacities, the fair treatment of our bodies and our spirits; the second enlarges our duty in all relations to our neighbour; the third contains the offices of direct religion, and intercourse with God."[1]

Asceticism for its own sake does not attract him, neither does he encourage it in others. People may choose pleasant food in preference to unpleasant, so long as it is not the mere delight of eating that is indulged. There is no glorification of celibacy. Marriage and single life are both states to which men are called by God, and neither is more or less holy than another. Taylor's intention was not to point out ways in which the soul can enjoy spiritual delights, or cultivate itself in solitary and superior perfection. He was concerned with outdoor Christians, and how they may best fulfil every duty they have to God, their brethren, and themselves. *Holy Living* therefore becomes to some extent a manual of casuistry. A section, for instance, dealing with the duties of merchants, headed "Rules and measures of justice in bargaining", treats the ethics of buying and selling with considerable detail. His opinion is that: "in prices of bargaining concerning uncertain merchandises, you may buy as cheap ordinarily as you can",[2] providing certain conditions are observed. There must be no violence, the prices must be governed, roughly, by what is customary in such cases; there must be neither monopoly nor what in modern language would be called cornering of products, and the good of the public as a whole must be considered. Wages must be paid promptly, and no one is to take in hand anything for a fee which he has not the ability nor some reasonable chance to perform. A doctor, for example, is forbidden to undertake the treatment of an incurable disease without first explaining to the patient that he considers the case hopeless. The whole section is of special interest since it shows that Taylor was fully aware of some of the difficulties which were being created by the increasing complexity of the nation's commercial life.

On the duties of subjects to princes he is as inflexible as ever. The doctrine of non-resistance is set out complete:

Lift not up thy hand against thy prince or parent, upon what pretence soever; but bear all personal affronts and inconveniences at their hands and seek no remedy but by patience and piety, yielding and praying, or absenting thyself.[3]

The reason for this is that the prince, like the father of the family, with whom Taylor links him throughout this section,

---

[1] *Works*, Vol. 3, p. 44.   [2] Ibid., p. 131.   [3] Ibid., p. 118.

holds his authority from God alone. This doctrine of passive obedience and the divine right of kings was not the mere sycophancy it is sometimes made out to be. There was a real need to find some basis for the fact of royalty. The time for government by force of arms had passed away, the time for government truly based on popular consent was not yet ripe. That for the moment the King's authority was overruled would make no difference to Taylor; he, like every other Royalist, would consider that his allegiance now bound him to Charles II, whom a few successful revolutionaries had deprived, rather than the nation repudiated. It was certainly not the government in power that Taylor had in mind when he wrote the passage which has just been quoted; the King was just as much King as he had ever been, and there was just as much need to show from whence his right to rule derived.

The final section in the book deals with the Holy Communion. This was a subject on which, doctrinally, Taylor was never very sure of himself. His teaching in different places is apt to seem contradictory. But one thing never changes. His devotional attitude toward the Blessed Sacrament is always the same; awe at the approach to an exceeding great mystery; complete abasement, coming from a sense of his own unworthiness to approach the altar to which he was commanded to come and from which his soul drew life and health.[1]

Holy Living contains one of the first attacks that Taylor ever made upon the idea that a death-bed repentance is sufficient to save a man who has consistently disobeyed God throughout his life. This was a crusade that he never gave up. It would be interesting to know what personal incident lay behind it; for, to one who felt more than he thought, the stimulus to such an abiding conviction would be almost certain to come from something actually experienced. No doubt a good many of those whom he met in his army days would be tempted to silence the exhortations of a too persistent chaplain with the promise to think of the repentance he advocated at a more convenient season; and it may have been that the body of some such a one carried in after a quick death in battle first impressed upon Taylor the wickedness of deferring the contrition which comes at any time later than it ought.

[1] Taylor's devotional writings are among the most original parts of his work, yet strangely enough it is here that there have been most attempts to prove him a plagiarist. It is said, sometimes, that *Holy Living* is indebted to St Francis De Sales' *Introduction to the Devout Life*, but the resemblances are few and the differences very many.

Most of Taylor's books have a few, slight, autobiographical touches in them. *Holy Living* has more than most. They throw light on both his mentality and his circumstances. It is hard to believe that he was not referring to himself when he wrote:

I am fallen into the hands of publicans and sequestrators, and they have taken all from me: what now? let me look about me. They have left me the sun and moon, fire and water, a loving wife, and many friends to pity me, and some to relieve me, and I can still discourse; and unless I list they have not taken away my merry countenance, and my cheerful spirit, and a good conscience: they still have left me the providence of God, and all the promises of the Gospel, and my religion, and my hopes of heaven, and my charity to them too; and still I sleep and digest, I eat and drink, I read and meditate, I can walk in my neighbour's pleasant fields, and see the varieties of natural beauties, and delight in all that in which God delights, that is, in virtue and wisdom, in the whole creation, and in God himself. And he that hath so many causes of joy and so great, is very much in love with sorrow and peevishness, who loses all, these pleasures, and chooses to sit down upon his little handful of thorns.[1]

Accepting this as autobiographical, it would seem that his first wife was alive at the time, since he could speak of his wife being left to him after the sequestration of his living. If the passage can be accepted as evidence, and there is no reason why it should not be, then it goes a long way toward clearing up the difficulty which surrounds Taylor's marriages, since it constitutes proof of the fact that his first wife was alive in 1650.

The same temper of mind which he exhibits in the passage just quoted continued throughout the section which deals with contentedness. It has a far truer ring than the conventional book-philosophy offered by those who desire to help others bear an adversity which they have never felt themselves. He is willing, for the sake of comparison, to take the reader into his confidence about his poverty, and to show how even an evil of that sort is only relative. If, he says to him, "God should send a cancer upon thy face or spread a crust of leprosy upon thy skin", would you not, to escape it, "gladly be as poor as I am or the meanest of thy brethren".[2] He refers to one who was in all probability the wife he was soon to lose, in terms which show how strong was the affection which bound them together.

[1] *Works*, Vol. 3, p. 91. In the same section Taylor uses the first personal pronoun in several other instances of men falling into adversity, but the passage quoted above corresponds so closely with what we know of his circumstances that it is reasonable to suppose the details are autobiographical.
[2] Ibid., Vol. 3, p. 93.

I have known an affectionate wife, when she hath been in fear of parting with her beloved husband, heartily desire of God his life or society upon any conditions that were not sinful, and choose to beg with him rather than to feast without him; and the same person hath upon that consideration borne poverty nobly, when God hath heard her prayer in the other matter.[1]

Possessed of the cheerful disposition and vigorous common sense as well as the domestic happiness which is mirrored here, Taylor must have found his retreat at Golden Grove a very pleasant one in spite of the apparent poverty which accompanied it.[2] Literary fame was coming to him, and *Holy Living* did a great deal to add to it. Writing a manual of direction for the conduct of ordinary life, Taylor does not give that full rein to his fancy or to his language which he allowed himself in *Holy Dying* and the *Sermons*, so from a literary point of view *Holy Living* falls below the other two books. But although there are no great, exalted, outbursts, a very high level of strong, interest-compelling prose is maintained throughout.

The argument of the book often suffers considerably through being broken. It is not so much one, evolving, train of thought that is offered, as a bundle of disconnected reasons, all, to some extent, bearing on the same point. Consequently, the reader finds his progress hampered a little. He goes forward by a series of leaps rather than steadily, and with increasing impetus, as he would do if each reason was the natural corollary of the one which went before.

Taylor's sentences lie like a handful of jewels, each one complete in its own beauty, neither borrowing from nor lending to its neighbour. There is scarcely any more warmth than there is in jewels. Taylor feels no devotional raptures himself and does not attempt to inspire any. All his concern is with action in this world. If you wish to be holy, says Taylor, this is what you must do; the visions which inspire action are outside his scope. It is the cumulative effect of so much sweetness, reasonableness, and trust in the goodness of God, and the air of pure holiness which hangs over all which is impressive, and only stops short of inspiration.

Almost as soon as the book was published the cheerful reliance upon divine goodness which it advocated was put to a still more

[1] *Works*, Vol. 3, p. 93
[2] In 1647, Parliament made an order that one-fifth of the income from their former livings should be allowed for the support of the dependents of the sequestered clergy. There is no indication that Taylor's family received any advantage from this.

severe test in Taylor's own life. Death took both his wife and his patroness. In a letter to Dugdale, dated 1 April 1651, he mentions his loss. "I have but lately buried my dear wife",[1] he writes, and goes on to refer apparently to an intention to write a tract upon baptism, and later in the letter, mentions that he is transcribing his *Rule of Holy Dying*. The dedication of that book is to Lord Carbery, and there again Taylor refers to his bereavement when he says:

Both your lordship and myself have lately seen and felt such sorrows of death, and such sad departure of dearest friends, that it is more than high time we should think ourselves nearly concerned in the accidents.[2]

All this dedication shows how keenly Taylor had felt the double blow which had fallen upon him. The consolation which he offers to his patron is the same as that with which he has fortified himself. Frances, Lady Carbery, seems to have been something more than a lady bountiful who had shown kindness to a distressed clergyman.[3] Both in the dedication to *Holy Dying*, and in the magnificent funeral sermon in which Taylor glorified her memory, he speaks of her as one who had shown him the fullest and deepest friendship. She had married Lord Carbery in June 1637, when she was very young. Her lot lay in a quiet place, but she seems to have been as notable a woman as any of her time, and it was an age of great women. She was clever, charming, of so spotless a character that "you might as well have suspected the sun to smell of the poppy that he looks on, as that she could have been a person apt to be sullied by the breath of a foul question".[4] Though her married life only lasted thirteen years, she was the mother of ten children and died, worn out by continual child-bearing, soon after she had brought her last child, a daughter whom she called Athamia, into the world.[5]

[1] Hamper, *Life of Dugdale*, p. 250.   [2] *Works*, Vol. 3, p. 258.

[3] Lord Carbery was three times married. First wife: Bridget, daughter and heiress of Thomas Lloyd of Llanllyr, Cardiganshire. Second wife: Frances, daughter of Sir John Altham, of Oxey, Oxfordshire. She was Taylor's patroness and died 9 October 1650. Third wife: Lady Alice Egerton, daughter of John, First Earl of Bridgewater. She was a pupil of Henry Lawes, Milton's friend, and an adventure of hers has been mistakenly supposed to have suggested the plot for Milton's *Comus*. See Masson, *Life of Milton*, Vol. 2, p. 227.

[4] *Works*, Vol. 8, p. 443.

[5] All Carbery's surviving issue were by her. Francis, the eldest son, died before his father in 1667. John Vaughan, Third and last Earl of Carbery, inherited the title and estate. Probably educated under Taylor. Appointed Governor of Jamaica, 1674, accused of extortion and superseded by the Earl of Carlisle, 1678. Was a patron and friend of Dryden, who dedicated to him, as a suitable offering to a man of his tastes, one of the filthiest of his poems. Pepys says he was "one of the lewdest fellows of the age, worse than Sir Charles Sedley", *Diary*, 16 November 1667. He was a bitter opponent of Clarendon.

The account of her end is without doubt the most moving passage Taylor ever wrote. It is all the more powerful because he attempts no set description, but turns, as it were, every now and then from his rapt contemplation of death itself to her who was passing through its shadow. Religion had been one of the great occupations of her life. As much time as she could spare from the management of a great household and the upbringing of her children she had spent in prayer and meditation. Every day she either read a sermon or listened to one, and almost the last plan she ever had was for collecting in "a large book" such religious "assistances as she would choose so that she might be readily furnished and instructed to every good work".[1] Her religion was as strong and deep as a mighty river and "in all her actions of relation towards God, she had a strange evenness and untroubled passage, sliding toward her ocean of God and of infinity with a certain and silent motion". And so she came to death, prepared for anything, and dreading nothing but the actual pain of her dissolution.

But so it was that the thought of death dwelt long with her, and grew from the first steps of fancy and fear, to a consent, from thence to a strange credulity and expectation of it; and without the violence of sickness she died, as if she had done it voluntarily, and by design. . . . And in this I cannot but adore the providence and admire the wisdom and infinite mercies of God. For having a tender and a soft, a delicate and fine constitution and breeding, she was tender to pain, and apprehensive of it, as a child's shoulder is of a load and burden. . . . But God that knew her fears and her jealousy concerning herself, fitted her with a death so easy, so harmless, so painless, that it did not put her patience to a severe trial. It was not (in all appearance) of so much trouble as two fits of a common ague; so careful was God to remonstrate to all that stood in that sad attendance that this soul was dear to Him: and that since she had done so much of her duty towards it, He that began would also finish her redemption, by an act of rare providence, and a singular mercy. Blessed be the goodness of God, who does so careful actions of mercy for the ease and security of his servants.[2]

It was with the thought of this death in mind, and the loss he had suffered in his own family, that Taylor wrote *Holy Dying*. That it did not spring suddenly out of his sorrow as has been suggested,[3] is quite clear from his own words in the dedication to Lord Carbery when, after references to the death of his lady,

[1] *Works*, Vol. 8, p. 446.   [2] Ibid., p. 448.   [3] Gosse, *Jeremy Taylor*, p. 89.

Taylor says: "this book was intended first to minister to her piety and she desired all good people should partake of the advantages which are here recorded".[1] This, as well as some words which follow a line or two later, show that Lady Carbery had prompted the writing of *Holy Dying*. But when the time of publication came she was dead, and Taylor could do no more than "dress her hearse with the bundles of cypress" which were intended to "dress her closet".[2]

A curious folding plate adorns the first edition. It represents the hall of a country house, where a divine is exhibiting the life-sized portrait of a skeleton to a lady who has her husband and child nearby. This rather gruesome work was executed by Peter Lombart, the French engraver who produced several of those portraits of Taylor which are to be found as frontispieces of many of his works.[3] In this case also the clergyman is said to represent Taylor, and the gentleman and lady to be pictures of Lord Carbery and his third wife.

It may be doubted whether the first paragraph of the dedication is in the best of taste, for the author very pointedly reminds Lord Carbery of what was then happening to the body of the wife whom he had buried such a little time before. This is not the only occasion in the book when the ghastliness of corruption is dwelt on a little more than the modern reader thinks necessary. There is the revolting story of the young German gentleman, which Taylor thought worthy of polishing into one of his most finished sentences.[4] But on the whole there is far less of the horrible side of human dissolution in this book than in other compositions on death which the age produced. He only goes into the charnel house when it is necessary to read his auditors a lecture upon what he finds there. He himself is neither attracted nor repelled by decay. The human body has none of the horrible fascination for Taylor that it had for Donne. He can see it near its end and feel neither curiosity, wonderment, nor regret at its fate. When a man comes to death he has come to "That harbour whither God has designed everyone that he may find rest from the troubles of the world".[5] There is neither fear of this end, nor longing for it, in his mind. It is inevitable, it is God-sent and

---

[1] *Works*, Vol. 3, p. 257.   [2] Ibid.

[3] Pierre Lombart, d. 1681. He came to England from Paris, *circa* 1640. Practised successfully as an engraver and portrait painter until a little after 1660. Returned to Paris and died there. Known to Pepys, a portrait of Mrs Pepys was by him. Known to Evelyn, who was probably the link with Taylor.

[4] *Works*, Vol. 3, p. 271.   [5] Ibid., p. 336.

therefore it is well. And just as Taylor avoids any extraordinary clinging to this world so does he refuse to go into raptures and dilate upon the glories of the next. There is no mention of harps, singing, or angel choirs in his book; but patience in sickness, self-examination, and repentance for sin, and then a cheerful abiding of the issue.

All this was new in the literature of the age. The refusal to see death as a macabre monster, a black figure hurling poisoned darts, or as the majestic subduer of tyrants and kings, was a break-away from a literary convention which had been observed by too many and lasted too long.[1] Taylor writes about death just as so many have undergone it before his day, then and since, quite simply and naturally. Part of the reason may have been that the death-bed of Lady Carbery, which the funeral shows had affected him profoundly, was still fresh in his mind. What he had witnessed at his wife's bedside we do not know; it belonged to that private life which he was never anxious to reveal. He delivered no funeral oration over his wife. He could not make his grief objective to that extent. But though recent experiences no doubt had their share in determining the tone of his writing, the main explanation lies in the extraordinary serenity of his religious faith. Whatever vicissitudes his exterior circumstances may have suffered, no waves or storms had gone over his soul. He served God in the beauty of holiness and the beauty of holiness was his strength. The theology which he professed avoided extremes. It neither threatened him with the pains of purgatory, nor the wrath of a God who delights in anger; and so he feels that one who has done all he can to fortify himself by a life of devotion can safely resign his spirit, when the time comes, into the hands of a Merciful Saviour.

Holy Dying has more personal feeling in it than any other of Taylor's books. There was nothing like it in English before he wrote, and he disagreed so profoundly with the Roman Catholic teaching about death, that it is doubtful if any Latin manuals influenced him. His continually reiterated objection to death-bed repentance, which finds vigorous expression here too, offers, even without his own testimony, sure indication that he would condemn extreme unction. But he does in fact make his position

[1] In the sixteenth century Montaigne and Shakespeare are almost alone in their attitude of quiet acceptance of death. In Donne the preoccupation with all that concerned it has the force of a morbid passion, but from then on the dread of mortality appears less and less in English literature. See Spencer, *Death and Elizabethan Tragedy*, London, 1936.

quite clear. He calls it a "charm"[1] and says "it must needs be nothing, for no rational man can think any ceremony can make a spiritual change without a spiritual act of him that is to be changed".[2] On prayers for the dead, he unhesitatingly condemns intercession for those who have lived evil lives, for their state is determined; but he neither expressly, or by the tone of the passage, condemns supplication on behalf of those that have lived faithfully and died trustfully. The book came straight from his heart and his experience. He writes of the difficulties a parish priest finds in actual ministration among his flock. Of the reluctance of sick people to send for a priest, until life is almost extinct, he writes so fully that he had doubtless had the same experience as many priests of to-day in this matter. Not all of this was remembered from his Uppingham days, for he seems to have exercised his pastoral office whenever he had the opportunity, right up to the Restoration.

In the first chapter of *Holy Dying* Taylor reaches the height of his literary glory. He did few things as well and nothing better in his after days. The grandeur of his theme is matched by the exaltation of his language and the range and beauty of his imagery. To read it for the first time is like turning into a tropical valley; one is overwhelmed by hitherto unimagined luxuriance. This fact has been recognized by most of the makers of anthologies, for in nearly every collection in which Taylor figures, something is taken from this chapter. His subject is the inevitability of death and the pathos of it coming suddenly to one who, like the dead captain in the shipwreck, strong in earthly hopes and confident of the future, meets a catastrophic end.[3] Every one of us has but the feeblest hold on life. "Death meets us every where and is procured by every instrument and in all chances."[4] Taylor had a poet's mentality, and though he could not write verse he proves himself in this chapter a master of prose rhythm. Almost every line will show how skilfully he matches his cadences to his thought. There is nevertheless very little that could be called merely fine writing in the book. He does, it is true, pile up arguments and images, but there is sincerity in them all. They are there because the writer felt that they might bring extra, and perhaps needed, persuasion to bear upon the reader: not because they gave him a chance to show how beautifully he could embroider a common, if noble, theme. Indeed the sincerity, the pathos, the beauty, of Taylor's meditations upon death do for

[1] *Works*, Vol. 3, p. 268.　　[2] Ibid., p. 269.　　[3] Ibid., p. 268.　　[4] Ibid., p. 269.

H

the moment trick us into believing that he is saying something new, when actually originality is entirely wanting in the basic ideas upon which he erects so lovely a fabric.

In essence the sum of the whole book is this: we must all die, we ought therefore to endeavour to die worthily—a stock reflection of every moralist, pagan or Christian. The author's debt to the classics throughout the book is conspicuous, not only in pointed stories skilfully borrowed, but in allusions, quotations and paraphrases. Our generation will never read *Holy Dying* with the complete understanding of, and joy in, the author with which our forefathers read it, because we are without that background of knowledge of the literature of Greece and Rome which educated men were wont to have. A moderately well-read man nowadays will probably recognize the names of the more famous authors to whom Taylor refers; he may make some effort to verify for himself how close the quickly appended paraphrase may be to the quotation which Taylor has just given in the original, but the hints, the fleeting glances, at something the ancients said, and which the author will assume because they said it, all these will be beyond him. Still, there is enough beauty of an inescapable sort to assure that *Holy Dying* will have its readers so long as anyone takes any interest at all in what Jeremy Taylor wrote.

Taylor did not intend it to be used only, or even chiefly, by those who are nearing their end. He wanted it to be read while men were in their health and strength, so that they might fitly prepare themselves for sickness and death.[1] The book is too long for any sick person except those whose illness does not make them incapable of sustained mental effort. Lovers of pure literature who have no objection to a solemn theme adequately treated, will always come to *Holy Dying* with delight. Its continuous publication with *Holy Living* has made it difficult to gauge how much popularity it has gained on its own merits, for the earlier of the two works so adequately filled an obvious need in the Church of England that it has regularly been republished for its devotional value ever since its first appearance.[2] The two books together have had a vast influence over countless lives. Captain Thomas Verney, that interesting if rather unstable member of a notable family, wrote home to request "a provision

[1] *Works*, Vol. 3, p. 258.
[2] Some idea of the great popularity of these two books may be gained from the fact that *Holy Living* reached its fourteenth edition in 1686 and *Holy Dying* its twenty-first edition in 1710.

for my soul, Dr Taylor his *Holy Living* and *Dying* both in one volume", when he was contemplating a voyage to the West Indies. Later, when the Duchess of Marlborough was attempting to reduce Queen Anne to her obedience again, she sent the Queen a lecture on the duty of forgiveness before coming to Communion and a copy of *Holy Living* and *Holy Dying*, with the leaves turned down at suitable places.

It was the reading of *Holy Living* and *Holy Dying* while he was at Oxford which caused the first spiritual awakening in John Wesley. So, though partially and indirectly, it had a share in the founding of Methodism.[1] It had an influence which might have been expected upon the man who launched the greatest religious revival in the Church of England within the next century. John Keble, writing to his friend J. T. Coleridge in 1817, says:

I never read *Holy Living and Dying* regularly till this spring, and I cannot tell you the delight it has given me; surely that book is enough to convert any infidel, so gentle in heart, and so high in mind, so fervent in zeal, and so charitable in judgement, that I confess I do not know any other author, except perhaps Hooker (whose subjects are so different that they will hardly bear comparison), worthy to be likened to him. Spenser I think comes nearest to his spirit in all respects. Milton is like him in richness and depth, but in morality seems to me as far below him as pride is below humility.[2]

The same great qualities appear in the *Sermons*, which Taylor made his next publication. He claims that they were all actually preached;[3] but although there are fifty-two of them, and they are arranged to fit the Sundays of the year, it is not very likely that they were consecutively produced, one a week, throughout any one year of Taylor's life. They were probably the flower of his preaching throughout the time he had been at Golden Grove, and therefore belonged to a period contemporary with *The Liberty of Prophesying*, *The Great Exemplar*, and *Holy Living* and *Holy Dying*. It is important to recognize this fact, although it is impossible to sort them all out and fit each sermon into its

[1] Robert Southey, *Life of John Wesley* (Hutchinson's Standard Lives), p. 28. Another writer on Methodism remarks: "But for Jeremy Taylor, it is conceivable that Wesley would never have doubted that he was in a state of salvation, and that the doctrine of assurance, in the extremely narrow and highly technical sense that Wesley imparted to it, would never have perplexed English minds philosophical or lay", F. J. Snell, *Wesley and Methodism*, p. 36. See also Trevor-Hughes, *Jeremy Taylor and John Wesley*, London Quarterly, Oct. 1949.
[2] J. T. Coleridge, *Memoir of John Keble*, p. 68.
[3] "Preached at Golden Grove" is on the title page of each half year, *Works*, Vol. 4.

proper place, in a graph of Taylor's literary ability, in order to show that his strength was still on the increase. It is probable that after *Holy Dying* Taylor never did anything else so good in the ornate style, and that many of the most gorgeous passages in the *Sermons* were written before that book, and some little time before their publication. From 1651 the calm which Taylor seems to have found so necessary to good writing was passing from him.

Taylor's main collection of sermons is divided into two parts; the first, containing "Twenty-seven Sermons", is called *The Summer Half*, the second, with "Twenty-five Sermons", entitled *The Winter Half*. The whole work is called *Eniautos*, or *A Course of Sermons for all the Sundays of the Year, fitted to the great necessities and for supplying the wants of preaching in many parts of this nation*.[1] The *Summer Half* was published in 1651, with some doubts about the reception which the sermons were likely to receive.[2] Taylor apparently had a very graceful delivery and was not quite sure how his sermons would bear being deprived of that aid. He was also afraid that they might not have learning enough to suit the tastes of the time, so he puts in his protest early: "It were well if men would not enquire after the learning of the sermon or its deliciousness to the ear or fancy, but observe its usefulness."[3] That was his excuse for publishing—these sermons were useful. Taylor did not leave Wales to see this book through the press. The fact that his wife was dead and his family now wholly in his care would make it impossible for him to get away. So Royston, his publisher, added a short note apologizing for any printer's errors which might be found. "The absence of the author, and his inconvenient distance from London hath occasioned many lesser escapes in the impression of these sermons", he wrote. Quite an important little statement, for in the absence of very much certain knowledge about Taylor, information even of the briefest kind is very welcome. It would appear from this statement that Taylor usually corrected his own books, as they passed through the press, if he was in or near London, but that this time he was at a distance, almost certainly in Wales.

The *Second*, or *Winter Half*, he carried up to London himself; he was still in close contact with the family of his late wife, as a letter of his makes clear.

DEARE BROTHER,

Thy letter was most welcome to me, bringing the happy news of thy recovery. I had notice of thy danger, but watched for this

[1] *Eniautos* = a year.   [2] *Works*, Vol. 4, p. 323.   [3] Ibid., p. 324.

happy relation, and had laid wayte with Royston to enquire of Mr Rumbould. I hope I shall not neede to bid thee be carefull for the perfecting thy health, and to be fearful of a relapse. Though I am very much, yet thou thyself art more concerned in it. But this I will remind thee of, that thou be infinitely (careful) to perform to God those holy promises which I suppose thou didst make in thy sickness; and remember what thoughts thou hadst then, and beare them along upon thy spirit all thy lifetime. For that which was true then is so still, and the world is really a vain thing as thou didst then suppose it. I durst not tell thy mother of thy danger (though I heard of it) till at the same time I told her of thy recovery. Poore woman! she was troubled and pleased at the same time, but your letter did determine her, I take it kindly that thou hast writt to Bowman. If I had been in condition you should not have been troubled with it; but, as it is, both thou and I must be content. Thy mother sends her blessing to thee and her little Mally. So doe I, and my prayers to God for you both. Your little cozens[1] are your servants; and I am

thy most affectionate and endeared brother,

JER. TAYLOR.

November 24, 1653,

To my very dear Brother, D. Langsdale, at his Apothecary's House in Gainsborough.[2]

Taylor was apparently struggling with debt; but Bowman had been written to and, no doubt, satisfied for the time being, so that worry was quietened. There was no uneasiness whatever in his mind about the reception the public would give to his new book. The tone of its dedication, which, like the first part, was to Lord Carbery, was clear and confident; the writer feels no need to prepare the ground for his readers as he has done earlier. The two parts of *Eniautos* were from the beginning intended to form one work, and are now always published together, though the order in which they are arranged, the *Winter Half* first, to coincide with the beginning of the Church's year, is not the best. Placed so, the reader comes first to the confident second dedication, and until he makes a comparison of dates, is a little puzzled by the tentative air of the earlier dedication, which he meets later in the book. The author is insistent that his sermons are a course for all the Sundays of the year. There are fifty-two of them and to that extent the description is correct, but apart

[1] Cozens, i.e. Taylor's own children. Cp. "How now, brother! where is my cousin, your son?", *Much Ado About Nothing*, Act I, Sc. 1, line 2.

[2] Sloane MSS. 4274, No. 125 (Brit. Mus.). Heber ("Life", *Works*, Vol. 1, p. xxv) misread the date as 1643, and then, reasoning from the fact that Taylor does not mention his wife in the letter, considered it as additional evidence that the first wife died before Taylor left Uppingham.

from the first on "Domesday Book; or Christ's advent to Judgement", which does in a measure fit Advent Sunday, and the first in the *Summer Half*, "Of the Spirit of Grace", which coincides with Whitsunday, there is no reference to, or apparent fitness of the discourse for the day on which it is to be preached. Easter and Christmas are both passed by unnoticed. It might have been suggested that this was in deference to the dominant party, if there had been anything else in Taylor's life which gave the least encouragement to the idea. But the man who dedicated the *Apology for Liturgy* to the King, whom a purged Parliament had just executed, is not likely to have ignored the feasts of the Church because notice of them would give offence. It is odd, because even if Taylor was only publishing a collection of the most presentable of his discourses, one would have expected that the mighty themes of the Incarnation and the Resurrection would have inspired him more than once. He had already inserted discourses on these subjects in *The Great Exemplar*.[1]

There is also very little direct reference to the life of Our Lord in this collection. There are sermons on prayer, godly fear, the flesh and the spirit, the house of feasting, the marriage ring, Christian simplicity, mercy, sin, the righteous cause oppressed, and the author's permanent bugbear, deathbed repentance, but nothing to do with the main incidents in the Gospel story. He is practical throughout. There is nowhere any set pursuit of theological controversy, and very little attention is paid to it as a side issue. He observed his own precept, given when he was Bishop of Down and Connor to his clergy: "let the business of your sermons be to teach holy life, obedience, peace, love among neighbours".

A good many people have speculated whether the sermons were preached exactly as they were printed, or if a simpler version was given from the pulpit and this was afterwards worked over and polished before it appeared in book form. It has been objected that these sermons would have been far above the heads of an ordinary country congregation, but in all probability the congregation gathered in Lord Carbery's private chapel at Golden Grove was not composed entirely, or even mainly, of country people. There would be the master of the house and his family, such guests as they might have, and possibly some neighbouring clergy would be sufficiently attracted by Taylor's

---

[1] At a later date when he was bishop he particularly commanded his clergy to "explicate" the great festivals, *Works*, Vol. 1, p. 110.

fame to obtain permission, should that be needed, from Lord
Carbery to hear his chaplain's sermons. These and the servants
of the estate would make up the congregation. But no matter
who was there to hear him, anything that Taylor preached would
be both beautiful and learned. He had the true artist's joy in his
work, the delight which comes from the creation of a lovely
thing. One who thinks beautifully must speak beautifully, and
Taylor shows an habitual love of beauty, so far as his aptitude
allowed. The Latin and Greek was a convention of the day
among Anglican divines, and even country people have shown
often enough that they value the appearance of those languages
in the sermons they hear even though the meaning be utterly
beyond their understanding.

In the seventeenth century the sermon was one of the greatest
of mental activities. Never since then has the pulpit exercised so
great an influence, or the clergy as a whole been so conscious
of the power the preaching office gave them, or so eager to utilize
that power. The severe training in rhetoric, which all except the
most illiterate of self-appointed apostles had undergone, ensured
that the preacher should come to his task fully equipped to
perform it adequately. In addition to the ordinary training in
school themes, the sacred art of pulpit oratory had been studied
by itself. All the methods of the seventeenth-century preachers
may be said to have grown out of the same soil, and only as the
cultural and theological outlook of the party to which they
belonged forced them to one side or the other, did they branch
out. On the whole the Puritan preacher's sermons were plain
and unadorned with anything save plenty of references to the
Bible; indeed, in some cases they were apt to become a mere
mosaic of texts, in which very little more was wanted from the
minister than the power to string isolated passages together.
They were sermons which suited well the temperament of the
party. But the Anglicans carried that same love of beauty which
made them embellish their churches and their ritual into the
enrichment of their sermons. Both sides displayed immense
learning, drawn in general from the same sources; though
selected to fit the tastes of the audience to which it was to appeal,
and to support the particular case which was being presented.
On the whole the Puritans made more use of the classical
moralists than the High Churchmen;[1] though Jeremy Taylor,
borrowing freely from the whole field of classical literature, is as

[1] Mitchell, *English Pulpit Oratory*, p. 203.

frequent in his appeal to them as Adams or Hall. The Anglicans loved the Fathers and turned to them with great frequency. Perkins, the oracle of the Puritans, condemned the habit[1] and Baxter at a later date concurred, though no doubt with that effort which the endeavour to agree with anybody always demanded of him.[2] But to whatever extent the theological predilections of the preachers influenced their methods, their work had much the same background, as it had the same end.

The sermon at this time was not solely a religious exercise intended only for the ears of those who might assemble to receive it from the preacher's lips; it was, as much as anything else, an exercise in rhetoric designed for the widest possible public. Consequently, every preacher of any ability had publication in view, and the market was deluged with their works. It did not, however, follow that the preacher who intended to publish his work later on wrote it down before going into the pulpit word for word as it appeared later. He might do so; on the other hand, he might submit it to an elaborate editing before parting with it, and then state on the title page that the sermon was published with additions, or he might preach from notes which he afterward wrote out in full. A good many of the sermons which found their way into the bookshops were there without the consent of their authors. Some pious hearer, struck by the power and godliness of the address, might take it down in shorthand and have it printed to advance the views of the party, or his favourite preacher's fame, or even to make a little money. Posthumous sermons, edited by the executors of the deceased, or spurious work fathered on him because his name had a sales value, added their number to the overflowing supply.[3] Jeremy Taylor, when he started to publish sermons, was entering the most popular as well as the most exacting field of literature open to him at the time, and he made it completely his own.

We know that none of the sermons in *Eniautos* came to the printer from any other hands than Taylor's own. In all probability he preached them from manuscript in the form in which we have them now. If they are read with attention there is nothing in them to suggest anything other than the spoken word or any hint that there is a mingling of what was suitable for a country congregation with what was intended to charm the wider world.

[1] Perkins, *Works*, London, 1631, Vol. 2, p. 664.
[2] Baxter, *Works*, London, 1707, Vol. 4, p. 428.
[3] For a full discussion of the subject, see Mitchell, *English Pulpit Oratory*, pp. 14 ff.

If all the quotations and highly wrought passages were taken away from some of the sermons there would be very little left. There are only two ways in which the sermons could have been produced. The teaching in them might first have been delivered, quite simply in an extempore manner, the preacher using only a few notes, and then when the time for publication arrived the whole ground gone over again and the elaborate work produced as we now have it. What inducement there could be for Taylor to use this method it is impossible to say, if his congregation did not consist mainly of illiterates. It is more reasonable to suppose that the other method was used and the sermons were preached to all intents and purposes as they are printed.

Unfortunate as the present arrangement of *Eniautos* is from a chronological point of view, it has the advantage of presenting the reader with some of Taylor's best work first. The three introductory sermons for the *Winter Half*, those on Domesday Book, are exalted in tone, full of awe and at times of loveliness. In construction they are similar to those which follow. Three sermons are preached on the same text. Sometimes Taylor did not attempt more than two, but in none of the discourses in *Eniautos* does the preacher try to exhaust his subject matter in one address. But the various parts of the sermons follow on one another, and could easily be delivered together as one if such length was desired. Not even in the full form would they have been much longer than the normal pulpit effusion of the age. Divided as they are, each is notably short and can be read through comfortably in twenty minutes or half an hour.

After the text has been announced some general considerations upon it are offered, and the subject divided into heads. A good deal of care is spent on the opening. Sometimes the hearers are to be startled into attention, as for instance at the opening of the first sermon on "The Descending and Entailed Curse cut off":

It is not necessary that a commonwealth should give pensions to orators to dissuade men from running into houses infected with the plague, or to entreat them to be out of love with violent torments, or to create in men evil opinions concerning famine or painful deaths; every man hath a sufficient stock of self-love, upon the strength of which he hath entertained principles strong enough to secure himself against voluntary mischiefs, and from running into states of death and violence. A man would think that this I have now said were in all cases certainly true; and I would to God it were for that which is the greatest evil, that which makes all evils, that which turns good into evil, and every natural evil into a great sorrow, and makes that sorrow lasting and perpetual; that which sharpens the edge of swords, and makes agues to be fevers, and fevers to turn into plagues; that which puts stings into every fly, and uneasiness to every trifling accident, and strings every whip with scorpions; you know I must needs mean SIN; that evil men suffer patiently, and run after it greedily, and will not suffer themselves to be divorced from it; and therefore God hath hired servants to fight against this evil.[1]

Sometimes interest is engaged by a brief textual discussion, such as that which introduces the first part of the three sermons on "Godly Fear". Sometimes the passage of Scripture lends itself to satirical comment like the tremendous outburst that stands at the head of the sermon quaintly named "The House of Feasting". For text Taylor has "Let us eat, drink and be merry for to-morrow we die" and for comment:

This is the epicure's proverb, begun upon a weak mistake, started by chance from the discourses of drink, and thought witty by the undiscerning company; and prevailed infinitely, because it struck their fancy luckily, and maintained the merry meeting; but as it happens commonly to such discourses, so this also, when it comes to be examined by the consultations of the morning and the sober hours of the day, it seems the most witless and the most unreasonable in the world.[2]

There are a good many classical illustrations in this sermon, more than in most, but the morality is all for the preacher's own age and the people who heard him. If any more evidence of Taylor's attitude toward eating and drinking were needed than that provided in *Holy Living* and *Holy Dying* it is given here.[3] Moderate pleasure in the table is not condemned, but for the surfeiting and beastliness of which his age saw a good deal, he can find no words too severe.

The two sermons on "The Marriage Ring" which follow on "The House of Feasting" have attracted a good deal of attention both because of the unusual charm of the thought and the carefully wrought literary beauty with which they abound, neither are they without that sort of common sense in matrimonial affairs which is never out of date. Taylor's advice on the early days of marriage might be given to-day:

Man and wife are equally concerned to avoid all offences of each other in the beginning of their conversation: every little thing can

[1] *Works*, Vol. 4, p. 356.   [2] Ibid., p. 180.   [3] Ibid., p. 202.

blast an infant blossom; and the breath of the south can shake the
little rings of the vine when first they begin to curl like the locks of a
new-weaned boy; but when by age and consolidation they stiffen
into the hardness of a stem, and have by the warm embraces of the
sun and the kisses of heaven brought forth their clusters, they can
endure the storms of the north and the loud noises of a tempest and
yet never be broken; so are the early unions of an unfixed marriage,
watchful and observant, jealous and busy, inquisitive and careful,
and apt to take alarm at every unkind word. For infirmities do not
manifest themselves in the first scenes, but in the succession of a long
society; and it is not chance or weakness when it appears at first,
but it is want of love or prudence, or so it will be expounded.[1]

A little later on we get one of those rare glimpses into his own
home life. He is among his children, so soon to be motherless
and demanding more of his love than ever.

No man can tell but he that loves his children, how many delicious
accents make a man's heart dance in the pretty conversation of these
pledges; their childishness, their stammering, their little angers, their
innocence, their imperfections, their necessities, are so many little
emanations of joy and comfort to him that delights in their persons
and society; but he that loves not his wife and children, feeds a lioness
at home, and broods a nest of sorrows.[2]

It is religion in the home and in individual lives which is
here, as elsewhere, Taylor's chief interest. He makes no reference
to Milton's acrimonious pamphlets on divorce, or to any other
of the theories of marriage which were being discussed in his
time. Neither does he think it necessary to make more than the
slightest reference to the Church's right to bless the union of her
children; though this might have been expected, for the sectaries
who were now strongly in power hated all religious ceremonies
and were soon to enact that only those marriages celebrated
before a justice of peace were legal. It has been conjectured
that Taylor preached this sermon somewhere about the time
of his wife's death, from the fact that it would occur in the
yearly course about Ascensiontide:[3] but *Eniautos* did not contain
Taylor's sermons for 1651 merely, and so that conjecture falls
to the ground. Jeremy Taylor was never a Boanerges, his preaching was for the increase of holiness; it did not degenerate into a
tirade against political or Church enemies, as many of the pulpit
effusions of his age were apt to do. He makes very few references

[1] *Works*, Vol. 4, p. 216.   [2] Ibid., p. 224.
[3] Macleane (ed.), *Famous Sermons*, p. 83.

to the events of the times and calls names only on the rarest of occasions. He does, however, rebuke what he considers the exaggerated zeal of the Puritans, and makes a reference to Charles I and Strafford.

Only one set of sermons seems definitely to have its origin in the events of the day. The three which were preached on 1 Pet. 4.17-18, and entitled, *The Faith and Patience of the Saints; or The Righteous Cause Oppressed*, by implication throughout, and here and there by direct statement, set themselves to the work of encouraging the distressed Anglican Church. Preached, as they probably were, at some time between 1647, the year of Charles II's abduction from Holmby House, and 1651, when the royal cause seemed to have met total extinction at the battle of Worcester, it is easy to imagine the effect which the lyrical descriptions of good men suffering wrong must have had upon a congregation Royalist in sympathy. But this was an exception, and just as he addresses his sermons to the universal needs of men rather than to the exigencies of the times, so he avoids a habit which was very widespread among his contemporaries, of giving sermons fantastic titles whose chief object was to catch the eye of a buyer. He generally gives his addresses simple titles, which sum up the subject, rather than extraordinary ones which would make them conspicuous.

Besides the collection in *Eniautos* there are extant eleven unconnected sermons, and the twenty discourses embedded in *The Great Exemplar* which probably represent Taylor's preaching before 1649. Of the addresses published separately only one falls within Taylor's greatest period, the wonderful years between 1647 and 1655, and that is the funeral sermon for Lady Carbery already mentioned. In none of his other funeral orations did he achieve quite the same union of exalted contemplation and deep personal loss as he did in that, for the tie which bound the deceased lady to the preacher was a peculiarly close one. The sermon preached at the funeral of the Lord Primate, was also an act of mourning for one of his own friends—though the relationship between Taylor and Bramhall was neither so close, nor so tender, as that between him and Lady Carbery. Yet here again it is the personal interest which the preacher had in him whom they mourned which inspired his eloquence.

Bramhall died in 1663. He had been a great scholar as well as a wise and kindly diocesan. In order to appease the wounds of the distracted Ireland he served so well, he was willing to go further in concessions to the Presbyterians than some of his brethren on the episcopal bench. If he had lived longer it is possible that his moderating influence would have had some real effect upon the disputes. When he died, Taylor, whose reputation as a preacher was greater than that of any other of the Irish bishops, was called upon to preach the funeral sermon. His oration took the form of a meditation upon the Resurrection. Very little Latin and Greek found their way into it, and for the most part the prose is as direct as it is strong:

But this article [the Resurrection] was so clearly proved, that presently it came to pass that men were no longer ashamed of the cross, but it was worn upon breasts, printed in the air, drawn upon foreheads, carried upon banners, put upon crowns imperial; presently it came to pass that the religion of the despised Jesus did infinitely prevail; a religion that taught men to be meek and humble, apt to receive injuries, but unapt to do any; a religion that gave countenance to the poor and pitiful, in a time when riches were adored, and ambition and pleasure had possessed the heart of all mankind; a religion that would change the face of things, and the hearts of men, and break vile habits into gentleness and counsel; that such a religion, in such a time, by the sermons and conduct of fishermen, men of mean breeding and illiberal arts, should so speedily triumph over the philosophy of the world, and the arguments of the subtle, and the sermons of the eloquent; the power of princes and the interests of states, the inclinations of nature and the blindness of zeal, the force of custom and the solicitation of passions, the pleasures of sin and the busy arts of the devil; that is, against wit and power, superstition and wilfulness, fame and money, nature and empire, which are all the causes in this world that can make a thing impossible this is to be ascribed to the power of God and is the great demonstration of the Resurrection of Jesus.[1]

The essential simplicity of a passage like this is easily seen, in spite of the long sentences made by the addition of clause after clause, where most people would have been content to put in a full stop and begin again. There is in this sermon only one of that elaborate type of simile with which he loved to adorn his earlier work and that is neither so striking, nor worked out at such length, as the earlier ones.[2]

The weakest of the three funeral orations which Taylor composed is that which he delivered at the burial of Sir George Dalston, and in that case it is important to remember that there were no personal ties between the preacher and the

[1] *Works*, Vol. 8, p. 399.   [2] Ibid., p. 405.

deceased. Taylor appears to have had no more contact with Sir George Dalston than with any other worthy Royalist to whom he occasionally ministered.[1] There is far more Latin and Greek quotation, and argument about etymologies in it, than there is in the other two. It is not until Taylor begins to speak from his own knowledge of the religious behaviour of Sir George, and his composure in his last illness, that the sermon warms up at all. From a theological point of view it is more interesting. Preaching from the text, "If in this life only we have hope in Christ we are of all men most miserable", the preacher takes the opportunity to develop his views about an intermediate state. He rejects the Roman theory of purgatory without hesitation but refuses to hold that the souls of the dead pass immediately either to Heaven or Hell. His belief is that the just wait in a place of peace and refreshment until the last day when they shall be admitted to Heaven. The intermediate state of the damned he is not so clear about, for them their final abode is in "tophet". Except for the few personal touches the sermon is dry and constrained. It is in every sense an effort, inspired by the smallest possible amount of feeling.

Each of these three funeral sermons is constructed upon the same plan. First of all comes the sermon proper, drawn out of the text in the usual manner. This is followed by a short sketch of the life of the deceased. In all three cases the transition from one part to the other is made by a similar remark.[2]

In considering Taylor's claims to originality these three sermons must not be overlooked. Before them there was little that could truly be called a funeral oration in the English language. Fisher delivered two noble sermons, one at the death of Henry VII, and one at the death of that King's mother. Donne produced a funeral sermon or two, but they were more by way of putting a sad occasion to religious use than an oration over the departed. So Taylor had to discover his own method, and he took his hint, so far as we can tell without his own direct confession, from St Basil and St Chrysostom.

---

[1] This is the only one of his funeral sermons which Taylor did not publish himself. Sir George Dalston was buried on 28 September 1657, but the sermon was not printed until 1683.

[2] "I have now done with my text, but yet am to make you another sermon", "Countess of Carbery", *Works*, Vol. 8, p. 442. "I have now done with my meditation of the resurrection; but now we have a new and sadder subject to consider", "Lord Primate", ibid., p. 402. "I have now done with my text, and been the expounder of this part of the divine oracle; but here is another sermon yet", "Sir George Dalston", ibid., p. 563.

Jeremy Taylor's abilities and methods as a preacher are fully
displayed in *Eniautos*, in the funeral sermons, and in the twenty
discourses in *The Great Exemplar*. They all belong to the time
before 1653, by which date his fame was made and his most
characteristic work done. The other sermons which were published on occasions later in his life add little to our knowledge
of him as a preacher, though the sermon at the opening of the
Irish Parliament throws some light on the state of his opinions
at that very interesting time. It is *Eniautos*, *Holy Living*, and
Holy Dying which are the richest of all Taylor's works in that
elaborate rhetoric which was the greatest contribution of his
genius to our literature. But when that has been said, it must
never be forgotten that Taylor excels not only in the highly-
wrought, superbly-decorated manner with which his name is
most often associated; he had also, when he saw fit to use it,
an excellent plain style which would have enabled him to take
his place among the writers of the generation which succeeded
his own. If we value this less than the other, it is only because
there are more writers who have attained distinction in it. His
ornate style is entirely his own. It is only natural that the great
beauty, as well as the great care bestowed in presenting that
beauty, which is exhibited in, say, the simile of the lark,[1] should
fix itself most firmly in the mind of posterity. This illustration is
particularly interesting because one very much like it is to be
found in a sermon of Henry Smith's.[2] Taylor may have found it
there, or, more probably, it was in fairly wide circulation among
preachers at the time. As he and every other student of rhetoric
had been taught to do, Taylor borrowed a beautiful and striking
simile from wherever he could find one. But a comparison of the
simile as used by Smith, and as used by Taylor, will show how
immeasurably he improved what he borrowed.

In his search for apt illustrations, Taylor turns, as might be
expected, most often to the classics. There was no other literature
which had such treasure to lend, none which would be so well
known to the public or with which the preacher was himself
more familiar. Taylor's work was intended for an educated
public, and for them a considerable portion of the delight they
drew from him would derive from the skill with which he treated
themes and similes well known to them. Lord Carbery himself

[1] *Works*, Vol. 4, p. 61.
[2] Henry Smith, "A Caveat for Christians", published in *Sermons and other Learned
Treatises*, London, 1675.

as a student had no doubt copied into his commonplace book
some of the passages from the classics which Taylor afterwards
hit upon for his sermons, and possibly noted with admiration
what excellent use his chaplain made of them. One of the most
exquisite little sections in *Holy Dying* is the development of a
passage borrowed from so common a school author as Virgil.
Taylor's greatness lies not so much in the coining of a new
comparison, as in the perfect elaboration of an old. There can
be no suggestion that the preacher hoped to fob off the image
as entirely his own; the new guise in which it appeared would
be all that he claimed as original. He has a catholic taste for all
classical literature and quotes from it all impartially, though, as
Sir Edmund Gosse has noticed, the particular book he was
reading at the time is apt to make its way into what he was
writing more than any other.[2] These borrowings from the
classics come under three heads. Sometimes, as in the cases just
mentioned, he takes, with or without acknowledgement, some
striking image and develops it with all his skill. More frequently
he is content with an allusion, the mention of a name or a glance
at a line, or a fact. He compares the feasting of his own day to
the Roman banquets, where they had "many vessels filled with
Campanian wine, turtle of Liguria, Sicilian beeves, wheat from
Egypt, wild boars from Illyrium and Grecian sheep".[3] In
another place when speaking of the omniscience of God, he says
that to him the thoughts of men, "are visible as the Chian wine
in the purest crystal". When he wants an example of that very
homely product, a bore, he fetches one from Rome and refers
to "the gentleman Martial speaks of", who, though he was good,
was not to be endured because "he would read his nonsense verses
to all companies".[4] Taylor is an adept at making these skilful
little references, not only to the classics, but to every part of his
voluminous reading. He has assimilated it all perfectly. When he
writes, it is already in his mind, and pours itself out naturally
upon paper. The *Sermons* are particularly rich in this type of
allusion but his other works, especially his devotional ones, have
much of the same sort.

His other method of utilizing the classics is in direct quotation.
Although he does this frequently, it is never so often as to overload
the page, and always he adds a translation of the passage he has
quoted or weaves a paraphrase of it into the next sentence or

[1] *Works*, Vol. 3, p. 319; Virgil, *Aen.*, Bk. 8, lines 4–11.
[2] Gosse, *Jeremy Taylor*, p. 103.　　[3] *Works*, Vol. 4, p. 191.　　[4] Ibid., p. 277.

two. Because of this it would not damage the sense of his work very greatly if all the Latin and Greek were removed. Neither the quotations nor the paraphrases are always as accurate as they might be, though in his controversial work he took more pains than he did elsewhere. In the quotations his memory may have been at fault, but what produced some of the ludicrous mistranslations it is impossible to guess, certainly it was not because he did not know better.[1]

Taylor's citations served two purposes—they were didactic as well as entertaining. In *The Great Exemplar* he expressed a high opinion of the moral value of the classics; "excellent moral, and perfective discourses" were to be found in "all the Greek and Roman poets, historians and philosophers".[2] For these, as well as for every other part of his voluminous reading he had the most amazing of retentive memories. When all allowance possible has been made for the use of a commonplace book, the word or two borrowed here, the hint of an author or a story, the mere mention of a name, these things are enough to prove how full of remembered learning he was. He must have read everything with which he came in contact, mediaeval legend, speculations, and chronicles; as well as casuistry, secular history, theology, and Hebrew. He refers, with the ease which only perfect knowledge can give, to all the major Fathers of East and West. He had read masses of school theology as well as the Rabbins "those poets of religion". His knowledge of Church history, martyrology, of monastic legends, and of Roman Catholic books of devotion was immense; and besides all this he seems to have found time to read everything of any importance which was produced in his own day.[3] Apart from bewildering the modern reader with such a number of reference to authors who are now forgotten, one result of all this learning is that Taylor's work very often seems strangely impersonal. He is content to give us life at second hand, what other people have thought and suffered, rather than any experience of his own. When the few references to natural scenery which seem to have been the result of his sojourn in Wales are discounted, and a brief allusion or two to a

[1] E.g. *Works*, Vol. 4, p. 426, where Taylor quotes a phrase from Arrian, obviously from memory, ὀβελίσκον καταπιόντες περιπατȣμεν, and translates, "We walk by the obelisk".

[2] Ibid., Vol. 2, p. 36.

[3] In the ten volumes of his collected works Taylor quotes or refers to over 1,300 different authors. Most of these quotations are short, but there are many from one author: St Augustine, 684 times; St Chrysostom, 286; Cicero, 216; Seneca, 190; Juvenal, 116.

I

soldier's life (possibly the result of his own soldiering days) are excepted, by far the greater part of the illustrations which remain are taken from books.

Besides the school training in rhetoric, which we have already suggested was partly responsible for this habit, the influence which Taylor's profession had upon his work is not to be over-looked. He was the personal friend, and spiritual adviser, of many of those who heard him preach and who would be among his earliest and closest readers. He would therefore avoid any reference, however veiled, to anything which those with whom he had come in contact might possibly consider a breach of confidence. During his best years his acquaintance lay within a very narrow circle. But when he does look up from his books it is a very engaging face that he shows us. He is fond of a mild joke now and then. In discussing the prohibited degrees of marriage, he remarks that some have held that there is con-sanguinity "as long as any memory of kindred remains and that will be very far in Wales where they reckon eight degrees and special names of kindred after cousin germain".[1] He has a gentle gibe at the celibate, who "like the fly in the heart of an apple, dwells in perpetual sweetness but sits alone, and is confined and dies in singularity".[2] Of things that turn out not quite as we intend he says, "he that threw a stone at a dog and hit his cruel stepmother, said that although he intended it otherwise, yet the stone was not quite lost";[3] and he even finds opportunity in his sermon at Bramhall's funeral for a sly dig at Rome, remarking that when St Peter came back and told the disciples that their Lord was risen as "he was not yet got into the chair of the Catholic Church they did not think him infallible and so they believed him not at all".[4]

Taylor produced several short tracts between 1651, the year when *Holy Dying* appeared, and 1653, the year of the *Winter Half* of *Eniautos*. The first of these, *Clerus Domini*, published in 1651, is a glorification of the ministerial office, and it claims on the title-page to have been written at the special command of Charles I.[5] It is probable that this order arose out of the King's reading of *Episcopacy Asserted*, for the book is to some extent an attempt to do for the priesthood what Taylor had earlier done

[1] *Works*, Vol. 9, p. 396. The whole of this passage is full of wit at the niceties of Roman Catholic canon law.
[2] Ibid., Vol. 4, p. 211. [3] Ibid., Vol. 3, p. 88. [4] Ibid., Vol. 8, p. 398.
[5] This is one of the rarest of Taylor's works. It can be found now and then bound up with *Eniautos*.

for the episcopate—provide a study of its divine origins and holy duties. The book reads like a collection of material for a larger work, and it is possible that when Taylor first received the royal command he set himself to produce an elaborate defence of a sacerdotal ministry, but while he was still brooding over the subject he discovered his talent for devotional writing, and in the end contented himself with putting in order and publishing what he had brought together.

Clerus Domini begins with an appeal to antiquity. The wisest of nations have always had their priests, which proves that the office of priesthood is at least reasonable in its institution. It is also divine, for Christ appointed a ministry and gave it specific powers. The first was that of binding and loosing, and by this Taylor means the exercise of disciplinary authority rather than the power of absolution exercised in the confessional. The second power was that of preaching the Gospel, and this leads the author into a discussion of the ministry of women, which he concludes was subordinate to that of men, and exercised either among women or in the care of the churches. This leads him on to a long argument against preaching by unauthorized and irresponsible people. Taylor's weakness in logic is sometimes commented upon, but he can use it effectively at times, and he was always fond of putting an argument in the shape of formal logic when he wished to be concise. He does so here. Another power received by the priesthood was that of administering baptism, a sacrament which in no circumstances can be bestowed by the laity, since Scripture has nowhere indicated that *rem sacramenti* can be conveyed by any other than a properly ordained minister. The hard case is not to be urged, for unbaptized children may safely be left to the mercy of God. The priest also celebrates the Holy Communion, "the great mystery of Christianity, and the only remanent expression of Christ's sacrifice on earth".[1] But before any of the functions inherent in this office can be exercised, the person on whom they are bestowed must be chosen and ordained of God, and the Church must proclaim the divine election. By the bestowal of the rite of Ordination the chosen are made ministers and stewards of the Gospel, separated and sanctified for their work. The ministry, when it grows corrupt, can be reformed, but it cannot be abolished. Altogether *Clerus Domini* is a very weighty little tract upon the dignity of the priesthood.

Two other short writings of Taylor's appeared in 1651, owing

[1] *Works*, Vol. 1, p. 33.

to the enterprise of a London publisher who collected the prayers which famous preachers were accustomed to use before and after their sermons. Taylor's contribution is quite interesting. The first prayer is rather long, its earlier part being taken up with expressions of repentance and the latter part with intercessions, rather on the lines of a bidding prayer. The prayer for use at the end of the sermon is much shorter, consisting of a few brief thanksgivings and intercessions.[1] In the next year Taylor put out a *Short Catechism*, with an explication of the Apostles' Creed for the use of schools in Wales.[2] It is possible to suppose from the title that the book comprised the teaching which the author gave in his own school, and that experience had taught him the need for something similar in other places in the vicinity. From the Reformation to the Civil War, poverty and neglect had done more to harm the Church in Wales than the Nonconformists had been able to accomplish. Year after year in Laud's *Annual Accounts* of his province, the Welsh bishops report that there is very little dissent among them, but the poorness of the livings and the want of good men to fill them are the chief causes for anxiety.[3] Although in George Herbert, Henry Vaughan, and John Donne, Wales gave to British religious life in the seventeenth century three of its greatest figures, and Pritchard, the Puritan Vicar of Llandovery, was scarcely less famous in his day, the general tone was very low. The two evils of poverty and lack of good men persisted throughout the Civil War, and long afterwards, until the neglect of church fabrics and church teaching in Wales became a byword, even in the moribund eighteenth century.[4]

In 1654 Taylor once more appeared in print as a controversialist, this time with one of the fullest examinations of Eucharistic theology which he ever made. It is clear from a letter to Sheldon dated 11 April 1653[5] that the work was already written by that date, and that Taylor was short of money; for he mentions, together with the fact that he is sending to Sheldon a "second volume of sermons, for the *Winter Half Year*, and the *Life of Christ* in a fairer character and with some enlargement and advantages",[6] that he is grateful to Sheldon for forgiving him a debt, and also that he has sent his *Real Presence* to the printer, "but first

---

[1] *Works*, Vol. 1, p. 64.   [2] London, 1652, 12mo.
[3] Laud's *Works*, Vol. 5, pp. 320, 354, 359.
[4] Saunders, *A View of the State of Religion in the Diocese of St David's*, London, 1721.
[5] Bodleian, Tanner MSS., No. 52.   [6] Ibid.

to My Lord Bishop of Salisbury to be perused".[1] What it was exactly that set Taylor to work upon *The Real Presence and Spiritual in the Blessed Sacrament* is obscure, though Taylor made some reference to it both in the letter to Sheldon just mentioned and in the dedication of the book itself to Warner, Bishop of Rochester. He states that he is engaged in controversy again by accident and against his will; but he had come in contact lately with one of the Roman emissaries, who, rather pleased with the distressed condition in which the Church of England found herself, were busy making hay while the sun shone. This man Taylor attacks, but without mentioning his name. He was one who had once belonged to the Church of England, but had "run away from her sorrow and disinherited himself because she was not able to give him a temporal portion".[2] This has generally been taken to refer to John Sergeant, who at one time had been secretary to Bishop Morton of Durham. Sergeant and Taylor were in opposition to one another more than once during their lives. It would seem from the concluding words of the dedication that Taylor was still in need of money, and that Warner had helped him as he helped so many others. Parliament had done its best to put acts of generosity of that sort out of the aged bishop's power. It sequestrated the revenues of his see, it had attempted to take from him the large private fortune that he possessed, but the indomitable old man still kept himself personally out of harm's way and managed to find money enough for himself and some to give to his friends.

The Real Presence and Spiritual in the Blessed Sacrament is an attack upon transubstantiation, that "horrible doctrine" that man can "create God".[3] Taylor begins his book in a tone very much resembling Hooker's famous statement of his attitude toward the Holy Communion.[4] It is in itself a mystery, and one that were far better left to every man to make his own explanation of according to his ability. Such a freedom Taylor alleges was allowed before the fourth Lateran Council, and he supports this with masses of quotation. The attempt to define has brought in nothing but the bitterest and saddest of controversies. He claims that the doctrine of the Church of England, and Protestants generally, is that after the minister hath "ritely[5] prayed and blessed or consecrated the bread and wine, the symbols become

---

[1] Bodleian Tanner, MSS., No. 52. The Bishop of Salisbury was Brian Duppa.
[2] *Works*, Vol. 6, p. 8.   [3] Ibid., p. 4.   [4] Hooker, *Eccles. Pol.*, Bk. 5, Chap. lxvii.
[5] Ritely, i.e. used liturgical prayer.

changed into the Body and Blood of Christ after a sacramental, that is a spiritual, real manner, so that all that worthily communicate do by faith receive Christ really, effectually to all purposes of His Passion; the wicked receive not Christ but the bare symbols only".[1]

The Church Catechism, he declares, supports this doctrine. He interprets "real" as meaning "present to our spirits only",[2] and it is significant that when he used this interpretation previously he supported it with a reference to Calvin, which probably shows where he was indebted for a good deal of his own thought on this subject. This he states is the Anglican doctrine. He now sets out briefly, the Roman Catholic position:

First, that after the words of consecration on the altar there is no bread, in the chalice there is no wine. Secondly, that the accidents, that is, the colour, the shape, the bigness, the weight, the smell, the nourishing qualities of bread and wine do remain; but neither in the bread, nor in the body of Christ, but by themselves, that is, so that there is whiteness and nothing white, sweetness and nothing sweet etc. Thirdly, that in the place of the substance of the bread and wine there is brought the natural body of Christ, and His blood that was shed upon the cross. Fourthly, that the flesh of Christ is eaten by every communicant, good and bad, worthy and unworthy. Fifthly, that this is conveniently, properly, and most aptly called Transubstantiation, that is conversion of the whole substance of bread into the substance of Christ's natural body, of the whole substance of wine into his blood.[3]

This teaching he now proposes to try by "Scripture—by Reason—by Sense—and by Tradition". The places of Scripture alleged by Roman Catholic apologists as proofs of their doctrine are John 6 and the words of institution; but many of their own theologians admit that these passages are not sufficient to prove transubstantiation, without the declaration of the Church, and Taylor comments that if the meaning is not there already and plainly to be seen, the Church cannot put it there. In a long examination of the teaching in John 6 Taylor asserts that the words of Jesus as they are given there do not refer to the act of

[1] *Works*, Vol. 6, p. 13.
[2] Ibid., p. 17. Upon this Bishop Gore remarks: "there is a passage in Jeremy Taylor in which he contrasts two meanings of the word spiritual as applied to the Eucharistic presence (A) the presence of the body after the manner of a spirit, and (B) a presence to our spirits only and he declares only the latter to be what we [Anglicans] mean. But the latter explanation proves to be highly ambiguous when analysed, because . . . subject and object cannot be thus put in contrast to one another". *The Body of Christ*, p. 235–6.
[3] Ibid., p. 19.

bodily eating at all, or to the Sacrament at all, and in accordance with the method, pursued throughout the book, of supporting his arguments from the mouths of his opponents themselves, he brings forward Roman Catholic theologians who support his point of view. If, he says, physical eating is there spoken of, then there is an obligation upon infants to receive the Holy Communion, as some of the Fathers have claimed; but since we suppose that the eating meant is spiritual and performed by an act of faith, then because infants are incapable of that act they are not commanded to receive the sacrament. This, which he claims to be the teaching of the Church of England, he also claims to be the more reasonable. In order to support his position still further, Taylor refers to our Lord's words to the men of Capernaum when they were scandalized at his teaching.[1] Jesus also said that whosoever eats has the life abiding in him, therefore the eating cannot be merely physical, for the wicked perform the bodily act of eating, but cannot on that account be said to have life abiding in them. Both our Lord and St Paul condemned transubstantiation, since both clearly affirmed that the natural eating of Christ's flesh, could it be done, would benefit nothing, while the spiritual eating gives life. Taylor just notes in passing that this spiritual eating can be done in other ways than the Sacrament, a thing plainly to be understood, since the Word of God, Christ's doctrine, is the flesh spoken of, and the receiving and practising this is what is meant by eating.

In considering the words of institution, Taylor asks how it can be proved that "take and eat" are not as effective as "this is my body", and that the act of eating does not of itself consecrate. Certainly Christ himself did not tell us which were the consecrating words. He bid us *do* something. It is difficult to determine the precise point of time when the consecration takes place. The Roman Church stresses "*Hoc est corpus meum*", but, supposing that these words are as important as is alleged, *est* states a thing in being, and therefore the consecration must have already taken place. A more reasonable supposition than this would be that the consecration had already taken place at the blessing of the elements. The Greek Church has been content to teach that consecration is brought about by the prayers of the minister. Taylor goes on to contend that "*Hoc est corpus meum*" is not to be understood literally, remarking that the same phrase in Hebrew and Syriac shows the usual tendency of those languages

[1] John 6.63.

to fuse the sign and the thing signified. The consecration of the chalice offers a greater problem even than the consecration of the bread, for the accounts given of the words of Christ differ, and therefore it is impossible to say which were actually used. The Roman Church, however, uses words which have no biblical authority at all.

Taylor turns from refuting the Roman argument to state a positive case of his own, and in doing so he builds a good deal more on our Lord's words in Matt. 15.17 than one would think either reverent or necessary. It is one more example of that bad habit of never letting well alone. If a thing occurred to him which seemed in any way making in his direction he must put it in. The same is true to a considerable extent of the next argument. If he had stayed to think it out he might have agreed that the properties of our Lord's risen body might not be the same as those of a normal human body, but he argues as if they were. If, he says, Christ is in heaven in a bodily presence, how can he at the same time be present on the altar? In the Bible Christ is spoken of as "going from hence and coming again", therefore, he urges, the Scripture does not lead us to suppose that Jesus could be in two places at once. When he promised his disciples to be with them always even unto the end of the world he meant "present in a spiritual manner".

The book now pursues another line of attack, pointing to the obvious fact that the doctrine of transubstantiation is against the evidence of the senses. To this it is useless to reply that the senses may perceive the accidents of a thing, but not the substance; for it is of the nature of the accidents to reveal the substance if they be sufficiently, closely, and accurately, observed. On no account must the value of sense perception be disparaged for, in the last resort, all the testimony regarding Christ's life upon earth depends upon its reliability. Since there are other explanations of the Sacrament more reasonable in themselves, Taylor concludes it is unnecessary to adopt transubstantiation, which involves so many difficulties and contradictions. Such a doctrine was undoubtedly not that of the primitive Church; and to prove this it will only be necessary to cite one or two of the Fathers, since their non-acceptance of this teaching will be sufficient to disprove its catholicity according to Vincent of Lerins' rule. Actually, however, Taylor quotes from a very large number including Tertullian, Origen, Clement of Alexandria, St Cyprian, St Ambrose, St Augustine, and many others whose names are less well known. None of these, nor any other of the Fathers, condemn what Taylor claims to be the Anglican theology of the Eucharist. Throughout the book the author arranges his arguments in numbered headings, which if they make for clarity do not prevent him repeating himself, and certainly help to make the book one of the driest he ever wrote, as it is one of the most important for the estimation of his teaching. It is not a book to recommend to the general reader in these days, when the appetite for religious controversy is not what it was, but for students of religious thought, especially thought in the English Church, it has much value.

While from *The Real Presence and Spiritual in the Blessed Sacrament*, and from other less complete studies of Eucharistic theology in Taylor's works, it is possible to gain something like a clear outline of what his faith about the Sacrament was, it is always a little difficult to be absolutely sure, since he was given to making apparently contradictory statements. It may be doubted whether in his own mind Taylor ever committed himself to any one school of thought about the Eucharist. He knew what he did not believe; he was not so eager to write down what he did believe. There is one important place in *The Great Exemplar*,[1] and one in *Holy Living*,[2] in which Taylor treats of the Eucharist; besides several relevant passages in *The Worthy Communicant*,[3] *The Collection of Offices*,[4] in *The Reverence Due to the Altar*,[5] and the *Dissuasive from Popery*.[6] Taking all these passages together, it would seem that if we were compelled to put Taylor into some category it would be with receptionists like Calvin, or virtualists such as Cranmer. But the warning that Taylor is a hard man to classify must always be kept in mind. His doctrine concerning the Eucharistic Sacrifice, for instance, was certainly not that which would be expected from his apparent views on the nature of the Presence in the Sacrament. In *The Great Exemplar*,[7] and also in *Holy Living*,[8] he is quite clear that the priesthood is a sacrificial office, and throughout the whole of this last passage the way in which he links up the Sacrament of the Altar with the perpetual pleading of Christ's sacrifice in heaven shows how much he was influenced by the Fathers, and Eastern, as well as Western liturgical writers of the early Middle Ages.

Taylor is undoubtedly far more Protestant in his teaching

[1] *Works*, Vol. 2, pp. 637–9.   [2] Ibid., Vol. 3, pp. 214–21.
[3] Ibid., Vol. 8, pp. 4–43; also pp. 96–114 and pp. 616–27.
[4] Ibid., Vol. 5, p. 330.   [5] Ibid., Vol. 6, pp. 572–600.
[6] Ibid., Vol. 6, pp. 201 ff.   [7] Ibid., Vol. 2, p. 642.   [8] Ibid., Vol. 3, p. 214.

than many of the clergy who belonged to the same political party
as himself. Both Andrewes and George Herbert would have
repudiated many of his views, and certainly Laud, whose doctrine
came fairly near to transubstantiation as stated by its more theo
logically minded exponents, would have found his teaching
uncongenial.[1] But his practice was more in line with the Laudians
than his theology, and in this he shows little hesitation and no
contradiction.[2] His attitude toward the Sacrament is at all times
that of the greatest awe and reverence. He insists over and over
again on the great benefits which a worthy reception of it confers;
but he is always more eager to spend his rhetoric on the glorification of these benefits than to describe them accurately. He
teaches that the Eucharist should frequently be celebrated both
for the sake of the communicant and as a solemn and efficacious
act of intercession.[3] It should, whenever possible, be received
fasting; but he will not lay down an invariable rule on this
point, for necessity and charity are always to be considered.[4]
Indeed, if transubstantiation were ruled out, Taylor was willing
to leave everything concerning the Sacrament to the individual
conscience, except the frequency and reverence with which it
was to be received; but since he believed devout communion to
be essential to the life of the soul he will accept no compromise
about these.

[1] Laud himself repudiated the charge of teaching transubstantiation. See his
Works, Vol. 3, p. 354, Vol. 4, p. 284.
[2] Taylor, though differing in other respects, comes near to Cosin both in rejecting
transubstantiation and insisting on the sacrificial element in the Eucharist.
[3] *Works*, Vol. 2, p. 655.
[4] Ibid., Vol. 8, p. 221. See also Vol. 10, p. 358.

CHAPTER VII

CONTROVERSY

FROM time to time during his life in Wales Taylor had left his retreat, either to superintend the publication of one or other of his books or to visit his friends. In 1654 we have incontestable evidence of his being once more in London. On 15 April 1654, John Evelyn noted in his diary: "I went to London to hear the famous Dr. Jeremy Taylor (since Bishop of Downe and Connor) at St Greg:[1] on 6 [*sic*] Math: 48 concerning evangelical perfection." This is the first light we get on another of the important friendships in Taylor's life. This faculty for making friends deserves to be noticed, for it fully bears out all the encomiums which George Rust bestowed upon the winning personality of his late bishop, and enables us to believe without hesitation the tradition that his character was as attractive as his sermons. Wherever Taylor went he made friends, and it was not until the last years of his life that he had anything like a personal enemy.

Evelyn had been a young undergraduate at Balliol College when Taylor preached his Gunpowder Plot sermon. The outbreak of the Civil War had driven him abroad, and he had spent most of the next ten years wandering over Europe, for some part of the time the companion of the poet Waller, and always keenly interested in every form of art and learning. In 1647 he married a daughter of Sir Richard Browne, who was for nineteen years Ambassador at the French Court. In 1653 he came back to England, and settled at Sayes Court near Deptford, where he remained for the greater part of his long and busy life.[2] In 1654 Evelyn was hard at work supervising the decoration of his new house, and the laying out of those famous gardens which his tenant in later times, Peter the Great, did his best to ruin by the curious pastime of riding in a wheelbarrow through the hedges.[3] Evelyn was as devoted to the Church of England as he was to the King, and his acquaintances among the dispossessed clergy were very numerous. He would be certain

[1] The Church of St Gregory stood near St Paul's Cathedral. Under the Commonwealth it was a favourite resort of the Anglicans, and the Government did not show themselves over-eager to interfere. Evelyn was in the habit of jotting down as much as he recollected of any sermon which impressed him. Notes of eight of Taylor's sermons occur in a manuscript volume of *Sermons Recollected* now in the possession of Evelyn's descendants. See *Times Lit. Sup.*, 11 Jan. 1952, p.25.

[2] *Diary* from the beginning to the year 1654.

[3] *Diary*, Vol. 1, p. lxxix. Evelyn had let Sayes Court to Admiral Benbow, who sublet it to Peter the Great.

to take the first available opportunity of meeting so well known an author and scholar as Jeremy Taylor. There is no indication, however, that the intimacy developed to any extent on this occasion. Taylor went back to Wales, but was not to be forgotten by Evelyn. We know nothing of the course of his life at this time and we can only suppose that he was spending a good part of his time on the next two books which he was to publish. These were *The Golden Grove* and *Unum Necessarium*. Both these books were entered at Stationers' Hall in 1655, but a letter from Evelyn to Taylor, written most probably in the early part of 1655, suggests that *The Golden Grove* was quite possibly in print by the end of 1654, and *Unum Necessarium* early in 1655.[1] There was no rule that a book must be entered before publication; a month or two afterwards was sufficient.

On 20 April 1653, Cromwell went to the House of Commons and with bitter words sent them about their business. From that time until his death in 1658 he, and the Army which supported him, were the rulers of England. With the passing of Parliament and the coming of Cromwell, Presbyterianism lost the ascendency, and the Independents came into their own. It was therefore a bold thing for Taylor to attack, as he did in the preface to *Golden Grove*, that total want of restraint and decency in religion which the Government now seemed to encourage. In place of the orderly worship of the Church he complains that "the people are fallen under the harrows and saws of impertinent and ignorant preachers".[2] These people think that all sermons ought to be libels, and as a result their congregations have "reaped the fruit that grows upon such crabstocks",[3] and "grow both idle and irreligious"; so in order to do what he can to convey religion "in all its material parts the same, as it was by a new and permitted instrument" Taylor published his book.[4] The teaching is to be conveyed under three heads, "what we are to believe, what we are to do, what we are to desire". This short explanation of the origin and aim of the book is given in a dedication to "the pious and devout reader". All of what followed was based upon the shorter catechism for children, which Taylor had written in 1651.

The Golden Grove[5] opens with a brief instruction cast in the popular seventeenth-century question and answer form, but by no means

---

[1] *Diary*, Vol. 3, p. 204.   [2] *Works*, Vol. 7, p. 590.   [3] Ibid.   [4] Ibid.
[5] A book called *The Golden Grove*, moralized into 3 books, was published in 1600, by William Vaughan, and recommended by Brinsley in his *Ludus Literarius*. So both the place of writing and a well known book by the uncle of his patron drew Taylor's attention to the attractiveness of the title.

so comprehensive or so succinct as the Prayer Book Catechism, for which no doubt it was intended to be a substitute. Taylor deals with the nature of God the Father and his work as Creator, with God the Son as our Redeemer and Mediator, but unaccountably makes no mention of the work of the Holy Ghost. It was perhaps natural, the times being what they were and Taylor wishing to avoid controversy, that little should be said about the nature of the Church. He makes up for this deficiency to some extent in the next section, of *Credenda*. There he expands, rather than explains, each clause of the Apostles' Creed and therefore necessarily includes these subjects, though he is careful to limit his teaching on the Church to those things with which a Presbyterian, at least, would agree. The next section consists of *Agenda*, or things to be done; which, though it is admirable in intention, offers too complicated a rule of life for an ordinary person nowadays, and must always have demanded more time for prayer and Bible-reading than an active life allows. Subjects for meditation are supplied in the next section, *Via Pacis*, many of which are taken from Thomas à Kempis' *Imitation of Christ*. There is a selection of prayers, including a number in which each set has for its keynote a phrase from the Lord's Prayer; four litanies, and devotions suitable for each day in the week conclude the book.

Together with *The Golden Grove*, Taylor published *Festival Hymns According to the Manner of the Ancient Church*; probably because there were too few of them to make a book by themselves. It is a pity he decided to make them known, for everybody who reads them must say the same thing; they are ingenious, they are full of fancy, they are written in a complicated metre, but they are not poetry or anything like it.[1] The verse on Ascension Day will serve as an example.

> He is risen higher, not set
>   Indeed a cloud
> Did with his leave make bold to shroud
> The sun of glory from mount Olivet.
> At Pentecost He'll show Himself again,
>   When every ray shall be a tongue
> To speak all comforts and inspire
> Our souls with their celestial fire:
>   That we the saints among
>   May sing, and love, and reign.[2]

---

[1] But such as they are they have been considered worth stealing. Samuel Speed, the bookseller, in his *Prison Piety* (1677), appropriated Taylor's verses and tried to pass them off as his own.   [2] *Works*, Vol. 7, p. 660.

A poet would have made something of the underlying idea in this verse; Taylor only leaves us with the impression that he is struggling with a task which is too difficult for him. It has been suggested that when Taylor chose to write in broken, irregularly rhyming lines he was influenced by the *Silex Scintillans* of Henry Vaughan the Silurist, and possibly by a friendship with the poet himself, since at that time they were living fairly near each other,[1] and had a common friend in Mrs Katharine Philips.[2] It may have been so, but the convention of religious verse at the time rather favoured oddity in style. However, the two attempts made by Taylor in a less ambitious metre, as well as the short verse translations scattered about his books, are very little better poetry than the rest and confirm the impression, if that is necessary, that Taylor, in such efforts, was working in a medium unsuited to his genius.

The other publication upon which Taylor was working during his last months at Golden Grove did him more permanent harm than anything else he ever wrote. This was the *Unum Necessarium*,[3] which estranged some of his most valuable friends and plunged him into controversy just at a time when he needed both friends and peace of mind. For a number of years Taylor had been meditating a great work on casuistry, which would take away from the English Church the reproach of neglecting that study, and remove the need for her priests to read Roman books on that subject.[4] He had spoken of his intention to Duppa as early as 1652 or 1653.[5] When he actually started the work he saw at once that it would be necessary to make a preliminary study of the doctrine of repentance, unless he was to assume a good deal more than he ought. He discussed this matter also with Duppa when they met in London in March 1655, and received some encouragement to go on with his project.[6] Taylor did not then mention that he intended to discuss original sin, and Duppa did not think he would do so, since the matter did not appear to him to be relevant.

Some time in 1655 Taylor published *Unum Necessarium*. There

[1] Henry Vaughan (1622–95). Entered Jesus College, Oxford, 1638. Began to practise as a physician at Brecknock, 1645. Removed to Newton-by-Usk, his native place, in 1650. Published first part of *Silex Scintillans*, 1650; second part, 1655.
[2] Gosse, *Jeremy Taylor*, p. 115.
[3] *The One Thing Needful.*
[4] The mediaeval casuists were, of course, common property. Of post-Reformation Roman casuists the most popular among Protestants were Cajetan (1469–1534), Vasques (1551–1604), Reginaldus (? –1623).
[5] Letter from Duppa to Bayly, Tanner MSS. No. 52.
[6] Ibid.

is some obscurity about the actual date of its appearance. Evelyn, in a letter which is sometimes assigned to February 1655,[1] says that he had already seen it, and the terms of his reference make it clear that the book was then widely enough known for its teaching to have come in for a good deal of criticism.[2] But *Unum Necessarium* was not entered at Stationers' Hall until the third of May 1655. That is, of course, no guarantee that it appeared at precisely that date. A letter of Brian Duppa to his friend Dr Bayly, dissociating himself from Taylor's views on original sin, would put the publication in July or August, for he dates the letter 26 October 1655, and states that some two or three months earlier Royston had sent him some loose sheets of *Unum Necessarium*, the book being then more than half printed.[3] Duppa's references to dates throughout the letter are all approximate, but they indicate the latter part of the summer of 1655 as the date of *Unum Necessarium's* appearance. Evelyn most likely saw the book in manuscript during the spring of that year; it could hardly have existed in anything like a finished state, even in that form, early in 1654. But Taylor, who had taken the opinion of his friends in Wales about the book, would be almost certain to obtain the still more profitable criticism of his London friends as soon as he had anything fit to show them. It was just at this time that the friendship with Evelyn was beginning to ripen, and Taylor would have no objection to helping it along by the little flattery of pretending to consult Evelyn about a matter which it would seem his own mind had decided for itself for a long time. The opinion of a possible patron is always of peculiar value.

Taylor dedicated his book to Lord Carbery. It was the last offering of this kind that he was ever to make, because their association was soon to end. Possibly Taylor's growing preoccupation with casuistry had found its way into his sermons more frequently than suited his congregation, for he apologizes to Lord Carbery for the increasing number of his discourses on repentance. It is because he feels the supreme importance of the subject that he has taken in hand to write his book. People turn

[1] *Diary*, Vol. 3, p. 203. This letter is dated 9 February 1654. The references in it to *Golden Grove* and *Unum Necessarium* make this date most unlikely. Evelyn probably followed the common practice of beginning the year at Lady Day, so that letter dated February 1654 would belong to the following year. It is possible however that he intended to use the modern style, but wrote 1654 by mistake for 1655, an easy thing to do while the change was still new.
[2] *Diary*, Vol. 3, p. 203.
[3] Duppa to Bayly, Tanner MSS. No. 52.

away from repentance; "they find sin pleasant, prosperous, gay and in the fashion",[1] and so it is hard to convince them that it is a thing which ought to be left. They may perhaps at times be brought to something resembling contrition, but it is of the sort which sees sin following again almost immediately, and that sin in its turn being wiped out by one more single act of repentance. But those who think so "infinitely abuse themselves". So Taylor has written this "severe book"[2] to set out the true doctrine and practice of repentance.

This dedication is followed by a preface addressed to Brian Duppa Bishop of Salisbury, and to John Warner Bishop of Rochester, both of them old friends and confidants of Taylor, and through them to the whole clergy of England. It is ironical, in the sequel, that the preface opens with an attack on the prevalent love of religious controversy, for this book was to fling Taylor deeper into disputation than he had ever been before, and draw from him a few examples of the acrimony which he here reprobates so strongly. Men had far better turn their attention away from that, and teach the ways of truth and holiness; for there are too many who are satisfied with themselves because they avoid crime and "sin like a gentleman".[3] In order to make the conduct of souls easier for the clergy, the author has been persuaded to set his own "weak hand" to the work of providing a book of cases of conscience; but unless he had previously made it plain that a state of repentance is necessary to a holy life, and that death-bed repentance is the weakest of all broken reeds, his book of casuistry would be in vain. He refers again to the Roman attackers of the Church of England who were saying that she was no Church because she was suffering persecution.[4] The charge is the same as that made in *The Real Presence*, and probably Taylor had the same person in mind. Two references in this preface are worthy of note. The one to Arnauld[5] because it shows that, occupied as he was with the affairs and needs of his own country, he still had breadth of mind enough to be interested in what went on abroad. The other is one of the few references he ever makes to his own religious life; he speaks of himself as one who had received "many of the mercies of a repenting sinner", and then goes on to reiterate his sense of a

---

[1] *Works*, Vol. 7, p. 4.   [2] Ibid., p. 5.   [3] Ibid., p. 11.   [4] Ibid p. 14

[5] Antoine Arnauld (1612–94). Lived chiefly in seclusion at Port-Royal. He was both doctor and priest and director of the nuns of Port-Royal, of which convent his sister was Abbess. He was a prolific author, writing chiefly for the Jansenists against the Jesuits. His works are published in forty-five volumes.

divine mission in writing the book.[1] There is more than usual eagerness, and a deep sense of responsibility, running through the whole of this preface. Necessity is laid upon him; his utterance is that of a profound conviction.

Unum Necessarium is hard to classify. It is generally accepted as controversial because of the dispute which raged round it, but it could equally well be described as devotional. Taylor plainly intended it for such use. The whole tone is calculated to arouse repentance in the reader, not merely to supply him with a theory of repentance. At the end of each chapter there are practical directions for the application to one's own life of what has been taught, and these are followed by the necessary prayers and meditations. It is theological in the sense that it goes very carefully into the grounds of all that is said. Though the author knew that his doctrine of original sin would provoke comment, he never suspected that the storm would be as serious as it proved, or that people could not easily be made to see that his teaching was compatible with Anglicanism.[2] He is transparently sincere and filled with a deep conviction of the goodness and justice of God; it is this profound feeling which is the inspiration of his work.

The first chapter declares that the law of God is, positively, to love him with all our faculties and degrees and, negatively, not to lust or desire. Since it is obvious that no one keeps this perfectly, all need repentance. God calls upon us to do all that we can, and to do it with utter sincerity. If we fulfil this command then the Christian life is one of "perfection all the way",[3] even though it is only perfection in the particular stage at which we have arrived, and must be followed by reaching out to the perfection of the next stage.

In Chapter II Taylor makes a detailed examination of what repentance is in itself, beginning with a discussion of μεταμέλεια and μετάνοια, concluding that, however the grammarians may distinguish them, the words are used promiscuously.[4] He follows this with various instances and descriptions of repentance taken from the Bible.

The next chapter makes an attack upon the practice of dividing sins into those which are mortal and those which are

---

[1] *Works*, Vol. 7, p. 17.   [2] Ibid., p. 17.   [3] Ibid., p. 44.
[4] Ibid., p. 61. "The distinction so often laid down between these words μεταμέλεια, μετάνοια seems hardly to be sustained by usage. But that μετάνοια is the fuller and nobler term is indicated not only by its derivation but by the greater frequency of its use." Thayer, *Greek English Lexicon of New Testament*, Edinburgh, 1898.

K

venial.[1] Taylor complains that men do not enquire after what is lawful, but what is mortal or only venial; consequently, no division could be more strongly condemned, for it suggests that there is some allowable sort of offence which can be committed with impunity, since pardon is easy and sure. Against this he declares that the smallest sin is destructive of our friendship with God, and therefore can in so sense be called venial. It is this strictly theological view of sin, arrived at it would seem, oddly enough, from practical considerations, which leads Taylor to discard a distinction which is Scriptural and often found very useful in actual dealings with souls. In such parables as that of the mote and the beam, and in that of the King and his servants our Lord himself clearly teaches that there are degrees of sin. Both St Paul and St John speak of sins which carry spiritual death as their penalty, and those which do not. The early Church was careful not to neglect so important an aspect of teaching committed to its charge. Indeed, if no such distinction were made it would be impossible not to treat all sins, either as if they were venial, with the subsequent lowering of all ethical standards; or fall into the opposite error by insisting that all sins were mortal, and thus drive many weak souls into despair. Actually Taylor himself does not discard all classification. He declares that one who sins deliberately, of malice prepense, in a small thing, is a greater sinner than one who is carried away by temptation in a larger fault. Accordingly, from the point of view of a modern casuist his repudiation of classification into mortal and venial cannot be said to be complete. What Taylor really attacks is a rigid classification of sins into mortal and venial, without consideration of the spiritual state in which they are committed.[2] He follows this discussion with a catalogue of those sinners whom we do not usually treat so hardly as the Bible does, numbering among them those who have too great a love of pleasure, busybodies, the fearful, and unbelieving, and those that take delight in other men's sins.

A discussion of sinful habits, as distinct from sinful acts,

---

[1] "Venial sin may be taken to denote sin in which the danger to the soul is not immediate or urgent, and which therefore admits of treatment by gradual and innocuous means. Mortal sin is sin in which the danger is great and urgent, and against which every means of treatment gradual or sudden, harmless or dangerous must be employed in spite of the risks involved." Kirk, *Principles of Moral Theology*, p. 248.

[2] Sanderson uses even stronger language than Taylor in repudiating this time-honoured division. He calls it "*putida illa distinctio, quo velut fermento totam theologiae moralis massam foede corruperunt (casuistae)*". De Juramenti Obligatione, Prael. iii, par. 15.

follows in Chapter V. Taylor's chief concern is to point out that one act of repentance cannot wipe out the effects of an ingrained evil habit. That can only be done by the introduction of the contrary virtue:

The Church of Rome, whose chairs and pulpits are dangerous guides in the article of repentance, affirms that sin, or any habit of sin, may be pardoned by any single act of contrition: the continued sin of forty years may be washed off in less than forty minutes, nay, by an act of attrition with the priestly absolution; which proposition if it be false, does destroy the interest of souls: and it cannot be true, because it destroys the interest of piety, and the necessities of a good life.[1]

This subject leads him back to death-bed repentance again. He concludes that for those who trust to it there is ground of hope but in the goodness of God "whose mercy is as great as His power".[2] How can such people really repent, he asks, when a change of habit is essential for true repentance and dying men have no time for this? But no one will bid them utterly despair, and therefore he concludes with some quotations from the ancient doctors to open a little door of hope to those dying and sincerely wishing to repent. If Taylor had thought out his doctrine of the intermediate state more clearly he might have found at least some of his difficulties with regard to death-bed repentance disappear.

It was in Chapter VI that Taylor put forward his views on original sin, which plunged him into so much controversy. In an effort to make his position quite clear he wrote, after the controversy had started, *A Further Explication of the Doctrine of Original Sin*, which he published in a later edition of *Unum Necessarium* as Chapter VII. Both these will be better examined when we have finished the rest of the book, and they can be taken in relation to the controversy which they aroused. So we pass on to Chapter VIII, which is occupied with the question of what are sins of infirmity. This section consists very largely of an examination of Rom. 7.15.20, and Taylor concludes that St Paul was speaking of himself as one unregenerate and under the law, from which state of sin the Gospel delivered him. The real sins

---

[1] *Works*, Vol. 7, p. 178. Taylor gives no authorities for this statement. He probably had the Council of Trent (Sess. xiv, c. 4) in mind. On this a modern Roman Catholic casuist writes: "The Council [of Trent] then, seems to teach that sorrow for sin because of the fear of Hell, or its moral turpitude, or on account of the punishment with which God afflicts the sinner even in this life [attrition] will be sufficient for the remission of sin in the Sacrament of Penance." Slater, *Moral Theology*, Vol. 2, p. 135.

[2] *Works*, Vol. 7, p. 222.

of infirmity are whatever natural imperfections each may suffer from, but not delight in; and are more in the nature of sins of omission than sins of commission. The remedy for them is to work and pray.

In the next chapter Taylor deals with the effects of repentance— namely, the remission of sins. There is nothing, he declares, which may not be pardoned if there is proper repentance. Even sins after baptism upon which the early Church was so severe, are not irremediable; but in every case the fullest, completest repentance which is in the sinner's power is the least that can be offered. Over and over again he stresses this point. Always there must be dissatisfaction with our own efforts, for none but God can tell if we have gone as far as we might. The sin against the Holy Ghost which shall have no remission, Taylor concludes, from the examination of the case of the Pharisees, to be refusal to recognize the truth. In a single, short, passage, Taylor summed up the fact which he felt to be vital for the Christian life, the one which is the gist of his whole book—namely, that repentance is an attitude rather than an act:

It a man repents of his repentance and returns to his sins, all his intermedial repentance shall stand for nothing: the sins which were marked for pardon shall break out in guilt, and be exacted of him in fearful punishments, as if he never had repented. For if good works crucified by sins are made alive by repentance, by the same reason those sins also will live again, if the repentance dies; it being equally just that if the man repents of his repentance, God also should repent of his pardon.[1]

The final chapter of the whole book Taylor devotes to a consideration of "Ecclesiastical Penance". The story already quoted shows that Taylor enjoined penance on those who came to him for spiritual help, and at the actual moment of writing his book he was soon to become Evelyn's confessor. This chapter is particularly valuable both for those who exercise, and those who receive, the benefit of that ministry. Taylor writes not only as one with a wide knowledge of the theory of the confessional, but as one whose actual experience of it was also great. He is by no means inclined to borrow slavishly from Rome. He has read the casuists of that Church, but with a critical eye. It is quite clear that, in his opinion, the practice of private confession in the Church of England is indigenous to it, and imitated from nowhere else whatsoever. He traces the origin of the rite to the

1 *Works*, Vol. 7, p. 417.

inconveniences which resulted from the public confession of sin, and looks upon the priest as the deputy of the Church rather than as one exercising in his own right the authority bestowed by our Lord to remit and retain sins. The priest does not grant absolution, but he declares to those in whom he sees signs of true repentance that God has forgiven their sin. Because of this, Taylor refused to believe that there could be a real confession of sin at all, until the sorrow for it was as deep as grace and human effort combined could make it. Such a confession does not consist in the mere enumeration before a priest of the sins committed, in the hope that by this one act of repentance pardon may be obtained; but in a deep-seated condemnation of ourselves and justification of God, with humiliation before him, and before those of our fellow men also who have been injured by them. It is obvious that where the priest is not the person injured, confession to him alone cannot be sufficient. It must be supplemented by acknowledgement of the fault to the actual person who has suffered by it. But on this account private confession to the priest is not to be neglected. Those who do so are "neither lovers of the peace of conscience nor are careful for the advantages of their souls".[1] There are some pages of admirable advice to direct the self-examination of those who intend to make a confession. In accordance with what he has advocated throughout the book, Taylor does not draw attention so much to the breaches of particular commandments, but aims at inculcating a horror of the whole body of sin, and suggesting ways whereby repentance may be made as perfect as possible. He advises that the penances given should be such as fit the gravity of the sin, but are not such as may endanger health or oppress the spirit.

To the book so far no objection was made, but in Chapter VII Taylor elaborated his doctrine concerning original sin and concupiscence, and it was this which involved him in the most serious controversy of his life, and the one which drew upon him that suspicion of semi-Pelagianism which persistently injured him in later life.[2] He did not reach his opinions suddenly.

---

[1] *Works*, Vol. 7, p. 446.

[2] Semi-Pelagianism, a modification of Pelagianism, was originated by Cassian (A.D. 350?–440?), who held that: 1. In the beginning man was deathless, sinless and gifted with special knowledge of nature and the moral law. 2. Because of the first sin, death, moral corruption and an impairment of freewill was entailed upon all mankind. 3. Baptism removes the imputation of original sin and is essential to salvation. 4. Man's free will co-operates with God's grace which is essential to salvation. 5. The predestination of a soul to eternal life or death is conditional upon the use it makes of divine grace.

Certainly in *The Great Exemplar* there are germs of the idea which was set out fully in *Unum Necessarium* and the resultant controversial literature. But these ideas upon original sin were in strong opposition to the Calvinism which was the official Presbyterian teaching, and from the theologians of that school Taylor expected criticism.[1] It differed to some extent from the Arminian theory which some of his friends held, but he can hardly have thought the difference serious enough to provoke the rebukes which he received. The story of Taylor's unorthodoxy has so often been glibly repeated that it is worth enquiring just what his position was.

He begins his chapter by stating quite briefly the effect which sin had upon Adam. It reduced him to the condition of his own proper nature—that is to say, it made him certain to die a bodily death and deprived him of all those extra gifts with which God had originally endowed him. What these were we do not precisely know, for God has nowhere revealed it to us. To see what the effect of this sin and loss was upon Adam's posterity, Taylor makes a careful study of Rom. 5.12 ff. The conclusion he comes to, after a minute examination of the passages involved, is that the sin imputed to mankind was a legal impurity only and not sinful in itself. Adam's sin neither made us "heirs of damnation" nor "naturally and necessarily vicious".[2] To say therefore that infants could be punished for Adam's sin, that is to say merely for being born into a state which they could not avoid, is to accuse God of the grossest injustice. It is to say that God treats men worse than devils, for he punishes them only for their own wilful sin, and not for something which they could not avoid. Sin, Taylor contends, is essentially a thing of the will; Adam therefore could not transmit his sin to us. We share Adam's loss, but not his guilt. Taylor's creationism comes into play here, for it strengthens his argument that the soul could not receive guilt from Adam, since it in no way derives from him. But, he goes on

[1] "Original sin is that wherewith all that naturally descend from Adam are defiled even from their first conception, infecting all the powers of their souls and bodies and thereby making them drudges and slaves of sin; for it is the immediate effect of Adam's first sin, and the principal cause of all other sins." Usshers's *Body of Divinity* p. 175. "The sinfulness of that state whereinto man fell, consists in the guilt of Adam's first sin, the want of original righteousness, and the corruption of his whole nature, which is commonly called original sin; together with all actual transgressions which proceed from it. . . . All mankind by their fall lost communion with God, are under His wrath and curse, and so made liable to all the miseries of this life, to death itself, and to the pains of hell for ever." The Assembly's *Shorter Catechism*, Answers 18 and 19.

[2] *Works*, Vol. 7, p. 252.

to say, it may be argued that God undoubtedly punishes the son for the sin of the father, and to this he replies that "He does not do to him as a judge, that is, He is not angry with him, but with the parent; but to the son He is a supreme Lord and may do what seemeth good in his own eyes".[1] This is rather inconclusive for the result seems to be the same whatever the motive.

Taylor passes on to consider the fact of universal sin. He concludes that it exists because we do not naturally know, nor yet naturally love those supernatural excellencies which are appointed and commanded by God as a means of bringing us to a supernatural condition. And things were made worse because God did not at first offer any reward to encourage men to strive after holiness. Another reason for universal sin is that God's laws place restraint upon our nature in things which, apart from the forbidden instances, are in themselves indifferent. The natural inclination of a man to a woman, for instance, in some cases becomes lust. Such an example emphasizes again the sanity of Taylor's views upon sex, a thing in itself lawful but which may in some cases become unlawful. How refreshingly different it is from St Augustine's idea of sex, as a thing in itself sinful but which may in some cases be redeemed into lawfulness. But no matter how strongly disposed towards sin Adam's fall may have left us, there remains to each freedom of choice. We are able to choose good or evil. Original sin, such as Taylor has described it, is nothing that we can repent of, though it be remitted in baptism.

Taylor had so far escaped pretty well from the persecution which had overwhelmed so many of his brethren, but some time in 1654 or 1655 he suffered imprisonment. A letter from Evelyn to Taylor is the only source of this information, and all that it gives is the bare fact that in February 1655 Taylor had been in prison, but was then released.[2] It then goes on to refer to the preface to *Golden Grove* in such a way as to make it almost certain that it was the strong outburst against the Independents contained there which was the cause of the imprisonment. However, he can hardly have been shut up for long on this occasion, for throughout the late spring of 1655 Taylor was incontestably free. On 18 March Evelyn heard him preach on Matt. 14.17, on "the conditions of obtaining eternal life" and on 31 March went to "confer with him about some spiritual matters using him thenceforward as my ghostly father".[3] Then a letter of Evelyn's again

[1] *Works*, Vol. 7, p. 271.   [2] *Diary*, Vol. 3, p. 205.   [3] *Diary*.

provides us with a puzzle in the matter of dates, because, writing from London on a date supposedly 18 March 1655, he says that he has just heard from Taylor and been relieved from "my apprehension of your danger".[1] He goes on to bewail the increasing severity of the persecution which the Anglican Church was suffering, and to suggest that Taylor might write something which would help the afflicted members of that communion to remain true to their allegiance.

In the course of the letter Evelyn remarks that he has not yet seen the papers in defence of *Unum Necessarium* which "Royston tells me are printing". That all this was written on 18 March of that year is an obvious impossibility, for on that day Evelyn listened to Taylor preaching on Matt. 14.17, and had no need of communication by letter. Heber proposed to amend 18 March into 18 May, but although this avoids an unmistakable difficulty, it is not nearly late enough to account for the contents of the letter, the whole tone of which belongs to a time after the publication of the edict of September 1655, and when, in all probability, Taylor was safely back home again after his visit to London. Every student of Taylor would be grateful to someone who would take in hand the whole subject of Evelyn's chaotic chronology.

Some time during the summer of 1655 Taylor was imprisoned in the Castle at Chepstow, probably for not more than two or three months, since on 31 March Evelyn conferred with him on spiritual matters,[2] and on 21 November Taylor answered "kind and friendly letters" which he received not long after his coming from prison.[3] The cause of this second incarceration is as obscure as the first. It has been surmised that some Welsh creditor had Taylor imprisoned for debt, and that Evelyn allowed him to remain under arrest in order to teach him prudence.[4] This can hardly be so, for not only does Evelyn's letter, misdated 18 March 1655, say that Taylor had been in danger through "the general

[1] In this letter, supposedly written on 18 March 1655, Evelyn remarks: "I have not yet been so happy as to see those papers which Royston tells me are printing, but I greatly rejoice that you have so happily fortified that batterie, and I doubt not but you will maintain the siege", *Diary*, Vol. 3, p. 205. This must be the *Further Explication*, but according to Taylor himself that was not sent to the printers until November 1655: Evelyn, *Diary*, Vol. 3, p. 208. One sentence in Evelyn's letter which has not had the attention it deserves conclusively proves that the date of writing was after the time of Cromwell's edict of November 1655, "*Julianus redivivus* can shut the schools indeed and the temples but he cannot hinder our private intercourses and devotions", ibid., p. 207. Perhaps the date should be 1655-6.

[2] *Diary*.

[3] Evelyn, *Diary*, Vol. 3, p. 208.

[4] Gosse, *Jeremy Taylor*, p. 117.

persecution",[1] but if it had been in Evelyn's power to have released his friend, as it would have been had a mere payment of a debt been required, all the solicitude the letter displays would have been sheer hypocrisy. Taylor answered this letter in January 1655-6, which would again suggest that it was not sent to him until the autumn of 1655. It is possible that on this occasion some zealous local official had anticipated legislation which he knew was bound to come, and imprisoned Taylor for no other cause than being an outstanding royalist clergyman who was still exercising his calling.

It was while he was in Chepstow Castle suffering a not too rigorous imprisonment, with a kindly gaoler who allowed him to borrow books in the neighbourhood, that the controversy round Chapter VII of *Unum Necessarium* began to reach Taylor. Warner must have written almost as soon as the book came into his hands, and quite possibly before it was generally published. The bishop's letter is now lost, but Taylor replied to it at some length, apologizing for his delay in doing so, which, he says, had arisen because Royston, who usually forwarded Taylor's correspondence, had kept this letter back from July until September "supposing that it could not come safely to me while I remain a prisoner now in Chepstow Castle. But I now have that liberty that I can receive any letters, and send any; for the gentlemen under whose custody I am, as they are careful of their charges, so they are civil to my person."[2] The letter is as polite as it can be, but it shows no sign of a disposition on the part of the author to retreat from his central position. Warner had apparently written as much to pass on the complaints of other people as to advance any himself, though his sympathies were certainly with Taylor's critics. His great concern was that the doctrine of the Church of England, as he believed it to be set out in the Prayer Book, should be upheld; he therefore begs that Taylor would carefully consider Rom. 5.17-19. In reply Taylor reiterates his contention that there is nothing in his doctrine which is contrary to the teaching in the Thirty-nine Articles, if they are interpreted with any liberality, and that in Rom. 5 St Paul means that death is imputed to us because of Adam, and righteousness because of Christ, neither was made ours absolutely.[3] This letter by no means silenced Warner's doubts, for he wrote again requesting Taylor to "weigh that of St Paul, Eph. 2.5" and a number of the Fathers whom he

[1] Evelyn, *Diary*, Vol. 3, p. 207. [2] *Works*, Vol. 7, p. 541. [3] Ibid., p. 550.

considered Taylor had overlooked, especially "St Austin who is so frequent so full and clear in his assertions, that his words and reasons will require your most judicious examination, and more strict weighing of them".[1] Taylor replied still very politely and still without the slightest suggestion that he would change his mind.

The affair was agitating all Taylor's old Oxford friends and acquaintances. In October Duppa wrote to Dr Bayly the letter already referred to, disclaiming any responsibility whatsoever for Taylor's doctrine, in which he claimed no more share than all the rest of the clergy of England whom Taylor had included in his dedication. Sanderson, now an old man and in retirement from Oxford, was deeply distressed and would have had some sort of authority invoked to silence these views, which he believed to be contrary to the teaching of the Church of England and harmful to her reputation.[2] He was also very eager that Thomas Barlow, who afterwards succeeded him in the See of Lincoln, should publish some refutation of Taylor, but Barlow declined.[3] This widespread alarm made Taylor write, while still in prison, a yet more complete explanation and defence of his position. He kept the manuscript by him until he was free, and it is most likely that he did not wish to let it out of his hands until he had been able to look up his authorities again, for he did not send it to Royston for publication until November 1655. He called the pamphlet *A Further Explication of the Doctrine of Original Sin* and issued it at first as a separate booklet, though in later editions he published it with *Unum Necessarium* as Chapter VII. The dedication was to Bishop Warner, emphasizing the author's unbiased desire for truth, his devotion to the Church of England, his hatred of any thought of schism in her, and at the same time reaffirming his belief that the doctrine he has set out is the one which most advances God's glory.

In the booklet itself he goes patiently over the old ground again. Once more he states what he believes to be the real significance of Adam's fall—the loss of those splendid gifts which were additional to his proper nature, and death consequent to their loss. This weakened condition is one which we all inherit as Adam's children, but it is in itself properly no sin, and from it Christ alone can save us. In order that there could be no possibility whatever of misunderstanding he sets out his teaching formally with lettered headings:

---

[1] *Works*, Vol. 7, p. 558.   [2] Sanderson's *Works*, Vol. VI, p. 382.
[3] Kennet's *Register*, p. 633.

a. Original sin is Adam's sin imputed to us to many evil effects.

b. It brings death and the evils of this life.

c. Our evils and necessities being brought upon us, bring in a flood of passions which are hard to be bridled or mortified.

d. It hath left us in pure naturals, disrobed of such aids extraordinary as Adam had.

e. It deprives us of all title to heaven or supernatural happiness, that is, it neither hath in it strength to live a spiritual life, nor title to a heavenly.

f. It leaves us in our natural concupiscence, and makes it much much worse.

Thus far I admit and explicate this article. But all that I desire of the usual propositions which are variously taught nowadays, is this.

a. Original sin is not an inherent evil; not a sin properly, metonymically: that is, it is the effect of one sin, and the cause of many; a stain, but no sin.

b. It does not destroy our liberty which we had naturally.

c. It does not introduce a natural necessity of sinning.

d. It does not damn any infant to the eternal pains of hell.[1]

This teaching Taylor defends with many references to the early Fathers and the continental reformers among them "the incomparable Hugo Grotius",[2] who obviously had a strong influence upon Taylor. With respect to the Thirty-nine Articles he takes up the modern position. They were, he says, framed in the interests of peace, therefore they ought not to be interpreted with rigidity but with all the latitude that is honestly possible.[3] This, however, does not prevent him entering into a phrase-by-phrase examination of the relevant passages in them in order to prove his own case. He ends this chapter with a very eloquent plea that men should be more zealous for God's goodness and justice than for their own opinions, or the doctrines of their sect.

Taylor made one more lengthy defence of his doctrine of original sin and wrote it also apparently in Chepstow Castle. It was, like its predecessor, the outcome of difficulties arising in the mind of one of his friends—Lady Christiana, the Countess Dowager of Devonshire.[4] This lady, who was a good Anglican, had been considerably troubled by Presbyterian attacks on her Church generally, but particularly on Jeremy Taylor and the

[1] *Works*, Vol. 7, pp. 319–20.   [2] Ibid., p. 330.   [3] Ibid., p. 331.
[4] Daughter of Edward Bruce, Baron Kinloss, and wife of William, Second Earl of Devonshire. Died, 1672.

supposed unorthodoxy of his views on original sin. From the tone in which he writes his dedication, it is clear that Taylor suspects that some people, whom he might have supposed to be his friends, have also been disparaging him to the Countess, but it is against the Presbyterians that he makes his chief defence. In fact, he goes so far as to lay all the blame for the misunderstanding of his views on them. He knows, he says, the arts of these men. They put him in mind of what he was once told by Mr. Sackville, the late Earl of Dorset's uncle, "that the cunning sects of the world (he named the Jesuits and the Presbyterians) did more prevail by whispering to ladies, than all the Church of England and the more sober Protestants could do by fine force and strength of arguments".[1] So in order to disabuse the mind of his patroness, Taylor writes his long letter, hoping that it will be some little return for the "divers obligations" to her under which he lies. Eventually the epistle was published under the title of *Deus Justificatus*, but without Taylor's authorization. Royston put it out on his own account, and appended a long explanation to the reader as to why he had done so. Apparently he was animated only by the noblest motives—the good of humanity at large—though there is a possibility that the postscript which made the profession was not only intended to declare the singular purity of the publisher's motives, but to placate the Countess, who might very well be displeased at seeing her property stolen. Accordingly, she is asked not to grudge to others the benefit she now feels, of being freed from her scruples. The letter must have come into Royston's hands in some surreptitious manner, for apparently neither the recipient nor the author let him have a copy. When Taylor himself authorized an edition of the booklet, as he did a year later, he suppressed the lady's name, though it was restored in the folio edition of 1673.

Deus Justificatus is the most eloquent of all Taylor's writings in this controversy. It is less technical, as befits something written for a lady, and he is at pains to set out the whole controversy clearly: what the Presbyterians believe about original sin as well as the objections put forward by his own friends against his doctrine. He puts his case with great force and skill, and in a very appealing fashion. Great emphasis is laid on the hideous cruelty and injustice of predestination. To affirm it of God is to charge upon the Almighty Father a savagery from which earthly parents would recoil in horror.

---

[1] *Works*, Vol. 7, p. 496.

Could you have smiled if the hangman had snatched your eldest son from his nurse's breasts, and dashed his brains out against the pavement; and would you not have wondered that any father or mother could espy the innocence and pretty smiles of your sweet babes, and yet tear their limbs in pieces, or devise devilish artifices to make them roar with intolerable convulsions? Could you desire to be thought good and yet have delighted in such cruelty? I know I may answer for you; you would first have died yourself. And yet I say again, God loves mankind better than we can love one another, and He is essentially just, and He is infinitely merciful, and He is all goodness, and therefore though we might possibly do evil things, yet He cannot; and yet this doctrine of the Presbyterian reprobation says He both can and does things, the very apprehension of which hath caused many in despair to drown or hang themselves.[1]

Here Taylor is most likely expressing the feelings which led him toward his doctrine. The tenderness of his nature, his affection for his children, his spirit of love and devotion toward God are far more likely than his reading to have caused his revolt against one of the most widely held theological tenets of his time. He never quite escapes from a legalistic conception of man's relationship to God, but he struggles against it more manfully than any other trained theologian of his day. In this pamphlet Taylor had nothing to add to his position and he clearly intended to retract nothing. The arguments against him which the controversy had brought out left him unimpressed, though for the Countess' sake he is at pains to deal with them all carefully, and at times with a colloquial force not usual with him. When, for instance, he mentions the objection made by some of his friends, that even supposing his doctrine were true he ought not to have troubled men's peace by its publication, he replies: "I will answer with the labouring man's proverb, a pennyworth of ease is worth a penny at any time; and a little truth is worth a little peace every day of the week."[2] The letter, as we have seen, fulfilled its purpose, the Countess was convinced.

In the autumn of 1655 Taylor was released from prison, but not from the toils of controversy, which dragged on until 1657. A Presbyterian named John Gaule of Slaughton, in Huntingdonshire, wrote a book called *Sapientia Justificata*, defending the Calvinist interpretation of Rom. 5, and Taylor refers, without naming them, to two or three others who had published attacks on him; most of them centring round this passage of the Bible. None of them was of sufficient note to draw any answer from him.

[1] *Works*, Vol. 7, p. 504.   [2] Ibid., p. 519.

The most important incident in the controversy occurred in 165
and in it a certain Mr T. C. of Bridgwater was the chief actor
Heber conjectured him to have been Thomas Cartwright, but
there is no evidence either to support or refute this guess. But
whoever Mr T. C. was, he was a friend of Henry Jeans, the
Puritan minister of Chedzoy in Somerset. Dr Raleigh, the
former incumbent, had been removed because he was a Royalist
According to Jeans' own account, he and Mr T. C. were chatting
together at Chedzoy in a clerical way when Mr T. C. broke ou
into "extraordinary praise of Dr Jeremy Taylor". Jeans agreed
with his friend to some extent. He admired Dr Taylor's "admir
able wit, great parts, quick and elegant pen, his abilities in
critical learning, and his profound skill in antiquity", but
expressed himself dissatisfied with the Doctor's opinions of
original sin. Taylor's *Further Explication* "lay then casually in th
window", and Jeans, taking it up, turned to a certain passag
and showed that "therein was gross nonsense and blasphemy"
Mr T. C., with great modesty, declined to take the dispute of
his own shoulders, but offered to tell Taylor what his friend had
said. Jeans agreed, and a little time later received a letter from
Taylor offering to give a good reception to whatever exception
Jeans might care to send him. So the exceptions were written
out and sent through Mr T. C.[1]

Jeans' criticism was focused on one very short passage in th
Further Explication. Taylor there states that "it is true that ever
man is inclined to evil but this is no sin properly. 1. Becaus
that which is unavoidable is not a sin: 2. Because it is accidenta
to nature, not intrinsical and essential; 3. It is superinduced t
nature and is after it."[2] This argument says Jeans, may b
reduced to two syllogisms—the first:

Sin, properly, is not accidental to the nature of man.
An inclination to evil is accidental to the nature of man: therefor
An inclination to evil is no sin properly.

A second syllogism is:

Sin, properly so called, is intrinsical, and essential to the natur
of man.
An inclination to evil is not intrinsical, and essential to the natur
of man:
therefore
An inclination to evil is not sin, properly so called.[3]

[1] Preface to *Certain Letters of Henry Jeans*, Oxon, 1660. Reprinted in Taylor's *Work*
Vol. 7, p. 572.   [2] Ibid., p. 335.   [3] *Works*, Vol. 7, p. 573.

The major premise of both these syllogisms Jeans declared to be false and went on to argue that Taylor had, at least by implication, declared sin to be essential to the nature of man, and this, says Jeans, is "nonsense blasphemy and libertinism".[1]

But before this paper was sent to Taylor Mr T. C. has given him an account of the conversation, and received from him a letter which, for some unknown reason, he did not show to Jeans until he had written out and despatched the objections just quoted. The tone of Taylor's letter is a little acid. He complains that if "Mr Jeans had as much ingenuity as he pretends to have logic"[2] he would have seen that for Taylor to say that sin is essential to man would be to contradict his whole book. Jeans probably knew that well enough, and if he had any purpose beyond love of a dispute, it was most likely a desire to upset Taylor's doctrine that concupiscence is not a sin by showing that in this case it was closely related to an absurdity. But Taylor had used other arguments, as he pointed out. Jeans, however, was not to be silenced by one letter, and so long as he could pin the discussion to these two syllogisms he was on logically strong ground. He replied at once to Taylor's letter again, through his friend Mr T. C., though he complained because the letter he was answering had not been shown to him earlier. This second letter was like the first, though longer. It was concerned with Taylor's bad logic. Jeans was obviously proud of his letters and stated his intention of publishing them; indeed, he quite clearly enjoyed the whole controversy. With a little touch of malice, he slipped in a paragraph well calculated to stir up his opponent still more:

> I have heard that the Doctor hath printed a very good Grammar. If he will also publish a Logic for the better information of such triflers as myself, I do assure you that I will very diligently peruse it; and if it be more solid, weighty, and serious, than those which I have hitherto read, give him many thanks for it.[3]

Mr T. C., who no doubt felt himself very much edified by the brilliance of his two friends, dutifully passed on Jeans' letter. If Taylor had been wise, he would have refused to be drawn any more. After all, his book was clear enough. Only by a logical contortion could he be made to assert that sin is essential to the nature of man. But so far as the strict rules of disputation were

[1] *Works*, Vol. 7, p. 575.　　[2] Ibid.　　[3] Ibid., p. 580.

concerned, Jeans was right, and Taylor should have let him alone. Instead of this, he replied with a very angry letter addressed to Jeans directly, explaining himself once again, but recommending his critic to pay more attention to theology and less to formal logic. This time he definitely closed the controversy, so far as he was concerned. But Jeans, who was enjoying himself very much, was not to be silenced in that way; he replied with another long letter, commenting sentence for sentence on the one which he had just received. In 1660, the year in which Taylor was made a bishop, Jeans published the correspondence. Why he delayed so long is hard to say, but certainly when the issue was made, it was at a time well calculated to do Taylor as much harm as possible by reviving against him the old charge of semi-Pelagianism, just when his fortunes seemed on the mend. But at the same time it showed what a clever person Mr Jeans was in arguing so well with such a great man. The whole controversy was rather on that level. Taylor's teaching was unmistakable; he had stated it often enough and clearly enough, and the fact that he was wrong in this particular logical exercise made no difference to his position. But all the misunderstanding and controversy which arose because of Chapter VII of *Unum Necessarium* was as unfortunate as it could be. It gained him a reputation for a leaning toward semi-Pelagianism which he never afterwards quite succeeded in throwing off; and though it was an accusation which was made against many people, often on slight grounds, Taylor's position differed sufficiently from that of his contemporaries to give the accusation some appearance of truth. It also alienated his Oxford friends at a time when he needed them very badly.

When Taylor formulated his teaching on original sin he had the whole Augustinian school of theologians against him. This included a very large proportion of the teachers of the West since the death of Augustine, including St Thomas Aquinas, and in his own day the bulk of the orthodox Roman Catholics and Protestants. Those men who, in spite of his plea, insisted on the Thirty-nine Articles as the complete standard of Anglican doctrine could only regard Taylor as a rebel against the teaching of his own Church. But in the wider sense it is impossible to call him a heretic. In the Fathers of the first three centuries, to whom Anglicans particularly loved to appeal, a great deal could be found to support him. The Scotists were full of help, and in spite of the *Remonstrance* the trend of opinion in such a leading

Arminian as Episcopius was toward a similar position.[1] Moreover, Taylor had time on his side. Long before the theory of evolution made theologians approach the problem of the evil from a different angle, men were beginning more and more to revolt from a doctrine which, Taylor truly said, fastened on God cruelties from which a human being of moderate standards would recoil with horror. In *Unum Necessarium* Taylor adopted much the same position as when writing the *Liberty of Prophesying*. He could find precedents in antiquity if he looked for them, there was some support in his own age, but the chief incentive toward the position he asserted was his own instinct for goodness.[2]

[1] Simon Episcopius (1583–1643). His chief works are *Confessio Remonstrantium* (1624) and *Institutiones Theologicae*. He stresses man's responsibility in the use of God's grace; first put on one side, and then denied, original sin; reduced the essentials of Christianity to those propositions of which the subject, predicate, and connexion can be plainly found in the Bible. Of Episcopius, Taylor remarks that his "whole works are excellent and contain the whole body of orthodox religion". Letter to Graham, in Dopping's Commonplace Book, Trinity College Library, Dublin.

[2] S. T. Coleridge wrote on the blank page of his copy of *Deus Justificatus* his opinion of that work. It is really his opinion of Taylor's position in the controversy as a whole: "This most eloquent Treatise may be compared to a statue of Janus, with one face, which we may suppose fronting the Calvinistic tenet, entire and fresh as from the master's hand; beaming with life and force witty scorn on the lip and a brow at once bright and weighty with satisfying reason—the other looking toward 'The something to be put in its place' maimed, featureless and weather bitten into an almost visionary confusion and indistinctness." *Aids to Reflection*, pp. 187–8.

L

CHAPTER VIII

MINISTRY IN LONDON AND IRELAND

WHEN Taylor was released from Chepstow he went, not to Golden Grove as might have been expected, but to Joanna Bridges' estate at Mandinam. It would seem that he never visited Golden Grove again. What the causes were which led to his separation from Lord Carbery we do not know. There is no indication in Taylor's writings that there was ever a quarrel and certainly the tone of the dedication to Carbery of *Unum Necessarium* shows no hint of any estrangement; but it had been the publication of that book which led Taylor to go to London, and so, by his absence at a time when he needed to be on the spot, weakened his hold upon his patron. Perhaps we need seek no further explanation of the break in the relationship between these two men than that which lies in the history of the time.

In September 1655 Cromwell's Government ordered that after 1 November no Royalist could keep a chaplain, or a tutor for his children, under pain of having his fine doubled. No clergyman might preach, or administer the Sacrament, officiate at a marriage service, use the Prayer Book or even keep a school, without running the risk of three months' imprisonment for the first offence, six for the second, and banishment for the third. It is not very likely that the actual persecution was as severe as the orders issued would lead one to suppose, but none the less another regulation in much the same terms as the first was issued on 24 November to come into operation in the following January.[1] Taylor was both a chaplain and a schoolmaster, and the ordinance forbade him to exercise either of his professions. Carbery was not very likely to take any risks in a matter like this. He had made his peace with Parliament once, and would have no wish to get into trouble again.

After his release from Chepstow Castle, Taylor retired to an estate at Mandinam which belonged to Joanna Bridges, a lady

---

[1] Gee and Hardy, *Doc. Illust.*, No. 112. But in spite of this Dr William Fuller, afterwards Dean of St Patrick's, Dublin, and Bishop of Lincoln, a known Royalist, kept a school at Twickenham up to the time of the Restoration. Sir Edward Montague, afterwards Earl of Sandwich, sent his sons to this school. Fuller was intimate with Pepys and Evelyn and became the patron of Taylor's friend, William Wyatt.

whom in all probability he had just recently married. It may be convenient to review here all the difficulties which have been previously mentioned belonging to Taylor's marriages. He was first of all married to Phoebe Langsdale, at Uppingham in 1639. It has been suggested, on very insufficient evidence, that this lady died in 1642 and that Taylor was quite possibly attracted to Wales by the prospect of a second marriage; that his hopes were fulfilled and he did marry, and that this wife was the plank on which he escaped from the shipwreck of which he speaks. It is then suggested that this second wife died in 1651 and that Taylor married a third wife, who survived him; and that one of these two later wives was Joanna Bridges, a lady of some property at Mandinam in Wales. All that there is to support this complicated hypothesis is a statement attributed to Lady Wray that Taylor buried his first wife before he left Uppingham; the silence of Taylor regarding his wife in the letter of 24 November 1653, but which Heber supposed to belong to 1643; and the fact that the youngest of Taylor's three daughters, Joanna, who was plainly the daughter of Joanna Bridges and received the reversion of her estate at Mandinam, was married in 1668. To deal with this evidence in order. Lady Wray's supposed testimony is in any case of no value for she started too many myths, and the Uppingham registers which, during Taylor's incumbency, seem to have been very carefully kept, contain no reference to this supposed death and burial. The letter proves nothing about what happened in 1642, since it was not written until eleven years later; indeed, the lively interest in the family of Phoebe Langsdale which the letter shows could hardly have existed if eleven years and another wife had intervened since her death. That the daughter of Joanna Bridges was married in 1668 does not prove that her own marriage to Jeremy Taylor must have taken place in 1643 or 1644, since in the seventeenth century brides were frequently very young: fourteen or fifteen would not be considered too early if a suitable match presented itself.[1] We have no absolutely indisputable evidence, for the marriage

[1] Lady Grace Grenville and "Sir George Cartwright's grandson" were married by the Bishop of Durham when the bride was six years old and the bridegroom a little over eight (Verney, *Memoirs*, Vol. 2, p. 176). This case aroused some comment and Crew, the Bishop of Durham, was blamed for his share in it. In 1672 Henry Fitzroy, first Duke of Grafton, then aged nine, married Isabella Bennet, aged five (Evelyn, *Diary*, August 1672). Pepys married Elizabeth de St Michel when she was fifteen and roused no comment. In 1668 Mrs Taylor was a widow, not very well off, and a match with Edward Harrison, a local landowner and M.P. for Lisburn, would be attractive enough to outweigh scruples, if any existed, on the score of the bride's age, who would then be fourteen or fifteen.

registers of Wales offer no help in straightening out this tangle; but Taylor's own words in *Holy Living*, the close connexion with Phoebe Langsdale's family shown in the letter of 24 November 1653, and the absence of any evidence to the contrary, point to 1651 as the year of Phoebe Langsdale's death. Taylor's retirement to Mandinam in 1655 when he left Chepstow would suggest that a recent marriage to Joanna Bridges had opened that retreat to him. It was this lady who shared all his changing fortunes in the next twelve years, and survived his death. There is no reason whatever for supposing that Taylor was married more than twice.

Taylor stayed quietly at Mandinam, occasionally making visits to London or to other parts of the country, but absorbed for the most part of his time in working at the great book of cases of conscience which he afterwards published as *Ductor Dubitantium*. He was poor, but we need not suppose that he suffered from actual want, or that his poverty approached destitution. Echoes of the original sin controversy reached him. In November he wrote again to Warner giving him notice that he was sending the *Further Explication* to the press, and also that he had asked Royston to let Warner have the manuscript to revise or suppress, as his Lordship thought best. He promises that if there are any letters from Warner on the way, offering advice or suggestions, he will see to it that they are included in the pamphlet. The controversy was dying down and Taylor was glad of it. All he wanted was leisure to continue his studies, so that he could publish fairly soon the first three books of his cases of conscience.

Throughout this winter he was carrying on a continual correspondence with Evelyn. On 21 November he wrote thanking him for several "kind and friendly letters" which he had found waiting for him when he came home from prison, and mentioning the fact that he had just sent up his *Further Explication* to be printed and also that he had some other papers by him relating to the dispute which he thought of publishing.[1] He was probably referring to *Deus Justificatus*. It had been written with care, and would naturally suggest itself for publication if the Countess of Devonshire, to whom it had been originally addressed, was willing. Royston's unauthorized edition interfered with whatever plans Taylor might have had in this connexion. A good deal of the correspondence which passed between Evelyn and his friend has undoubtedly been lost. In the letters which remain persecution is a perpetually recurring subject, and the tone of every

[1] Evelyn, *Diary*, Vol. 3, p. 208.

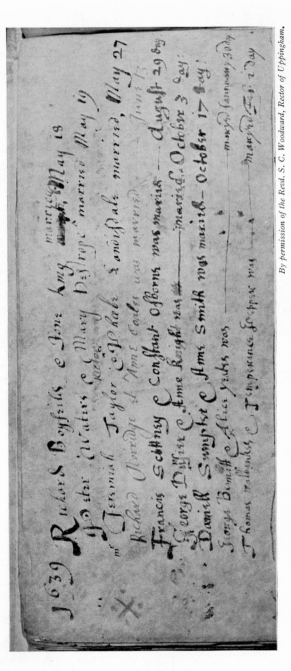

Entry of Jeremy Taylor's Marriage. From the Register Books of Uppingham Parish Church.

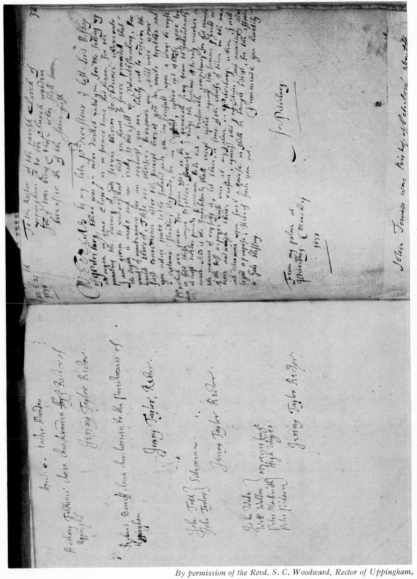

Samples of the handwriting of Jeremy Taylor. From the Register Books of Uppingham Parish Church.

reference makes it certain that Taylor had suffered from it recently, and that Evelyn himself felt none too safe. The next letter, dated "St Paul's Conversion, 1656", throws some light on the subjects which had been discussed between them. There had been a suggestion that Taylor should write a book of religious consolations for the use of Anglicans in those distressing times. Taylor readily agreed that a book of that kind was most desirable, but thought it would be better done by someone who was nearer London, and who therefore had a more precise knowledge of the need to be met. He had, however, thought about it very seriously, and had brought together such of his papers as might be useful in such a design before he decided that his cases of conscience took up too much of his time for him to carry out the idea.[1] He says rather sadly:

I know not when I shall be able to come up to London; for our being stripped of the little reliques of our fortune remaining after ye shipwrecke, leaves not cordage nor sailes sufficient to beare me thither. But I hope to be able to commit to the presse my first bookes of conscience by Easter time; and then, if I be able to get up, I shall be glad to waite upon you.[2]

It would seem from this that he thought of publishing his cases of conscience a few books at a time, and was working hard to get a presentable amount done by the spring. But either he changed his mind, or the publisher dissuaded him, for when the work did appear it came out as a whole, not, however, until 1660. "The little reliques" of fortune of which he had been stripped might possibly have been some part of the Mandinam property, certainly it was not the whole, for he continued to live there for a little while yet, and there was property at Mandinam for Mrs Taylor to hand on to her daughter in years to come. If it had been confiscated she might have got it back at the Restoration, but it is not very likely. Probably the letter means that every spare penny that could possibly be scraped together had gone in getting him out of Chepstow Castle, and there was nothing left to spend on travelling. But money was forthcoming from more friends than one during this period.

[1] The task which Taylor declined was adequately performed by an unknown author. *The Whole Duty of Man*, which appeared in 1658, has been attributed to Henry Hammond, to Richard Allestree, and to John Fell, as well as to some others; but to none conclusively, though Hammond, who put his initials to a prefatory letter, must have known the author. It set a commonly accepted standard of Anglican piety for a century and a half.

[2] Evelyn, *Diary*, Vol. 3, p. 210.

Warner, as we already know, had lent him various sums. Evelyn seems to have frequently done so, and it appears from a letter written about this time that he was indebted to Sheldon as well.[1] However much Sheldon might dislike what seemed to him Taylor's theological vagaries, he was not prepared to see him want if he could give help. To the end of his days Taylor never seems to have quite understood how Sheldon regarded him. They corresponded with every appearance of friendliness, Taylor could "not express how much" he loved and honoured his friend, and he seems to have expected the same complete trust in return, but it was not forthcoming. Sheldon had been financially generous. Twice at least he had advanced money: once as a gift and once as a loan, which Taylor confidently hopes to be able to repay to Sheldon's nephew by Candlemas.[2] He had also sent "prudent and friendly advice" about the cases of conscience, but he seems to have been quite unable to understand Taylor's doctrine of original sin, or the motives which led him to enunciate it.

At first he did not let Taylor know of his objections, but while his doubts and displeasure were smouldering, a friend stepped in and as Taylor remarked, spent a little time in "blowing the coals". The result was a letter of complaint which drew from Taylor one of the manliest replies he ever wrote.[3] Sheldon demanded that his correspondent should recant or "fairly explicate" the seventh chapter of *Unum Necessarium*, or if he could do neither of these things he should write no more on the subject. Taylor answers that, because he felt himself in duty bound to do so, he has spent a good deal of time over replies to the objections which the Bishops of Salisbury and Rochester sent to him though they were all such as he had considered before while writing his book. When he began to formulate his doctrine of original sin he could not avoid supposing that it was one that the bishops would sincerely accept, however much prudential reasons might prevent its open avowal. Whatever freedom he had claimed in his treatment of the Thirty-nine Articles, it was no more than the bishops had "approved under their hands to Mr Chillingworth". As to recantation, says Taylor, "you would pity and despise my weakness if I should".[4] The work which he has begun is the work of God, and as he ought not to be reproved

1 Brit. Mus. MSS. Donat. 4162, Art. 19.   2 Ibid.
3 Bodleian, Tanner MSS., No. 52. The letter is dated 19 January 1655–6.
4 Bodleian, Tanner. MSS., No. 52.

in it, so neither will he be discouraged. Whatever he is publishing on the question he is publishing in response to the demands of the two bishops, though he had thought that he "had not needed to give satisfaction for doing that which I had intended as an honour to them". The whole controversy was a weariness and a vexation, and it had come upon him merely for doing what he conceived to be his duty.

"But I shall by that time I am ready to die, and shall have little use of it, learn to be more prudent. You are a happy person, private and unharmed; my folly and forwardness hath wrought my trouble; but yet there was zeal in it, and I thought there was much reason, and I am sure I intended piously, and there are very many that do still think so. But Sir, I hope to have an opportunity of coming into Nottinghamshire for a fortnight. If I do I shall wait upon you, and discourse those things which I must not write concerning this trifling affair. I am used ill, and I yet think that truth and piety are discouraged even now that they ought not. But I will complain of no man."[1]

Whether Taylor did go to Nottinghamshire and explain his position personally or not we do not know, but the controversy was to cost Taylor more than he ever realized. At the Restoration Sheldon became the great man in the Church of England, virtually Archbishop during Juxon's life and actually so after his death, and Sheldon never forgot that Taylor was not a safe man.

Money for the journey to London was forthcoming, possibly a little earlier than was expected, for on 12 April Taylor dined at Sayes Court with Evelyn. Berkley, Boyle, and Wilkins were there also. After dinner Evelyn presented Dr Wilkins with a rare burning glass and the whole party went off to see "Colonel Blount's newly invented plows".[2] Evelyn must have thought this entertainment insufficient, for he wrote to Taylor making some excuses for the hospitality which had been offered; Taylor replied in a very lengthy, courtly, letter praising Sayes Court and its owner's translation of Lucretius, and suggesting that some of the poetical gifts which that work had exhibited should be used in the production of some Christian hymns. Praise of his translation of Lucretius was a subject of which Evelyn never grew weary. It was published on 12 May following.[3] Taylor hardly ever wrote to his friend after that date without inserting a little

[1] Bodleian, Tanner MSS., No. 52.
[2] Evelyn, *Diary*, 12 April 1656.
[3] *An Essay on the First Book of T. Lucretius Carus De Rerum Natura, interpreted and made English Verse*, London, 1656, sm. 8vo.

flattery of the work in his letter, although it was badly printed and not very successful. Evelyn and Taylor saw one another at least twice more during this visit to London. On 6 May Evelyn took a young Frenchman named Le France to talk with Taylor and they discussed the *Unum Necessarium* view of original sin in Latin. This interview was something in the nature of an ordination examination, because after Taylor had professed himself very satisfied with the young man, he was persuaded by Evelyn to recommend him to the Bishop of Meath for ordination. The candidate was accepted and ordained both deacon and priest on the same day. Evelyn paid the fees and the Bishop was glad to get them, for he "was poor and in great want".[1]

Soon after this Taylor went home. He wrote to his friend from Wales on 19 July. In the letter he shows how much he wished to be near London both for the sake of the company and also for the books he would find there. Mr Thurland, afterwards one of the Barons of the Exchequer, has made some financial offer which would apparently make the removal possible, but Taylor does not intend to write directly to him about it until after the publication of *Deus Justificatus*, which was then in the printer's hands. It is clear that he had learned caution from the episode with Warner and Duppa, and would commit his friends to nothing which they did not fully understand. We get from this letter one of the rare pieces of news about Taylor's family. He had lost a "little child, a boy which lately made us very glad".[2] This is just mentioned, and is then followed immediately by a compliment about the *Lucretius*. It was the first sign of disasters which were to touch him more closely than controversy or imprisonment. The next letter to Evelyn is about the *Lucretius* again. A printed copy had just come into Taylor's hands and his enthusiasms are renewed. He would like Evelyn to translate the whole, and suggested to him that it would be an excellent thing if someone were to turn the ancient Church hymns into English. The *Dies Irae*, for instance, would make a "divine song" if it were a little changed. Evelyn took the hint. He translated the *Dies Irae*, but when Taylor wrote next, although he had heard of the version, he had not seen it. Compliments did not

[1] Evelyn, *Diary*, 7 May 1656. The See of Meath had been vacant since 1650, and it was not filled up till 1669, when Bishop Leslie was translated thither from Down and Connor. Leslie had, however, been intended for that preferment for some time; it is therefore possible that he was the bishop whom Evelyn had in mind. This would be an interesting early association of Taylor with Leslie.

[2] Evelyn, *Diary*, Vol. 3, p. 217.

all come from one side. Evelyn said some nice things about Taylor's English poetry, though the writer of it was not to be beguiled for he had "certain knowledge of his own great weakness in it".[1] It appears from this letter that the *Unum Necessarium* controversy had become known in foreign countries, for Taylor had lately received certain extracts of Eastern and Southern antiquities from "a learned person beyond the sea", which had greatly confirmed him in his opinions.[2] *Deus Justificatus* was just out and Evelyn approved of it.

A few days after this, a letter was sent off to Dugdale acknowledging the receipt of his History of Warwickshire, and complimenting him on it. Taylor and Dugdale were old friends and correspondents, and it is a great pity that their letters do not seem to have survived. *Deus Justificatus* was the only work which Taylor published in 1656. An attempt has been made to fasten on him the authorship of a rather silly little book in defence of women painting their faces, which appeared in that year under the title of *A Treatise on Artificial Handsomeness*.[3] It is not now generally considered to be Taylor's, so that discussion of it can best be undertaken later with the rest of the pseudo-Tayloriana.

Taylor was once more forced to suffer imprisonment, either in January 1657 or January 1658. The only knowledge we have of this incident again comes from a letter of Evelyn's, one which he sent through a common friend to the Lieutenant of the Tower of London. After some apologies for the trouble he is causing, Evelyn writes:

Sir I speak in behalf of Dr Taylor, of whom I understand you have conceived some displeasure for the mistake of his printer, and the readiest way that I can thinke of to do him honour and bring him into esteem with you, is to beg of you that you will please to give him leave to waite upon you, that you may learn from his owne mouth, as well as the world has done from his writings, how averse he is from anything that he may be charged withall to his prejudice, and how great an adversary he has ever bin in particular to the popish religion, against which he has employed his pen so signally, and with such success.[4]

[1] Evelyn, *Diary*, Vol. 3, p. 218.
[2] Possibly Isaac Barrow, who was at this time travelling in Southern Europe.
[3] Wood, *Ath. Ox.*, Art. "Jeremy Taylor"; Kennet, *Register*, p. 787. Evelyn, *Diary*, 11 April 1654, noted that the habit, which had previously been considered disreputable, was now becoming common.
[4] Evelyn, *Diary*, Vol. 3, p. 227. Bray, in a note to this letter, remarks: "Dr Jeremy Taylor had been committed prisoner to the Tower for setting the picture of Christ praying before his *Collection of Offices* contrary to a new act concerning scandalous pictures as they called them."

It would be hard to find another Dr Taylor whom the description in the letter would fit, and it is therefore practically certain that Jeremy is the person referred to. The mistake of the printer is generally supposed to have been the insertion, by Royston, of a print of Christ in an attitude of prayer as the frontispiece of the *Collection of Offices*. But Evelyn's letter is dated "From Greenwich, 14 Jan. 1656-7" and the *Collection of Offices* was not published until 1658, so either the commonly given reason for the imprisonment is wrong or, what is more likely, Evelyn's letter is wrongly dated. If 1658-9 was the time of its writing then every incident in the story falls properly into place. Taylor was then living in London, so the Tower would be a possible place of imprisonment, and the *Collection of Offices* was published with the frontispiece to which objection might have been taken. The records of the Privy Council contain no mention of Taylor's commitment to the Tower, but neither do they of his imprisonment at Chepstow. England was at this time under the rule of the Majors-General and the legal preliminaries of imprisonment were not always observed. Evelyn's letter would lead one to suppose that the actual prosecutor was the Lieutenant of the Tower. But in whatever year it occurred the imprisonment was of short duration.

Taylor's life in this period can only be seen by piecing together odds and ends, but when we have done so we do get a picture, faint and shadowy perhaps, of the man himself apart from his books; a picture all the more valuable because at no time in his life before 1658 is the view we have of him altogether clear. An unaddressed letter of his shows him in the February of 1657 once more suffering bereavement in his family.[1] Two more of his children had died. The recipient was a friend of Taylor's and acquainted with Thurland, and was therefore in all probability Evelyn. Whoever he was, Taylor could open his heart to him and be sure of understanding. He has passed, he says, through a dark cloud which has wetted him deeper than the skin. God has been pleased to send smallpox and fever among his children so that he has buried two, sweet, hopeful boys. He has now but "one son left",[2] whom he intends to bring up to London before Easter, and then he will wait upon his correspondent, and hopes in his friend's society to relieve his sorrow. The real quality of Taylor's religion comes out in this letter. In spite of all the crushing pain which he has been called upon to endure he can

---

[1] Evelyn, *Diary*, Vol. 3, p. 233.   [2] Ibid.

still see, even in this trial itself, mercies which are infinitely sweet and judgement that is inexpressibly gracious.

Taylor had now within a short time lost three children and had but one son and one daughter left. This letter caused Heber a good deal of trouble, for it clashes with a supposed statement of Lady Wray in which she claimed to have had two uncles who lived to manhood, both the sons of her grandfather by his first marriage. Heber ingeniously proposed to get over this obstacle by assuming that the children of the first wife were living with their mother's family. But even if that were the case, they were Taylor's children still; and he could hardly leave them entirely out of his reckoning when speaking of the number of his family, and he is emphatic that he has but one son left. In later life also one adult son is all that can be traced.[1] Once more no confirmation whatever can be found for a statement attributed to Lady Wray; both she and the fictions connected with her could have been ignored had they not been accepted by Heber, whose *Life of Taylor* has such a deservedly high reputation.

It was while he was still feeling the first bitterness of his loss that Taylor wrote the defence of infant baptism which he inserted in the new edition of the *Liberty of Prophesying*. No doubt, much of the gentle brooding over the sweet innocency of childhood which finds a place there was due to the memory of the little ones he had just lost. As his earlier letters to Evelyn show, he had for some time been conscious of the inconvenience of living in Wales, so far from books and friends. The loss which he had just sustained made him all the more eager to leave the country and go to London. It has been pointed out, that once he had moved to Town one would expect the friendship with Evelyn to have grown much closer, but it seems to have gone on much as before.[2] If the *Diary* records all their meetings, they were no more frequent than they would have been if Taylor had been living in the country, and going up to London only once or twice

[1] Charles, buried 2 August 1677 at St Margaret's, Westminster. The son Edward, who was buried at Lisnagarvey, 10 March 1661, was, according to Lady Wray's supposed letter, a captain in the Guards and killed in a duel near Oxford. But as Heber himself points out, it is unlikely that (a) a captaincy in the Guards would have been given to anyone so early as 1661, and (b) if a fatal duel of this sort had taken place near Oxford it is difficult to believe that it could have gone unnoticed by Wood. But in spite of this Heber does not consider himself "justified in withholding all credence" from the story. Yet it is much more probably that Edward was the child whose birth was expected in August 1659. Murray MSS., letter dated 26 February 1658–9.

[2] Heber, "Life", *Works*, Vol. I, p. cccxxiii.

a year. But whatever the cause of this, that Taylor removed to London cannot now be doubted. Both Rust[1] and Anthony Wood are emphatic that soon after the death of his children he went to live in London, and Wood adds that he "for a time officiated in a private congregation of loyalists to his great hazard and danger".[2] Taylor's standing among the London clergy, for whom he was both a spokesman and a channel of Royalist bounty, as well as his connexion with Lord Conway's London household, do away with whatever doubts may have been entertained on this subject. A great deal of his usefulness during this period seems to have consisted in dealing with cases of conscience which were sent to him from all over England. Probably it was this same sort of business which took him now and then on journeys into different parts of the country, journeys of which his letters give one or two indications.

From time to time Evelyn lent or gave Taylor money. A letter of 15 May 1657 acknowledges the receipt of a letter and a "token" from Evelyn, for both of which Taylor is very grateful. From this date on, these "tokens" came to Taylor with such regularity that they were probably part of a settled pension. Certainly the gratitude expressed in this letter is so warm that the writer must have been under some more than usual obligation at the time, possibly the promise of this pension. On the 9th of the following June, Taylor wrote to Evelyn again, to congratulate him on the birth of another child and accede to a request that he should baptize the baby. Evelyn may have been behind with his diary and muddled the dates when he wrote it up later on, for it is the entry for 7 June which records: "My fourth son was born, christen'd George (after my Grandfather): Dr Jer. Taylor officiating in the drawing-room." Nine days later, on Taylor's solicitation, the ever-helpful Evelyn went out to Eltham to use his influence with the patron of that living to get it for a young man named Moody.

Taylor had just published a new edition of the *Liberty of Prophesying* in folio with the additional argument against the Anabaptists, and was discussing with Evelyn the need for a treatise *De Providentia*. Evelyn had got into difficulties about the immortality of the soul. He found it difficult to understand how it could exist in the interval between death and the Day of Judgement, when, according to the teaching of the Church,

---

[1] Rust, "Funeral Sermon", *Works*, Vol. 1, p. cccxxiii.
[2] Wood, *Ath. Ox.*, Art. "Jeremy Taylor".

eternal life or death are bestowed. Taylor sent him a long letter
on the subject, arguing that even if the soul is quiescent during
the time spoken of, it would not follow that it was dead. He
promised to talk the matter over when they next met. Evelyn was
apparently in deep water, for he had also asked how it appears
that God made all things of nothing. This is dealt with very
shortly. Either God is the sole eternal or he is nothing.[1]

A faint touch of the bitterness engendered by the original sin
controversy found its way into the most notable of the works
Taylor issued in this year. It is a little duodecimo volume entitled
*A Discourse of the Nature and Offices of Friendship in a letter to the
most ingenious and excellent M.K.P.* The initials stood for Mrs
Katharine Phillips. This lady was a provincial blue-stocking of
some note. Aubrey, who was her contemporary and knew her
as a child, left an account of her precocious learning and goodness. Her father was a London merchant, and like most City
men a Presbyterian, but as soon as the girl was old enough she
thought things out for herself and became enthusiastic for Church
and King. This was probably about the time of the outbreak of
the Civil War, for in 1646, when she was seventeen years old,
she married a Royalist and changed her maiden name of Fowler
for that of Phillips. Her husband lived at Cardigan Priory in
Wales and soon the young wife was intimate with all the literary
society in the neighbourhood. Almost certainly she would
become known at Golden Grove, where, ever since William
Vaughan at the beginning of the century, there had been a love
of books and authors. She published nothing until 1651, when a
congratulatory poem to Henry Vaughan the Silurist made its
appearance. It revealed her as a capable poet of the type of
Waller and Denham. Her friends called her the Matchless
Orinda. She made friendship her speciality and she sought
friends with avidity. Among them were Henry Lawes the musician
and Samuel Cooper the miniature painter, as well as Henry
Vaughan and a good many other men and women notable in
their day. Jeremy Taylor's connexion with Golden Grove and
his literary repute gained him admittance to her circle, and in
accordance with Orinda's custom of decorating her friends
with romantic names, he was called the Noble Palaemon. This
appellation did not come to him brand new, for she had previously called Francis Finch, first the Excellent Palaemon and later
the Noble Palaemon. The name was obviously too good to lose.

[1] Evelyn, *Diary*, Vol. 3, p. 240.

Friendship was the theme of nearly all her writing, an generally it was the excellence of it as exhibited in her fema friends. She was feeling after a new school in literature, somethin of the sort that Sterne afterwards founded, though without h snigger. The friendship with Taylor was as lasting as any sh made, since she pursued it as late as 1662, when they enjoye each other's society in Ireland. This lady wrote to Taylo probably about the beginning of 1657, asking him one or tw questions about the legitimacy of friendship for a Christian The enquiries were rather of the kind which a good many divine with a reputation for skill in casuistry were wont to receive, bu Taylor's reply was very different. He produced not a considere theological opinion, but a charming little essay on friendshi which must have gladdened the heart of the literary lady t whom it was sent. Taylor could be a courtier when he chose His ability in writing agreeable dedications has already bee noticed. He opens his letter with the remark that his corresponden was really far more able to deal with the question herself, tha he whose advice had been asked. But when he comes to answe the actual question which had been propounded to him—that how far Christianity authorizes a perfect friendship—he answer at once that the New Testament takes no notice of friendshi at all. He then bids his reader hasten on, and not think this i the least strange, for if by friendship is meant "the greates love, the greatest usefulness, and the most open communication and the noblest sufferings, and the most examplar faithfulnes and the severest truth, the heartiest counsel, and the greates union of minds of which brave men and women are capable", this is what the New Testament calls "charity" and bids us exten to all the world. He quotes Cicero in support of this contentio that friendship is applicable to all the world and says that he glad to be able to produce such authority on his behalf for, h continues:

I have been so pushed at by herds and flocks of people that follo anybody that whistles to them, or drives them to pasture, that I ar grown afraid of any truth that seems chargeable with singularity.[2]

It is difficult to avoid thinking that this little piece of irritatio comes in rather oddly, just where the author is celebrating th duty of universal charity. Friendship, he goes on, is of the wides possible application. He himself, good man, is touched by ever

[1] *Works*, Vol. 1, p. 72.   [2] Ibid.

:ale of distress. "I am troubled when I hear of a pretty bride murdered in her bride chamber by an ambitious and enraged rival; I shed a tear when I am told that a brave King was mis-understood, then slandered, then imprisoned, and then put to death by evil men." This last reference was too obvious to escape the notice of anybody who read the book, and Taylor showed a good deal of courage in making it, since his previous difficulties with the authorities must have made him to some extent a marked man.

The answer to the specific question asked had now been given, and Taylor would have fulfilled his obligation had he written no more, but he goes on to deal with it in more detail and to discuss who it is that may be chosen to a special and particular friendship, how far such a friendship may be carried, and how it is to be conducted. The answer to these questions, he con-cludes, will be neither useless nor unpleasant. They occupied the rest of the book, but they may be given here briefly. The answer to the first is that a good man is the best friend, since from him we may get most real good. In answer to the second, it is his opinion that a friendship of this sort must only be limited by some former duty either to God or ourselves or some "pre-obliging relative". In answer to the third question, he gives a list of ten rules for conducting a friendship which really amount to this—there are limits to the closest attachment and they ought to be respected. For example, too great demands ought not to be made upon it and neither treachery nor backbiting should be tolerated. If two friends are in a dispute, then a third should give them the best counsel he can, but must on no account allow himself to be made the judge between them, because whichever way his decision goes, one is sure to be offended, and possibly irretrievably. Taylor exemplifies his own wisdom in dealing with his friends by introducing this section with another little compli-ment, this time to the abilities of women for friendship:

A woman can love as passionately, and converse as pleasantly, and retain a secret as faithfully, and be useful in her proper ministries; and she can die for her friend as well as the bravest Roman knight.[1]

This comes with particular force in a composition intended for a lady who was a connoisseur in female friendship. The *Discourse of Friendship* is the only secular theme which Taylor ever handled and he treated that very like a divine. The subject is stated and

[1] *Works*, Vol. 1, p. 94.

split up into its appropriate divisions as if it were a sermon, texts are quoted and explained in support of what is said, and a gently pious air hangs over the entire writing. In spite of this gravity, the whole essay is delightfully mellow and spontaneous. There are Greek and Latin quotations, for the Matchless Orinda was a learned lady. There are also references to Madame de Scudery's *Grand Cyrus*,[1] to George Whetstone's *Promos and Cassandra*,[2] and to "a pretty apologue that Bromiard tells".[3] This last, the story of the thrush and the fowler, is very old, but Taylor puts it well, and uses it to point a moral very much in the manner of the elaborate similes in the *Sermons*:

A fowler in a sharp frosty morning having taken many little birds for which he had long watched, began to take up his nets, and nipping the birds on the head laid them down. A young thrush espying the tears trickling down his cheeks by reason of the extreme cold, said to her mother, that certainly the man was very merciful and compassionate that he wept so bitterly over the calamity of the poor birds. But her mother told her more wisely, that she might better judge of the man's disposition by his hand than by his eye; and if the hands do strike treacherously, he can never be admitted to friendship, who speaks fairly and weeps pitifully. Friendship is the greatest honesty and ingenuity in the world.

Taylor wrote with the possibility of publication in view. He probably knew that the lady, having persuaded one of the most popular religious authors of the day to write her so long a letter, was not likely to keep her treasure hid, so he added a postscript to the effect that if the papers were to pass further than the lady's own eyes it was his wish that they should first be submitted to the scrutiny of Dr Wedderburne, whom Taylor reckoned among the best of physicians and the best of friends. This Dr Wedderburne was at the beginning of his career Professor of Philosophy at St Andrew's, but afterwards gained a great reputation and a great fortune as a doctor of medicine. He was

---

[1] *Works*, Vol. 1, p. 81. Madame de Scudery, 1607–1701. While she was still young she became a notable figure at the Hotel Rambouillet. She and her brother between them composed many romances, which were issued in the brother's name. *Artamene ou le Grand Cyrus* (1649–53), is a meandering romance of 15,000 pages and its dullness is only relieved by its *naïveté*.

[2] Ibid., George Whetstone, 1544?–1597?. Served in the Low Countries and wrote considerably both in prose and verse. *Promos and Cassandra* (1578) is a play in rhyming verse which was never acted. Its plot is in some ways similar to Shakespeare's *Measure for Measure*.

[3] *Works*, Vol. 1, p. 96. John de Bromyarde, *fl.* 1390. A Dominican friar, scholar of Oxford, a prominent Thomist and opponent of Wycliff. His *Summa Praedicantium* is a collection of anecdotes similar to the *Gesta Romanorum*.

a staunch Royalist and well known to all the King's friends. We have no more information than this about his friendship with Taylor, though the tone of the postscript would suggest that there was a particularly warm attachment between them. But one of the most remarkable things in Taylor's life is the great number of his friends, and the small records of these friendships which remain. We know very little more of his acquaintance with the Matchless Orinda beyond the visit she paid him in Ireland which has just been mentioned. The lady's literary reputation continued to increase. The *Discourse of Friendship* made her widely known, and the long poem in which she returned answer to Palaemon on his incomparable *Discourse of Friendship* added to her fame.[1] She translated Corneille and Horace and wrote poems which were published with commendatory verses by Cowley, Flatman, Tyrrel, and others. She died in 1664.

In the summer of 1657 Taylor was doing what he could to give spiritual help to members of the Church of England who were living in or near London. Among them was Sir George Dalston, a Loyalist knight. One day while this gentleman was in church, listening to a sermon, he was suddenly taken ill, and through the fairly lengthy sickness which followed he was attended by Jeremy Taylor, to whose sermon he had probably been listening. When Sir George died, in September 1657, Taylor preached at his funeral the sermon which has already been noticed.

A good many of the dispossessed clergy had found their way up to London and lived there as best they could, very often in great poverty. It was the duty of such Anglicans as had the means to help them to the best of their power, and they did so. Taylor seems to have been one of the regular channels through which this generosity found its way to the proper quarters, an indication that, compared with the rest of his brethren, he was moderately well off. In February 1657-8 Robert Rich sent him a letter couched in very pious phrases, and ten pounds to bestow on such Episcopal ministers as should be in want.[2] This was probably an early instalment of a collection made among Anglicans during the following March for their "persecuted and sequestered ministers".[3] But as Hammond, particularly, was aware, if an educated priesthood was to survive in the Church

---

[1] It has been suggested that this poem was addressed to Francis Finch. The mistake is due to the circumstance, mentioned earlier, that both had been called Palaemon.
[2] *Abstracts of some Letters written by Mr Robert Rich*, London, 1680.
[3] Evelyn, *Diary*, 23 March 1658.

M

of England, not only must the older men be kept from starving, but students at the universities must be helped as well.[1] He did not get all the support he had counted on for this work, but he managed to achieve something. Jeremy Taylor seems to have shared his views on this subject, and he assisted a number of promising young men, among them Isaac Barrow and Clement Ellis, a poor poet but a very good theologian.[2]

Juxon, who had presented Taylor to his first living, was now residing at Richmond as unobtrusively as possible. It was, however, natural that his house should become the centre of all the Anglican work which was being attempted in London. Not that there seems to have been any deliberate effort to organize such clandestine ministry as could be given, but anybody who had a problem to discuss, or who wanted help, or wished to get into touch with somebody, could generally find what he was in search of at Juxon's house. Taylor had considerable influence in the circle which gathered there, and was sufficiently trusted by the rank and file of the clergy to act as their spokesman. His Church policy, like his theology, was not always acceptable to his old Oxford friends. Hammond, writing to Sheldon during this period, says:

> Your presence will be very useful at Richmond, where some of our ecclesiastical affairs are now afoot, and by what I hear concerning a report made to the Bishop of London by Dr Jeremy Taylor concerning the clergy's sense to have the Common Prayer taken off and some other forms made, I cannot but wish you were there to interpose your judgement and authority. I heard also from the Bishop of Sarum this week who much depends upon your coming.[3]

It was probably never intended that the Prayer Book should be wholly withdrawn but only that, in order to tide things over for a time, it should be allowed to fall into the background. Such an appearance of complying with the Government would undoubtedly make it easier to keep a flock together. But the older men would not hear of change, and their opposition was justified, though for the time being it meant that the Church must follow the harder road. English people loved the Prayer Book more than anything else in the Anglican system, and to cling to it and if necessary to suffer for it was the surest of all ways to increase their respect for the clergy. Alternative forms were, however, licensed for use in special circumstances.

[1] Fell, "Life of Hammond", Wordsworth, *Eccles. Biog.*, Vol. 5, p. 376.
[2] Ibid., note.   [3] Harleian MSS., No. 6942.

It was in order to provide this alternative use that Taylor produced his *Collection of Offices*. On the title page he describes his compilation as having been made from "the scriptures and the ancient liturgies of several churches, especially the Greek".[1] In all probability they were the forms which he himself used in public now that the Prayer Book was suppressed. The book was prefaced by a vindication of the liturgy of the Church of England, which was afterwards taken from its place in the *Offices* and published with the *Apology for Liturgy*. Besides this, he added an advertisement directing how the prayers were to be said, and emphasizing their temporary nature with a short paragraph stressing that they were only to be used publicly if the bishops gave consent. Most of the corporate devotional needs of the Church are satisfied by this book. There are forms of morning and evening prayer to be used in public as well as shorter forms for a family, and both are provided with additional devotions for special occasions. These are followed by an office for the Holy Communion and one for baptism, with two other short forms of prayer, one for a safe delivery and one for thanksgiving after childbirth. This seems to be an improvement on the Prayer Book, where only the short petition for "women labouring of child" and a thanksgiving office are provided. Taylor kept the needs of women well in mind. He furnished prayers for a newly married wife, prayers for the gift of children, for an afflicted wife, on behalf of children, and prayers to be used by widows. It would go far to solve many problems to-day if the needs and duties of family life were as prominent in the authorized prayers of the people. Following on these is an office to be used in time of persecution, prayers for an army or navy, an office for prisoners and a form of prayer for mariners. These are succeeded by prayers before a journey, various prayers including one on behalf of "fools and changelings", a service for the visitation of the sick and the burial of the dead, prayers to be used in sorrow and affliction, a form of thanksgiving, and a penitential litany.

Of all these, the service for the Holy Communion is the most interesting liturgically. Taylor does not indicate his sources beyond saying that he has taken his prayers from the Greek. In fact, many of them are from the *Liturgy of St James* and are translated with singular beauty. The cherubic hymn, "Let all corruptable flesh be silent",[2] is a piece of prose full of the loveliest

---

[1] *Works*, Vol. 8, p. 571.

[2] Ibid., p. 642. See Brightman, *Liturgies Eastern and Western*, Vol. 1, p. 41.

harmonies. But besides the prayers there are a good many extracts from the Bible. Taylor divides his service into three parts: the Ante-Communion, the Communion, the Post-Communion. The Ante-Communion contains prayers for purity, and the Beatitudes said in place of the Commandments with the response "Lord pardon our faults, and incline our hearts to obey Thee that we may inherit this blessing". Then comes a rather expanded version of the prayer of the offertory from the *Liturgy of St Basil*,[1] which is itself followed by an Epistle and Gospel, and what Taylor called an Eucharistical Hymn made up of passages of Scripture strung together, and comminatory readings from the Apocalypse. Next comes confession and absolution, collection of the alms, and reading of the offertory sentences and an address to the Holy Mysteries. This is followed by the beginning of the Anaphora, as far as the Trisagion, from the *Liturgy of St James*.[2] There the Ante-Communion ends.

The Communion begins with the cherubic hymn and goes on to the Consecration, which again follows in a modified form *The Liturgy of St James*.[3] But it is interesting to note that the priest communicates the people with words which are a paraphrase of those in the Prayer Book. The Post-Communion begins with the Lord's Prayer. It is strange that Taylor should imitate the Prayer Book here, since the Lord's Prayer is not usually found in this position in other liturgies. It is followed by a prayer for the catholic Church, which is reminiscent of the prayer of intercession, which in most of the ancient offices comes before the Consecration. The rite closes with three Eucharistic prayers and the blessing.

The Baptismal Service is based on that in the Prayer Book, being in many places hardly more than a paraphrase of it. The structure of the morning and evening services again follows the Prayer Book, though in this case the resemblance does not extend to the wording of the prayers and canticles themselves. The King is not prayed for by name, but there is an intercession for all Christian kings, princes, governors, and states. Both Morning and Evening Prayers are provided with a good selection of collects for use on the great festivals and other special occasions. The most noteworthy perhaps of all the prayers in the private offices is the confession "taken out of the prayer of Ephraim the

---

[1] *Works*, Vol. 8, p. 618; Brightman, *Liturgies Eastern and Western*, Vol. 1, p. 401
[2] Ibid., p. 623; Brightman, ibid., p. 49.
[3] Ibid., p. 625. Brightman, ibid., p. 52.

Syrian".[1] All the four prayers provided for use in time of war
are taken from the special office published by the authority of
Queen Elizabeth in 1597. It would seem that, perhaps because
he thought the Puritans might object, Taylor did not attempt to
provide direct and obvious translations of the ancient liturgies,
but he kept them in mind and modelled his own prayers on
them, only using now and then, where it suited him, their
exact phraseology. In the Holy Communion Service he naturally
felt himself least free to depart from precedent.

In 1658 Evelyn's two sons, Richard and George, died, and on
17 February, as soon as he heard of his friend's loss, Taylor sent
the bereaved father a manly and sympathetic letter of condo-
lence,[2] and six days later called to offer his sympathies in person.[3]
On the 7th of the following March Evelyn entered in his diary:
"To London to Dr Taylor in a private house on xiii Luke 23-24.
After the sermon followed the Blessed Communion of which I
participated. In the afternoon Dr Gunning at Excester House
expounding part of the creede." At this period Taylor and
Gunning seem to have been working in conjunction. Gunning
made it his business to dispute with the multitudinous sects
which were springing up everywhere at that time, and the
practice developed in him a hypercritical turn of mind. Taylor
regretted this, but thought that when once Gunning had published
something of his own, he would be a little less censorious of
others.[4]

While he was living in London Taylor became acquainted
with the Conway family and thus began an intimacy which was
to rival his earlier friendship with the Carbery family at Golden
Grove. In 1658 Edward, the Third Viscount Conway, was thirty-
five years old. An ardent Royalist, he had served the King's cause
well both in Parliament and in battle. He had large estates in
Northern Ireland, where the main strength of his family had
always lain. His grandfather had bought a great house at Ragley
in Worcestershire, where Lord Conway spent as much time as
he could spare from his duties in Ireland and London. In 1651
he married Anne Finche, who, partly because her weak health
made it necessary for her to spend much of her time within reach

---

[1] *Works*, Vol. 8, p. 606.
[2] Dated 17 February 1657-8.
[3] Evelyn, *Diary*, 25 February 1658.
[4] Letter to a person unnamed, Tanner MSS., No. 52. Peter Gunning, 1614–84.
Fellow and tutor of Clare Hall, Cambridge, 1633. Ministered during the Commonwealth at Exeter Chapel, Strand. Bishop of Chichester, 1669–75. Bishop of Ely,
1675–84.

of doctors, lived mainly with her mother at Kensington House, a place which nearly a century and a half later was to become famous as the birthplace of Queen Victoria. It was inevitable that Taylor should come into contact with the Kensington House circle. Lady Conway corresponded with Henry More at Cambridge and would hear of Taylor from him, if her own eager interest in philosophy and theology had not already made her seek out so admired an author. There was another connexion with the Conways through Evelyn; he was known to both them and Taylor, whose ministrations to the London Royalists would in any case have brought him to notice. A letter dated 17 April 1658 is the first to survive of the correspondence which passed between Taylor and his new patron.

April 17th 1658.

MY VERY GOOD LORD,

I have till now deferred to write to your Lordship because I could not sooner give an account of the time when I could attend your Lordship at Ragley. But now that my wife is well laid and in a hopeful condition, I hope I shall not be hindered to begin my journey to my Lady Chaworth on the 26th of this month, and from thence by the Grace of God I will be coming the 3rd of May towards Ragley, unless your affairs call your Lordship from thence before that time; but if they are like to do so, and I have intimation of it from your Lordship I will begin my journey that way and from thence go on to Nottinghamshire. My Lord, I suppose by the first return of the Carrier, you will receive those pieces of Thom: Nash which I received by your Lordship's command to put into order and to make as complete as I could. Upon the views of them and comparing them with what I had, I found I had but one to add, which I have caused to be bound up with the rest; but I have as yet failed of getting that piece Castalis against Beza, which your Lordship wished to have; but I shall make a greater search as soon as it please God I am well, for I write this to your Lordship in my bed being afflicted with a very great cold and some fears of an ague, but these fears are going off, because I see my illness settling into a cold. My Lord, I have not yet had an opportunity to wait upon the Swedish Ambassador according to your Lordship's command because I have attempted to procure a great Bible at 11£, but found it impossible, they being resolved to let none of the supernumaries go under 15£, besides ruling and binding, and not perceiving how I could be serviceable to him, I did not think it necessary to be troublesome: but if your Lordship still persists in your commands that I should wait upon him, I will presently address myself to him. My Lord, I have yet wanted confidence to go to Dr Ridgeley either to visit him or to obtain that part of yours *de revelatione Divinae Majestatis*, but if your Lordship will be pleased by the first post to write two lines to him; under that warranty I shall satisfy two very great desires I have, one to be acquainted with the Dr, the other to peruse that book: And now My Lord having given your Lordship an account of these little impertinences, my great business which I shall ever be doing but shall never finish is to give your Lordship the greatest thanks in a just acknowledgement and publication of your greatest, your freest, your noblest obligations passed upon me : for the day scarce renews so often as your Lordships favours to me. My Lord, I have from the hands of your excellent Lady received 30£, for your Lordship not only provides an excellent country for me, but a viaticum and Manna in the way, that the favour may be as much without charge to me as it is without merit on my part. Truly My Lord, if your Lordship had done to me as many other worthy persons have, that is, a single favour, or a little one, or something that I had merited, or something for which I might be admitted to pay an equal service, or anything which is not without example, or could possibly be without envy to me, I could have spoken such things as might have given true and proper significations to my thankfulness; but in earnest My Lord, since I have understood the greatness of the favour you have done and intended to me, if I had not also been acquainted with the very great nobleness of your disposition, I should have had more wonder than belief, but now My Lord, I am satisfied with this, that although this conjugation of favours is too great for me to have hoped for from one person it is not too great for your Lordship to give; and I see that in all times, especially in the worst, God is pleased to appoint some heroical examples of virtue, that such extraordinary precedents might highly reprove, and in some measure restore, the almost lost worthiness of mankind. My Lord, you read my heart, which with the greatest simplicity and ingenuity sends forth some of its perpetual thoughts; but if I can have my option I shall not receive this heap of favours with so great joyfulness as I shall with earnestness beg this greater favour, that it may be in some measure put into my power to express how much I love, how much I honour, how willingly I would serve, so excellent, so Dear a person. My Good Lord I am

Your Lordship's most humble, most obliged, and most affectionate servant,

JER. TAYLOR.

I pray my Good Lord present my humble service to your excellent and pious Lady Mother and to good Mr Whitby.[1]

The journey to see Lady Chaworth, who lived at Annesley Park near Nottingham, was no doubt similar to others which Taylor seems to have undertaken to great houses in the country

[1] Murray MSS.

where there were Royalists who valued his services. It is obvious from this letter that the acquaintance with Lord Conway was already of sufficient standing for Taylor to be employed by him in various pieces of business of a literary and semi-literary nature. The Thom. Nash whose works he was editing was possibly the Thomas Nash who had published in 1633 a work called *Quaternio*. He was a keen Royalist, and his death in 1648 was said to be due to his great grief at the misfortunes of Charles I. But Taylor, who seems to have read everything that came his way, may have been interested in the exuberant journalism of the more famous Thomas Nash of Elizabethan times. It would also seem that the plan for Taylor to move to Ireland and become chaplain to the Conway household at Portmore was already sufficiently settled for Lady Conway to advance £30 for the expenses of removal. For a long time Lord Conway had been looking for an Anglican priest who would be more acceptable to his Irish establishment, and that of his brother-in-law, Major Rawdon, who commanded the garrison at Lisnagarvey, than the minister who since 1651 had been intruded upon them by the Government. This was a man named Andrew Wyke, an Ana-baptist whom Adair described as "void of human learning, never educated in that way but a tradesman and impudent".[1] Such a person was not very likely to be pleasing to a Royalist household. Mrs Dorothy Rawdon, Lord Conway's sister, in particular had taken a violent dislike to the man. She wrote to her brother in London: "There is nothing I dislike here but Mr Wyke, whom I never can like. You would very much oblige me if you would send a good minister here, as it is hard to live by such a one as he." Accordingly, Conway had been looking out for a suitable man. He would have been very glad if he could have induced either Henry More or Cudworth to go out, but both declined. Whether More, who probably knew Taylor well enough, sug-gested him instead is hard to say. Taylor's letter shows how thankful he was for the opportunity. The postscript may indicate that he had been to Ragley already and met the Dowager Lady Conway, to whom he presents his humble service and "good Mr Whitby" who, according to a note written at the bottom of one of the later letters in this series, was the chaplain.

Lord Conway seems to have found the gratitude of his corres-pondent embarrassing. He replied by return of post:

[1] Adair, *True Narrative*, p. 186. The name is sometimes spelled Wyke, sometimes Week or Weeks.

Sir,

I should have troubled you long before this with enquiries after your health, if my friends at Kensington who know my inclination had not frequently endeavoured to satisfy me therein. I perceive the joy of your lady's safe delivery, and the birth of a fine boy, hath wound you up to so high a pitch of complacency that you are pleased to let it fall in showers upon the commonest objects, so Princes release felons, on the like occasion, there being a time where it is lawful to do as well as say anything, I being in this number a partaker of your favours, am so far from deserving your expressions that I am sure it was never in my power to do you the least kindness. Truly Sir I read your letter with many intermissions, and much trouble and it drives me to beg three things of you. The first is that you would never think of me otherwise as one that hath done you the ordinariest, the commonest civilities. Secondly that you would never mention me in discourse to others but as one you are not well acquainted with, and thirdly, that you would never injure any book of yours by putting my name in the dedication. These are so essential to that notion of justice which I have and so far sympathize with my Genius that I shall account them the highest obligations. I shall wait for your coming out of Nottinghamshire that I may be happy in your company to London, the fourth of May by your own account I may expect you, but if you stay beyond the fifth I shall conclude you in the jaws of a committee. I have little time to write to Dr Ridgely, and I think you would have as little to deliver it and therefore I defer it, but I pray do me the favour to visit the Swedish Ambassador if you can. Mr Bee told me that he had Castellio against Beza and promised it to me. I am exceedingly joyful for your lady's safety, and the blessing that God hath sent you. I pray present my humble service to her and esteem me.

Sir,

Your most affectionate and faithful Servant,

E. C.

Ragley. 21 April, 1658.
For my honoured friend
Dr. Taylor at London.[1]

The committee, which Conway feared might get Taylor into its jaws, was no doubt one of those groups which had been set up to administer Cromwell's edict of 1655 against sequestered ministers. Any clerical functions which Taylor performed at Annesley Park would put him into the power of such a body if news of them leaked out. But the journey to Ragley had been put off for a few days. Taylor was ill, yet not so as to prevent

[1] Murray MSS.

him writing a lengthy defence of his indiscreet enthusiasm for his connexion with Conway. He still seemed to think that modesty was the only reason why the dedication he had hinted at was unacceptable, and pleaded his own seeming ingratitude if he was not to be allowed to make some public acknowledgement of his indebtedness. A little more worldly wisdom would have enabled him to understand that, circumstances being what they were, the best way to show his sense of obligation was to say as little about it in public as possible. He is pained that Conway bids him keep silence:

But my Lord, I shall be more careful to please your Lordship than to serve any little end of my own vanity; only this I shall beg of your Lordship that you will do me this right not to think me so unjust an estimator of things as that I ever can suppose than a hundred dedications can assoil my obligations to your Lordship, or that I can pay my debt by receiving a new favour. For I conceive that dedicating a book is like dining with my friend, he will thank me for my company, and I shall account myself bound to thank a worthy patron that shall own my book. But, my Lord, when your Lordship hath conversed longer with me, you will discover more imperfections in me, yet because I know you shall never discern my unworthiness, I hope your Lordship will in time love me so well as not to prejudice me in all my possibilities of doing myself right by endeavouring to wash away from myself all the outsides and colours of unthankfulness. This, my Lord, I will promise, that if ever your Lordship will be pleased to give me leave to inscribe your honoured name before any of my books I will, in the address, discourse upon some worthy subject and not spend three lines upon anything that shall press upon your modesty.[1]

In actual fact, he never did dedicate a book to Conway, though no doubt at this time he was intending to offer him *Ductor Dubitantium*, since Conway greatly admired Taylor's vast knowledge of casuistry. That great work, however, was not published until after the Restoration, and was then dedicated to Charles II. The letter goes on to deal with the writer's circumstances:

My Lord I have been so very ill with a cold that I have been forced to put off my journey to Nottinghamshire, and shall better finish it by going that way into Wales. So that I purpose, by the Grace of God, to be at Pershore on Saturday morning in the Worcester coach, whither, if your Lordship will be pleased to send a horse to bring me to Ragley, I shall not fail to attend your Lordship that night and so wait on you to London without being occasion of any longer stay than

[1] Murray MSS., Taylor to Conway, 24 April 1658.

our first intentions. The Worcester coach comes from hence on Thursday morning, April 29th and on Saturday morning will pass through Pershore, and there I shall stay expecting your Lordship's favour of a horse, for I suppose that to be the nearest stage to Ragley. Your Castellis and Beza I shall bring along with me, and in the meantime I shall endeavour to wait upon the Swedish Ambassador according to your commands. On Monday I am to wait upon your most excellent lady at Kensington, and give her honour an account of this my intendment, though already she is acquainted with my purpose in general, but then I did not know how the motion of the coaches would determine me. My Lord I humbly thank your Lordship that you are pleased to be concerned in the good of my little family, you cause much good to it and rejoice in the rest.[1]

That letter was dated 24 April, and one written by Lady Conway to her husband on the 27th completes the picture of Taylor at this time, which is the clearest and fullest description we have of him at any period of his life. He had made the visit to Kensington which he had spoken of, but on a day when Lady Conway had been so ill that it was as much as she could do to get up and entertain him, and the company that came with him. In spite of that, they had stayed so late that she had scarcely been left time enough in which to write to her husband. Dr Taylor, she writes "hath lost his boy, which I believe is a very great grief to him, but he seems to bear it cheerfully" and she goes on to tell her husband of the arrangements for the journey to Ragley which Taylor himself had already described.[2] So in the fortnight or so which these letters cover Taylor had been thrilled with the generosity of his new patron, dashed a little by the chilly response to the outpouring of his thanks, his child had been born and died, quite possibly from the influenza which he himself had suffered from, and now he was setting out on what he expected to be a pleasant journey to his new friend's house and back again, but which might very well put him in gaol once more if it was suspected that he was travelling in performance of his duties as an Anglican priest. When Taylor taught that a Christian should live serenely, putting his whole trust in the goodness of God, it was not because he himself had never been tested.

In the following May, Evelyn, who possibly regretted that his friend was going so far away from him, was the intermediary

[1] Murray MSS., Taylor to Conway, 24 April 1658.
[2] Brit. Mus. Add. MSS., 23,214, Fol. 14, printed, *Conway Letters*, p. 147.

through whom another offer was made. The details of it are onl
to be gleaned from the letter in which Taylor refused it.

I like not [he says] the condition of being a lecturer under the dispos
of another, nor to serve in my semi-circle, where a Presbyterian an
myself shall be like Castor and Pollux, the one up and the othe
down, which methinks is like worshipping the sun, and making hin
the deity, that we may be religious half the year and every night serv
another interest. Sir, the stipend is so inconsiderable, it will not pa
the charge and trouble of removing myself and family. It is wholl
arbitrary; for the triers may overthrow it or the vicar may forbid it
or the subscribers may die or grow weary, or poor or be absent
I beseech you Sir, pay my thanks to your friend who had so mucl
kindness to me as to intend my benefit, I think myself no less obliged
to him and you than if I had accepted it.[1]

The letter is incomplete but in what remains Taylor goes on to
answer some doubts which Evelyn had passed on to him abou
the lawfulness of taking interest on money. Even without the
full argument, Taylor's reply is fairly clear. In his opinion, i
you may let your farm to another man for hire you may justly
allow him the use of your money on the same kind of terms.

It has been usual for Taylor's biographers to consider tha
this letter referred to some hitch in the negotiations about the
post in Ireland, and that Evelyn, acting as a friend of botl
parties, was trying to put things right. But Taylor's own letters
to Conway quoted earlier make that view very difficult to hold
It is obvious from them that the Irish plan was already settled
in April, and that preparations for carrying it out were sufficiently
advanced for Taylor to have accepted a "viaticum". It is hardly
likely that it could have gone so far without the difficulties which
appeared so insuperable coming to light long before. The post
Evelyn offered on behalf of his friend was a lectureship with a
Presbyterian. The post in Ireland was a chaplaincy, and Wyke,
if he had much authority over Conway's personal chaplain,
which is doubtful, was an Independent. The difference was too
glaring to be overlooked. Again, the salary in the case of Evelyn's
offer was to be provided by a subscription in which it would
seem that a fair number of people were involved. In the Irish
post only Conway and Rawdon were concerned, and it was not
very likely that either of them would give up their interests at
Portmore so that Taylor would be left stranded, as he feared in
the other case. Certainly there was not much likelihood that

---

[1] Evelyn, *Diary*, Vol. 3, p. 248, letter dated 12 May 1658.

ither Conway or Rawdon would "grow poor". The fact that
he Triers could forbid it would seem to indicate that Evelyn
was putting forward a lectureship in England or Wales; they
were not concerned with an appointment to Conway's household
in Ireland.[1] If Evelyn was acting for Conway, there was no
reason why Taylor should refer to him remotely as "your friend",
he was himself perfectly well acquainted with him, and had
conveyed his own thanks profusely enough already. Taylor's
letter to Evelyn only becomes understandable on the supposition
that it concerns a totally different position than the one he had
already accepted in Ireland.

The news of his coming had certainly stirred up opposition
here, which distressed Conway considerably when he heard of
it from his brother-in-law, Major Rawdon. Writing on 15 June,
when Taylor was already on his way, he says to Rawdon, "That
which you writ me in your letter of the second of this month
concerning Dr Taylor was sufficient to have discouraged him and
all his friends from any further thoughts of that country", and
he goes on to say that it was for no personal reason that he
persuaded Taylor to go to Ireland but because he had a mind to
do "an act of Piety toward him, and an act of piety toward all
such as are truly disposed to virtue in those parts; for I am
certain he is the choicest person in England appertaining to the
conscience, and let others blemish him how they please, yet all
I have written of him is true". He goes on to detail the steps he
had taken to make Taylor's life in Ireland more agreeable to
him. Dr Petty, afterwards the famous Sir William Petty, had
been induced to write to Dr Harrison and several others on his
behalf. Harrison, who was the minister of a Nonconformist
church in Dublin, had been very critical of Taylor's appointment,
and as he was influential with the Government, Petty's intercession with him was valuable. Through Dr Petty's agency, for
he had been appointed to survey the many forfeited estates in
Ireland, Taylor was also to be given the opportunity of purchasing
land cheaply; Rawdon was to be consulted later on about other
schemes for Taylor's benefit. Conway himself had seen that he
was furnished with letters of recommendation to Sir Mathew
Tomlinson, to the Chancellor, and to the Lord Chief Baron.
It would seem that Taylor was already known to Dr Dudley
Loftus, the Irish Vicar-General and Judge of the Prerogative
Court. The Lord Protector himself had shown some favour, for

[1] For Baxter's opinion of the Triers, see his *Autobiography* (Everyman), pp. 70-1.

Conway adds that Cromwell had given Taylor a pass for himsel
and his family under his own "sign manual and privy signet".
If these introductions were of any use, Taylor began his life in a
new country with a phalanx of friends to help him.

When Taylor went to Ireland the entire country was under
going a drastic change. By the Articles of Kilkenny, which wer
signed in May 1652, the wars, which with brief intervals had
devastated Ireland for eleven years, were brought to an end
Shortly after the outbreak of the rebellion of 1641, the Long
Parliament had formulated a plan for the permanent subjugation
of the country by the confiscation of its lands. This design wa
carried out by the Act of Settlement of 12 August 1652. By it the
whole of Ireland was regarded as forfeited property, and many
owners, in addition to the loss of their estates, were condemned
to lose their lives also, unless they could prove their complete
innocence of any taint of rebellion. To this Act was appended a
list of those for whom no pardon of any kind was available
among whom were both Ormonde and Bramhall. The vas
tract of land made vacant by this Act was divided into two parts
one consisting of the Province of Connaught and County Clare
the other the rest of Ireland. Into the first were huddled all the
native proprietors who by hook or by crook had managed to
retain a title to some parcel of land; the other was to be divided
between the friends of the Parliament, who were mostly English
and Scottish adventurers. With unsparing strength, the forfeited
lands were cleared of their former owners, satisfactorily measured
by Sir William Petty, and by May 1659 the new possessors were
settled upon their new estates. The landless Irish either emigrated
as soldiers, were indentured to labour in the West Indian planta-
tions, or wandered about their native country begging their
bread. No attempt afterwards made to overthrow this settlement
had more than slight success.[2]

Toward the end of June 1658 Taylor arrived in the North of
Ireland. He intended at first to live in Lisnagarvey, which was a
town of fairly recent growth in Taylor's day. It had sprung up
round the castle which Sir Fulke Conway had built when he
obtained the territory of Killultagh about 1609. Sir Fulke had
brought with him a number of English and Welsh settlers, and
it was these who built the town. The Conway family erected

[1] *Rawdon Papers*, pp. 187–91, Conway to Rawdon, 15 June 1658.
[2] S. R. Gardiner, "The Transplantation to Connaught", *Eng. Hist. Review*, Vol.
XIV, pp. 700–34.

for themselves a castle and a church, and settled down to enjoy their new possessions in a land of pleasant fields, water brooks, rivers full of fish, forests full of game. In 1641 the rebels burnt the whole town, together with the church and the castle, but they were driven from the site by a small force under Sir George Rawdon. Everything was rebuilt as soon after the rebellion as possible, and the town received its old name of Lisnagarvey again. It was not until 1662 that it is referred to in the parish registers as Lisburn, the name by which it is known to most of those who are acquainted with the life of Taylor.[1]

It was from that town that he wrote to Lord Conway on 26 February 1658/9 in a strain of lyrical gratitude:

"My Noblest, My Dearest Lord, If amidst the throngs of your joys and the crowds of summer friends who come to congratulate to your Lordship these late counsels and levees of heaven for your avail, you have leisure to read the heart of him whom, of all persons in the world, you have most obliged, then my Lord be pleased to believe that though since my coming into Ireland by God's blessing and your Lordship's favour I have had plenty and privacy, opportunities of studying much and opportunities of doing some little good yet I cannot say that I have had joy till now."

This special cause for rejoicing was the birth of a son to Lord and Lady Conway on 6 February 1658/9, and Taylor goes on to develop at length his theme of the goodness of God in hearing the prayers of Conway's family and friends and granting this great blessing in response:

"My Lord if I talk wildly and that which civil men call meta-physically, but angry persons (it may be more truly) call extravagantly, be pleased to impute it to my excess of joy which is not always the soberest inventor of sense and reasonable discourse. My Lord you have made all my comforts under God to depend upon you and you have satisfied all my desires and filled all my needs and relieved all my necessity and I have nothing to do (next to the service of God) but to combine with all your interests."

But he has forgotten his greatest joy: he has been told that Lord and Lady Conway intend to settle in Ireland. "It may be it will be so, but the asperity of my fortune does not use to entertain to great advantages. If it comes all that I can say is that I did not certainly expect that in this world also I should receive so great content-ments." He intended to go up to Hillsborough that afternoon to

[1] The origin of the name Lisburn is unknown. For a reasonable explanation and an interesting account of the town, see Carmody, *Lisburn Cathedral and Its Past Rectors*, pp. 1–7.

talk over the good news with Mrs Rawdon. Major Rawdon was in England, and now that he was away the country was "without law and justice and nothing in Kilultagh" was "good". Mrs Taylor herself would be unable to go to Hillsborough with him, as she was expecting a child, though not till August. In the last few lines of his letter Taylor begs leave to "throw a little myrrh into my full goblet of wine and complain that I have not these five or six weeks had the honour to receive a letter from your Lordship though I have written four and have thought myself strangely concerned in the expectation of this blessing".[1]

Conway must have replied at once to this entreaty, for Taylor's next letter is dated from Portmore on 10 March, and is obviously an answer to one from his patron. Conway had once more objected to the rapturous expressions into which Taylor's unrestrained gratitude was leading him. He had put some of them down to the "remaining effects of a high distemper". "But", says Taylor, "truly my Lord they are not, but it may be I did not express my meaning prudently, I was only troubled that things were here so that I could neither serve your Lordship nor your sister, but I must be like a cistern under a conduit pipe ever receiving fresh waters and returning nothing back."[2] The letter is a long one and deals mainly with the theories of Cardan about the occult influences of precious stones, ideas which Lord Conway seemed to think had something in them. Taylor treats the subject with common sense and gentle humour. "I could not but smile when I read in Cardan[3] that the hyacinth will increase riches and authority, indeed it is the truest thing in all the 7th book, good store of them will, but so will pearl and diamond, . . . but a ragged coat has as much secret effort as a jewel, for it will make a man lie." He still harps on the prospect of the Conways coming to live in Ireland, but since that was not immediately likely and he himself could not be at Ragley he intended "not to stir" that summer, but to "make myself the fitter to come to England if it please God". He had in mind no doubt the finishing of his *Cases of Conscience*, which was already far enough advanced for him to think of sending the greater part of it over to the printer by one of his servants or by a friend. "I am", he says, "almost at an end of this tedious work, and then I shall more carefully look after my health, that I may live long

---

[1] Murray MSS.   [2] Ibid.
[3] Girolamo Cardano, b. 1510, d. 1576. An Italian mathematician, physician, and astrologer. He wrote 122 books on these and other subjects. He cast the horoscope of Edward VI and foretold a long life for him.

to serve God and your Lordship." What he had particularly in mind was that he might be the tutor of Lord Conway's son. Though the baby was not two months old yet and it was early days to think of tutors, the first hint of such a possibility seems to have come from Conway himself.

In the first months of his life in Ireland Taylor seems to have lived partly at Portmore and partly at Lisnagarvey, settling finally at Portmore. It was no doubt safer as well as quieter, and certainly far more splendid, than anything to be found in an ordinary Irish country town. Portmore had been built from designs by Inigo Jones soon after the rebellion of 1641. Nothing remains of it to-day but a few broken traces of brick walls, and some old trees which may or may not have formed part of Lord Conway's garden.[1] The house was beautifully situated on the eastern bank of a small lake which was sometimes called Lough Beg and sometimes Portmore Lough. It had a charming view across the lake and away to Lough Neagh, where the old round tower on Ram Island stood up against the sky. On both sides and behind it were green meadows and bog land. There was a church nearby in which Taylor ministered to Lord Conway's household, but neither church nor house lasted long. The church was dismantled by Taylor himself when, a little before his death, he built his new chapel at Ballinderry, and the house was pulled down in 1761, when the Conway peerage became extinct. From Portmore Taylor rode over most Sundays to Lisnagarvey to preach in the church there. But in view of the shortage of efficient ministers Taylor was not able to content himself merely with doing his duty in Lisnagarvey. He is said to have preached also at Templecormac and once a fortnight at Ballinderry, Soldierstown, Derriaghy, and Magheragall.[2] Tradition only is the authority for this statement, and it is possible that he did not preach in all these places. No doubt many churches aspired to be associated with Taylor.

A month after his last letter Taylor wrote again to Lord Conway, a little apologetically this time but feeling that he had business enough to justify it.

Portmore. April 9th 1659.

MY NOBLEST, MY DEAREST LORD,

I have so lately tired your Lordship with my many and tedious letters that as it was my duty to write them, so I think it were charity

---

[1] See a short paper entitled "Jeremy Taylor at Portmore", by Classon Porter, printed in the *Northern Whig* and reprinted in *Ulster Biographical Sketches* (Second Series), Belfast, 1884. [2] Ibid.

N

sometimes to forbear, but I cannot unless you chide my diligent impertinence. I have now my Lord finished my great employment all except two little chapters, which I reserve to give the printer law before me, that he may be doing with what he hath. I have sent my servant over with my papers and commanded him to wait upon your Lordship to know your pleasure and to receive your commands and hope he may receive something in order to your Lordship's coming over and abiding here, and if your Lordship hath anything to be carried that is not very great, he will take care of it. I hope my Lord you will be pleased to send over all your library, both from Kensington and Ragley, and I cannot imagine how you will give yourself your usual entertainments and divertisement without such a retinue and therefore I shall flatter myself much with that expectation, and if it fails me not, look on it as an indication of your Lordship's abode here with your servants who long for it passionately. My Lord I am now sending for my two girls that I left behind, the eldest in London and the youngest in Wales, and then my Lord I shall give hostages to your Lordship and to those of your relations and friendship, who are so kind to me as to be willing and to seem desirous I should live and die in Ireland, and I have often thought of a passage in one of your Lordship's first letters to me in Ireland when I had recounted the troubles and mighty inconveniences of removing a family, you were pleased to say, you were confident I should find that to be the last of this kind in my whole life. Now, though sometimes I did dream your Lordship might fancy I should quickly die, yet because the apprehension of dying is not intolerably afflictive, I rather now begin to suppose your Lordship did prophesy of that event which God's providence, and your own bounty, and my gratitude, and my inclinations do very much determine me to prosecute.

My Lord I am to beg a favour of your Lordship that when Royston sends to your Lordship the sheets of my second volume, which I have ordered him to do, you will be pleased to let some of your servants convey them speedily to me. My Lord I would not have moved this trouble to your Lordship if I could have found another way so safe or so tolerable, save only that your Lordship's trouble ought to be intolerable to me. They will be brought by 8 sheets or 10 at a time, and it may be a fortnight after so many more, that they may not be too grievous or troublesome. My Lord that excellent person at Hillsborough, Mrs Hill, is likely to be at a great loss for want of a chaplain to minister in her family and to the parish. I have attempted a very worthy person in Ireland to accept it but unsuccessfully. It is possible my Lord, my son Birkenhead may hear of a fit person if your Lordship will be pleased to engage him to enquire, and to name the person to me when he hath found him. But my Lord it will be of concern to us all by reason of the neighbourhood that he be good and worthy company, and in Kilultagh we are like to be wholly destitute, for Mr Watwood is leaving Glanavy for a living of almost £200 per annum, and Joseph Dunbar is now at Dublin in pursuance and acquist of a good living, and declares his purpose of leaving us and possibly Lisnagarvey will be more uneasy or unprovided than they that have none at all, so that it will not appear unreasonable that your Lordship in time think how to supply your own estate with that which will be pleasing to your Lordship and necessary to others. There is one here which was servant to Colonel Hill, that is a very honest person, a converted papist, understands Irish well and Latin pretty well, and studies divinity hard in order to undertake the ministerial function the right way, if he may be encouraged, but this will be but too poor a supply for the great needs of this great Lordship concerning which you will be pleased effectively to consider. I pray my Lord be pleased to honour me with an account of what health your excellent lady does enjoy. Is the miracle of her recovery and perfect restitution still in greater probability of being effected? How does her nursery? I pray present my humblest service to her Ladyship. The next time I write I shall be bold to call her eyes from looking upon her sweet baby to read a letter from her humblest servant. My Lord when you go to Ragley be pleased to present my humble service to your most virtuous Lady Mother and my kind regards to Mr Whitby. I shall wish myself there to attend that excellent company, but I hope ere long to do it longer, and with more advantages of pleasure and content in Ireland, but before I can obtain that I must wish myself nearer to my grave, it will be a long year first and that is a great part of my life, but however I very much long for it for it will be one of the greatest comforts of the remaining portion of the life of

My Noblest Lord
　　Your Lordship's most obliged, most affectionate and most humble servant,

JER TAYLOR.[1]

Taylor had obviously left his two daughters each with their maternal relatives, the elder with the Langsdales in London and the younger with the Bridges in Wales, he and his wife and possibly his son having gone over to Ireland to find somewhere to live before bringing the whole family together. The reference to "my son Birkenhead" is obscure. Sir John Birkenhead, the political satirist, had been acquainted with Taylor as early as 1647 and was also known to the Conway family. He was only three years younger than Taylor himself, but it is possible that he had been baptized late in life and was a godson of Taylor's.

[1] Murray MSS.

There is no trace of an actual son of that name. On the same day, 9 April, Taylor wrote to Evelyn. He always seems more at ease with him than with any other of his correspondents.

He asks for news of the outside world, what scholars are making a name for themselves, what new books have been published since he left England. He particularly wishes for some information about the new sect of the "Perfectionists" which was said to be rising in England. He believes that the chief opinion of these people is one that they have borrowed from Castellio—namely, that it is possible to give God perfect and entire obedience in this life. The leaders of this new body, he says, are Dr Drayton W. Parker and Dr Gell.[1] He himself has been busy all the winter with his *Cases of Conscience*, which are now ready for the press.[2] Evelyn still continued his generosity, since, writing from Portmore on 4 June 1659, Taylor expresses himself obliged "much for your pension but exceeding more for your affection". The rest of his acquaintances were beginning to forget him, and he quotes a little sadly the Spanish proverb which says "the dead and the absent have but few friends". Evelyn's brothers had also helped Taylor in some way, probably monetary, for he writes: "I shall be ashamed to make any address, or pay my thanks in words to them till my rule of conscience be publicke and that is all the way I have to pay my debts."[3] In this letter, as in the one which preceded it, Taylor still shows himself very anxious to find out more about the Perfectionists. In addition to his own curiosity on the subject, there was Lady Conway in the background, wanting to discuss the matter with her chaplain no doubt, since Gell was a friend of Henry More, her chief and most interesting correspondent in England. Indeed, most of More's letters to the Conways in Ireland were sent by carrier from Cambridge to Dr Gell's house in Bow Lane, London, and were picked up there by one of the Conway servants.[4] It would no doubt help Taylor a good deal in his conversations with his patroness if he knew what well-informed London people were thinking of the Perfectionists. Evelyn, who had a ready curiosity for every form of intellectual activity, had promised to enquire, and Taylor is

---

[1] Dr Robert Gell, 1595–1665. He was a Fellow of Christ's College, Cambridge, and at this University his friendship with More probably began. Rector of St Mary's, Aldermanbury. The book of his which Taylor had in mind was probably his *Essay toward the Amendment of the last English Translation of the Bible*, 1659. Gell was at one time chaplain to Sheldon.

[2] Evelyn, *Diary*, Vol. 3, p. 253.

[3] Ibid., p. 256.

[4] Letter from Henry More to Anne Conway, *Conway Letters* (ed. Nicholson), p. 54.

very grateful. He points out that "Parker hath written something lately of it, and in Dr Gell's last booke in folio there is much of it".[1] In the earlier letter he had told Evelyn that he thought an *Examen of the Westminster Confession*, put out by Gell and two of his friends, was well worth reading. They studied the Scriptures a good deal, but gave them very largely a mystical meaning. They were also indebted to Jacob Behmen, whom, says Taylor, they understand "as nurses do children something by use and much by fancy".[2] Nevertheless, he has heard that "some very learned and very sober persons have given up their names to it". Taylor maintained a regular system of transmitting letters from London. At one time he asks that communications for him may be sent to Mr Allestree, stationer, at the Bell in St Paul's Churchyard;[3] at another time to Mr Martin, bookseller, at the Bell in St Paul's Churchyard.[4] Possibly, since the address is the same, these two men were successors in the same business. Royston, Taylor adds, would also send letters, but he did not often employ him.

Though the London friends were becoming a little forgetful, Taylor was gaining new acquaintances in Dublin. Among them was Dr John Sterne who, after the Restoration, founded the Irish College of Physicians, and for whose *Thanatologia*, published in 1658, Taylor wrote a Latin letter, the only composition of his in that language which has survived, except the long epitaph on Lady Carbery. Sterne was at this time a Fellow of Trinity College, Dublin; and Cowley, Sheridan, and Graham, also members of that college, were friends of Taylor. It was in reply to an enquiry which these gentlemen made of him that Taylor sent them a list of books which he considered suitable as the nucleus of a theological library. The suggestions are divided under four heads: Prayer Book, Government and Discipline of the Church, Doctrine, and School Divinity. It is amusing to see how in every section except the last Taylor recommends his own books as among the indispensable minimum.[5]

All this time Taylor was writing as hard as he could, struggling to finish his *Cases of Conscience*, the progress of which is mentioned in almost every letter to Evelyn. There is a tradition in the neighbourhood of Portmore that he did most of his work in a little study which Lord Conway ordered to be built for him

[1] Evelvn, *Diary*, Vol. 3, p. 256.   [2] Ibid.   [3] Ibid., p. 253.   [4] Ibid.
[5] Letter in Dopping's *Common Place Book* (Trinity College Dublin, Library), printed *Irish Eccles. Journal*, January 1849. The letter is dated 13 January 1659. No doubt 1659/60 is meant.

on a small island in Lough Beg, which was called Sally Island because of the many willows which grew there. He is also said, with less probability, to have studied on Ram Island which is about a mile from Portmore, in Lough Neagh. But even here he was not to have uninterrupted quiet. In the letter to Evelyn which he wrote on 4 June 1659, he complains: "I fear my peace in Ireland is likely to be short; for a Presbyterian and a madman have informed against me as a dangerous man to their religion; and for using the sign of the cross in baptism. The worst event of the information which I fear is my return into England; which although I am not desirous it should be upon these terms yet if it can be without much violence, I shall not be troubled."[1] Probably the Presbyterian and the madman were the same person, for Lord Conway writing to Rawdon ten days later about the same affair only mentions one name, that of a Mr Tandy:

I received a letter yesterday from Dr Taylor; it hath almost broken my heart. Mr Tandy hath exhibited articles against him to the Lord deputy and council, so simple, (as Colonel Hill writes) that it is impossible it should come to anything: the greatest scandal being that he christened Mr Bryer's child with the sign of the cross. I have written to Hyrne to supply him with money for his vindication, as if it were my own business. I hope therefore, when you come over, you will take him [Tandy] off from persecuting me, since none knows better than yourself whether I deserve the same at his hands. I would have sent you the Doctor's letter to me but I know not whether this will ever come to you. The quarrel is, it seems, because he thinks Dr Taylor more welcome to Hillsborough than himself.[2]

The Hillsborough mentioned in the letter was Colonel Hill's house a little way from Lisnagarvey. It would seem from the letter that Tandy's real spite was with Lord Conway, whom he wished to strike through his chaplain, at the same time desiring to get a little revenge on Taylor for being more popular than himself. Possibly Tandy was an Independent preacher, though his name does not appear in any of the lists of ministers.[3] Conway remarks that he would do better to set himself against the Anabaptists and Quakers than to trouble his best and most peaceable neighbours.

Whatever influence Conway used, he could not prevent the

[1] Evelyn, *Diary*, Vol. 3, p. 256.
[2] *Rawdon Papers*, p. 195, Lord Conway to Major Rawdon, 14 June 1659.
[3] Nicolson, *Conway Letters*, p. 159.

prosecution going on. On 11 August the council ordered Lieut.-Colonel Smyth, the Governor of Carrickfergus, to see that Taylor was sent in safe custody to Dublin to answer for his offences before the commissioners. The order was not obeyed at once. When he wrote again to Evelyn, on 3 November, Taylor either did not know of its existence or did not think the threat of it sufficiently serious to mention to his correspondent. He is concerned with the state of England. On account of a recent disturbance there, a letter from Evelyn, written on 23 July, was not received until All Saints' Day. Taylor writes as one who is puzzled and not a little worried by the state of affairs. He is not very clear about the disturbance he has mentioned, whether it was for or against the Church, but it is clear, he thinks, that God did not intend to send relief by its means. He was probably referring to Sir George Booth's rebellion, but his remarks are cryptic.[1] Taylor obviously did not want anybody to get into trouble should his letter go astray.[2]

But his distresses, and those of the Church, were coming to an end. Cromwell died in September 1658 and Richard Cromwell's rule only lasted until May 1659. It was succeeded by a confused scene of struggle and intrigue, in which generals and party leaders sought to realize either their own personal power or their own ideal of government. On 2 January 1660, Monk crossed the Tweed into England, and began to bring this chaos to an end. One last piece of persecution Taylor was called upon to endure. According to his own account of it, written to Evelyn in February 1660, the delayed warrant for his arrest was executed about Christmas-time, and he was forced to travel to Dublin in the worst winter weather. As a result he was ill on the journey to Dublin and worse on the way back, but by February he was well enough to write in comfort.[3] Allowing for a journey to Dublin and back and an illness, however short, there seems little time left between Christmas and February for him to have been detained by the Commissioners. In all probability, the charge was dismissed as soon as he arrived. It was not a time for petty persecution, especially of a churchman, for a change of régime was already well under way. In the previous year Lord

---

[1] Sir George Booth, first Baron Delamer (1622–84). Joined the parliamentary forces and was military commissioner for Cheshire. Changed to the King's side, and commanded forces for him in the same county and in Lancashire and North Wales during 1659, but was defeated by Lambert at Nantwich. Raised to the Peerage at Charles II's Coronation.

[2] Evelyn, *Diary*, Vol. 3, p. 274.   [3] Ibid., p. 275.

Broghill, who commanded parliamentary troops in Munster, and Sir Charles Coote, one of the commissioners for the Government of Ireland, had opened correspondence first with Ormonde, then with Charles himself. Everything being in train, the two made a bold stroke for the King by seizing Dublin Castle, and sending Sir Hardress Waller the regicide as a prisoner to England. The Army as a whole was on their side. A convention Parliament met at Dublin in February 1660, the very time when Taylor was writing his letter. The members decided both to restore Charles and to grant him large sums of money. In the following May the King was solemnly proclaimed in Dublin.

All that winter, as his letters to Evelyn show, Taylor was looking forward to the spring, when he intended to go to London. His "cases of conscience", which he considered the great work of his life, was now finished, and as he seems always to have liked to see his publications through the press himself, the issue of this latest book was drawing him to London. Ireland had not been so pleasant a place to live in that he did not welcome the distraction of visiting his old friends again. Although every letter to Evelyn acknowledges a "token" and it would seem that his chaplaincy was not very profitable, he makes no suggestion that poverty may keep him from effecting the journey. Rust leads us to suppose that it was the news of the unrest and excitement in England which made him decide to go over to London.[1] He had an excellent excuse if he wanted one, for the manuscript of *Ductor Dubitantium* was ready at last and needed to be seen through the press. If, on his way to England, he passed through Dublin, he would see how promising the affairs of the Royalist party were beginning to look. The Church was already receiving a great deal more respect than had been her lot for a good many years. With the prospect of the King's return becoming clearer every day, the leading Presbyterian laymen were beginning to pay their court to the bishops. Churchmen, who a few months before had been refused access to the commissioners and were either ignored or insulted in the streets, now found themselves sought after, their salaries paid to them, and even their proper ecclesiastical titles afforded them again.[2] There was no outstanding personality among the Presbyterians who was capable

---

[1] Rust, "Funeral Sermon", *Works*, Vol. 1, p. cccxxiii. "This loyal subject went over to congratulate the prince and people's happiness, and bear a part in the universal triumph." But, as Taylor's letters show, he had been looking forward to visiting London for some time.

[2] Adair, *True Narrative*, p. 240.

of becoming their leader, or even of showing them a way of dealing with the exceedingly difficult situation they were in.[1] None of them had any more love for bishops now than he had ever had, but many of them were eager for the King's return, and the bishops were among the King's closest friends. It was hard to continue to ignore one and yet court the other.

Taylor arrived in London in March 1660, and so was in time to affix his signature to the declaration which the Loyalists published on 24 April in support of the measures which Monk had initiated.[2] On 29 May, his birthday, the King entered London. Charles II had come into his own again. With a heart as full of thankfulness as any man in England, Taylor sat down to write a short dedication of his *Ductor Dubitantium* to the King. The great book which he confidently expected to establish his fame was now on the eve of publication. Two joys had come to him together: the return of the King, bringing an end to the persecution of the Church which Taylor so dearly loved, and the close of a great labour which had extended over many years, and in its preliminary studies brought him so much distress of mind and misunderstanding. When he wrote his dedication he probably knew that he was certain to receive some preferment. His joy overflowed:

God has left off to smite us with an iron rod and has once more said to these nations "they shall serve the Lord their God and David their king whom I have raised up unto them" and now our duty stands on the sunny side; it is our work to rejoice in God and in God's anointed, and to be glad and worthily to accept of our prosperity in all our business; for so good a God we serve that he hath made it our duty to be happy and we cannot please Him unless we be infinitely pleased ourselves.[3]

His dedication goes on in a strain of overflowing gratitude to God and welcome to the King, to whom he begs to present his two volumes, which, like the widow's two mites, make up a contemptible sum and yet are all that he has. This dedication must have been rushed through the press, and the original one, to whomsoever it was offered, hastily suppressed. The book appeared very soon after the King's return. While he was writing it, Taylor generally referred to it as his "cases of consciences". Evelyn once, in March 1657,[4] mentions is as *Ducto Dubitantium*, a title only a little different from that under which it finally appeared.

[1] Adair, *True Narrative*, p. 229.   [2] Kennet's *Register*, p. 121.
[3] *Works*, Vol. 9, p. 1.   [4] Evelyn, *Diary*, 25 March 1657.

It was not to be expected that so large a work, written for specialists, should have the immediate success which Taylor's other publications generally received. But *Ductor Dubitantium* was not given to a world which was entirely heedless of casuistry. Since the Reformation, controversy had taken up so much of the theologian's time that very little had been written on anything else. But the discussion which originated in the divorce of Henry VIII found expression in a good many pamphlets on marriage which really belong to moral theology. Andrewes, in his *Tortura Torti*, had discussed political issues from a theological point of view, and therefore may be said to have made some contribution to casuistical literature. Every scholar of any pretentions had read books of casuistry, and fitted himself to take a part in debates on nice points of personal conduct. But there were very few attempts on the part of Protestants to treat casuistry at any length. Dr Perkins,[1] an Elizabethan divine who had an extraordinary reputation among the Puritans, published a book of *Cases of Conscience* in 1606. Among the Lutherans, Frederick Baldwin, who was Professor of Theology at Wittenberg and died in 1627, had written on morals. In Jeremy Taylor's own generation a good many of the outstanding men had published books which, however restricted in scope, showed their authors' interest in casuistry. Cosin, for instance, wrote on *The Dissolution of Marriage*, and Hammond between 1645 and 1650 published three quarto volumes, one *Of Conscience*, another *Of Sins of Weakness and Willfulness*, and another *Of the Power of the Keys*. Selden was writing on a subject very near akin to casuistry when in 1640 he published his *De Jure Naturali et Gentium juxta Disciplinam Ebraeorum*,[2] in which he set himself to examine the opinion of the Jews on what moral obligation existed outside the Mosaic Law and which was therefore binding on all men.

A far greater book and one which had a profound influence on European thought for many generations to come was Grotius' *De Jure Belli et Pacis*.[3] In it he examined the foundations of justice among men and nations, and particularly the rights and duties connected with war. On the Continent this book received wide recognition immediately; in England it made its way more slowly. But Taylor, who greatly admired Grotius, had studied it

---

[1] William Perkins, 1558–1602. Fellow of Christ's College, Cambridge. A strong Calvinist, his works were considered almost the equal of Calvin's own. His books were translated into Dutch, Spanish, Welsh, and Irish. Fuller published a short sketch of him in his *Holy State*, Bk. 2, Chap. 10.

[2] London, 1640.   [3] Paris, 1635.

and made considerable use of it in both *Unum Necessarium* and *Ductor Dubitantium*.

Bishop Hall of Norwich, among his many other interests, found time to write *Cases of Conscience*, but his treatment of the new problems which were beginning to arise through the great changes in commercial life shows that he was hardly at home in cases for which authority had not provided. Another Anglican, Thomas Barlow, Bishop of Lincoln, who managed to accommodate himself successfully to the political changes of a life which stretched from 1607 to 1691, wrote a number of casuistical works, but it was Sanderson, his predecessor in the See of Lincoln, who was "esteemed the most known casuist this nation ever produced". His *De Obligate Conscientiae*[1] was most outstanding. Taylor probably saw it in manuscript, and undoubtedly it had an influence on his own work, though to say, as Bishop Wordsworth did, that "*Ductor Dubitantium* seems to be derived from it,"[2] is to overstate the case. Walton mentions the very extensive correspondence which Sanderson carried on with individuals upon cases of conscience. On the Puritan side, Baxter's *Christian Directory* attempted to cover every problem with which a minister might be confronted, whether in theology or the practical direction of souls. Possibly because Puritanism was strong among the merchant class, Baxter shows himself particularly well aware of the difficulties which are apt to arise between masters and servants, and buyers and sellers.[3] But with all this interest in casuistry and all this practical application of it to daily life no Protestant had attempted to provide a complete system. The mediaeval and later Roman manuals were the only full and authoritative books on the subject which were to be had. There was therefore a recognized need for a Protestant text-book. Fuller, in his *Life of Mr. Perkins*, complains:

> In case divinity Protestants are defective. For (save that a smith or two of late have built themselves forges, and set up shop) we go down to our enemies to sharpen all our instruments, and are beholden to them for offensive and defensive weapons in cases of conscience.[4]

Taylor himself says much the same thing, and uses the same Biblical illustration in his preface.[5] After mentioning by name

---

[1] London, 1659. The lectures were delivered at Oxford in the academic year 1647–8.
[2] Sanderson's *Lectures on Conscience and Human Law* (ed. Wordsworth), p. v.
[3] The Puritan interest in casuistry seems to indicate that the neglect of that study after the Restoration was not due to its supposed taint of Romanism, as is sometimes suggested, but to the lack of a pastorally-minded clergy.
[4] Fuller, *Holy State*, Bk. 11, Chap. 10, par. 4.   [5] *Works*, Vol. 9, p. v.

almost all the Protestant writers on casuistry, he goes on to acknowledge both the debt which the moral theologians of his time owed to Rome, and also to point out how unsuitable for Protestants were many of the books furnished from this source, which they were compelled to use for want of others. And because nobody else would undertake it he has essayed the task himself. He admits that his book is rather long, but even then he has not been able to do what some will expect, produce a "collective body of cases of conscience", for such cases are infinite and life is not so. Instead, he has taken for his pattern Tribonianus who made a digest of the Roman Law to fit all cases; in the same way the cases of conscience which he discusses will be found to fit all, or nearly all possible combinations of circumstances.[1] If there could be any doubt on such a subject, his words make it quite clear that he never intended his work for the general reader, but only for the director of souls. Taylor concludes his preface with words of thankfulness to God who has given him health and leisure in which to write. As his letters and Evelyn's *Diary* show, it had taken a vast amount of labour, and several times when he believed that he had got it ready for the press, he had withdrawn it again, in order to spend more effort still upon it. No wonder it had taken a long time, but it would have taken longer still, he points out, if "God by the piety of one of His servants had not provided comfortable retirement and opportunity of leisure."[2] No doubt this was Lord Conway who, if Charles II had not returned, would most probably have received the dedication.

Ductor Dubitantium is divided into four books. "The first of Conscience, the kinds of it and the general rules of conducting them; the second of Divine Laws and all collateral obligations"; the third of Human Laws; and the fourth of "the nature and cause of Good and Evil". It would have simplified his task a good deal, and made the result much clearer, if he had adopted more divisions. The first chapter begins with a definition of conscience. Taylor declares it to be "The mind of man governed by a rule, and measured by the proportions of good and evil, in order to practice; viz. to conduct all our relations, and all our intercourse between God, our neighbours, and ourselves; that is in all moral action".[3] If, in the effort to be precise, he

---

[1] *Works*, Vol. 9, p. xix.   [2] Ibid.

[3] *Works*, Vol. 9, p. 3. Cp. Sanderson, *Conscience and Human Law*, p. 2: "Conscience therefore I define in short to be, a Faculty or Habit of the Practical understanding, which enables the mind of man, by the use of reason and argument, to apply the light which it has to particular moral actions."

had not been so wordy, his meaning might have been clearer. After a general introduction he spends one chapter each in discussing the right or sure conscience, the confident or erroneous conscience, the probable or thinking conscience, the doubtful conscience and the scrupulous conscience. In all of these he is at pains to stress the paramount claims of conscience, declaring in the third chapter that it is a greater sin to do a good action against our conscience than to do an evil action in obedience to it. He is, however, careful to add that "this rule is true only in equal cases and when there is no circumstance aggravating one part".[1]

The fourth, on the probable or thinking conscience, is as might be expected, chiefly occupied with probabilism in one or other of its applications. Taylor insists that the probable conscience must make itself certain by the accumulation of such aids as it can obtain, and that where, after every effort, two courses of action lie open, the safer course must be followed. In some cases, even if the balance of probability seems to incline against what appears to be the safer course, still, safety must be sought. As an example he takes the case of gains from usury; it is, he says, safer to restore them, "but it is more probable that a man is not obliged to it. In which case the advantage lies not on that side that is more probable but on that which is more safe".[2] The reason for this, of course, is that while in the one case there may be a negative avoidance of sin, in the other there is an active virtue. In order to convince the doubting conscience, Taylor inserted in this chapter his famous "Moral Demonstration or a conjugation of probabilities proving that the religion of Jesus Christ is from God".[3] The argument, which is rather lengthy, takes the form of enumerating many of the incidents in the Incarnation, and claiming that each one of these is so remarkable in origin and result, that all of them, taken together, may be considered as cumulative proof that Jesus was divine. There is more sustained eloquence in this passage than elsewhere in *Ductor Dubitantium*.

Taylor gives a very salutary warning to one who is in doubt, against enquiring of several teachers, until he finds one who is willing to answer in the way he wants, though he concludes that there are cases, as for instance when a man is tempted to despair, when it is legitimate to go from priest to priest until one can be found who is able to give comfort on grounds that are acceptable

---

[1] *Works*, Vol. 9, p. 139.   [2] Ibid., p. 181.   [3] Ibid., pp. 156–78.

as well as right.[1] In the discussion of the doubtful conscience, Taylor illustrates his point with a little incident which may have happened to himself at Golden Grove or Mandinam:

A little child came to my door for alms, of whom I was told he was run from his mother's house and his own honest employment; but in his wandering he was almost starved; I found that if I relieved him, he would not return to his mother, if I did not relieve him, he would not be able. I considered that indeed his soul's interests were more to be regarded and secured than his body, and his sin rather to be prevented than his sickness, and therefore not to relieve him seemed at first the greater charity. But I weighed against these considerations, that his sin is uncertain, and future, and arbitrary, but his need is certain, and present, and natural; that he may choose whether he will sin or no; but he cannot in the present case choose whether he will perish, or no; that if he be not relieved he dies in his sin, but many things may intervene to reform his vicious inclination; that the natural necessity is extreme, but that he will sin is no way necessary, and hath in it no degrees of unavoidable necessity; and above all, that if he abuses my relief to evil purposes which I intended not, it is his fault not mine; but the question being concerning my duty and not his, and that therefore if I do not relieve him, the sin is also mine and not his; and that by bidding of him to do his duty I acquit myself on one side, but by bidding him be warm and fed, I cannot be acquitted on the other, I took that side which was at least equally sure and certainly more charitable.[2]

It is a pleasing picture. The beggar boy waits outside and hopes for his dinner while the moralist inside debates, with many weighty reasons for and against, whether he should give him any. The result is never in doubt, but kindliness is not allowed to prevail until it can call itself tutiorism. In the course of the same chapter on the doubtful conscience Taylor examines the extremely difficult question whether it is ever right to advise a lesser sin in order that the greater may be avoided. He gives as an instance the action of Pilate in the trial of our Lord. Pilate knew that Jesus was innocent; nevertheless, in order to save himself from being forced to crucify a just man, he proposes to satisfy the hatred of the crowd by scourging Jesus and then letting him go. Was this lawful? Taylor answers no, for Pilate's conscience was not perplexed and he had it in his power to free Jesus; but if circumstances had been different, and he had seen

[1] Taylor is much less severe on this point than Sanderson. Cp. *Concience and Human Law* (ed. Wordsworth), The Third Prelection, *passim*.
[2] *Works*, Vol. 9, p. 229.

the Jews absolutely insisting on some punishment so that to
save Jesus utterly was out of his power, then the suggestion of
scourging would have been lawful as a means of preventing the
crucifixion.[1] In the last chapter of this book, that on the scrupulous conscience, he defines a scruple as "a great trouble of mind
proceeding from a little motive",[2] and his best advice to one
disturbed in this fashion is to rely on the judgement of a prudent
guide.

Having dealt so very fully with the act of judging and applying
laws, Taylor now feels himself free to go on and discuss law
itself. In spite of, or possibly because of, many words it is not very
easy to find out what Taylor meant by the law of nature, the
part of his subject with which he opens his second book. He says
it is "the law of mankind, concerning common necessities, to
which we are inclined by nature, invited by consent, prompted
by reason".[3] It is incumbent upon us solely by the command of
God, who alone can dispense us from it. The two chief bands of
this law are punishment and love. As, perhaps, is to be expected,
there is more of his old strain of eloquence in discussing the appeal
and power of holy love than there is in other parts of this work.
But although to love virtue for virtue's sake is a noble thing, it
does not, as Taylor is careful to point out, put all idea of a
reward out of the question. The man who "serves God for hope
of glory, loves goodness for goodness' sake, for he pursues the
interest of goodness that he may be filled with goodness, he
serves God here that he may serve Him hereafter, he does it
well that he may do it better, a little while that he may do it
over again for ever and ever. Nothing else can be loving virtue
for virtue's sake; this is the greatest perfection and most reasonable and practical sense of doing it."[4] Rewards of a right kind
must be a proper inducement to the service of God, for if they
were not, the Bible would not be so full of gracious promises.
Christianity perfectly comprehends the law of nature in itself
as it does all that is of perpetual obligation in the law of Moses.
Taylor is willing to admit that there are some situations which,
at first sight do not seem to be provided for by the law of Christ.

[1] *Works*, Vol. 9, p. 239. Cp. Sanderson, *Conscience and Human Law* (ed. Wordsworth),
p. 50: "I observe thirdly that if two sins are proposed to a person's choice, and he is
persuaded in his conscience that both of them are really sins, he ought to make
choice of neither but to avoid both."

[2] *Works*, Vol. 9, p. 262.

[3] Ibid., p. 279. For the first two chapters of this book, Taylor drew largely on
Selden's *De Jure Naturali*.

[4] *Works*, Vol. 9, p. 317.

War is such a one. But, he quickly adds, Christianity has nothing to say about war as such, because it aims at making war impossible by uprooting all the seeds of it in individuals. If men be subject to Christ's law they can never go to war with each other, if they do so they are at once in revolt. Such a one, beginning his act of aggression, cannot ask how he may conduct it in accordance with morality since he is engaged in a completely immoral act. The innocent party is not forbidden by the law of God to defend himself. If it be a citizen or group of citizens within the State that is suffering in this way, then an appeal to the laws must be made; if it be a commonwealth, then it must defend itself by force, for it is necessary to protect the laws and what is necessary is lawful. Taylor's rules are excellent, except for modern wars where both parties are vociferously innocent on their own showing.

In addition to the law of nature and equally binding for ever upon all persons, there are certain superinduced laws given by Christ himself and from these there can be no dispensation. It would seem that Taylor not only considered Holy Orders to be of divine origin but held that the ritual bestowal of them was an intrinsic part, for he notices the claims of some Roman theologians that the Pope can "with one word and without all solemnity consecrate a priest or a bishop", he concludes that these pretensions are "insolent and strange".[1] In the same passage, during a further consideration of the Pope's dispensing power, he examines the case of a man who has solemnly vowed himself to a woman and then changed his mind and wished to enter a monastery. Taylor supposes that the Pope would give him a dispensation to do so and holds that such an action would be wrong, unless it could be clearly proved that a celibate life in religion is better than holy matrimony, a thing which Taylor refuses to believe.

Human laws, while not absolutely binding, are yet in most circumstances obligatory upon men's consciences whether they have been accepted by them or not. Only when they are not just or good can they be set aside, or if they are founded upon a false presumption. Neither do they compel us to an active obedience if to obey would involve us in some moral evil, or place us in some danger of death which had not been envisaged by the law-giver. But, "the supreme power can command the curate of souls to attend a cure in the time of a plague, to go to sea in a storm, to

[1] *Works*, Vol. 9, p. 560.

stand in a breach for the defence of an army".[1] In these cases the danger of death is of the essence of the law; it was indeed made because it was necessary for the risk of death to be run. This leads on to a discussion of how far a man may defend himself from the penalties of the law, or from any other danger, by a lie. Taylor affirms unhesitatingly that lying is in all instances wrong, but an ingenious definition which he supplies allows him a good many opportunities of providing for hard cases. "Lying is to be understood to be something said or written to the hurt of our neighbour, which cannot be understood otherwise than to differ from the mind of him that speaks."[2] This would seem to make a lie which was told to save someone from danger, or a subterfuge which could possibly be made to fit the "mind of him that speaks", properly no lie. Taylor grounds the obligation to speak the truth upon a universal contract, implied in all discourses, that the persons engaged will faithfully declare their mind. Children and madmen, because they have no power to distinguish true from false, have no right to the truth, provided that the lie told to them is charitable and useful. Taylor has sometimes been taken to task for not allowing the full right of children to the truth, but it is doubtful if he meant more than to allow that it is right to use harmless deceptions with children at times; even the most scrupulous do not always think it necessary to point out that there is a pill in the jam. The similar contention, that madmen may be deceived for their own good, he illustrated in an earlier part of his work with an odd story of a man who imagined himself to be the prophet Elijah and under an obligation to fast, whose life was saved by the doctor sending him "a fellow dressed like and angel" who bad him rise and eat.[3]

As soon as he begins to treat of the spheres in which Church and State operate, Taylor shows an Erastianism unexpectedly complete. Kings, he says, must be supreme in religion or they are but half kings at best, for the affairs of religion are more than half the interests of mankind. The civil power is supreme in all causes, ecclesiastical as well as secular, for under no circumstance is it lawful for a subject to rebel or take up arms against it. In the matter of excommunication, the bishop can be restrained in

[1] *Works*, Vol. 10, p. 37. Cp. Sanderson, *Conscience and Human Law* (ed. Wordsworth), The Fifth Prelection, *passim*. After discussing the question very carefully in a manner rather more academic than Taylor's, he concludes "that whenever a law forbids what is so simply necessary that it cannot be omitted without sin, or commands what is so unjust that it cannot be obeyed without sin, that law does not lay any obligation upon the conscience", ibid., p. 129.
[2] *Works*, Vol. 10, p. 102.   [3] Ibid., Vol. 9, p. 254.

O

the exercise of this part of his spiritual authority "if there be anything in it of temporal concernment".[1] Considering the close texture of modern life, which allows so little separation of interests, it would seem that excommunication is a weapon which the Church has for ever lost. The power of the Church, Taylor insists again and again, is solely spiritual. She may make laws which bind the conscience, but until they have been accepted by the State they can only bind those who are willing to submit to them. After the civil power has accepted them, their enforcement is on a different footing, for since they are now ordinances of the commonwealth even the wicked are compelled to obey them. In this case they become of double obligation to the Christian. The ancient canons of the Church oblige the conscience only in so far as they are accepted by the modern Church, but all that is of divine institution is perpetually obligatory. The mere fact that a custom is laudable, and in use in modern times, does not give it power over the conscience unless it is formally accepted by the Church to which the person belongs. No Church can bind the consciences of any but its own members; the Pope, for instance, has no power except over those of his own communion. Taylor saw the modern Church as a collection of national or provincial churches, each one of them catholic in so far as they held to the apostolic teaching.

Taylor occupies Chapter V of Book III in asserting the absolute sway, qualified only by what is owed to God, of the father's authority over his children. Chapter VI is an enquiry where the power to dispense or abrogate human laws may lie. Laws become obsolete when the reason for which they were made ceases, or when the power that made them abrogates them. Whether they have been accepted by the people or not makes no difference since the prime source of power is not in the people:

As a law hath not its beginning so neither can it have its perpetuity dependently upon them; and no man thinks it hath but he who supposes the supreme power to be originally in the people, and in the King by trust; and there are too many to think that, for there have been so many democratical governments that many wise men have said so, because then they had reason, but so many popular governments have also produced popular opinions, which being too much received even by wise men, have still given the people occasion to talk so still, and to very many to believe them.[2]

[1] *Works*, Vol. 10, p. 314.　　[2] Ibid., p. 540.

The republican theories of his time had made no impression on Taylor. The uttermost relief he will allow is to say that if the letter of the law is burdensome, and unjust, then the spirit of it only obliges the conscience. In matters of this sort political theorists nowadays would not see eye to eye with Taylor. His views on the ethics of contracts would no doubt be more popular. His opinion of human nature is not over-exalted, but there is common sense in it. In business arrangements of this kind "we must suppose that the contractor did intend that sense that is the wariest, because that is the most likely; nothing being so reasonable as to think the man intended that which all the world does, that is, to buy cheap and sell dear. If this will not" settle our difficulty "then we must run to the custom of the country".[1] As usual, Taylor illustrates his meaning with a case or two.

The last book of *Ductor Dubitantium* is the shortest, yet it is in many ways the most interesting. In it Taylor discusses "the efficient causes of all human action, good or evil".[2] He finds this in the will, for which he claims entire freedom: "God intending to be glorified by our true obedience hath set before us good and evil; we may put our hand to which we will; only what we choose that shall be our portion."[3] In the rest of this section he stresses as vigorously as ever he had done in *Unum Necessarium* the necessity of free will in men if God is to be considered a moral Being. And the same doctrine, he asserts, brings emancipation to men; for nothing external to ourselves can ultimately determine our fate. It matters nothing whether we are born illegitimate, or of evil parents, or whether we suffer injustice from other men, "God will judge us according to our works, not according to his or any man's else, or by any measures but by his own law and our obedience".[4] Obviously the man who wrote *Unum Necessarium* was still unrepentant of his supposed heresies. Taylor's dealing with the everyday moral problems of his time was very human. To the question whether the host sins when he provides the wine on which his guests get drunk, he replies that though for our guests we should "do something more than ordinary, yet our greatest care should be for ourselves, that we do nothing which may misbecome the house of one of Christ's servants".[5] We ought therefore to provide all that is necessary for hospitality, but nothing which may abuse it. On the old problem of betting and gambling, which was as hotly debated

---

[1] *Works*, Vol. 10, p. 508.   [2] Ibid., p. 548.   [3] Ibid., p. 548.
[4] Ibid., p. 555.   [5] Ibid., p. 581.

by the moralists of his day as it is in ours, Taylor again takes up what might be called the man-in-the-street's point of view:

That cards and dice are of themselves lawful I do not know any reason to doubt. For if they be unlawful, it is because they are forbidden, or because there is in them something that is forbidden. They are nowhere of themselves forbidden: and what is in them that is criminal or suspicious? Is it because there is chance and contingency in them? There is so in all human affairs; in merchandize, in laying wagers, in all consultations and wars, in journeys and agriculture, in teaching and learning, in putting children to school or keeping them at home, in the price of the market and the vendibility of commodities. And if it be said that there is in all these things an overruling providence; though no man can tell in what manner or by what means the divine providence brings such things to a determinate event, yet it is certain that every little thing as well as every great thing is under God's government, and our reactions as well as our wages. But what if it be, and what if it be not? He can never be suspected in any criminal sense to tempt the divine providence, who by contingent things recreates his labour, and having acquired his refreshment, hath no other end to serve, and no desires to engage the divine providence to any other purpose; and this end is sufficiently secured by whatsoever happens. I know nothing else that can be pretended to render the nature of these things suspicious; and this is perfectly nothing.[1]

As will be seen Taylor looks at the matter purely from the point of view of those who play moderately, and can afford to lose. The effects of gambling as a habit upon individuals and ultimately on the nation as a whole is beyond his ken. Yet it is to gambling as a social evil, undermining thrift and transferring property without adequate return that it is most often objected to in these days.[2] But Taylor is willing to admit that there are evil appendages to this as to every other kind of sport, yet he considers that these lie chiefly in immoderate use, and a Christian, who in everything remembers the duty which he owes to God, will not be likely to fall into them.

It was natural that at the end of so vast a work the author should be aware of the task which he had accomplished. Taylor concludes with the words *Nomini Tuo Da Gloriam*, and he never seems to have doubted that glory would accrue. In fact the success it met with was reasonable but not overwhelming. There were

---

[1] *Works*, Vol. 10, p. 592.
[2] Cp. W. Temple, *Personal Religion and the Life of Fellowship*, p. 43: "The fundamental objection to gambling is that it is a distribution of wealth on the basis of chance, and that is socially unwholesome."

four editions of it printed between 1660 and 1696. A book of the same scope would be thought to have done very well nowadays if it were printed as often.

Because some of the cases cited in *Ductor Dubitantium* are by no means pleasant, Taylor has been accused of a certain "perduration of mind", and his great familiarity with the classics is given as the cause.[1] But such a criticism entirely leaves out of account the object with which the book was written. Physicians of souls have unfortunately to deal with as many disgusting cases as physicians of bodies and Taylor, who aimed at a textbook which would meet every need the casuist has, would have entirely failed in his purpose if he had refused to consider certain sins merely because the treatment of them did not afford nice reading. If religion be real it must often handle things which are revolting. Taylor's age probably had no more moral turpitude than our own, but it did state itself more plainly. His long experience as a confessor had given him a peculiarly wide acquaintance with the sins and difficulties of his times, and it is not its least value that *Ductor Dubitantium* shows us what these were. Hallam offered a deeper and more pertinent criticism. "Taylor", he says, "seems too much inclined to side with those who resolve all right and wrong into the positive will of God." Taylor would have been the first to admit that since God is the source of all reason his acts spring from reason, and therefore the motives which underlie his commands may, to some extent, be sought out and comprehended by man. But when he wrote *Ductor Dubitantium*, Taylor's aim was not so much to discover principles, as to offer a trustworthy guide which depended upon a consensus of opinion and experience.

Casuists still quote Taylor's conclusions with respect and it is probable that they will continue to do so. His book was founded upon an extensive personal experience in the conduct of souls, and upon extraordinarily wide reading in the best casuistical literature of all ages. Although Taylor's splendid gift of prose is not so evident in this as in some of his other works, it is still present, here and there, in sufficient quantity to encourage the reader at least to turn over the pages in search of it. The greatest fault of the whole book, and the one which has done it most harm, is its length. This could easily have been avoided if Taylor had controlled himself a little more and paid more attention to method. Dr Kirk complains that "*Ductor Dubitantium* is erudite,

[1] Gosse, *Jeremy Taylor*, p. 166.

tortuous and garrulous, and its author's promise to 'avoid all questions which are curious and unprofitable' and to give rules 'whereby a wise guide of souls will be enabled to answer most cases which shall occur' is altogether forgotten in a maze of discussion, illustration and digression".[1] This is true, but in spite of so heavy a drawback, no one who is interested in either Jeremy Taylor or casuistry will wish to leave *Ductor Dubitantium* unread.

[1] K. E. Kirk, *Conscience and Its Problems*, p. 205.

CHAPTER IX

THE REORGANIZATION OF TRINITY COLLEGE, DUBLIN

CHARLES II did not live up to the expectations which the Presbyterians, at least, conceived of him at Breda and at his first coming home. There is a good deal to be said for him. Parliament and people showed such loyalty that it was hard for him to be kind to those who were reckoned his, and the Church's, enemies. It was perhaps too much to expect that Charles would risk popularity of this easily acquired sort on behalf of men who, though they had welcomed him back, had undoubtedly helped to drive him out. Neither did his personal predilections lead him to offend the Loyalists, in this matter at least. Charles liked Anglicans better than Presbyterians, and he probably liked Roman Catholics better than either. If he had any religion of his own it was nothing more than a hesitant deism. As the chief of a state in which Anglicanism was the established religion he attended the services of the English Church and listened to its sermons, though he liked them plain and short. But the all-pervading loyalty transformed even this last, quite human characteristic, into an exhibition of superior taste, springing from the high principles of art which the King had learned in France, and from the royal fancy the simplification in sermon style, which became marked about this time, was supposed to derive.[1]

When so many of Taylor's old friends were receiving English bishoprics it might have been expected that one would be found for him. His reputation for learning was as great as any, he had never wavered in his devotion to Church and King, he had suffered for his loyalty, and he had sufficient friends with influence to expect that his name would be brought forward at an opportune moment. Yet his chances of preferment were much more slight than he probably realized. After the shocks administered to orthodoxy, first by *The Liberty of Prophesying* and then by *Unum Necessarium*, those in authority considered him unsafe. Sheldon,

[1] Burnet, *History of His Own Times*, Vol. 1, p. 267. No doubt the King's taste had its influence, but the simplification of sermon style was only a part of a general movement for simplicity manifesting itself throughout all English literature at this time.

writing in August 1667, when the news of Taylor's death had just reached him, referred to him as "a man of dangerous temper, apt to break out into extravagances",[1] and no doubt this was what he thought of him in 1660. Such an opinion in such a man would be fatal to all chance of English preferment; because after the Restoration, though Juxon was nominally Archbishop of Canterbury, he was too old to exercise much real authority, and all effective power was in the hands of Sheldon. There was no open breach, and Taylor on his side does not seem to have been aware that there was any cause for reserve between them; but Sheldon was running no risks. It is ironic in the sequel that *The Liberty of Prophesying* and *Unum Necessarium*, the two greatest proofs we have of the width of Taylor's charity, should have caused lasting distrust of him in his friends. Taylor was given a bishopric, but it was an Irish one. On 6 August 1660, the King nominated him under the privy seal to the diocese of Down and Connor. A little later the Duke of Ormonde, who was now once more Chancellor of Trinity College, Dublin, recommended him for the Vice-Chancellorship. Perhaps Taylor received less than he might be thought to have deserved, but in spite of its general low standard, the Irish Church had been served by some famous men. Ussher and Bramhall, to mention only two among its seventeenth-century bishops, have their names among the greatest. Taylor was not dishonoured when sent to join their company. There were, of course, obvious reasons why he should be made Bishop of Down and Connor. His residence in the district had given him a knowledge of the conditions prevailing there; Colonel Hill and Sir George Rawdon would like to have a man whom they already knew and respected for their neighbour.[2]

Ireland at the Reformation produced no outstanding figures similar to those of England and Scotland. Whatever reforms came to that country arrived from the Government in London and did not greatly recommend themselves on that account.[3] The Englishmen who went over in Elizabeth's day carried their theological opinions with them, but little effort was spent in

---

[1] Carte MSS., fol. 222.

[2] Heber ("Life", *Works*, Vol. 1, p. xciii) building on the fantastic story attributed to Lady Wray that Joanna Bridges was a natural daughter of Charles I, suggests that possibly the fact of her union with Taylor had something to do with it, since the King would not wish the pious husband of his half-sister to be near enough to see and reprove his vices. But it may be doubted whether a possible rebuke in the future for sins he had not yet committed would influence Charles to that extent.

[3] "Historical Collections of the Church of Ireland", *Harleian Misc.*, Vol. 5, p. 600.

trying to convert the natives; therefore the majority of the people remained devoted, if ignorant, Roman Catholics, ready to receive the Jesuit missionaries which the Counter-Reformation brought over. Spenser attributed the slow progress of the Reformation in Ireland to the perpetual disturbances there. It was, he said, "an ill time to preach amongst swords".[1] Yet he also drew attention to the poverty of the livings, the remoteness and insecurity of habitation which discouraged respectable men from coming over from England, and above all the fact that none of the Protestant ministers who had any ability understood Irish. The truth was that Anglicans and Presbyterians were too busy settling their respective differences at home to have able men to spare for Ireland. With the noble exception of Bishop Bedell, no one made any attempt to reach the people in their own language. Bedell learned Irish himself and wrote a grammar of it; he corrected a version of the Old Testament in Irish; in his day, though it had been long in coming about, the New Testament and the Prayer Book had both been translated, and he did his best to promote Irish-speaking priests to the livings in his gift. But in spite of this one admirable effort, the history of the Irish Church for many years is one gloomy story of war, neglect, robbery, and wretched incompetence.

When Bramhall went to Ireland in 1633 he wrote to Laud an account of what he found there:

In Dublin we find our parochial church converted to the Lord Deputy's stable, a second to a nobleman's dwelling house, the quire of a third to a tennis court and the vicar acts the keeper. In Christ Church, the principal church in Ireland, whither the Lord Deputy and the Council repair every Sunday, the vaults, from one end of the minster to the other, are made into tippling rooms for beer, wine and tobacco, demised all to Popish recusants, and by them and others so much frequented in time of Divine Service, that though there is no danger of blowing up the assembly above their heads, yet there is of poisoning them with fumes. The table used for the administration of the Blessed Sacrament in the midst of the choir, made an ordinary seat for maids and apprentices.[2]

He goes on to report that the clergy are below all contempt for poverty and ignorance. One bishop held three and twenty benefices with cure, and the Earl of Cork had obtained the "whole Bishopric of Lismore at the rent of forty shillings or five

[1] Spenser, "View of the Present State of Ireland", *Works* (Globe ed.), p. 646.
[2] Bramhall, *Works*, Vol. 1, p. lxxix.

marks by the year".[1] Bramhall mentions the vigorous measures
which Wentworth had put into execution to try to remedy
this appalling condition, and Bramhall himself was behind them
all. On his side, Wentworth, also writing to Laud, drew a picture
as gloomy as Bramhall's. The clergy were ignorant and without
any of the outward appearance of ministers. The churches and
parsonages were in ruins, the people untaught, and in many
cases without hope of teaching, since their clergy were non-
resident. Where the services were said, they were run over
without decency of habit, order, or gravity. Some of the clergy
had wives and children who were recusants. Most of the incum-
bents were wretchedly paid and consequently tried to hold as
many livings as they could possibly get into their clutches. In
Ulster at the time of the Plantation things were as bad as any-
where. Often there had been no service for years together. There
was the old story of bishops holding livings *in commendam*, or by
sequestration, and making no attempt to provide for the people.
There were but very few in the whole land who seemed to feel
any responsibility for the souls of the native Irish.[2]

In 1615 a convocation of the clergy was held at Dublin which
set itself the task of providing a series of articles embodying
reformed principles for the Church of Ireland. Up to that time
Mathew Parker's eleven articles had been the only legal confession
of faith; in Ireland they were twelve in number. In their place
was now substituted a list of 104, grouped under nine heads.
They were mainly the work of Ussher, and were based on the
articles of 1559—which had been in use—those of 1562, and the
Lambeth Articles. They were violently Calvinistic and anti-papal,
and they did not contain any reference to clerical orders or any
form of ordination. Apparently no one was compelled to subscribe
to these articles, though silence and deprivation was the punishment provided by the Convocation for anyone who openly laughed
at them. They lasted more or less unchallenged until 1634, when
it was proposed in the Irish Convocation that the English articles
and canons should be adopted by the Irish Church. The scheme
met with Ussher's strenuous opposition, chiefly on the ground that
to accept the proposal would derogate from their position as a
national Church. Bramhall was eager for their adoption. The

---

[1] Bramhall, *Works*, Vol. 1, p. lxxxi. Ussher, who was appointed to the see of Meath
and Clonmacnoise in February 1620/1, in his Certificate of the State of the Diocese,
issued 22 May 1622, gave an equally depressing account of the Church in his
jurisdiction. Elrington, *Life of Ussher*, Appendix v.

[2] Wentworth, *State Letters*, Vol. 1, p. 187. Also Carte, *Life of Ormonde*, Vol. 1, p. 68.

canons were rejected, although in November 1634 the articles were accepted mainly because of Strafford's vigorous insistence. The Irish articles were never formally repealed, it was hoped that if they were neither affirmed nor denied they would in time quietly die out. Undoubtedly Bramhall and Laud considered them to be suspended; but one or two of the bishops, notably Bedell of Kilmore, are said to have insisted on a double subscription though the point has been disputed.[1] If they did, it was only in a few cases and the practice soon died out.

This insistence on a less Calvinistic standard of doctrine was only one sign of the interest which Charles I, and his servants Strafford and Laud, took in the affairs of the Irish Church. The King issued a royal letter against abuses, in 1633 he made a royal visitation, he encouraged education and appointed better bishops. A commission was issued for the repair of church buildings, and Parliament passed several Acts for the betterment of church finances. With the King's full support behind them, the three men, Strafford, Laud, and Bramhall, had done great things for the restoration of religion in Ireland when the rebellion of 1641 and the subsequent wars came and nullified their efforts.[2] During and immediately after that time, conditions could do nothing but grow worse. The desperate slaughter which characterized the rebellion led to an irremediable hatred between settlers and natives—that is to say, between Protestants and Roman Catholics. Archbishop Ussher returned to England and stayed there until his death in 1656. Bramhall, apart from one visit to Ireland in 1648/9, was also an absentee from the outbreak of the Civil War until the Restoration. With Anglican clergymen proscribed and persecuted, nothing could be done for the distressed Irish Church from the English side, and there were neither men nor means to help in Ireland herself. But in 1660, with the Restoration an accomplished fact, it looked as if all good things were soon to come. Ormonde, who had left his post as Lord Lieutenant in 1650, came into authority again

---

[1] "There was no thought of two distinct standards at that time. And if any Bishop had been known to have required any man to have subscribed to the Irish articles after the English were received and authorized under the great seal of Ireland, he would have been called to account for it." Bramhall, "Discourse of the Sabbath", *Works*, Vol. 5, p. 81. Heylyn in his *History of the Sabbath*, Chap. 8, par. 9, and again in his *Life of Laud*, pt. 2, pp. 271–4, asserted that the Irish articles were called in, which occasioned an angry dispute with Bernard, Ussher's biographer. A case instanced by Bernard in which Bedell is supposed to have examined Thomas Price on the Irish articles, when conferring priest's orders on him, must have occurred before 1634, since at that date Price was Archdeacon of Kilmore.

[2] Phillips (ed.), *History of the Church of Ireland*, Vol. 3, Chap. 1, *passim*.

automatically as soon as the King's return was certain.[1] His
resumption of power meant that Anglicanism would be restored
in Ireland. Although the Presbyterians made some efforts to
state a case for themselves, the feeling of the gentry was definitely
in favour of episcopacy. No law had been passed to do away
either with the office of a bishop or with the liturgy while
Ormonde had been away; consequently, his first act was to
recommend that the vacant sees should be filled with the best
men available. Since the death of Ussher there had been no
Primate of all Ireland. Now Bramhall, who since 1634 had been
Bishop of Derry, was chosen for that preferment. He was an old
man, but he had struggled bravely to reform the Church of
Ireland in earlier years, and he had all the courage necessary to
begin the work again. How much of all this depressing history
Taylor knew it is hard to say. He had lived in the country for
some years, and therefore it could not have been entirely unknown.
One thing can be said with certainty, he was aware that he would
meet with bitter opposition from the Presbyterians from the very
first moment of his appointment.

When Ulster was planted in 1609 a good proportion of the
settlers were Scots. They were not men of remarkably high
moral standards and at first they had very little religion among
them.[2] But when episcopacy was restored in Scotland there were
a good many Presbyterian ministers in that country who could
not reconcile their consciences to it, and these left their homes
and began evangelistic work among their countrymen in the
North of Ireland. They were devoted, and many of them able,
men as well as unflinching believers in the divine right of
presbyters. Soon they were one of the strongest influences in the
colony. With such a history of self-sacrificing and continuous
opposition to episcopacy, extending over half a century, the
Presbyterians of Ulster were not likely to accept any bishop
willingly, no matter how learned and holy he might be. They did
their best to prevent one being sent over to them. First they held
a large synod at Ballymena with all the presbyters in North of
Ireland present.[3] Patrick Adair, one of their leaders who had
just come back from Dublin, gave them an account of the state
of affairs there. He had managed to get them warrants to receive
their tithes for that year and the next, until the bishops were
established. The brethren solemnly considered what might be

---

[1] He was not formally reappointed until 4 November 1661.
[2] Dunlop, *History of Ireland*, p. 90.   [3] Adair, *True Narrative*, p. 241.

their duty at this juncture, and, as a second step in their opposition, decided to send two of their number to the King with an address. "They humbly reminded His Majesty of God's wonderful dealing with him in his preservation and restoration, on which they heartily congratulated him; but withal, they humbly petitioned the settling of religion according to the rule of Reformation against Popery, Prelacy, heresy, etc., according to the covenant."[1] Everybody signed the address, and it was taken to London by the hands of Mr Richardson of Killeagh, and Mr Keyes of Belfast. Keyes was chosen chiefly because he was an Englishman. The deputation started in May 1660, but the nearer they got to England the lower their hopes sank. When they arrived in London they went first to Sir John Clotworthy, who, as an Irish Presbyterian magnate, was their natural patron. He took them to see Drs Calamy, Ashe, and Manton; they at once told the deputation that "the plainness of the address, for the covenant and against prelates, would make it unacceptable to the court".[2] Richardson and Keyes hardly knew what to do. They had no authority to alter the address, but they wanted to get an interview with the King. Matters were complicated still more by the fact that bishops had already been nominated to the Irish sees, and some of them were getting ready to go to their new duties. Quick as the Presbyterians had been, they had not been quick enough. The deputation went the rounds of everybody who might be expected to help them: Lord Manchester, Lord Broghill, and Mr Annesley; and at last, after a good deal of difficulty, they managed to see General Monk, the new Duke of Albemarle. He would have nothing to do with the address, but told them that if they would petition the King he would help them. His advice was taken. Mention of the covenant and prelacy was dropped.

After that all went well. The deputation was introduced to the King and their expurgated address was read by Mr Annesley. Charles listened with "an awful, majestical countenance",[3] but he spoke kindly to the delegation and told them that he had appointed a deputy for Ireland who would be their friend, and that he would give him the royal commands concerning them.[4] The two ministers went back to Ireland, not feeling very pleased

---

[1] Adair, *True Narrative*, p. 241.   [2] Ibid., p. 242.   [3] Ibid., p. 243.

[4] John, second Baron Robertes, 1606–85. Colonel in Essex's army and a strong Presbyterian. At the Restoration he was made Lord Deputy of Ireland, but he exchanged the office for that of Lord Privy Seal. On Ormonde's recall in 1669 he was appointed Lord Lieutenant of Ireland, but was recalled in the following year. Created Earl of Radnor, 1679.

about their mission and uneasy about the reception which awaited them with their brethren. They had indeed seen the King, which was more than another Irish Presbyterian delegation had managed to do, but they had accomplished nothing else The deputy whom the King said would be their friend was never sent. Richardson and Keyes' fears were realized; they got more blame for leaving out the covenant and prelacy than praise for seeing the King. The Presbyterians saw clearly that their effort had failed. Taylor must have been well aware of the presence of this deputation in London, and the knowledge that such strong efforts were being made in opposition to episcopacy among his new flock can hardly have cheered him to his task. It is essential to an understanding of the situation which afterwards developed to realize that antagonism to bishops in Down and Connor was deep-rooted and irreconcilable from the start. The Presbyterians there would not be placated with concessions which might have satisfied Baxter and Calamy in England. Episcopacy in itself was hateful and nothing could make it otherwise.

Before leaving for Ireland, Taylor handed to Royston the manuscript of his next book, *The Worthy Communicant*, and this was published in the late summer of 1660. Taylor dedicated his book to Princess Mary of Orange.[1] This lady, whose court in Holland had been a refuge for so many of the exiled Royalists, was in the summer of 1660 expected to come over to England to share in her brother's triumph. She did not actually arrive until 30 September, and by that time Taylor had gone back to Ireland. But although he had probably never met her personally he was not unknown to her, since he thanks her for the great honour she had done him in "reading and using divers of my books".[2] It was on account of the notice she had taken of his previous writings that "he made bold" to offer her the dedication of this one. It was not his intention this time to write a controversial book, he wished "not to dispute but to persuade; not to confute anyone, but to instruct those who need; not to make a noise but to incite devotion".[3] But since he intended to produce a manual of instruction it was necessary first to lay down the theological assumptions upon which his practical direction would be based. This he does quite briefly in the first chapter

[1] Princess Royal of England and Princess of Orange, 1631–60. A very beautiful and able woman. Eldest daughter of Charles I and Queen Henrietta. Mother of William III of England. Visited England at the Restoration and died there of smallpox
[2] *Works*, Vol. 8, p. 4.
[3] Ibid., p. 9.

His point of view is unchanged since the time when he wrote *The Real Presence*. The bread and wine are "symbols and sacraments" of Christ's natural body; "not to be or to convey that natural body to us, but to do more and better for us, to convey all the blessings and graces procured for us by the breaking of that body".[1] Taylor uses all his magnificent powers of language to express the overwhelming veneration which he has for the Blessed Sacrament, and his deep sense of its necessity to Christians. By means of it our faith is increased. It is of "great efficacy for the remission of sins",[2] not because of any formal power, but because it is "the ministry of Christ's death". "It is the greatest solemnity of prayer, the most powerful liturgy and means of impetration[3] in this world."[4] By means of it our bodies "are made capable of the resurrection to life and eternal glory".[5] These and similar expressions occur on almost every page.

Taylor's purpose in writing was to teach Christians how to receive this Sacrament worthily. According to his usual method when composing devotional books Taylor ends every chapter with a collection of prayers suitable for those who wish to apply the lessons which have just been taught. Many of them are of great beauty; all breathe the most intense sincerity, a feeling more easily conveyed in these intercessions than in some others of Taylor's writing because the style is less florid. The second chapter deals with self-examination, which must not be for gross sins only, but for the smallest act of uncharity; to the end that we may come to the Sacrament, if not without sin, then at least cherishing none. To effect this our examination must not content itself with the interval between this and the last Communion, but must spread over our whole life, and establish itself in a continual state of watchfulness against sin. But it must continually be borne in mind that self-examination deals only with the negative side of preparation; there must be the positive possession of faith, charity, and repentance before "we can ever approach to these divine mysteries with worthiness or depart with joy".[6]

This necessity for faith leads Taylor on to the enquiry whether infants, innocents, fools, and madmen may be admitted to the Holy Communion. He concludes that, as no command has been given, the practice of the Church must be our guide. The early Church communicated infants, the later Church did not, and

---

[1] *Works*, Vol. 8, p. 25.   [2] Ibid., p. 35.
[3] Impetration, from *impetro* = to accomplish, effect.
[4] *Works*, Vol. 8, p. 37.   [5] Ibid., p. 40.   [6] Ibid., p. 87.

there is reason on both sides. Therefore the best we can do is to obey the commands which our own Church lays upon us. In the other cases mentioned the priest must use his own judgement. But it must ever be kept in mind that all who come must not only have faith but also that faith must issue in good works. In the actual reception of the Blessed Sacrament itself the office of faith is not to contradict the evidence of sense, but so to enlighten the heart that "it tastes more than the tongue does but nothing against it".[1] This faith is entirely necessary to the reception of the Sacrament. "For unless a man be a member of Christ, unless Christ dwells in him by a living faith, he does not eat the bread which came down from Heaven."[2] Taylor closes this chapter with a meditation and prayer of St Bernard and a confession of faith from the Clementine Liturgy.

The chapter which follows deals with forgiveness and is mainly occupied with the discussion of seven different cases of conscience all of them bearing on this duty. A similar method is followed in the chapter on repentance. With his usual insistence on practical religion Taylor is at pains to point out again and again that repentance is hardly worthy of the name until it has resulted in changed deeds.

The Blessed Sacrament should be received frequently. "It is without peradventure very much better to receive it every day than every week; and better every week than every month." Only for the very gravest reasons ought a Christian to abstain from frequent Communion, and only those who are excommunicated or publicly known to be guilty of grave and unrepented sin are to be refused. Taylor had no doubts about the usefulness of private confession, not only for the removal of these greater obstacles, but also as a normal part of preparation. "Concerning this thing I shall never think it fit to dispute, for there is nothing to enforce it but enough to persuade it; but he that tries will find the benefit of it himself, and will be best able to tell it to all the world."[4]

No one can read this book without being impressed by the solemnity of spirit with which Taylor approached the altar. That he was a popular writer, and this book a popular manual, says a great deal for the spiritual earnestness of our ancestors. It is humiliating for those who like to think that religion has at least grown in depth in these last 250 years to compare this with the little books of theological colouring matter which are supposed

[1] *Works*, Vol. 8, p. 106.   [2] Ibid., p. 114.   [3] Ibid., p. 184.   [4] Ibid., p. 205.

to supply the needed preparation for communicants today. *The Worthy Communicant* has aroused different opinions regarding the date of its composition. On the one side it has been described as hastily written in order to teach the Royalists their duty, and on the other as composed while Taylor was surreptitiously ministering in London in the days of the Commonwealth.[1] To some extent both these theories are right, for the book bears every mark of being compiled from previously existing papers. It includes cases which could easily have come from the vast collection accumulated for *Ductor Dubitantium*, sermons which might have been preached at any time when the Holy Communion was celebrated, and a brief résumé of the general line of argument used in *The Real Presence*. The summer of 1660 would not seem to have been a very propitious time for a bishop-designate to engage in serious writing. It would be a far easier task for him to occupy what leisure he had in arranging, and welding into one, some of his scattered papers. But, however it was achieved, the result is a book of devotion deep, persuasive, and sincere. The style is attractive, but as a whole it is less enriched than that which characterizes Taylor's most abundant period. It is interesting to note that the only elaborate simile the book contains occurs in what might easily be a fragment of an early sermon.[2]

Taylor's first work in Ireland was to visit the University. He began his task at once though he did not take the oaths which admitted him legally to his office until 2 January 1660/1.

Under that date he wrote to Lord Conway: "This day I am to take my oath as Vice-Chancellor of the University,[3] it is to be given me by our Chancellor and I hope we shall pass our seals speedily that I may go into the North and take care of my friends and my enemies." Conway was still continuing his generosity for Taylor thanks him because "in your most obliging letter by the last post . . . you were pleased to settle my temporal affairs by the measure of piety and charity rather than of severe justice". Conway had also given him good advice about trying to gain the friendship of Lord Massereene, one of the Presbyterian magnates in Northern Ireland, and Taylor promises that "when he comes over I will, according to your Lordship's counsel, address myself to him in a confident and affectionate way". He asks Conway to get him appointed to the Irish Privy Council, an idea which

[1] Gosse, *Jeremy Taylor*, p. 169.   [2] *Works*, Vol. 8, p. 8.
[3] Taylor never uses the name Trinity College; he always refers to it as "The University" or "The University of Dublin".

P

had originated with Conway himself, but which Taylor had not encouraged as he thought it would take him out of his diocese too much. It would, however, obviously help him in his disputes with the Presbyterians in his diocese, and since "it is already made necessary that I be sometime at Dublin in order to the University and giving degrees, at these times it will be sufficient for me to attend the council, but so I shall have countenance and reputation enabling me to do my duty comfortably".[1]

There was a great deal of work for him in Dublin. Since its foundation in Queen Elizabeth's days, Trinity College, Dublin, had suffered many vicissitudes, but it had always retained a close connection with Cambridge, and, though its teachers were predominantly Puritan, had always been remarkably tolerant in matters of religion. Bishop Bedell, who was appointed Provost in 1627, found everything in the greatest disorder, a description which occurs with ominous regularity in very many early accounts of the College. Its estates were scandalously mismanaged, it was involved in lawsuits which nobody seemed to understand, discipline was in abeyance, and when Bedell became Provost there had been no observance of religion for years. The task of reconstruction was made the more onerous by lack of any proper constitution, since although there were statutes they had never been put in order, but remained as a bundle of loose papers, some in Latin, some in English. Bedell set to work with great energy. Once more the fellows and masters were made to attend prayers. The Holy Communion was regularly celebrated again, the statutes were collected and revised, and the accounts were kept on an orderly system which began to promise the College something like solvency. One of the most striking of all Bedell's accomplishments was the introduction of Irish into the curriculum, and the day-to-day life, of the College. It has often been said, and probably with truth, that if only Bedell's labours in this direction had been continued, the Reformation might have been as successful in Ireland as it was in England and Scotland. But he was only at Trinity College for two years. In 1629 he was made Bishop of Kilmore, where his devoted life ended in the midst of the rebellion of 1641, when the chiefs of the insurgents, out of respect for his memory, fired their muskets over his grave as they shouted, "*Resquiescat in pace, ultimus anglorum*".

[1] Murray MSS.

Bedell was succeeded at Trinity College by Robert Ussher, a kinsman of the Primate. He was a conscientious man, but too weak to govern the unruly elements which Bedell had controlled. He tried to keep on his predecessor's work, but he was a failure, and so he was promoted to make way for a better man.[1] Then the vigorous hands of Laud took up the task of providing Trinity College with an ordered constitution. He became Chancellor in 1633. A new charter was procured from Charles I. It was narrower in its religious sympathies than the previous statutes, for by it Roman Catholics were debarred from fellowships, and the Provost was bidden to drive away all heretical or popish doctrines. None the less, Roman Catholics were admitted as students, provided that they renounced the Pope's temporal authority over the realm of England. The charter also made the government of the College considerably less democratic, but it proved its usefulness and was adhered to on the whole until modern times. At Strafford's suggestion, Laud appointed William Chappel, Milton's old tutor at Cambridge, as Provost. He was not a success. Martin, who followed him, fled to England during the rebellion of 1641, and although he came back again later on, things still continued to go to rack and ruin.[2] When Martin died, Cromwell appointed a strong Puritan, Samuel Winter, as Provost, and in 1653 Henry Cromwell became Chancellor in place of Ormonde. The times were difficult, but Winter seems honestly to have done his best for the College. Poor scholars were helped out of the Provost's own pocket, he did what he could to promote the study of Irish and mathematics, and tried to get the chronically involved finances straight. But when at the Restoration Ormonde came back to power again, Winter and his associates were dismissed, and Jeremy Taylor was appointed Vice-Chancellor, with Thomas Seele as Provost, the first graduate of the College to hold that office. Taylor thus became heir to the thirty years of perpetually changing government and unsuccessful attempts at reform which have been sketched.

By 3 October Taylor had completed a preliminary survey of his task, for on that day he sent a first report to Ormonde. "I found", he writes, "all things in a perfect disorder indeed so great as can be imagined consequent to a sad war, and an evil

[1] Anthony Martin, appointed provost of Trinity College, Dublin, 1641. He was Bishop of Meath from 1625 until his death of the plague in Dublin, 1650. See Ware, *Works*, Vol. 1, "Irish Bishops".
[2] Dixon, *Trinity College, Dublin*, pp. 1-51.

incompetent government set over them."[1] To call Winter evil
and incompetent was not very just. The greatest obstacle to
reform was that no one now on the staff of the College had any
lawful right to his place. Taylor says "there is indeed a heap of
men and boys, but no body of a college, no one member, either
fellow or scholar, having any legal title to his place but thrust
in by tyranny and chance".[2] According to the College statutes
no election could be made except by the provost and four senior
fellows. Taylor proposed to remedy this situation by obtaining
from Ormonde authority for himself, the Provost, and the
Archbishop of Dublin as visitor, to appoint seven senior fellows
who would be able, legally, to proceed with all the necessary
elections. Ormonde agreed to the suggestion in principle, but
asked for five persons to be recommended to him so that they
might be made fellows by royal authority. Taylor sent the names.
Among them was that of Dr John Stearne, his old friend. He
was a married man and therefore, strictly speaking, ineligible
for the office for which he was proposed, but Taylor begged that
this disability might be overlooked, both on account of his learning
and his great familiarity with the College affairs. Stearne's future
career more than justified the choice. The others proposed were
Joshua Cowley, Richard Lingard, William Vincent, and Patrick
Sheridan. Sheridan and Cowley were acquaintances of Taylor,
and as they had previously asked for his guidance in their
reading, it is reasonable to conclude that he had personal knowledge of their abilities. In the same letter in which these names
were sent up for the Chancellor's approval and the King's
confirmation, Taylor also asked for authority to "collect and
frame" necessary statutes. We have, he says, "no public statutes
relating to an university, no established forms of collating degrees,
no public lectures, no schools; no Regius Professor of Divinity,
and scarce any ensignes academical".[3]

Taylor and Seele worked hard at their task. While the Vice-
Chancellor saw to the organization of the University, the Provost
restored discipline. But funds were short, and there were few
able men available for the vacant positions, for the troublous
times through which Ireland had been passing had not been
conducive to study. The disorderly bachelors and scholars were,

[1] Letter from Taylor to Ormonde, Carte MSS. fol. ss. Carte inserted an account
of Trinity College at the restoration in his *Life of Ormonde*, Vol. 2, p. 208. He based
his statements on the letter quoted above.
[2] Carte MSS. fol. ss.
[3] Taylor to Ormonde, 19 December 1660, Carte MSS. fol. ss.

however, brought under control; services in chapel were regularly conducted once more, and both an organist and a University preacher were appointed. Seele continued to be Provost after Taylor's death and went on with the excellent work which they had begun together. They firmly and finally set Trinity College on its feet.

Taylor had sent down orders to his diocese that while he was away in Dublin the Presbyterians should be closely watched, and their activities reported to him. In accordance with this order he received early in October 1660, a letter from his agent which was anything but reassuring. It conveyed the news that a week or two before the Presbyterians had called a meeting and appointed a committee of four people, Mr Greg, Mr Drysdale, Mr Ramsay, and Mr Hutcheson, to examine Taylor's writings, and draw up a list of what they considered objectionable features in them.[1] The committeemen must have had the greater part of their task done before they were appointed, or else they were very familiar with the works of their diocesan, for they presented the result of their labours to their brethren only a week after they had been chosen. Their report stated that Taylor was a Socinian, that he denied original sin, that he was an Arminian and "so heretic in the grain".[2] The synod accepted the indictment, and decided to send the four men who had drawn it up to carry it to Dublin and there, if they could get a hearing, they were to lay it before the authorities; if not, it was to be sent to their correspondent in England to be presented to the King. In the meantime all ministers were to preach vigorously against bishops, and the Book of Common Prayer.[3] One of their number, Mr Richardson, carried out this part of the resolution very thoroughly. After some wholehearted abuse of bishops and the Prayer Book, he warned his hearers that it would be as well for them to get the Bible by heart, for the time was coming when no man would be allowed to have a copy of his own, and when it

---

[1] *C.S.P., Ireland, CAR. 2, CCV*, No. 7. These four men were associated on many occasions. Drysdale came over from Scotland as a layman to preach in Lord Claneboye's regiment and was ordained by the presbytery at Carrickfergus. He was afterwards sent as a special deputy from the presbytery of Northern Ireland to the Assembly in Scotland. Ramsay was the minister of Bangor, County Down. All four were arrested in 1663 for alleged complicity in Blood's plot. Drysdale retired to Scotland with Ramsay; Hutcheson was protected by Lord Duncannon; Greg, who seems to have really been implicated, suffered imprisonment and "hard usage". All four were again in trouble in 1670, with Taylor's successor. Adair, *True Narrative*, pp. 27, 277, 281.

[2] *C.S.P., Ireland, CAR. 2, CCCV*, No. 7.

[3] Ibid.

would be safer to break the sabbath than a holy day. He concluded with a prayer of thanksgiving for "the little mite of liberty which the King had granted them".[1]

Taylor immediately laid his agent's letter before the Lords Justices, and wrote an account of what he had heard to Ormonde. It must have thrown Taylor into a fit of the profoundest depression, for he asks either to be removed "from this insupportable burden" or to be supported under it. Intrigue in England was what he chiefly seemed to fear. He knew perfectly well that, as soon as he was consecrated and at work in his diocese, he would be compelled to face an open clash with the Presbyterians, unless he was content to betray both his commission and his order by staying on while his authority was ignored and his person insulted; so he leaves Ormonde in no doubt about his wish to be removed from the diocese or, if he is to stay, to be unequivocally supported by the Government. The King and Ormonde both, he says, intended to prefer him when they sent him to Down and Connor, but the income is not what it was represented to be, and many of the rents are uncertain, but that is not the subject of his complaint. He has been thrown into a place of torment, and the chief offenders are the Scotch ministers. The nobility and gentry, all except one, "are very right", but the ministers are implacable:

They have for these four months past solemnly agreed, and very lately renewed their resolution, of preaching vigorously and constantly against episcopacy and liturgy; they defy them both, publicly they disparage his Majesty's government; they slight and undervalue his most gracious concessions in his late excellent and princely declaration; they talk of resisting unto blood, and stir up the people to sedition, doing things worse than can be expressed by any but themselves.

My lord; I have invited them to a friendly conference, desired earnestly to speak with them, went to them, sent some of their own to invite them, offered to satisfy them, in anything that was reasonable; I preach every Sunday amongst them, somewhere or other; I have courted them with most friendly offers, did all things in pursuance of his Majesty's most gracious declaration; but they refused to speak with me; they have newly covenanted to speak with no bishop, and to endure neither their government nor their persons.[2]

The Presbyterians were trying to undermine his popularity with "the better sort of people" by calling him an Arminian, a

[1] C.S.P., Ireland, CAR. 2, CCCV, No. 7.
[2] Taylor to Ormonde, 19 December 1660, Carte MSS., fol. ss.

Socinian, and a Papist or half a Papist. They had bought his books and appointed a committee of "Scotch spiders"[1] to see whether they could find any poison in them, and the spiders having found one or two little things they had put them into a paper which they were sending across to London for their agent to present to the King. Taylor thinks that the object behind all this is not so much to remove him as to discredit him. Against this attack Taylor asks for the "countenance" of the authorities. If he does not receive that, then it is better for him to be "a poor curate in a village church than a bishop over such intolerable persons".[2] Appended to this letter was a list of some of the more outrageous things which were being said in Down and Connor against the bishops and the Government; they seem to be chiefly drawn from the agent's report. This letter and the list of charges were sent with a covering letter to Sir George Lane, Ormonde's secretary, asking for his help. In this communication, after giving most of the details which had already been sent to Ormonde, Taylor adds his opinion that a great deal of the trouble with the Scotch Presbyterians arose from the delay in the justices coming over, and delay in the consecration of the bishops.[3]

Taylor's difficulties with the Presbyterian ministers in his diocese have been the occasion of some disputes and misunderstandings, but the facts are not too difficult to obtain. Taylor's own letters on the subject are lengthy, and Adair, one of the Presbyterian leaders, wrote their full story with personal knowledge of what had happened and at a time when the events he described were fairly recent.[4] There are, of course, some things slurred over which we should like to have in more detail, but nothing really necessary is missing. In all essentials, allowing for the inevitably different points of view, the two accounts agree.

There was a chance toward the end of 1660 that Taylor might be able to avoid for a little while longer the battle which he knew was awaiting him in his diocese. The Irish Church proposed to send a deputation, consisting of a bishop and a clerk, over to

[1] Taylor to Ormonde, 19 December 1660, Carte MSS., fol. ss.

[2] Ibid. Taylor signs this letter *Jerem. Dunensis Elect.*, a wrong style, since the Irish bishops were appointed by the King's letters patent simply.

[3] Taylor to Lane, 19 December 1660, Carte MSS., fol. ss.

[4] *A True Narrative of the Rise and Progress of the Presbyterian Church in Ireland*, by the Revd Patrick Adair, Minister of Belfast. Adair intended to bring his work down to the beginning of the reign of William III, but he died in 1694, leaving his MSS. unfinished, but fairly complete up to 1670. The book stayed unprinted until it was edited by W. D. Killen and published, Belfast, 1866.

England with a petition to the King for the reorganization and settlement of Church finances. The episcopal representative was to be either Jeremy Taylor or Michael Boyle of Cork and Ross; but before the actual person was chosen a letter from the King gave the clergy the prospect of obtaining their wishes, the deputation therefore was never sent.[1]

Taylor had probably been waiting for his consecration before he did more than take stock of his diocese. On 27 January 1661, he and nine other bishops were consecrated in St Patrick's Cathedral, Dublin, and Taylor preached the sermon.[2] He took Luke 12.42-3 for his text and the address, drawn out of the picture of the faithful and wise steward, was a defence of episcopacy on the lines of his former work. It was published in response to the desire of those who heard it, without a dedication, but with a short address to the Christian reader. It is a sermon of no great distinction and is chiefly valuable for indicating the state of mind in which the preacher was about to take up the active administration of his diocese. He is as strongly convinced as ever that episcopacy is the divinely ordered system of Church government. In his address to the Christian Reader he quotes the words of St Cyprian "he that is not with the bishop is not in the church".[3] Yet that is only one half of Taylor's thought; the other is the heavy sense of responsibility which a bishop must feel for those who are the lost sheep of his flock.

[1] Bramhall, *Works*, Vol. 1, p. cii, Letter of Bramhall to Ormonde, 5 December 1660.

[2] Bramhall himself drew up the order of service. The paper entitled "The Manner of Consecration of the Bishops in Dublin by the Lord Primate in the Year 1660" was lost until it was republished for controversial purposes in the eighteenth century, in a book entitled *The Pillars of Priestcraft and Orthodoxy Shaken*, by Richard Baron, 8vo, London, 1768. It consists of a careful programme of Procession, Service, Anthem, Sermon; and was sent by the Primate to those concerned "to the end that all things might be done in order". See also Mason, *St Patrick's Cathedral*, p. 192.

[3] *Works*, Vol. 8, p. 306.

CHAPTER X

TAYLOR IN HIS DIOCESE

WHEN Taylor went down to live in his diocese he was still without a home of his own, and therefore he and his family stayed at Hillsborough House. It belonged to Colonel Hill and had been built in the reign of Charles I as a stronghold against the rebels. There was a little church nearby which served as the bishop's chapel. In a letter to Lord Conway, written on 2 March 1661, he says that he hopes soon to have a house of his own at Lisnagarvey:

"My Lord I have so great an encouragement from your Lordship's favour and the assistance you have contributed that I hope I shall not be long ere I can abide wholly at Lisnagarvey, whither if your Lordship's affairs will at last suffer you to come I shall have a double joy and constant stock of comfort. My Lord there is a gentleman in Dublin, to whom I gave the degree of Doctor of the Laws, that hath very good skill in architecture and hath drawn me a very pretty design for my house. I forbear to send it to your Lordship for approbation because we flatter ourselves that we shall before May see your Lordship in Dublin."[1]

He apologizes for the shortness of the letter "because the time of the post passing is near". All that morning he had been with Major Hill, who had been so ill with a quinsy that at one time his life was despaired of, though Taylor was happy to say that the crisis was passed. Taylor himself had suffered from a disorder which had made him feverish and full of pains all over. This was an illness from which he suffered a good deal, for hardly a letter goes to Conway without an attack of it being mentioned. The Lord Primate had paid them a visit and had found an amicable settlement to a dispute between Colonel Hill and the Church authorities and "considering my Bishopric was greater in charge than in revenue, and less in value than it was in promise, hath added to my see some impropriate tithes which he formerly purchased. He was conducted in and out by your Lordship's troop and Major Rawdon's." There is a final request that if Lord Conway brings any horses over he "would be pleased to let his groom buy a good strong nag" for the Archbishop, who will gladly return him the money, for good horses were not to be had in Ireland. Taylor is about

[1] Murray MSS.

to ask for a similar favour for himself but "Just as I am writing this Dr Colvil sends me a pretty nag".[1] There is no mention in this particular letter of disputes with the Presbyterians, possibly because their leaders were away in Dublin at the time. They had been forbidden by a proclamation issued by the Lords Justices[2] in the previous year to hold any meeting; but they had again managed to gather at Ballymena, and transact their business, before the party of horse which Sir George Rawdon sent to disperse them reached the spot.[3] This must have happened in the early part of February 1661, for Taylor arrived in Down about the middle of the month,[4] and this meeting had taken place a little before. The synod decided to send four of their number to Dublin to remind the Justices of the King's gracious dealings with Richardson and Keyes in London. They were encouraged the more to hope for favour because Sir John Clotworthy, who had lately become Lord Massereene, had won a promise from the King that the Presbyterians in Ireland should be treated with special leniency. But although the deputation saw the Irish Privy Council, they did not get much encouragement.[5] There were several bishops belonging to the Privy Council at the time, of whom Jeremy Taylor was one; but as Adair himself says that the deputation was in Dublin when their Bishop came to his diocese, it is unlikely that he was sitting when his own complainants appeared. As soon as they came back Taylor summoned them all to meet him at his episcopal visitation at Lisnagarvey. They were expecting some such command and were at loss what to do, since the proclamation forbidding their holding a meeting seemed to make it impossible for them to consult together on possible lines of action. But Lady Clotworthy, the mother of their patron, died just at this time, and since her son was so strong a supporter of their cause, the Presbyterians of Down and Connor flocked to her funeral, and so were able to talk over the Bishop's summons.[6] But even so they could not come to any unanimous agreement on what was best to be

---

[1] Murray MSS.

[2] Ireland was under the rule of three Justices: Lord Broghill, Earl of Orrery, Sir Charles Coote, Earl of Mountrath, and Sir Maurice Eustace, the Chancellor.

[3] Adair, *True Narrative*, p. 246.

[4] *Rawdon Papers*, p. 125.

[5] Adair, *True Narrative*, p. 247.

[6] There is a doubt about the actual date of the funeral, but, according to the entry in the Office of Arms, Dublin Castle, it must have taken place between 5 December 1660 and 5 March 1661. Since Taylor did not arrive in his diocese until about 17 February 1661, it narrows the date of the visitation down to late February or early March.

done. The majority seem to have thought that they ought to be somewhere in the neighbourhood of the visitation, so they met together next day at Belfast and rode over to Lisnagarvey. The Bishop was staying at Hillsborough House, so, as soon as they arrived, the Presbyterian ministers sent three of their number as a deputation to see him. As they had already gathered and made a journey that day, the dusk of the spring evening must have been beginning to fall as the three men traversed the short distance between Lisnagarvey, where they had left their brethren, and Hillsborough. Their diocesan awaited them with an anxious heart. He was probably well enough aware of what had happened at old Lady Clotworthy's funeral, and even if he had never seen these four men before, he no doubt knew the sort of persons they were and the sort of message they brought to him. It was, that they could on no account appear at his episcopal visitation or submit to his jurisdiction; but in order to show that they were acting on principle they would, if he cared to, meet him privately and explain their position.[1] The Bishop asked that they would let him have what they had to say on paper, but this the deputation declined to do, on the ground that many of their brethren were not present. Taylor's tone sharpened at this reply. He told them that he could neither receive anything from them as a body, nor consider them as a body. They answered, unmoved, that whatever they were or however he regarded them, it was their wisest course to consult together on matters of importance. This attempt to get written proof of the recalcitrance of the ministers, and their refusal to supply it seems to have been by way of a preliminary.

The discussion began with a question from Taylor which went straight to the heart of the dispute. Did they consider government by presbyters to be *jure divino*? At once the deputation replied that they did. Taylor answered that if they held to that there could be no further talk of accommodation. The other side saw their opportunity; they wanted to avoid the visitation and get a private interview, and the Bishop's words had given them an argument which helped their case. They were persuaded in their consciences, they said, that their form of government was *jure divino*, and if to give that answer would only cause trouble then it was best for them to stay away from the visitation. The bishop answered that if, on that occasion, they made any profession contrary to the law they would smart for it, and he

[1] Adair, *True Narrative*, p. 247.

advised them as a friend not to appear. The tables had been neatly turned; by implication, both sides had admitted that Presbyterianism was something the authorities would take exception to if it were openly discussed. Seeing "their foot in a snare",[1] the deputation thanked him, but thought none the less that they might still hold government by presbyters to be *jure divino* and not break the law, since they were not actually using that form of government. It would seem from this remark that the presbytery had ceased to function in an organized way, and that their churches were in a similar situation to the Independents. Possibly this had been the case since Major Rawdon's troop of horse arrived at one of their meetings, but they still acted in concert so far as they were able and were certainly no nearer accepting any government other than that of presbyters. Taylor continued to insist that the government they then exercised was contrary to law, and went on to say that, though the King's declaration on matters of religion were extended to Ireland, it would not do them any good.[2] The Presbyterians had obviously hoped for a great deal from that declaration, but Taylor, who had been nearer to the centre of things than they, knew how much or how little it was going to be acted upon. But still the deputation insisted. There were, they said, a good many in England who thought as they did and yet enjoyed the benefit of the King's declaration. Taylor disagreed. His next question was about the oath of supremacy. Would they take it? They replied that they could not answer for their brethren, but they thought that if it was put to them in the sense in which Archbishop Ussher had explained it, and King James accepted it, then most of their friends would take it; though they admitted, when pressed, that such an interpretation was contrary to law. To get over this difficulty, the Bishop said that he would offer them the oath in its grammatical sense, but he had never known anyone take it in that way except Jesuits and Presbyterians "who were the greatest enemies to monarchy and most disobedient to Kings which he instanced in the case of the Assembly of Scotland, and in Calvin, Knox, Buchanan, etc.".[3] The Bishop went on to stress that disagreeable parallel. Adair adds that none of the bishops did actually administer the oath to Presbyterians,

[1] Adair, *True Narrative*, p. 248.
[2] The King is said to have promised Lord Massereene that the "declaration concerning ecclesiastical affairs" would have "some favourable addition put to it for the Presbyterians in Ireland". Adair, *True Narrative*, p. 246.
[3] Adair, *True Narrative*, p. 249.

because by law they were not allowed to force it on any except officers of Church and State. As the bishops did not recognize Presbyterian orders, they could not admit the holders of them to office in the Church, neither did they think it possible for such people to take office under the King.[1] Not much good had come from the meeting so far, nor did it seem that much could be gained by prolonging it. They parted with something like an expression of sympathy from the Bishop. He saw, he said, that they were in a difficult position, for "if they did conform contrary to their consciences they would be knaves, and if not they could not be endured contrary to law"; he wished therefore that they would lay aside their mistaken scruples of conscience.[2] The Presbyterians were very upset at being classed with Jesuits and by the Bishop's reflection on the Assembly of Scotland, and the worthy reformers, and they did their best to disabuse his mind. They were not successful, since on one point, at least, the likeness was too clear, as Taylor and many more of his contemporaries recognized.[3] And so the meeting came to an end. No possible opening for compromise had ever risen. On both sides it had been root principles which had been called in question.

On the next day Taylor held his visitation, at Lisnagarvey. Only two Presbyterians attended. The Bishop's sermon was on "The Minister's Duty in Life and Doctrine". As we have it now it is in two parts "as it was preached in so many several visitations", a phrase which probably means that the sermon was preached twice in its entirety, for it undoubtedly reads as one work. Possibly the first half was delivered on one morning and the remainder in the afternoon or on the next day, but both at the same visitation. The first part is an exhortation to those present to live a holy life and preach sound doctrine; it is plain and simple and never rises to any great heights. In the second half the substance of what the minister is to preach is dealt with more precisely. It is all to be taken from Scripture, sensibly expounded with the best aids that can be got. Taylor recommends

[1] Adair, *True Narative*, p. 250.
[2] "*Deponere conscientiam erroneam*" were the actual words. Adair, *True Narrative*, p. 250.
[3] The Protestant reformers based their claim to limit the King's authority on the rights of the people, the Romanists on the Pope's power to absolve subjects from allegiance to wicked sovereigns. Buchanan's *De Jure Regni apud Scotos* claimed that the right to put tyrannical kings to death was scriptural, Taylor was probably thinking of that as well as the language which John Knox and the Assembly had used to Queen Mary. Bellarmine, and the Jesuit controversialists generally, had reclaimed for the Pope the power to take away and bestow kingdoms for the good of souls. See Bramhall, *Works*, Vol. 3, pp. 300 ff.

a few books, but none of them are in English.[1] With a good
many of the ministers of the district rebellious and absent,
the Bishop might have been expected to refer to the situation
at some length. But only toward the end of the second of the two
sermons does he make any mention of it. There he exhorts his
hearers to preach such things as shall be useful. They shall teach
the people:

> To fear God and honour the King, to keep the commandments of
> God; learn them to be sober and temperate, to be just and pay their
> debts, to speak well of their neighbours and to think meanly of them-
> selves; teach them charity, and learn them to be zealous of good
> works. Is it not a shame that the people shall be filled with sermons
> against ceremonies, and declamations against a surplice, and tedious
> harangues against the poor airy sign of the cross in baptism? These
> things teach them to be ignorant; it fills them with wind, and they
> suck dry nurses; it makes them lazy and useless. Troublesome and
> good for nothing. Can the definition of a Christian be, that a Christian
> is a man that rails against bishops and the Common Prayer Book?
> and yet this is the great labour of our neighbours that are crept in
> amongst us; this they call the work of the Lord; and this is the great
> matter of the desired reformation; in these things they spend their
> long breath, and about these things they spend earnest prayers, and
> by these they judge their brother, and for these they revile their
> superior, and in this doughty cause they think it fit to fight and die.[2]

Besides the sermon, Taylor delivered a pastoral charge which
is quite unaffected by the dispute. It took the form of eighty-
three short "Rules and Advices to the Clergy of Down and
Connor for their deportment in their Personal and Public
capacity". Their form makes it unlikely that they were read
aloud to the assembled clergy, most likely they were handed to
them in print, but however given they are wholly admirable.
Although time has necessarily made some part of them obsolete
by changing the circumstances of men's lives, even to-day no
minister could read them without profit. They are divided into
five sections: "First, Personal duty; second, of prudence required
in ministers; third, the rules and measures of government to be
used by ministers in their respective courses; fourth, rules and
advices concerning preaching; fifth, rules and advices concerning catechism." It had been an oft repeated charge of the
Presbyterians that the bishops were too much lords of this world
and too little fathers of God's people, yet it would be difficult

[1] See Appendix G.   [2] *Works*, Vol. 8, p. 532.

to find among any body of Christians a book which has in it more of the true spirit of pastoral care than these eighty-three brief paragraphs. Once again Taylor had enriched Anglicanism. From time to time since the Reformation responsible persons had put out papers of legal directions, and good advice, for the benefit of the clergy; but no one had ever concerned himself in such an intimate, or searching, fashion with the souls of the priests, and through them with the souls of their people. The temptation is to quote, and go on quoting, so that the reader may judge for himself, but two extracts, those numbered x and xv in the first section must suffice:

x. Let every curate of souls strive to understand himself best; and then to understand others. Let him spare himself least; but most severely judge, censure and condemn himself. If he be learned, let him show it by wise teaching and humble manners; if he be not learned, let him be sure to get so much knowledge as to know that, and so much humility, as not to grow insolent, and puffed up by his emptiness. For many will pardon a good man that he is less learned; but if he be proud no man will forgive him.

xv. Pray much and very fervently for all your parishioners, and all men that belong to you, and all that belong to God; but especially for the conversion of souls: and be very zealous for nothing, but for God's glory, and the salvation of the world, and particularly for your charges: ever remember that you are by God appointed as the ministers of prayer, and the ministers of good things, to pray for all the world, and to heal all the world, as far as you are able.[1]

It is a pity that some early publisher did not bind up this little gem with *Holy Living and Holy Dying*, so that it could have become more widely known.[2]

The Bishop repeated the names of all the absent Presbyterians when he called the roll of his clergy at the visitation, but did nothing further about their non-attendance. When he had returned home, and had finished his dinner, another group of the malcontents arrived to see him. Again there were three of them; two had belonged to the deputation of the night before; the other was new. What had happened to the man whose place he took, Adair does not say. The object this time was to try to get Taylor to call all the Presbyterians together for a private conference with him at his house, and they thought that his words on the previous evening gave them some hope of his

---

[1] *Works*, Vol. i, pp. 102, 103.
[2] It was republished at Oxford in 1847 in a volume called *The Clergyman's Instructor*, together with seven other booklets on the ministerial life.

doing so. There must have been some misunderstanding, for Taylor's words, as Adair reports them, only convey that it was wisest in the Bishop's opinion for the Presbyterians to stay away from the official visitation if their going would cause trouble; and at the same time he had pointed out that he could not consider them as a body or treat them as such. At this meeting also he told the representatives the same thing over again: he could not consider the possibility of negotiating with them as a body and "fell angrily on reflections on presbyterial government".[1] He also told them that contempt was the real cause of their not appearing at the visitation. They replied that it was awe of God and their consciences. To which the Bishop responded that a Jew or a Quaker would defend himself with the same argument or anybody else who was on a wrong course. This was the last attempt that the Presbyterians made to obtain some collective terms from their diocesan. It was hopeless for them to persist, since he would only consider them as a number of individuals who were stubbornly refusing to put themselves right with the law. As such he did his best to get them to see their mistake. He interviewed those whom he thought most likely to respond, one by one, and "gave them offers of great kindness and preferment but he obtained not his purpose".[2] Both singly, and as a body, the Presbyterians remained staunch in their opinions. Judging by their past history, time was not likely to make any change in their attitude. But thirty-six of them were in possession of church livings. It was obviously an intolerable position for any bishop to have to endure. Taylor had shown himself not only willing, but eager, to resign; but the Government had not wished him to do so. All that was left for him to do was either to stay on, at best ignored by a large part of the diocese for which he was legally and spiritually responsible, or do as his superiors clearly intended that he should, and exert his authority. He did exert it and declared the thirty-six churches vacant.[3]

The date of this action is uncertain, but as it followed on Taylor's first visitation it must have been about the end of March 1661. The justice, and even the legality, of what was done has frequently been questioned. It has been pointed out, quite truly, that the Irish Convocation which examined and approved of the Prayer Book which had just been revised and settled by law in England, did not do so until November 1662,

[1] Adair, *True Narrative*, p. 250.   [1] Ibid., p. 251.   [3] Ibid.

and its use was not enjoined under penalties by the Irish Parliament until 1666. But it was not for refusal to accept the revised Prayer Book that Taylor deprived the thirty-six ministers, but because they were not episcopally ordained persons, and therefore not qualified by law for the livings which they held. It has also been pointed out, again quite truly, that the Irish Articles do not demand episcopal ordination, and that the English Articles are not specific on that point. It was unnecessary that either of them should be so, for the Ordinal left no doubt about the matter. As part of the Prayer Book, it had been passed into law by the Irish Parliament of 1560, and it had not been legally superseded by anything which happened during the Commonwealth. Its preface is uncompromising. No man shall be "suffered to execute any of the said Functions (of Bishop, Priest or Deacon) except he be called, tried, examined and admitted thereunto, according to the Form hereafter following, or hath had formerly Episcopal Consecration, or Ordination". The Presbyterians had not been ordained according to the forms provided; Taylor therefore held them to be no ministers and ejected them from the livings they had obtained.[1]

Some authorities, without examining too closely into the charges, have been willing to allow that Taylor was guilty of persecution, and that he repudiated by his action the principles which he had so eloquently expressed in *The Liberty of Prophesying*. To do so is to miss entirely the point of that book. It pleaded that all men of goodwill should be allowed to keep their own opinions so long as they were not inimical to good morals or the welfare of the State, not that they should be allowed to receive the emoluments belonging to another body. Taylor never had a hand in punishing a Presbyterian as such, but he found it harder and harder as time went on to believe that some of their teaching was not dangerous to the country.[2] His linking the Jesuits and the Presbyterians together in the accusation that they were underminers of monarchy has already been mentioned, and he never quite forgot that the Presbyterians had been leaders in the Civil War which put one King to death and exiled another. Of course, whenever discipline is brought to bear, the cry of

[1] Adair bears out this point of view: "He did not make any process against the ministers, nor suspend or excommunicate; but simply held them not to be ministers they not being ordained by bishops." Adair, *True Narrative*, p. 251.

[2] Taylor was instrumental in arresting Drysdale and holding him for trial, but it was on the ground of suggested complicity in Blood's plot. Letter of Taylor to Ormonde, 11 June 1663, Carte MSS., fol. ss.

Q

persecution is raised by those who are penalized. But no organized body can exist without discipline. It must have principles which bind it together, and these must be enforced if the organization is to continue its existence. And episcopacy is a root principle of Anglicanism; by 1661 that had been established beyond hope of removal; though, from time to time, some limitation of the bishops' power might be proposed. How could any part of that Church tolerate within itself those who resolutely stood for the complete extirpation of episcopacy, and who would neither submit to it as even a temporary expedient, nor even recognize any authority in it? Those who deny the fundamental laws of a society have no place in it, though they may rightly claim the liberty to organize a body of their own. This is what Taylor's action forced the Presbyterians to do. We may regret the schism, but it was unavoidable if each side was to keep its self-respect. To say, as is sometimes done, that Taylor was the cause of a separated Presbyterian Church existing in Ulster is to put the fact the wrong way round. More truly, it was due to him that the Anglican Church continued to exist there. The case against Taylor is that he deprived men whose Presbyterian orders previous bishops had not called in question, whose work had been blessed, and who were men of ability. None of this alters the fact that they were legally incapable of holding the preferment they had, and therefore in justice could not complain when it was taken from them. The negligence of previous bishops could make no difference to this, and was all the less likely to be favourably construed, since it was but a part of a scandalous mismanagement which extended through all their work. In this affair with the Presbyterians Taylor has had less than justice done to him. Neither is it entirely an academic concern to us, for if he was ever a persecutor, then his whole character becomes a puzzle. There was, then, something inherently wrong in all the holy atmosphere and pious teaching of the Golden Grove days if, the moment that Taylor was made a bishop, he was no longer ruled by it, but was either swept away by a burst of irritation, or was filled, on the advent to power, with pride and self-will. If love and mercy have been the principles of a lifetime, an honest man is not likely suddenly to be converted to tyranny. But persecution is hard to prove against him. There is every sign that the task which Taylor was compelled to perform was distasteful, and yet it is difficult to see how he could have acted otherwise and been true to himself. His opponents were implacable. He was met from the beginning with a resolute hostility by men whose consciences told them that hostility to bishops was what God required of them. It is perhaps too much to expect that those same men should have given him as much credit for being true to his conscience, as they took for loyalty to their own.

The authorities in Dublin supported Taylor's action though the Presbyterians had powerful friends. Writing to Conway at this time, Taylor says:

"I am greatly pleased with the conduct of the church affairs at the Council board concerning the Scotch ministers, there was no fear that anyone should suspect your Lordship to be a Presbyterian, they know you have too much reason and are too much a gentleman to be undone with such principles, but how my Lord Massereene will forgive your Lordship for that contrast or me for silencing his two chaplains at Antrim and Killead I cannot imagine.[1] However I have learned to be valient by your Lordship's example and to do what I think is fitting and leave everyone to be pleased or not pleased as they see cause for."[2]

Taylor filled the vacant livings with new men; some he brought over from England, some were able persons then in Ireland, and willing to accept ordination, but these too were all of English extraction. It is a pity, perhaps, that when Scots had to be displaced, Irishmen should not have been preferred, but conditions had not been such as conduced to the training of scholars. Among the newcomers was George Rust, who became Dean of Connor and ultimately Bishop of Dromore. Taylor seems to have had no particular person in mind when he sent over to Cambridge for some "learned and ingenious man" who might be suitable for the vacant deanery.[3] Henry More recommended George Rust, his friend and pupil; and since there was a long-standing friendship between Taylor and More, as well as between More and the Conway family, his nominee was naturally appointed.

[1] Adair, *True Narrative*, p. 252, says: "Mr Hamilton of Killead and Mr Cunningham of Antrim . . . through my Lord Massareene's intercession with the bishop, obtained about half a year's liberty after their brethren were silenced, only they must not lecture before preaching, according to their former practice."

[2] Murray MSS.

[3] Cambridge University Library, Baker MSS., c. 2. 24, fol. 109. Also, *Diary of Dr John Worthington* (Cheetham Soc.), p. 301. There were complaints later on that Rust did not keep in touch with Taylor. He lived at Carrickfergus and was Rector of Island Magee and was nearly always absent from Lisburn. The complaints about this were many (*Rawdon Papers*, 5 September 1665, March 1666, 25 April 1666). His name does not occur once in the Lisburn register. A letter of his to Lord Conway is a little highly coloured even for the seventeenth century: "I thought Ireland a pleasant country and Lisburn a delightful place, but now I see it was your presence made it so. The sun does not shine as it used to when you were here and the verdure of the fields is not the same. I love my dear Lord as my Guardian Angel". Carmody, *Lisburn Cathedral and Its Past Rectors*, pp. 23–5.

Thomas Bayley was another of the able men whom Taylor brought into the diocese. He had at one time been chaplain of Christ Church, Oxford, and was appointed in 1664 Bishop of Killala. Taylor's own chaplain, Lemuel Mathews, was a Welshman who settled down in the Church of Ireland, but the new Archdeacon of Down, Jeremiah Piddock, was ordained priest by Taylor himself on 3 March 1661.[1] The new Chancellor of the diocese, James Mace, was an Englishman, who although receiving his early education in his own country at the Perse School and Trinity College, Cambridge, had been in Ireland longer than Taylor. He was ordained deacon and priest on the same day at the same ordination as Piddock.[2] In all these cases there are circumstances which suggest possible links with Taylor before the Restoration. Certainly in training and ability the newcomers were the equals of the men they displaced.

By the summer of 1661 Taylor had appointed most of the officers of his diocese, but as yet he had no cathedral. The old one at Down had been in ruins for 150 years. Bishop Leslie in days before the civil war had tried to get something done and had not succeeded. The church at Lisnagarvey was suitable for the purpose, and since there was no money either to restore or to build at Down, it became the cathedral. Its new importance was recognized in a charter granted by the King in 1662, in which it was not only styled cathedral, but such provision was made for its endowment out of the impropriations granted to the Church, as the Bishop of the diocese, the Archbishop, and the Governor-General should see convenient.[3] It is odd, as Dean Carmody observes, that when these three offices were held by zealous churchmen the cathedral should never have obtained any endowment.[4]

On 10 March 1661, Taylor buried his son Edward at Lisnagarvey, or, as it was now increasingly called, Lisburn.[5] In all probability he was the child whose birth was expected in August 1659. With such a blow to his hopes, and in the midst of his struggle with the Presbyterians, it is no wonder that Taylor felt neither happy nor settled. In the same month Bishop Leslie of Meath, that courageous old man, lay dying. He had been translated from Down and Connor at the Restoration, and

[1] Carmody, *Lisburn Cathedral and Its Past Rectors*, p. 20.

[2] Ibid., p. 25.

[3] The original charter is in the keeping of the Rector of Lisburn. It is printed in Carmody, *Lisburn Cathedral and Its Past Rectors*, p. 93.

[4] Ibid., p. 99.

[5] Ibid., p. 87, quoting the Burial Register of Lisburn, Book 2, 1661–1720.

Taylor hoped that the precedent might be of use to himself; accordingly, he wrote to Ormonde asking to be preferred if a vacancy should occur.[1] Meath lay near to Dublin and would therefore make his attendance on his duties as Vice-Chancellor much easier. He claims that he has now "broken the knot of the Scotch ministers" in Down and Connor, and so his successors would find a comparatively easy task. The tone of the letter hints that the writer thought his request so reasonable that he hardly contemplated refusal. In a postscript it is stated that the "nobilitee and gentree of this diocese are something passionate" for the little Diocese of Dromore to be added to that of Down.[2] It had, besides dignitaries, only five clergy. Its Bishop at the time was Robert Leslie, a son of the Bishop of Meath. Taylor suggests that when the father's expected death occurred the subsequent changes would be almost certain to involve the son, and so make it easy to carry out the idea which he was putting forward. His meaning is not exactly clear, but he seems to have wished the two dioceses to be united under Leslie. The request made in the body of the letter was ignored. When the See of Meath became vacant it was filled by transferring Henry Jones from Clogher. But the postscript had more effect. Robert Leslie was sent to Raphoe, and on 30 April Taylor was made administrator of the Diocese of Dromore. He is often referred to as Lord Bishop of Down Connor and Dromore,[3] as if the two sees were united, but this can hardly have been the case. Before such a union could have been brought about, it would have been necessary to get an Act of the Irish Parliament and a petition to the Privy Council, and there is no trace of either of these things being done. A similar process would have been required to separate them again, but at Taylor's death Rust became Bishop of Dromore without any special legal proceedings.

Taylor still continued to live at Hillsborough for some part of his time, visiting both the dioceses in his charge from there. Dromore Cathedral, like many other buildings, had been laid in ruins during the rebellion of 1641. Taylor rebuilt it in simple style, the nave from public funds, the chancel out of his own pocket. One of his family, a Joanna Taylor, who may have been

[1] Taylor to Ormonde, 28 March 1661, Carte MSS., fol. ss.

[2] Ibid. Thackeray used the same spelling 200 years later in the attempt to convey what he considered to be a comic Irish accent.

[3] Matthews, on the title-page of his elegy, calls Taylor "Lord Bishop of Down, Connor and Dromore". In the circumstances, it would be quite natural for the Bishop's household to give him that title, even though strictly he had no right to it.

his daughter, but is far more likely to have been his wife, presented the Communion plate. It was while he was struggling with the reorganization of his diocese, and when the knowledge that there was to be no immediate escape from conflict with the Presbyterians was fresh in his mind, that Taylor went up to Dublin to take his seat in the House of Lords and, on 8 May, preached before the new Parliament. A few days later the Two Houses publicly thanked him for his sermon, and asked for it to be printed.[1] Both the short epistle dedicatory and the sermon itself are occupied with the duty of obedience. It is such a great virtue that none but the very weightiest reasons can discharge us from it. He was inclined to think that the plea of tenderness of conscience was overworked. So many different people were demanding exemption from so many different things on that account. It amounted to a disease and "must be cured by anodynes and soft usages, unless they prove ineffective, and that the lancet be necessary".[2] All sense of proportion must not be lost. "To stand in a clean vestment is not so ill a sight as to see men stand in separation; and to kneel at communion is not so like idolatry as rebellion is to witchcraft."[3]

The whole sermon throws a most interesting light on Taylor's own attitude toward Nonconformity. He saw himself, and his fellow bishops, as the executives of the law with only a limited discretionary power. So far as the laws allowed them they might tolerate differences, provided such toleration did not increase the discontent it was meant to cure. But outside certain narrow limits the granting of liberty was not in their hands. In any case, obedience for its own sake is a great virtue, and he refers to the ritual laws of the Jews, which, in his opinion, were of no value except for the opportunity they offered of giving unquestioning obedience to God. Even Christ himself was baptized on the ground of obedience, and his submission was approved by the witness of the Holy Ghost. He repeats in several parts of the sermon that scruples are not to be endured longer than the ignorance which begets them remains incurable, nor can any man's opinions "be suffered to do mischief, to disturb the peace, to dishonour the government".[4] The gist of all the advice which Taylor has to offer to Parliament can be summed up in two short quotations:

[1] *Journals of the Irish Parliament*, Commons, 11 May; Lords, 9 May.
[2] *Works*, Vol. 8, p. 337.
[3] *Journals of the Irish Parliament*, Commons, 11 May; Lords, 9 May.
[4] *Works*, Vol. 8, p. 347.

You have no other way of peace, no better way to appease and quiet the quarrels in religion which have been too long among us, but by reducing all men to obedience, and all questions to the measures of the laws: for they on both sides pretend scripture, but one side only can pretend to the laws.[1]

But at the same time they must remember that,

as religion teaches us to pity the condemned criminal, so mercy intercedes for the most benign interpretation of the laws. You must indeed be as just as the laws, and you must be as merciful as your religion; and you have no way to tie these together, but to follow the pattern in the mount; do as God does, who "in judgement remembers mercy".[2]

Taking these two extracts together, there does not seem to be any very marked contradiction between this sermon and *The Liberty of Prophesying*. A man with responsibility and a man without will state the same principles with a different emphasis. One is concerned with winning converts, the other with the more difficult matter of practice. Taylor as an obscure priest presses the claims of conscience; Taylor as a bishop is concerned to point out, to those who are pushing the plea of conscience as far as it will go, that if it is to keep its right to be respected, it ought only to be used on the gravest occasions. If any proof is needed that Taylor's action in his diocese had not proceeded from a burst of irritation it is supplied by this sermon. It shows quite clearly two trains of thought in his mind. He and his fellow bishops were the executives of the law, bound to discharge it faithfully and, while mercy is owed to everyone, a great deal of sympathy is not due to those who resist the law on trivial occasions. The only comment which seems necessary on this sermon is that the governors and the governed naturally take a different view of what are trivial occasions. Taylor had the greatest reputation of any preacher in Ireland, and though he did not add to it by this work he did not bring it into danger. It was in the quieter style which Taylor used more and more toward the end of his life, either because the new fashion approved or because the old exuberance was beginning to fail.

In the August of that year Archbishop Bramhall made his visitation of Down and Connor. The magnificent hospitality which Taylor offered on this occasion is said to have done a great deal to increase his popularity with the local gentry. Taylor was again the preacher, and the sermon which he delivered

[1] *Works*, Vol. 8, p. 349.   [2] Ibid., p. 358.

was afterwards expanded and given to the "little, but excellent, university of Dublin", and finally published as *Via Intelligentiae*.[1] His duties at the University and in his diocese must have necessitated a good deal of travelling up and down between the two. As Vice-Chancellor he had a regular lodging in Trinity College.[2] On 4 November 1661, Ormonde was made Lord Lieutenant of Ireland and Taylor sent him a graceful letter of congratulation.[3] He was himself in Dublin at the time, probably to take part in the celebrations with which the news was received. On 16 November he wrote to Evelyn, the last letter which we have of their long correspondence.[4] It is short, but full of the warmest feeling of friendship and praise of Evelyn's recent literary activity, which Taylor probably knew would give the recipient as much pleasure as anything in the world. For his part, he laments that he is so full of business that he has little time for his "old delightful employment", but Royston has in his hands the *Rules and Advices to the Clergy*, and two sermons, of which he will present copies to Evelyn, or any other of the Bishop's acquaintances who may wish to have them. One by one Taylor's English friends were beginning to lose touch with him. He had tried to recall himself to his old patron, Lord Hatton, but without success. With Thurland he must still have been on good terms, for he sends him his "love and dear regards". In 1661, it might, if winds were difficult, take a long time to travel between England and Ireland, and most of Taylor's influential friends were desperately busy with the rehabilitation of the monarchy. It is no wonder if, without any special diminution of regard, the correspondence between them should grow less. But Henry More, in the academic calm of Cambridge, had time to keep in touch with his old friend; sometimes by letters, sometimes by affectionate messages and books enclosed in packages for Lady Conway.[5] When More produced a defence of his *Cabala*, Taylor read it with interest and suggested that it ought to be made larger. To this More responded with the request that the Bishop would "polish and adorn it with the richness of his style", but again Taylor was too busy to comply.[6] Dean Rust was also a frequent writer to people

---

[1] *Works*, Vol. 8, p. 361.

[2] "The middle chamber in Sir Richard Scot's Buildings adjoining unto the steeple", Dixon, *Trinity College*, p. 50.

[3] Taylor to Ormonde, 20 November 1661, Carte MSS., fol. ss.

[4] Evelyn, *Diary*, Vol. 3, p. 281.

[5] *Conway Letters*, pp. 193, 196, 213, 218, 219.

[6] Henry More to Lady Conway, letter undated, *Conway Letters*, p. 218.

in Cambridge, so that there was a good deal of news and intellectual speculation exchanged between that University and Northern Ireland.

We catch a glimpse of Taylor again in a letter of his to Lord Conway written on 18 January 1662 from Portmore. The opening sentences offer us another of those puzzles over an event in his life which Taylor's love of oblique statements produced more than once. "My Noblest and Dearest Lord", he begins.

"You are ever the same to me, all nobleness and bounty, for the child's life in Portmore, it is true I am desirous of it but I will rather want that expression of your favour than give any the least suspicion of trouble to any of your relations, to yourself or your posterity, by occasioning the introduction of a troublesome tenant. It is true that I never expect the blessing of another child, much less a son, but if I can obtain this instance of your favour for my daughter it will be great in my eyes and a rest to my cares in a very great measure, but I will not press it beyond your own liking, and had not done so much of it as I have, but that I have observed your Lordship is more pleased to do actions of favour to me, than to receive thanks for what is already done. I will trouble your Lordship no more in this affair but to lay it at your feet and to resolve to be perfectly pleased with what you shall do, for I am sure it will be kind."

The most likely interpretation is that Taylor was begging a position in the Conway household at Portmore for one of his daughters. Phoebe, the child of his first wife, would certainly be old enough to go to a great house as half maid, half pupil, if such a position could be found for her. It would be looked on as part of her education and would not be derogatory even to a bishop's daughter. But there is no means of knowing whether that happened or not. Whatever the real meaning of the request, it was the main reason for Taylor's letter, though he goes on to thank Lord Conway "for the book of verses, besides my own pleasure I receive in seeing the little productions of my old friends, it entertains my clergy here who come in numbers to see Portmore", and concludes with the promise to hasten to Dublin to kiss Lord Conway's hand so soon as he can get away from some pressing business with his clergy.[1]

With the Presbyterians the battle still went on. They sent up three of their number with a petition to Parliament subscribed by them all.[2] It was no use; they could not get it presented, and their friends in Dublin advised them to go home again. It was

[1] Murray MSS.   [2] Adair, *True Narrative*, p. 256.

clear that they would get no help from the authorities, so they decided that their most effective line of action would be to go to what had formerly been their parishes and do what they could in an unobtrusive way to keep their influence alive. Some of them owned houses of their own, and nobody interfered when they went to live in them. Whenever they could do so, without drawing too much attention, they held meetings and preached and tried to keep the people strong in Presbyterian principles. This was probably the work of the older and wiser men. After all, Ireland had seen vicissitudes enough in one generation to make reasonable people think their best course to consist in maintaining their party as well as they could, while they waited for a change. In the meantime they intended to resist, and continue to resist, episcopacy, and at the same time keep in favour with the Government if they could. It was fortunate for them that their patron, Lord Massereene, had influence and could do them useful service by continually putting their side of the case to the Throne.

But this policy did not satisfy them all. Adair, who had more than a little quiet irony in his composition, remarks that "at this time there were two or three young men who had come from Scotland, and had been but lately ordained by the Presbytery here and who intended to return to Scotland and put themselves out of the bishop's reverence[1] in this country, resolved to do some good before they went".[2] Their idea of "doing good" was to stir up trouble and leave others to bear its permanent effects. They held great field preachings and "spoke much against the bishops and the times".[3] While they could keep out of the hands of the authorities it was all very gratifying. They went about over the country "under disguise and oft in the night time" and in general behaved in a way that Adair evidently considered more heroic than necessary. As a result, they were tremendously popular among the more hot-headed section, who liberally contributed to their support, while they neglected the less conspicuous but really far more difficult services of the steadier men. But the deepest injury which the field preachers did to their own cause was to give it just that taint of rebellion which Adair and his friends were anxious it should not have, with the consequent injury to their chances of gaining favourable treatment from the Government. It was probably young men of this sort who provided all the talk about "resisting unto blood"

[1] Reverence, i.e. authority.   [2] Adair, *True Narrative*, p. 258.   [3] Ibid.

which was brought to Taylor, and made him and the rest of the magistrates in the district genuinely suspect that a rising was being planned. It was hard for men who had known so much upheaval to decide what was mere vapouring, and what had a meaning. Taylor was hearing stories of this kind from all sides. He went about his diocese a good deal, preaching in one or other of the parishes every Sunday, getting to know the spiritual needs of his people, holding confirmations and visitations. It was while he was at Dromore for a visitation in the autumn of 1662 that one of the best-known incidents in his life occurred.

For some time all the usual stories of ghostly visitations which were common over the countryside had been subordinated to one, which seemed particularly well authenticated. A young man named Francis Taverner, in the service of Lord Chichester, was riding back to Belfast from Hillsborough one night when he was overtaken near Drum Bridge by two horsemen whom he could not see, though he "could hear the treading of their feet". After them came a third, who was wearing a white coat and had the likeness of James Haddock, incredible though that was, for James Haddock had been dead nearly five years. The apparition spoke and told Taverner his name, and went on to prove his identity by reference to some nuts which he had received from him on one occasion. Taverner asked why the ghost had appeared to him, and was answered that it was because he was a man of greater resolution than others, and if they could ride together for a little way the spirit would let him know some business which he had for him. Taverner refused, and being at a cross-roads went off homeward, so that the two were forced to part, at which there was a great wind and "very hideous screeches and noises". The next night when Taverner was sitting quietly at home, the ghost came again and informed the young man that he must go to a woman named Welsh, who had been Haddock's wife, but was now married to another man, and tell her that she must stop robbing Haddock's son of a certain lease. It was not a very pleasant task, and Taverner put off doing it. He had no wish to be thought either officious, or mad, according to the degree of credulity in those to whom he spoke. But for a month he was haunted by the spirit, every night wearing a more terrible shape. He made one half-hearted attempt to do as he had been told, but finding that there were two women called Welsh he gave it up. At last, hoping to get out of the way of the ghost, who was becoming more and more obnoxious, he moved down to Belfast to the house of one Pierce, a shoemaker, and sat up all night with him and one or two of Lord Chichester's servants who adventurously wished to see a ghost. They were not disappointed. Again it came and this time in a more threatening guise than ever, so much so that next morning the young man went and told his trouble to his master's chaplain and on his advice and in his company went and related it to Dr Downs, the minister of Belfast. All three then went off and delivered to Mrs Welsh her late husband's message, at which Taverner felt a "great quietness in his mind" and, thanking the gentlemen for their help, went off to his brother's house at Drum Bridge. That night the ghost appeared again, this time considerably pleased at what had been done, but, wishing to make sure that justice would prevail, he ordered the story of the lease to be told to his executors.

This was the tale which was brought to Jeremy Taylor, and which aroused his curiosity so much that he wished to investigate it himself. Taverner was ordered to meet the Bishop at Dromore and relate what had befallen him. After the fullest enquiry, the Bishop was convinced that this "strange scene of providence", as he called it, was true. He did nothing more about it then, but on the way home was told that Lady Conway, who, because of her friendship with Henry More if for nothing else, would certainly be interested in the occult, was waiting at Hillsborough and would like to hear the details of the case. So Taverner was sent for, and the whole affair was told over again "to satisfy the curiosity of the fresh company". This time the Bishop advised Taverner, if the ghost should ever trouble him more, to ask these questions:

Whence are you? Are you a good or bad spirit? Where is your abode? What station do you hold? How are you regimented in the other world? And what is the reason that you appear for the relief of your son in so small a matter, when so many widows and orphans are oppressed in the world, being defrauded of greater matter, and none from thence of their relations appear, as you do, to right them?

Lady Conway must have gone home and told her husband all that she had heard, for the poor haunted young man was sent for again that same night to Lisburn and, after being examined once more, was ordered to stay the night. But not even yet was he to be left in peace. About nine or ten o'clock "his countenance changed and he fell into a trembling", the usual signs that the apparition was about to present itself. So, in order not to make any trouble, he and his brother went out of doors and saw the spirit coming over a wall. The ghost asked if his message had been delivered and when told that it had, promised not to hurt Taverner, but threatened the executors if they did not look after the boy. Taverner was too occupied to remember to ask the Bishop's questions, but his brother reminded him. The ghost, however, refused to answer, but crawled on his hands and knees over the wall again "and so vanisht in white, with a most melodious harmony".[1]

Defoe included this story in his *Secrets of the Invisible World*, and Increase Mather, that inveterate believer in ghosts, noted the incident in his *Diary for the Recording of Illustrious Providences*, and chided Taylor for what he considered impertinent curiosity in matters beyond his ken.[2] Taylor himself does not seem to have been over prone to believe this kind of story. When he examined Taverner he appeared to be convinced, but it would have taken a very hardened scepticism at that period to have resisted so many witnesses. Of his suggested questions, the first five were of a type more or less usual, the last proceeded from Taylor's own shrewdness, and hints that in spite of what he had heard there were still some doubts in his mind.

He had one other opportunity of studying the ways of the spirit world. His own neat-herd, a man named David Hunter, was carrying a log of wood into the dairy one night when he was startled by the apparition of an old woman. That time he managed to get away, but she came again night after night, and the poor man was compelled to follow her all over the country. His wife went too, and so did his little dog. At last, when the apparition came on him very suddenly one day, Hunter called out, "Lord bless me, would that I were dead, shall I never be delivered from this misery." This pleased the ghost very much, for apparently she had no power to speak first. Now that her tongue was loosed, she told him about some money, the not very large sum of twenty-eight shillings, which she had buried and now wished to be recovered and used for paying her debts. She also gave him a message to a refractory son of hers. Hunter did as he was told and the ghost appeared once more, to thank him. This time she said that if he lifted her up from off the ground she would never trouble him again. This he did and

---

[1] Glanvill, *Sadducismus Triumphatus* (ed. More), Pt. 2, London, 1682, pp. 243 ff.
[2] Boston, 1684, pp. 223–9.

thought that she felt like a bag of feathers in his arms. "So she vanisht, and he heard most delicate music as she went off, over his head, and he never was more troubled." What Taylor thought about this is not recorded, but Lady Conway took a great interest in it; and Thomas Alcock, the Bishop's secretary, wrote the story down.[1]

Archbishop Bramhall, who, although he was over seventy and had had two strokes, was active to the last, died in June 1663. At the funeral Taylor preached the best of all his post-Restoration sermons. The biographical details which the preacher furnished according to his usual manner in the second half of his sermon are full and interesting. They form indeed one of the most valuable sources which we have for the life of Bramhall. There is a curious passage in which Taylor refers to one of the most open of the attempts made to convert Charles II, while he was in exile, to the Roman Church; the wording of it suggests that the King did not repel the attack very vigorously. It was made by a Frenchman named M. de la Milletière, who made the statement, astounding on the face of it, that the King's conversion to Romanism would hasten his return to his kingdom.[2] But the King did not change his religion, and the fact that he did not do so Taylor attributes to Bramhall, who produced a strong *Answer to M. de la Milletière*. Taylor published this sermon himself soon after it was preached, but it seems to have been twice pirated before he had the opportunity to bring out his own edition.

He also issued in this year, with a short dedication to the Duchess of Ormonde, three sermons: "*The Righteousness Evangelical Described*," "*The Christian's conquest over the Body of Sin*," and "*Fides Formata, or Faith Working by Love*." They are plain and sensible, but a little dry. One sentence in the dedication gives the only indication we have of Taylor's preaching practice. To the sermon preached before the Duchess he has joined two more which various people had asked "to be made fit for the use of those who hope to receive profit by them".[3] This suggests that the spoken word was revised before it appeared in print, and hints at a little more difficulty in creation than formerly.

---

[1] Glanvill, *Sadducismus Triumphatus*, p. 251.

[2] Théophile Brachet, Sieur de la Milletière, was originally a French Protestant, but, his doctrines gradually approximating to those of Rome, he was expelled from the Reformed Church and joined the Roman Catholic. He was an eager controversialist. His *La Victoire de la Vérité pour la Paix de l'Eglise, au Roy de la Grande Brétagne*, Paris, 1651, provoked Bramhall's *An Answer to M. de la Milletière*, published, not by Bramhall himself, The Hague, 1653, 12mo.

[3] *Works*, Vol. 8, p. 245.

Taylor published in the same year Χρίσις Τελειωτική,[1] *A Discourse on Confirmation*, a work which Canon Ollard, in his exhaustive survey of Confirmation in the Anglican Communion, calls "the greatest of all English books" on this subject.[2] In spite of covering so much ground, with so much attention to detail, the work is quite short compared with some of Taylor's writings. It is dedicated to Ormonde, whom the writer describes as the great restorer of the Church of Ireland; one who, both by inclination and duty, was zealous in the interests of religion. In the discourse itself the writer undertakes to prove the divine origin of the rite of confirmation, its continuous use from the earliest times, the necessity of bishops to administer it, and he adds some directions for preparing to receive it, and for its reception. Even in a book of this kind, which was mainly to concern itself with the historical justification of the rite, Taylor's insistence on the practical side of religion had to show itself. He refuses to consider whether it is a sacrament or not, for it is clear that it is not of the same necessity as baptism and the Lord's Supper and any further discussion would be useless. "But that it is an excellent and divine ordinance to purposes spiritual, that it comes from God and ministers in our way to God, that is all we are concerned to enquire after."[3] Taylor finds the origin of baptism in the baptism of Jesus by John in the River Jordan, and the origin of confirmation in the descent of the Holy Ghost which followed. This was not his own idea. He frankly admits that he had learned it from Optatus and St Cyril.[4] This gives him his first argument to establish the difference between baptism and confirmation. The theory that the descent of the Holy Ghost shows that confirmation is part of baptism giving "fulness and consumation to it" he finds unacceptable for "reason and context are both against it". He goes on to strengthen what has been said by pointing out that the two are different mysteries because, although many were baptized in Christ's lifetime, none received the Holy Ghost until after the Ascension. Christ himself made water and the Spirit the means of entrance to the Kingdom of God and, naming them so carefully as separate, clearly intended them to be separate things. From the Acts of

---

[1] In the introduction (*Works*, Vol. 5, p. 616) Taylor quotes the phrase which gave him his title from the *Ecclesiastical Hierarchy* of the so-called Denys the Areopagite (Cap. ii, par. 85). Dr Mason (*Relation of Confirmation to Baptism*, p. 380) translates the title of Taylor's book, *The Unction which Perfecteth*.

[2] *Confirmation*, S.P.C.K., Vol. 1, p. 154.

[3] *Works*, Vol. 5, p. 619.

[4] Ibid.

the Apostles he takes the often quoted example of the journey of Peter and John to Samaria to lay their hands on the believers there. He refers also to Heb. 6.1 and 2, unhesitatingly ascribing the authorship of that Epistle to St Paul; and he is at pains to defend his interpretation of this last passage from the charge that the "laying on of hands" is that of ordination. These examples from the apostolic age are followed by a large number of quotations from the Fathers of the first four centuries, to prove the claim that the rite had unbroken use. The strength of this patristic testimony which Taylor marshals in order to show the high opinion of confirmation held by antiquity, and its historic continuity, is another proof of the wide range of his scholarship and of his ability to bring together facts and arguments from the most recondite sources.

Taylor goes on to prove that the ministers of confirmation were always bishops, and this gives him an opportunity to introduce an interesting discussion of the chrism in the early Church. This ceremony he contends was never an actual part of the confirmation, though it was sometimes administered at the same time. Anointing by the priest with oil consecrated by the bishop could never take the place of confirmation, though he complains that the "Regulars, the Friars and the Jesuits misled the people of England with that teaching".[1] Earlier in the book he has blamed the Jesuits as being partly responsible for the neglect of confirmation in Ireland. He affirms again that there can be no way of receiving this rite except by prayer and imposition of hands by the bishop. This he says has so well been understood by ordinary people that their common name for confirmation is the "bishoping of children".[2] In Taylor's opinion, confirmation is not so necessary as baptism but it is "a conditional necessity", the same sort of necessity as there is for a man to eat his food if he would be strong.[3] Baptism gives life, confirmation gives vigour to that life. Because these two rites were often administered together, some people have mistaken them for parts of the same thing; but this is clearly not the case, since some time must have elapsed between the baptism administered

---

[1] Compare a modern Roman casuist: "The ordinary minister of Confirmation is a bishop, but the Pope may, and in the missions frequently does, delegate facilities to a priest to administer the sacrament (of confirmation) with crism blessed by a bishop". Slater, *Manual of Moral Theology*, Vol. 2, p. 89. It would seem that in the seventeenth-century Ireland priests sometimes claimed to have received this power from the Pope, though they had not done so. The Roman Synod of Armagh (1614) denied that any priest had received authority to confirm.

[2] *Works*, Vol. 5, p. 650.   [3] Ibid., p. 654.

by Philip at Samaria, and the journey of the Apostles to that city to bestow confirmation.

In his concluding section, Taylor stresses very earnestly the need for confirmation to be given while those who are to receive it are very young:

A little thing will fill a child's head; teach them to say their prayers, tell them the stories of the life and death of Christ, cause them to love the holy Jesus with their first love, make them afraid of sin; let the principles which God hath planted in their very creation the natural principles of justice and truth, of honesty and thankfulness, of simplicity and obedience, be brought into act and habit, and confirmation by the holy sermons of the gospel. If the guides of souls would have their people holy, let them teach holiness to their children, and then they will, at least, have a new generation unto God, better than this wherein we live.[1]

It is with plain, practical, wisdom of this sort that Taylor illuminates the great learning of his book. His words on the relationship of the external rite to the inward grace offer another example. When St Paul says that we are "sealed by that Holy Spirit of promise",[2] these

"and some other words of Scripture relating to the sacraments or other rituals of religion do principally mean the internal grace, and our consignation is by secret power, and the work is within; but it does not therefore follow that the external rite is not also intended: for the rite is so wholely for the mystery, and the outward for the inward, and yet by the outward God so usually and regularly gives the inward, that as no man is to rely upon the external ministry as if the *opus operatum* would do the whole duty, so no man is to neglect the external because the internal is the more principal".[3]

If that was kept in mind how much argument in defence of the functions of organized religion should we be saved! It is by the outward that God usually and regularly gives the inward.

Canon Ollard in his examination of Anglican teaching on confirmation from 1500 to 1850, speaks of Taylor's work as "the fullest treatment of Confirmation on its doctrinal, historical, and practical sides, put forth by any theologian of the English Church".[4] His learning was never more apparent in anything he wrote, of his wisdom and common sense many more examples might be given than the two just cited, and in this work he has at last become aware of a fault which robbed his earlier books

[1] *Works*, Vol. 5, p. 666.   [2] Eph. 1.13.   [3] *Works*, Vol. 5, p. 634.
[4] *Confirmation*, S.P.C.K., Vol. 1, p. 162.

R

of some of their effectiveness: the inclination to pile up every sort of argument which seemed to be making his way, whether it actually fitted into his scheme or not. "I shall add no more, lest I overset the article and make it suspicious by a too laboured defence"[1] is the remark with which he draws near to the end of his proofs of the unbroken tradition of confirmation in the early Church. But the want of leisure for writing of which he had complained to Evelyn left its mark upon his style. The discourse shows many indications of having been put together from previously existing papers. Taylor would be almost certain to preach at the confirmations which he held in his diocese, and these sermons would provide some of the necessary material when he came to consider writing a book. Passages such as that on "the many great graces and blessings consequent to the worthy reception and due ministry of confirmation"[2] irresistibly suggest the sermon form. Similarly, the concluding section on the preparation for, and reception of, confirmation was no doubt teaching that he had given himself to the candidates whom he prepared. Even if he needed specially to get together the references to the Fathers, and all the learning for the basis of his work, yet his long and minute familiarity with the theologians of past days would not make that as formidable a task as it sounds. The want of unity in style which resulted from bringing together different papers, composed on different occasions, could only be overcome by a rigorous polishing, and for this his business in the diocese and the University left him no leisure.

His letters to Lord Conway were now less frequent and were more confined to business matters. On 28 January 1665 he wrote about the progress that was being made with the Cathedral at Lisburn and the plans he has made for providing the see with a bishop's house. He had taken a lease of Donagh Magee's house and hopes that it may be possible to buy it outright later on. If Lord Conway will let him have "a void place of thirty-four foot in front" which lies next to the house and which had at that time "only a dirty smith's shop upon it" he will be able to provide his successors with "a very convenient seat at Lisburn". How troubled the times were his letter goes on to show: "My dear Lord we do live here in so great fear of the Irish and of a sudden rebellion that I have been forced several nights to call in my neighbours and arm them and my servants, the fear is not yet over but something abated. We infinitely miss your

---

[1] *Works*, Vol. 5, p. 642.   [2] Ibid., p. 654.

Lordship here as for many other things so particularly for your care and defence of us." It cannot have been a congenial atmosphere for a man to live in who loved peace as much as Jeremy Taylor did, but who none the less had spent so large a part of his life harassed by the afflictions which come from civil war. The England which he had left in order to find peace now possessed it while he was plunged in further strife. His health, which for years had not been very good, was now beginning to fail seriously.[1]

In a letter written to Sheldon on 25 May 1664 he pleads once more to be removed from his diocese.[2] The Bishop's ostensible purpose in writing was to recommend Sir Richard Kennedy, a judge whose circuit had covered Down and Connor and who was now being recalled to England for being a little too vigorous against the Presbyterians. Taylor says: "I have been informed from a good hand in England that your grace was pleased once to say that I myself was the only hindrance to myself of being removed to an English Bishopric."[3] He tries, most eagerly, to remove this impression from the Archbishop's mind, and beseeches with a humility that is very touching that "your grace will not wholly lay me aside, and cast off all thought of removing me; for no man shall with greater diligence, humility, and observance endeavour to make up his other disabilities, than I shall".[4] One feels that Jeremy Taylor ought not to have begged like this. It all came to nothing, as it was bound to do so long as Sheldon thought Taylor's intellectual restlessness was likely to cause new embarrassment to his friends. It was at this time that Taylor was reported to have sent his chaplain over to England to buy up all the copies of *The Liberty of Prophesying* which could be found; and then, when they had been sent to him in Ireland, burned every one as a protest against its misuse by Noncon-formists.[5] Up to now the Bishop and his family had lived for the greater part of their time at Portmore, but in 1664 Lord Conway

[1] Murray MSS.

[2] Heber, "Life", *Works*, Vol. 1, p. cxix, note. The source of the letter is not specified.

[3] Ibid.

[4] Ibid.

[5] This anecdote is given in a letter from Dr Lort to Bishop Percy, the relevant part of which is printed in Nichol's *Illustrations of Literary History*, Vol. 7, p. 464. Its probability is strengthened by the inclusion of copious extracts from *The Liberty of Prophesying* in at least two post-Restoration Baptist tracts. See *A Plea for Toleration*, by John Sturgion, a member of the baptized people, London, 1661. Also *Sions Groans for her Distressed*, 1661 (no place of issue mentioned). Both these tracts are printed in *Tracts on Liberty of Conscience* (ed. Underhill), London, 1844. The quotations from Taylor occur on pp. 330, 333, 335, 337, 339, 378, and 382.

rebuilt the house on a magnificent scale, and the Bishop and his family were forced to find accommodation elsewhere. But the need for his patron's hospitality existed no longer, since by this time Taylor owned several houses of his own. One was called Homra House;[1] another was a small residence, with a farm of about forty acres attached to it, and was called Megheralave. He is also supposed to have had a cottage by Lough Neagh, as well as a town house in Castle Street, Lisnagarvey, or, as it was now called, Lisburn.

In 1663 the ordinary state of tension and suspicion in which the people of Northern Ireland lived was intensified by news of a plot against the Government. Colonel Blood, a desperado who gained notoriety in more ways than one, got himself introduced to some of the Presbyterians in Ulster and attempted to get them involved with him in action against the Government.[2] No responsible person from among them would have anything to do with him, and the whole plot was soon discovered and broken up. Blood himself managed to get away to England to continue his nefarious career among richer opportunities. Two days before Taylor heard the news of the conspiracy, he discovered that a Mr John Drysdale was back in the neighbourhood again after an absence in Scotland. Taylor and his brother magistrates, Lord Conway and Major Rawdon, had such a poor opinion of Drysdale's loyalty and such a strong opinion of his capacity for mischief that they at once had him arrested, as soon as they knew of the plot, though they had nothing to charge him with except a general suspicion that he would be certainly mixed up in any disaffection.[3] They had some thoughts of sending him up to Ormonde, but compromised by letting him go on a £500 bail while information was passed on to Dublin. Taylor, when writing to the Lord Lieutenant about this affair, took the opportunity to stress the fact that in his opinion there would be no peace in the countryside while the ejected ministers were

[1] It was two miles to the west of Hillsborough, on the Comber road.

[2] Lecky, who was in the plot, was a Presbyterian minister and Blood's brother-in-law. Blood himself at one time professed to be a Presbyterian. His main supporters, according to Adair (*True Narrative*, p. 270), were Independents. In 1671 Blood nearly succeeded in stealing the crown jewels from the Tower of London.

[3] Adair does not mention any arrests made by Taylor on this occasion. He says "Within three weeks of it [Blood's Plot] breaking up, the whole ministers of Down and Antrim who could be found were in one day apprehended, in the middle of June 1663", *True Narrative*, p. 276. They were, he says, "seven in number, viz: Messrs. John Drysdale, John Greg, Andrew Stewart, Alex. Hucheson, William Richardson, Gilbert Kennedy, and James Gordon". Reid thinks Kennedy a slip for Ramsay, *Hist. of Presby. Ch. in Ireland*, Vol. 2, p. 279, note.

allowed to remain.[1] It seems to have become his firm conviction
that the Presbyterians were rebels who, at best, were only biding
their time. He returned to the same accusation in a letter which
he wrote to Ormonde, only a little before his death, giving it as
his opinion that "the Scotch rebellion was either born in Ireland
or put to nurse" there.[2] Undoubtedly in this matter Taylor
misjudged the real local leaders among the Presbyterians. Their
attitude was one which it was very difficult for him to understand.
The law enjoined episcopacy upon all, and in his view those
who refused to accept it dishonoured the Government. From
dishonouring a government to attempting to overthrow it is
but a step. This, together with the memories of past troubles in
England, and the ominous reports of what was being said and
done in his diocese, convinced him that every Presbyterian was
suspect.

[1] Taylor to Ormonde, 11 June 1663, Carte MSS. fol. ss.
[2] Taylor to Ormonde, Feast of St Stephen 1666, Carte MSS., fol. ss.

CHAPTER XI

THE LAST SCENES

ANGLICANISM, wherever it exists, is compelled to resist attacks from extremists on opposite sides, from the Protestant as well as from the Romanist; but in Ireland the strength of the forces on either wing has always called for a more vigorous defence of the central position than has been necessary in other countries. The bishops in Taylor's day were well aware of that. The rising tide of loyalty which swept away the popularity of all bodies that had opposed the King, while weakening Presbyterianism, was having the opposite effect upon Romanism, which had always been peculiarly identified with the royal cause. The Church of Ireland had been mainly the Church of the invaders; the bulk of the native population, while giving it some small, nominal, allegiance had in their hearts continued to belong to the Church of Rome. This covert fealty Roman missionaries during the Commonwealth had set themselves the task of bringing into the open, and they had met with conspicuous success. So as soon as they had time to take stock of the country's needs, Taylor and his brother bishops decided that it was time to check "those enemies which had put fire into the bed straw".[1] It was settled that they should counteract the Roman propaganda with a book, and Taylor was asked to write it. He was not very eager for the task, for he had never enjoyed controversy, but he could not well refuse;[2] so in 1664 he published *A Dissuasive from Popery*.

Although this is the fullest and most careful examination he ever made of the grounds of difference between the two Churches, it is not the only time that he wrote on the subject. "The Gunpowder Plot" sermon of his earlier days was chiefly occupied with the particular problem of Roman Catholic teaching on the obligations of subjects to their princes, but in *Five Letters to Persons changed, or tempted to change, in their Religion* he

---

[1] *Works*, Vol. 6, p. 172. In 1672 Petty estimated the population of Ireland at 1,200,000; of these, 800,000 he classed as Roman Catholics. Of the other 400,000 he thought that a little more than half belonged to the Church of Ireland and the remainder were chiefly Presbyterians and concentrated in Ulster.

[2] Ibid., Vol. 6, p. 173. When the work was decided on, Bramhall was alive, and he was undoubtedly the ablest anti-Roman controversialist in the Anglican communion at that time, but he was too old and too busy for such a thing.

deals with various difficulties which were affecting the lives of individuals. The first letter was to a lady who had already gone over, and Taylor rebukes her rather sharply for leaving the Church of England during a time of persecution. He was writing under the Commonwealth, apparently from Golden Grove or Mandinam, though no address is given. The letter goes on to make a strong appeal to the recipient's sense of loyalty. It then sets out, with perhaps too much violence of contrast, the disadvantages of the Church of Rome compared with the Church of England. The lady had passed on some of the questions which had been the means of changing her allegiance. They were not profound, and Taylor deals with them a little scornfully. "Where was your church before Luther?"[1] and similar enquiries perhaps deserved no better treatment. But the letter seems too rhetorical to be convincing, though it is possible that if the lady had been converted by the type of question she propounds, a confident statement was more effective than argument to change her mind.

The second letter was also written to a lady, but in this case to one who had reversed the process and been converted to the Church of England. It seems to belong to the time of Taylor's ministry in London, though again there is no indication. The opening phrase is interesting: "I bless God that I am safely arrived where I desired to be after my unwilling departure from the place of your abode and danger."[2] The lady obviously lived at a distance and a visit to her entailed risk. The whole tone of the letter is such as will encourage the recipient to persevere in her devotion to the Church of her adoption. Taylor is at particular pains to stress that although Anglicans do not compel their people to use private confession they "advise and commend it".[3]

The other three letters are all to the same person, to a man who could not make up his mind whether to go over to Rome or not. He had enquired of Taylor if the apostles had received of our Lord a tradition of things not written down in Scripture, and whether the things in which the Roman Church differed from the English were due to tradition, or innovation. Taylor answers that all that is necessary to salvation is written in the Scriptures, and he quotes the Fathers to prove his case. It follows from this, of course, that whatever the Roman Church claims to

---

[1] *Works*, Vol. 6, p. 652. This was a common question for Roman Catholics to put to Protestants. See Walton, "Life of Sir Henry Wotton", Wordsworth, *Eccles. Biog.*, Vol. 5, p. 43. The usual answer was: "Where was your face before you washed it?"
[2] *Works*, Vol. 6, p. 661.
[3] Ibid., p. 663.

be necessary to salvation, which is not in the Scriptures, is an innovation. This letter contains a particularly vigorous repudiation of the stories that Taylor himself was going over to Rome.[1] It was written in January, but in February the gentleman was still "much troubled" and in "great danger", as Taylor remarks in the short note that is his fourth letter.[2] In March the gentleman wrote twice more about his difficulties. The first time his communication went astray; the second Taylor answered, dealing with the question whether we may adore the Blessed Sacrament. He answers it is all a question of the theology in which you believe: if you are convinced that transubstantiation is right, then you may adore the Sacrament, but if you hold the true doctrine, such as Taylor has explained in his book, then plainly you may not.[3] These letters also would seem to have been written while Taylor was living and working in London. They give us a very valuable glimpse of his actual dealings with souls.

But for a complete exposition of his attitude toward Rome we must turn to *The Dissuasive from Popery*. The preface is particularly interesting for its description of the superstitions which were common among the Irish peasantry at that time. There was much swearing, especially by St Patrick's Mass Book, but also by their father's soul and their gossip's hand. There were visits to holy wells and the leaving of votive offerings there in the shape of "pins, ribbons, yarn and thread".[4] Fasting was particularly severe, abstaining from both eggs and fish in Lent and keeping a special fast on Saturdays in honour of our Lady.[5] They were specially desirous of being buried "with St Francis' cord about them".[6] If pressed by the parson to come to church, their reasons were more ingenious than truthful, such as "now they are old and never did, or their countrymen do not, or their fathers and grandfathers never did, or that their ancestors were priests and they will not alter from their religion".[7] Taylor suspects that the real reason for it lay in the rigid hold, reinforced by fear, which the Roman priests kept on their people.

He tells an odd story of an incident, in which he was personally concerned, to illustrate the superstition which was the real, basic religion of Ireland. A few months before the time when he was writing he had been very much troubled by petitions about a bell. During the rebellion this had come into the hands of a person of quality, who had no intention of giving it up,

---

[1] *Works*, Vol. 6, p. 667.   [2] Ibid., p. 668.   [3] Ibid., p. 670.   [4] Ibid., p. 175.
[5] Ibid.   [6] Ibid.   [7] Ibid.

though he was willing to pay the full value of it to the former owners. This may have been Colonel Hill or Major Rawdon, and if so Taylor was appealed to because of his friendship with them. He was completely puzzled by this eager persistence in getting a thing back which was of no great worth, so he began to look into the affair more closely. The first reason he was given was that "a dying person in the parish desired to have it rung before him to church, and pretended he could not die in peace if it were denied him".[1] His family had anciently been the keepers of the bell. This ought to have convinced Taylor, but it did not. Enquiring further, he found that the bell was one of the most powerful pieces of magic in the neighbourhood. It was supposed to have fallen from heaven, and all oaths sworn upon it were of the greatest sanctity, so that it was in much demand. It was also used at funerals, for if it was rung before a corpse on its way to the grave, it would help the soul out of purgatory. All this produced a respectable little income for the owners. Taylor does not say what happened to this coveted piece of property, but we may be fairly sure that the people never got it back. Taylor blamed the priests and the friars for not ridding the nation of degrading beliefs of this kind, as he did for encouraging the people to keep to the Irish language.

The three chapters of Taylor's book correspond to the three charges, increasing in gravity as they proceed, which he brings against the Roman Church: that her distinctive doctrines are innovations; that she teaches things which in themselves, or in their results, are impieties; and that she teaches things which are destructive to monarchy and even of Christian society itself. The very claim to declare things to be matters of faith, which are not plainly stated to be so, he contends is an innovation, and possibly the greatest of them all, since it lies at the root of so much else. Among other instances he mentions indulgences. He is willing to admit that certain of the early Fathers refer to them, in the limited sense of remitting a penance imposed by a confessor; but indulgences, as they were commonly understood during the Middle Ages, he claims to have no catholic warrant whatsoever. Neither has Purgatory, "the mother of Indulgencies".[2] The early Church in her prayers recommended the souls

[1] *Works*, Vol. 6, p. 176.

[2] Ibid., p. 193. Taylor seems unwilling to give the Roman Church credit for her persistent attempts to reform the abuses which she was willing to admit did exist in relation to indulgences. Yet he must have been well aware of Council of Trent, *Sess. XXI*, cix.

of the faithful into the hands of God and prayed that they might find a good resurrection. This kind of prayer for the departed the Church of England has left open, her children may use it or not as they see fit, but prayers for the dead in any other sense are an innovation. As may be expected, transubstantiation and the "half communion", as he called it, are among the intruded doctrines;[1] but, considering Taylor's attitude toward the use of Irish expressed only a few pages earlier, it argues some want of self-criticism when he stresses here Rome's wrongdoing in retaining Latin for her liturgy. English would certainly be as obscure as Latin to the native Irish. He is a little sweeping in his next instance of innovating—the adoration of images. With passages quoted from the iconoclastic Fathers, he seems to forbid the simple hanging of pictures in churches. The last and strongest of the charges he brings against Rome is in opposition to her claim for the Pope's universal power. The object of all these accumulated accusations is to prove that "their religion as it is distinguished from the religion of the Church of England and Ireland, is neither the old nor the catholic religion, but new and superinduced by arts known to all who with sincerity and diligence have looked into their pretences".[2]

The subjects dealt with in the second chapter, those which Taylor contends produce impiety, are mostly to do with sin and repentance—for example, the teaching that repentance, though it must take place at some time, can be deferred; and the mechanical use of private confession, which results in the sinner doing what evil he wishes and then trusting to "the circular and never failing hand of the priest"[3] to rid him of his guilt. He goes back again to indulgences, to which he had referred in his first chapter as an innovation. This time he studies them chiefly to show their evil effects on morality. That form of probabilism which makes the opinion of one teacher an allowable guide, even though it contradicts the main current of the Church's teaching on the point at issue, the invocation of saints as deliverers,[4]

---

[1] *Works*, Vol. 6, p. 208. The Roman Church, of course, denies that Communion in one kind is half Communion. She argues that by reason of the hypostatic union and of the indivisibility of the glorified humanity of Christ, our Lord is really present and is received whole and entire under either species alone. Council of Trent, *Sess. XXI*, ciii.

[2] *Works*, Vol. 6, p. 224.   [3] Ibid., p. 230.

[4] Ibid., p. 254. Taylor supports this with numerous quotations. He proves that many Roman Catholic theologians were unguarded in the language they addressed to the saints; but not all are, and as usual Taylor does not put the other side. See, Bellarmine, *De Laud Beatif.*, 1, 17; also Council of Trent, *Sess. XXII*, ciii, where it is stated that in Masses celebrated in honour of the saints the sacrifice is to God alone, while from the saint addressed the priest desires prayer and patronage.

and exorcism, are also cited as leading to bad conduct. The section on exorcism provides some curious reading. Taylor had perused a good many books on this subject, some of them with the authority of the Roman Church behind them; but some, although put out by mediaeval priests and never definitely condemned, she was not so proud of. He spends five pages analysing these with a good deal of sarcastic and humorous comment, ending with the remark that "whatever the devil loses by pretending to obey the exorcist, he gains more by this horrible debauchery of Christianity".[1] The last chapter, in which the Roman Catholic teaching which Taylor considers destructive to society is discussed, goes over much the same ground as that covered by the Gunpowder Plot sermon, dealing with equivocation, the right of the clergy to be exempt from secular authority, and the Pope's power to depose and excommunicate kings.

Throughout the book Taylor is much too prone to accept the common practice of some parts of the Roman Church as the authoritative teaching of the whole. It was part of his case that Romanism led to a degraded and superstitious life, but it would have been a much fairer method if he had pointed out what superstitions she encouraged, what she only acquiesced in, and what she condemned. No Church ought to be judged solely by the popular practice of the most ignorant of her believers, any more than she has a right to be judged entirely by the devotion of her saints and the most guarded statements of her theologians.

Roman Catholics have never been slow in defence of their doctrines, so it was not to be wondered at that such a sweeping attack, coming from so well-known an author, was promptly answered. One of the replies published under the initials J. S. was by his old adversary, John Sergeant, whose activities in Wales had formerly provoked Taylor into writing his *Real Presence*.[2] Another was by an anonymous writer referred to by Taylor as A. L. who issued *A Letter to Friend, touching Dr. Jeremy*

[1] *Works*, Vol. 6, p. 266.

[2] John Sergeant, 1622–1707. Educated at St John's College, Cambridge. Secretary to Bishop Morton for about a year. His researches in the works of the Fathers led to his joining the Church of Rome. Studied in the English College at Lisbon, was encouraged to write controversial works and did so voluminously for about forty years. His best-known efforts were directed against Bramhall, Jeremy Taylor, and Tillotson. "He must doubtless be distinguished from the John Sergeant whose evidence with respect to the Oates' plot was printed by the House of Commons in 1681", *D.N.B.* See *Literary Life of John Sergeant*, ed. Kirk, London, 1816. The attack on Taylor was in the form of "An Appendix subverting fundamentally and manifoldly, my Lord of Down's *Dissuasive*" added to the second edition of his *Sure Footing in Christianity*.

Taylor's Dissuasive from Popery, discovering about an hundred and fifty false or wrested quotations in it. A third was by Edward Worseley, the Jesuit procurator and missioner at Antwerp, who published, with his initials only, a book called *Truth will out, or The Discovery of some Untruths smoothly told by Bishop Jeremy Taylor*.[1] Of all the attacks this was the most damaging, though in the second part of *The Dissuasive* which Taylor wrote specially to confute his critics, he only makes a few references to it and to A. L., spending most of his time on Sergeant. In his "Epistle to the Reader" Worseley brings up the old charge of Taylor's reputed Pelagianism. More seriously, he accuses him of misquoting both the Fathers and Roman Catholic divines. His method is to go through *The Dissuasive* with a running criticism rather than producing a general line of argument against Taylor. But all the way through, recurring like the rhyme in a song, is a heading "The Doctor's quotations not true", "The Doctor's quotations not right", "The Doctor's quotations still amiss". In some cases the mistakes which Worseley pressed home so relentlessly were apparently due to Taylor's quoting as much as he thought fit and neglecting the rest of the passage as unimportant. In a few instances he seems to have relied more than he ought to have done upon his memory.

Though Taylor left Worseley almost unanswered, he dealt very fully with Sergeant's criticism in the introduction to the *Second Part of the Dissuasive*, which occupied the last years of his life. The art of vituperation was a very valuable part of the controversial divine's equipment in former days. Now that a few centuries have elapsed, and there are no feelings to be hurt, the student is often grateful for a few passages of ingenious invective, since they lighten many a volume of defunct theology. But Taylor's life is, in general, so full of life and beauty that we can well be content with the very little of this lesser inducement which he offers us. The opening of his attack on Sergeant is probably the longest piece of personal abuse he ever wrote, though it only runs to a page and a half. He referred to the Appendix in which he had been attacked as "a viper", remarking neatly that though it be "but little, it is a viper still though it hath more tongue than teeth".[2] He then takes the eight methods of criticism which Sergeant had used, and considered unanswerable and overwhelming, and refutes them in their order. They were rather far-fetched, and the gist of them all was that Taylor had no real authority for what he said, since he had admitted

---

[1] At Liége, 1665.   [2] *Works*, Vol. 6, p. 289.

that "Scriptures, Fathers, councils, reason, history and instances" were all liable to err. Taylor's retort is simple in essence, though going into details, as it does, it takes up a fair amount of space. No person or thing, not even Sergeant himself, is infallible; but that does not make it impossible to arrive at a reasonable degree of certainty.

The book which followed this lengthy introduction goes over much the same ground as the first part, though there is a fuller discussion of the authority of Scripture, which aims at showing that Anglicanism in relying upon the Bible has a surer basis than Rome, who chooses for her main support the authority of the Church. For the rest he was content to underline, and expand, the main items in his former attack on innovations in general, purgatory, indulgences, *Index Expurgatorius*, auricular confession, transubstantiation, and the worship of images. In this last section he defended some of the quotations which Worseley had attacked, in one case by criticism of his adversary's scholarship in a minute point of translation,[1] in another by pleading a printer's error. Only the necessity of defending what he had written justified Taylor in producing a second part. He had already stated his position with respect to Rome fully, and clearly. Against that, the main criticisms which can be offered are the faulty quotations, which his opponents laboured, and, what weighs more with us today, the tendency to judge Rome solely by what was objectionable in her. There is no doubt about Taylor's general position. He is as energetic in his defence of reform as he is in his claim to be catholic.

In 1665 England was at war again with the Dutch, and a mutilated letter from Taylor to Lord Conway belonging to this time, though undated, describes the rejoicings in Dublin when the news of a great naval victory arrived. "We are here so full of joy at the newly received news of the Dutch defeat, that we can do nothing but give God thanks and rejoice with one another, and tell the story over a thousand times. . . . As soon as we heard this [news and the pac]quet was opened, the Lord Deputy and Council went to Christchurch [attended by the] horse guards in arms and the Mayor and Aldermen in scarlet [where Te Deum] was sung solemnly, besides public prayers and proper anthems."[2] The letter refers, possibly, to the Duke of York's

---

[1] Worseley claimed that εἴδωλον should always be translated by *simulacrum*, whereas Taylor contended that *formula* could be used. *Works*, Vol. 6, p. 618.

[2] Murray MSS. The words within brackets are suggested by the transcriber of the Murray MSS. to supply passages which, obviously, were missing from the original.

victory off Lowestoft in June 1665. But the war with the Dutch was not over yet. Taylor mentions it again in a letter he wrote to Conway on Lammas (1 August) 1666 when the news that Lord Conway was in Ireland had just reached him and awakened some of the old enthusiasm.

"My Dearest Lord it is very well that this degenerous age of the world hath preserved your Lordship as a great example of the noblest friendship. We all here long to see your Lordship, but I could not stay the leisure of your Lordship's affairs but that I must endeavour some way to converse with your Lordship beforehand, and to express the true pleasure I have in your Lordship's coming over and in the very precious imagination of your being near us. . . . I heartily pray for your Lordship that you may have the great joy and pleasure of a victory over the Dutch sent you into Ireland for your welcome hither. . . . My Dearest Lord I have not much good Irish as to bid your Lordship welcome home when you are about sixty miles from home, but I have a true English and thankful heart to love and honour you greatly."[1]

For the last year or two Taylor's health had been failing. Lord Conway was eager that he should see Valentine Greatrakes, the stroker, and profit by the marvellous healing power of that extraordinary man, which was astonishing England.[2] But ill though he was, Taylor was still active in his diocese. For many years the complaint all over Ireland had been that the churches were in ruins. Conditions in Down and Connor were no better than they were elsewhere, and so, although there was very little money to spare, Taylor had perforce to be a builder. Only one of his churches now remains in anything like the condition in which he left it. That is the Church at Ballinderry, which Taylor began to build in 1665. To obtain the oak fittings for it he dismantled the chapel of Lough Beg, where he had officiated in his early days in Ireland before he became a bishop. There is nothing very remarkable about the building; it is plain and becoming to its time and its purpose, with high oaken pews, a

[1] Murray MSS.
[2] Valentine Greatrakes, 1629–83. Was born of middle-class parents at Affane in the County of Waterford. Was intended for the University, but, owing to the troublous times, entered Cromwell's army and became a lieutenant in the Earl of Orrery's Regiment. When the soldiers were disbanded in 1657, he retired to his farm at Affane. There discovered his gift of healing. He was invited over to England in 1666 to help Lady Conway (*Conway Letters*, p. 247). He failed with her, but had great success with others in the neighbourhood and at Worcester and London. Though attacked as an impostor, he was modest in his claims and often successful. Accused of being a protégé of Presbyterians and his power as "intrenching" on the King's claim to cure by touch (*Har. Misc.*, Vol. 6, p. 160). See his own *Brief Account of Mr Valentine Greatrakes*, London, 1666, and many other tracts.

lofty pulpit topped in spite of the low roof with a sounding board, and windows set with small bull's-eye panes. Originally it was roofed with slates from Wales. By the beginning of the present century it had fallen into ruins, but was then restored to exactly its first condition, as an act of homage to Taylor's memory. His connexion with Trinity College, Dublin, still continued, and seems to have given him as much pleasure as anything in Ireland. It offered him also from time to time opportunities of helping his friends. He is said to have sent students there at his own expense, and in 1666 he was willing to use his influence with the College to obtain for a Mr Dodwell a dispensation from the statutory obligation on Fellows who were Masters of Arts of three years' standing to proceed to Holy Orders.

In addition to ill health, distresses outside and inside his family harassed the last months of his life. Colonel Hill died in 1663, and in the settlement of his estate Taylor became involved in a lawsuit with Moses Hill, his old friend's son. The cause, with Viscount Conway and the Lord Bishop of Down as the defendants and Moses Hill as the petitioner, came before both Houses of Parliament in March and April 1666. Its only effect was to bring on a dispute between the two Houses, and the cause was left undetermined when Parliament was dissolved. Taylor was not the aggressor, but such a quarrel with an old friend's son must have pained him greatly. But the whole history of the Church of Ireland showed that only the most resolute defence of her financial rights could keep them from being alienated. This is another example of Taylor's sense of duty forcing him to act in a way which must have been contrary to his inclination. Another sorrow touched him more nearly still, although the full weight of the blow fell upon him too late for him to be fully conscious of it. Charles was the Bishop's only remaining son. He was now a young man of twenty-four and is said to have had some sort of position in the Duke of Buckingham's household. He died in 1667 and was buried on 2 August in St Margaret's, Westminster. It is not clear what his complaint was; possibly it was consumption. Nevertheless, the romantic imagination at the back of the Jones MSS. ascribed his early death to the wild debaucheries into which his master had initiated him.

While the son was dying in London, the father lay sick in Lisburn. He had visited a fever patient, and caught the disease. On 10 August, when the Bishop had been "very ill for three or four days", Sir George Rawdon wrote to Lord Conway to say that the Bishop was that morning a little better than he had been the day before, "when the Lord Primate took leave of him",[1] so much so that now the doctors gave him a little hope of recovery. He had been in a violent fever for some days, too ill to make his will, for which there was luckily no necessity, since Rawdon had pressed him to this last duty before the illness had grown too severe;[2] though he had "not in all two thousand pounds to dispose of, of which six hundred pounds is for his lady and two daughters".[3] On the thirteenth the Bishop died. It was his wish that he should be buried in his new church at Ballinderry, but as that was not yet consecrated he asked with his last breath that he should be buried at Dromore. On the 14th Rawdon again wrote to Lord Conway, this time to announce the Bishop's death. He "died yesterday about three in the afternoon and hath left a sad family".[4] There was no money in the house and "two doctors from Dublin to be paid and his lady cannot pay them without borrowing".[5] Of the £2,000 he had left, £1,500 was in the hands of Lord Donegal, and another £600 was being kept by Lord Conway, but of this £100 would be needed at once to pay the funeral expenses.[6] Already a scramble was going on among those who hoped to succeed to his offices. Rawdon, who showed himself now as kind a friend as he had ever been, had suggested to the Primate during his visit five days earlier that Dr Marsh, Taylor's son-in-law, who was then Dean of Armagh, ought to succeed to the Bishopric of Down, and Dr Rust to that of Dromore.[7] Both these men were intimate friends of Taylor's, and their succession is what he would himself have wished. While the Bishop's body lay in "searcloth" waiting to be buried, Dean Marsh hurried off to Dublin to push his claim for preferment, and Rawdon wrote to Lord Conway to use his influence with the Lord Lieutenant on behalf of both Marsh and Rust and, what was less legitimate, to get Ormonde to stop any letters which others who sought this preferment might try to send to London.[8]

---

[1] *C.S.P., Ireland, Car. 2*, CCCXXIII, No. 56, Rawdon to Conway, Lisburn, 10 August 1667. The Primate was Archbishop Margetson.

[2] Ibid., No. 62, Rawdon to Conway, 14 August 1667.

[3] Ibid., No. 56, Rawdon to Conway, 10 August 1667.

[4] Ibid., No. 62, Rawdon to Conway, 14 August 1667. Harris, *History and Antiquities of Ireland*, 1764, Vol. 1, p. 210, says that Taylor left £10 to the poor of each of the parishes of Dromore, Lisburn, and Ballintobber.

[5] *C.S.P., Ireland, Car. 2*, CCCXXIII, No. 62, Rawdon to Conway, 14 August 1667.

[6] Ibid. Rawdon's figures were, of course, approximate, but the £2,000 was no doubt what would be left of the estate when all expenses were paid.

[7] Ibid., No. 56. Rawdon to Conway, Lisburn, 10 August 1667.

[8] Ibid., No. 62, Rawdon to Conway, 14 August 1667. Searcloth, or cerecloth, i.e. linen smeared with wax or gum.

Mrs Taylor was also in Rawdon's mind. At Michaelmas half a year's rent on the Bishop's lands would be due and he had already been "very importunate with the Primate and the Lord Chancellor that this should be paid to the widow".[1] When next Rawdon wrote to Conway he had received a letter from the Primate which made him think that all his requests would be granted. It only remained for Conway to use all the influence he had in England to see that nobody upset this plan. As if these greater troubles were not enough, local thieves had taken advantage of the distress in which the Bishop's household was plunged to break into his orchard on the very night he died and steal all his fruit, as well as a quantity of loose timber which was intended for flooring the dining-room, and was lying there to season.[2] By this time the Bishop's body had been sent across to Dromore in Rawdon's old coach, and was there awaiting the funeral which was to take place on Tuesday following Rawdon's letter, which would be 3 September.[3] So Jeremy Taylor's last request was granted and his bones were laid to rest in the cathedral he had built.

It is entirely fitting that the one funeral sermon in the English language which approaches those which Taylor himself composed should have been delivered over his grave. It was by George Rust, now soon to be Bishop Rust. The method was the one which Taylor had himself invented; first the text and the meditation upon it, then the biographical details. It was a dangerous thing to attempt, when everybody present must have remembered how adept the one whose obsequies they were celebrating had been in this manner, but it was entirely successful. Its eloquence was worthy of the subject and it would be difficult to find higher praise than that. The sketch it gives of the Bishop's life supplies a very large part of the total information we have about him. Its accuracy has been questioned at times, but further research has almost always shown Rust to be in the right. And quite apart from the facts of his life Rust is the only one who gives us anything like a picture of Taylor as he lived, and moved, and we welcome it all the more since it shows to us that the man himself was as gracious as his works. Says Rust:

[1] *C.S.P.*, *Ireland*, *Car. 2*, CCCXXIII, No. 87, Rawdon to Conway, 31 August 1667.
[2] Ibid.
[3] Rawdon, writing on 14 August, refers to his letter of 10 August as written on Saturday. On 31 August, which would therefore also be a Saturday, he says that Taylor's body is to be buried on the following Tuesday, which would be 3 September, as stated in the text. Gosse, *Jeremy Taylor*, p. 209, gives the date of Taylor's burial as 21 August, which is clearly incorrect.

S

Nature had befriended him much in his constitution; for he was a person of the most sweet and obliging humour, of great candour and ingenuity; and there was so much of salt and fineness of wit, and prettiness of address, in his familiar discourses, as made his conversation have all the pleasantness of a comedy, and all the usefulness of a sermon. His soul was made up of harmony, and he never spake but he charmed his hearer, not only with the clearness of his reason, but all his words, and his very cadences were strangely musical.

But that which did most of all captivate and enravish was the gaiety and richness of fancy; for he had much in him of that natural enthusiasm which inspires all great poets and orators; and there was a generous ferment in his blood and spirits that set his fancy bravely to work, and made it swell and teem, and become pregnant to such degrees of luxuriancy, as nothing but the greatness of his wit and judgement could have kept it within due bounds and measures.[1]

Taylor's learning which seems to us so prodigious seemed wonderful even to his own learned age:

There were very few kinds of learning but he was mystes[2] and a great master in them. He was a rare humanist, and hugely versed in all the polite parts of learning; and had thoroughly concocted all the ancient moralists, Greek and Roman, poets and orators; and was not unacquainted with the refined wits of the later ages, whether French or Italian. [But] notwithstanding his stupendous parts, and learning, and eminency of place he had nothing in him of pride and humour, but was courteous and affable, and easy of access, and would lend a ready ear to the complaints, yea to the impertinencies of the meanest persons. His humility was coupled with an extraordinary piety and I believe he spent the greatest part of his time in heaven; his solemn hours of prayer took up a considerable portion of his life. . . . But he was not only a good man God-ward, but he had come to the top of St Peter's gradation, and to all his other virtues added a large and diffusive charity; and whoever compares his plentiful incomes with the inconsiderable estate he left at his death, will be easily convinced that charity was steward for a great proportion of his revenue. But the hungry that he fed, and the naked that he clothed, and the distressed that he supplied, and the fatherless that he provided for; the poor children that he put to apprentice, and brought up at school, and maintained at the university; will now sound a trumpet to that charity which he dispersed with his right hand, but would not suffer his left hand to have any knowledge of it.[3]

It is a great tribute to the memory of a man whose life touched greatness at more points than it is given to many to achieve.

[1] Rust, "Funeral Sermon", *Works*, Vol. 1, p. cccxxv.
[2] Ibid. Mystes, i.e. one who has been initiated.
[3] Rust, "Funeral Sermon", *Works*, Vol. 1, p. cccxxvi.

After it the other literary offering which was made in Taylor's honour seems merely bathos. Lemuel Mathews, his chaplain, published in Dublin *A Pandarique* [*sic*] *Elegie* of which all that can be said is that no doubt Mathews meant well, but that there must have been very few chaplains in Ireland who could have written anything worse. Stanza V of the poem will be a sufficient sample:

> So vast his knowledge, he
> Had tasted oft of each allowed tree
>   On all their sweets had daily fed.
> The Bird of Paradise, he kindly bred
> A guileless dove within the serpent's head:
>   The cherubs bowed, and sheathed their swords;
> For's tongue had all the charm of words,
>   All that language and wit affords,
>   And new and fitter names did wear;
> And 's lucky pen (as if a pencil twere)
> Made gold, by guilding it, more golden to appear.
>   Ye, wisdon's sons with him there lost
>   A Vatican of learned things which cost
> A treasury of precious time; but grieve ye most
>   For undiscovered Arts and Sciences,
>   And what is excellent in those or these;
> What never was, what never shall be found,
>   With him lye buried under ground.
>
>   .   .   .   .
>
> Such was our mitred man,
> Our great Diocesan.

No effort was made to raise other monuments to his memory than these. There is even a story that "about a century after", his bones and those of his friend Rust were disturbed from their vault to make room for another bishop,[1] but that they were piously gathered together again, and restored by Bishop Percy. Happily, such an act of desecration has been proved by Bishop Mant to have been extremely unlikely.[2] Between 1713 and Dr Percy's appointment in 1781 only one bishop died in possession of the see. That was Dr Marley, whose death occurred suddenly in Dublin on 13 April 1763. Though his burial place had not been discovered, his lineal descendant in Mant's day was sure that it could not have been at Dromore. The story is itself later

---

[1] Heber, "Life", *Works*, Vol. 1, p. cxxi. Again the source of this misinformation was the Jones MSS.

[2] Mant, *History of the Church of Ireland*, Vol. 1, p. 673.

than Bishop Percy's time. His domestic chaplain, when asked
about the incident at a later date, had no recollection either of
the happening itself or of the Bishop ever referring to it. Obviously
tradition has again been muddying the pure stream of history.
No record was kept of the exact spot in which Taylor's body was
laid. It was always supposed to have been under the altar, and
when, early in the nineteenth century, the vault there was
opened, a leaden coffin with the initials J. T. on the lid was
discovered and assumed to be that of Taylor. In 1827, through
the efforts of Bishop Mant and his clergy, a white marble monument, bearing on either side of the inscription a crosier, and
above it a sarcophagus surmounted by a Bible and a mitre, was
erected in Lisburn Cathedral. Bishop Mant himself composed
the epitaph in a style of elaborate eulogy.

But Taylor needed neither monument nor epitaph, his books
are his remembrancers wherever the English language is found.
Ever since his first beginning to write, his literary output had
been very large, so that there could not have been much left
unpublished at his death. The second part of *The Dissuasive from
Popery* was in the press when its author died, and a number of
sermons which had been issued as pamphlets when they were
first preached were afterwards given a permanent form. Apart
from these, there are only two works of which we have certain
knowledge. One was *A Discourse upon the Beatitudes*, which the
Bishop was actually writing when his final illness overtook him.[1]
This unfinished manuscript seems never to have been printed.
The other is a small tract entitled *The Reverence Due to the Altar*.
Its existence was quite unknown until the manuscript of it was
discovered early in the nineteenth century in the library of
Queen's College, Oxford. It was printed first as a separate booklet
and then included in Heber and Eden's edition of Taylor's works.
Possibly it was written when Taylor was in residence at All
Souls College, and if this is so, it has the considerable interest
attached to it of being the first known writing of his that we
possess. It does not bear Taylor's signature, but the handwriting,
the vocabulary, the cast of thought, all proclaim it to be his.
Put in letter form it is addressed to someone who desired "an
account of those reasons which move the Church in her addresses
to the place of public worship, but especially the Altar, to adore
God Almighty with lowly bendings of the body".[2] The argument,

[1] Rust mentions this in his sermon, *Works*, Vol. 1, p. cccxxiv.
[2] *Works*, Vol. 5, p. 317.

which is stated briefly, with very little development, takes the form of asserting that the altar is to be reverenced as the place of God's special presence, and although this is not explicitly formulated, the implication is of God's special presence in the Eucharist. This in accordance with Taylor's usual custom is reinforced by reference to the practice of the early Church. Perhaps the manuscript survived because Taylor had some idea of publishing. It would be a fitting thing for Laud's chaplain to do, at a time when the new regulations about the position of the altar were causing opposition.

S. T. Coleridge, in a hastily jotted note, once criticized his generation for allowing a manuscript volume of Jeremy Taylor's sermons to lie unpublished when so much ephemeral rubbish found its way through the press.[1] No one since has succeeded in finding this disregarded treasure, though a number of people have tried, the present writer's own extensive enquiries having failed, like all others, to bring it to light. It is possible that John Wilson Croker had come across such a volume among the papers which he received from the Marquis of Hertford and that Coleridge had seen it. If that is so then the book has disappeared. Or Coleridge may have had the Jones MSS. in mind and mistakenly supposed some part of them to be sermons.

[1] S. T. Coleridge, *Omniana* (1888 Ed.), p. 365.

CHAPTER XII

TAYLOR'S CHARACTER AND ACHIEVEMENT

FROM the all too few accounts of those who knew Jeremy Taylor, and from the indications of his personality which we can find in his works, it is possible to put together a fairly complete picture of what the man himself must have been. All agree that he was strikingly handsome, an advantage of which he seems to have been fully aware, for it was his usual practice to adorn his books with his portrait. That published with *Eniautos* shows him in his prime. The face is oval, with large, vivacious eyes set beneath a wide brow. His hair curls gracefully up from beneath a closely fitting skull-cap. The cumbrous, and sombre, garments of a divine which he is wearing serve to emphasize the more than usual facial beauty. It is the portrait of a man who is both sensitive and highly intelligent; and one who is certain to be an artist in some medium or other. Taylor was of a very good height, and had a charming manner. The comment of nearly all those who recorded their impression of his preaching was, that the grace of his appearance and delivery matched the grace of his style. His personal attractiveness was not limited to the pulpit. Alcock, his secretary, said that it was a pleasure to hear him speak even to common people. Among his intimates he had that same humour and gaiety of conversation which, in the generation before his own, had endeared the character of Bishop Andrewes to many who did not love his opinions.

For a large part of his life Taylor associated on intimate terms with some of the most polished society in Britain. No one who was welcomed into, and retained his place in, such company could be without personal gifts, though in Taylor's case these might never have reached their full development if the exercise of them had been limited to the narrow circle of college society and a country rectory. But just at the most critical time of his life, when he might have settled down into a dull, good, learned man, he was thrust into the wider world of the King's army, into Oxford when all the Royalist world was flocking there, and Golden Grove. There he associated with men who had been formed in the most polite courts of Europe, statesmen nursed in great events, prelates whose advice swayed the actions of the King, and men who had tested the learning they had gathered from books by travel and experience in many lands. Such experience was of inestimable value in the formation of his character. It provided scope and incentive for his innate gifts, and congenial acquaintanceship for the further development of them. Taylor's life is a record of friendships, none of which was ever marred by a serious quarrel, or ended except by time and distance. The unfortunate thoughtlessness which dedicated to Duppa a book which he had not read considerably irritated that good man; but it produced no bitterness, and in no way injured the respect and love which each had for the other. Right until the last years of his life there is only one trace of a grudge against anyone. In that case, however, it must be admitted that Taylor found it hard to forgive Sheldon his opposition to Laud's bestowal of the Fellowship at All Souls. That was perfectly understandable. Taylor a young and ambitious man, had just had his feet planted on the bottom rung by a patron who had the power and the wish to help him climb. It would be difficult for most men as near to their youth as Taylor was then, not to harbour some resentment against one who, in the face of everybody else's agreement, opposed his advancement. But Taylor and Sheldon were both too good to let a difference of this sort rankle over long. When it came, Sheldon's distrust of Taylor was on other grounds. The disagreement with Jeans can hardly be called a personal quarrel. It was a clash between two theological points of view rather than two men, for they had never met. Remarkable as it may seem in a day when personal animosities were many and bitter, Taylor had to wait until the latter part of his life and go to Ireland before he found an enemy. This fact alone speaks eloquently for his personal charm.[1]

The same society which did so much to help his development in one direction hindered it in another. Because of it, Taylor never had that wide acquaintance with all classes of people which he would ordinarily have gained if he had continued to fulfil the normal duties of a parish priest. Consequently, in his sermons there is a complete lack of those homely, intimate, little

[1] Adair shows us how Taylor appeared to the opposite side: "There was set in the Bishoprick of Down and Connor, one Dr Taylor, a man pretending civility and some courteous carriage especially before his advancement, but whose principles were contrary to the Presbyterians . . . not only in the matter of government, modes of worship and discipline but also in doctrine. He had sucked in the dregs of much of Popery, Socinianism, and Arminianism, and was a heart enemy not only to Nonconformists but also to the Orthodox." *True Narrative*, pp. 244–5.

stories of everyday people which some of the Puritan preachers could use to such good effect. He knew two sections of life well, the rest but little. The society to be found in universities, and the Loyalist groups in London and Oxford, and the similar types in a great country house, dominated his experience. In none of these spheres did he deal mainly with either the middle or the working classes, and the fact that he began life in a barber's shop never seems to have drawn him towards them. Consequently, his writings lack a certain width and humanity. Had he chosen to write about people, he would have been able to depict one or two characters exquisitely, but he could never, as Bunyan did, have populated a highway with all the diversities of human kind. The nature of his genius in no way compensated for his narrowness of experience, by allowing him to supply from within what he had not been able to gain from without. A similar straitened outlook was a defect common to most of the High Anglicans of his day. They understood the spiritual needs of the Hall excellently, but not many of them had any message for the shop, and the cottage, except that the dwellers therein should, so far as was practicable, model themselves on the Hall. Such a restricted point of view was not all loss. It left its holders free to develop, so far as they wished, that literary art, and learning, in which they delighted. If Taylor had been habitually set to preach to middle-class congregations, it is doubtful if we should have had the unique treasure of *Eniautos* permanently to enrich our language.

Taylor's surroundings entirely suited his nature. He absorbed learning easily, and reproduced it as easily. Certain forms of beauty he loved passionately, and his hearers welcomed him in the elaborate presentation of them. These beauties he found principally in books, but now and then he came across them in a garden, in some aspect of nature, or in the intimacies of family life. He never spoke with any clarity about his wife and children, but little domestic cameos with no names attached decorate his work with some frequency. Judging from these, he would seem to have had a very happy family life, which, together with the more than ordinary calm of his religious experience, produced that inner serenity which is so noticeable a feature of all his writings. There is nothing whatever resembling egotism in his life. He was totally dependent upon the effect his abilities might have upon those in high places for any advancement which he might gain, since he had by birth no influential connexions. That he had great powers he must have known perfectly well, and yet, so far as we can learn, he never scrambled for preferment. When he wrote that sad letter to Sheldon asking that he might be removed from Down and Connor, it was relief from an intolerable position for which he begged, not a better diocese.

His courage was as great as his modesty. Change for the worse in his circumstances produced no word of complaint from him. The shipwreck of all his fortunes at the beginning of the Civil War merely left him with the determination to begin again, and without books as he was, or any help, furnish the world with something by which he might be remembered in after ages. Years of hard work, not very lavishly rewarded, followed upon this resolve. Imprisonment, misunderstanding, no settled home and continually reoccurring poverty, and what he felt more keenly, the loss of his quiet—none of these abated his sense of God's goodness, or forced him into peevishness. Great courage, as well as originality, was needed to revive those humane doctrines concerning man's free will which, though they were not unknown to the ancient world, the majority of theologians in Taylor's day could only execrate and condemn. A book of moral theology seemed to him to be needed, and his wide reading in that subject appeared to fit him for the task, so he set himself to its accomplishment, though the deliberate restraint of his artistic faculties must have been at least as formidable as any other of the difficulties involved. During the Civil Wars his conduct, so far from being timid, might at times seem rash. The most loyal of men might have thought it unnecessary to advertise his sentiments by dedicating a book to the King who had just been executed, or by a vigorous attack on the religious favourites of a Government which seemed at the height of its power. But Taylor never forgot that he had been a chaplain to Laud, and to the King, and was for ever bound in duty to them. That some parts of *The Liberty of Prophesying* were said not to please his majesty must have given him great pain; for all the talk of toleration which was in the air when he wrote would lead him to suppose that what he had to say would be sympathetically received. From beginning to end of the Civil Wars his political opinions were never for one second in doubt, and his Anglicanism was likewise without thought of change.

There seem to be extraordinarily few failings to set against so many virtues. Taylor has been accused of flattery, and it is true that he produced many dedications, a species of composition in which adulation is hard to avoid. Yet judged by the standard of his time—the only standard fairly applicable—such a charge is difficult to substantiate. It was an age of compliment, and Taylor paid many graceful ones, which were designed to appeal as much to the artistic sense of the recipient as to his self-love. A good deal of the rest was nothing more than the suitable and expected language on those occasions, with not much more meaning in it than "yours sincerely" has to-day. There is no trace in Taylor's dedications of the crude vulgarity with which Disraeli cynically heaped his trowel. A more serious, and more easily proved, charge is that of unfairness in controversy. This shows itself particularly in the two volumes of his *Dissuasive from Popery*, where, instead of occupying the far stronger position which would have been his had he placed Romanism in its best light, and dealt temperately with it, he was content, in addition to picking out and demolishing a few local absurdities, to repeat the often-made Protestant charges without adequately considering the Roman defence. So many different theologians, in so many different ages and countries, have taken upon themselves the explanation of the Roman Faith that foolish arguments and unworthy teachings are sure to abound. Taylor was certainly not the best critic of the Roman position which Anglicanism has called forth. The fault which Chillingworth mentioned in his early days handicapped him to the end. He could neither listen to the other side long enough, nor sufficiently respect its conclusions. This is the fault of many quick thinkers, and ready speakers, and does not necessarily imply an overbearing disposition.

Inconsistency is another fault with which he is frequently charged, and with much truth. Isolated extracts prove almost nothing about what was the balance of his opinion, since he was always ready to revise his views as some new piece of study showed him another facet of the truth. At all times he clung to the Apostolic Succession, he consistently and utterly repudiated the Calvinistic theories of sin and predestination, and the doctrine of transubstantiation, but it would not be easy to find any other major theological position to which he adhered throughout his life with complete wholeheartedness.

Nothing that he did suggests that he possessed that cool, and judicial, habit of mind which befits the controversialist. He was a generous-hearted man, who inherited some of his views from his teachers and was guided toward a good number of the rest by his emotions. Taylor's attitude toward Rome was one which he shared with most of the Laudians. They discovered the Church which seemed to them ideal in the Church of the first three or four centuries. Rome, they held, had corrupted the purity of the tradition to which the early times had clung, and to which it was the mission of Anglicanism to bring the world again. This tradition could be explained, but nothing should be added to it ; and yet Rome had been so false to her trust as to add continually to a system of order and teaching which was essentially simple. In the first three centuries Taylor and his contemporaries found the two great sacraments, a ministry of bishops, priests, and deacons; and an apostolic doctrine carefully preserved by a Church which was the Body of Christ. They could not assure themselves that they found there papal supremacy, purgatory, indulgencies, and many minor points on which the Church of Rome placed great value. Anglicanism therefore repudiated these things, or set them in a far less important light than did the Romanists.

It is essential to an understanding of the Laudians and those who sympathized with them, to realize that they did not reach their position by way of premeditated compromise, a concession here to Protestantism and there to Catholicism, so that they might appeal to reasonable men on both sides. They came to it by way of study. In the ages of the Church which seemed to them the purest they found such and such things; to them therefore they would hold, rejecting all later accretions. Such a resolve did indeed place them midway between the extreme Protestant and Roman positions. It had all the advantages and disadvantages of the deliberately sought compromise which it was not. It lay very open to attack. Rome could argue that if the Church is the Spirit-guided Body of Christ it will necessarily, as time goes on, bring new treasures of doctrine into the world, since it was not deserted after the first centuries by its promised guide. Protestants, on the other hand, could argue that decay had set in long before the Laudians were willing to allow, and that those who wished for a pure Church must seek it nearer to the times of Christ. On both these fronts the High Churchmen fought a long and successful fight, in which Taylor bore his full share of the battle. They staked their whole position on learning. Everything must be brought to the test of that primitive, catholic rule which Vincent of Lerins had laid down; and this necessitated a scholarship both wide in its range and minute in its attention to detail.[1]

[1] See McAdoo, *Structure of Caroline Moral Theology*, pp. 4 ff., for numerous references to Caroline authors on this point.

The amazing extent of Taylor's knowledge has already been commented on, but many other men in his day had read almost as widely. Archbishop Williams in the midst of a busy life regularly studied from six at night till three in the morning, would sleep until seven, and then be ready again for the round of duties which would keep him occupied until evening. Burton, living a college life, with leisure and the Oxford libraries close at hand, had perhaps more opportunities; but even then the vast and curious mass of his learning, brought together from so many different sciences and countries, is amazing. Selden once remarked that "all agree that we have never had a more learned clergy",[1] though another saying of his shows that he had only theological learning in mind.[2] Taylor did not differ from his contemporaries in being, as a rule, uncritical in his scholarship. It is true that he seems fairly certain that the Athanasian Creed was not written by Athanasius,[3] but he is quite willing to attribute the Apostles' Creed to the Apostles.[4] Yet as time went on learned men grew more and more inclined to compare texts in order to arrive at the most trustworthy reading, to estimate the importance of different sources, and to judge the value of various traditions.

With this deference to learning the Laudians combined a great reverence for the historic continuity of the Church. If they objected to Rome because she had inserted things which did not belong to the true line of descent, they objected to Puritanism because it severed itself from the past altogether. In such matters as liturgical worship, for instance, the extreme Protestants wished to make a clean break, and either begin again with forms of their own devising, or leave men untrammelled by any forms whatsoever. Taylor and his friends retorted by upholding the Prayer Book as a system of worship approaching the ideal, for it was catholic in that it accepted all that was best in the Church's traditional worship, and it was reformed in that it was purged of all mediaeval errors.

In the general cast of his mind, Taylor was at one with the Anglicans of his time. Laud's loved phrase "the beauty of holiness" exactly described what he, and those with whom he sympathized, were aiming at; and what he so conspicuously achieved. They adorned their churches with carving, with silk, fine linen, and precious metals; they adorned their theology with poets, philosophers, and the Fathers; and in their lives they showed forth

[1] *Table Talk*, Chap. XXI, par. 5.   [2] Ibid., Chap. LXXIX, pars. 2 and 3.
[3] *Works*, Vol. 5, p. 407.   [4] Ibid., p. 371.

that grace and charm, unshaken by the ills of life, which have always been considered indisputable marks of saintliness. It is perhaps an unavoidable evil that a number of men, sharing a common trend, should be given a common name and classed as a school, but it is a habit which can be most misleading. If the word "Laudian" or the phrase "Anglo-Catholic" is taken to mean a group of men whose doctrines upon all except the minutest points were in agreement, a serious mistake is made. The thing which bound them together was a common attitude, rather than a common theology or a common teacher. With this in mind, it is not surprising to find that Taylor's opinions differed in a number of ways from the complete Catholic position, and that he had clear affinities with what was later on called "Latitudinarianism". In this connexion, Taylor's early acquaintance with Chillingworth, and his close friendship with Henry More, are significant. According to Baxter, More was the leader of this group who "were mostly Cambridge men, Platonists or Cartesians, and many of them Arminians with some additions".[1] Whether or not Taylor belonged entirely to the group, he had drunk of the same fountain as they. He loved Plato, had eagerly studied Descartes, and of his Arminianism there can be no doubt. But there was more than that.

His catholic side can be partly illustrated by the study which we have attempted to make of his Eucharistic doctrine. In his continual emphasis on the sacrificial element in the Eucharist, and his consequent insistence that the Anglican minister is in a true sense a sacrificing priest, he was above most Laudians; in his views on the nature of the Presence in the Sacrament he was below them. Similarly, not all those who upheld episcopacy as a practical system would have been so emphatic and clear in their assertion of its divine origin. In his wholehearted love for the ancient liturgies, in his desire for beauty of worship in his own day, and in his vigorous claims for the continuity and necessity of confirmation, Taylor was completely catholic. On his Latitudinarian side his insistence on the paramount claims of reason, his willingness to tolerate all who would make themselves tolerable, his inability to accept the infallibility of either Scriptures or councils, stand out in clear relief. But Taylor was not a man with a divided mind, keeping an uneasy allegiance to two schools, for there were not yet two schools. Everything tended to hold together men who might otherwise have emphasized one side

[1] *Autobiography of Richard Baxter*, ed. Lloyd Thomas (Everyman), p. 177.

of their teaching to the detriment of the other. The rigidity of Puritanism and Romanism on either hand drove into the centre those who claimed their right to hold fast by tradition and at the same time to test it by an appeal to reason.

When the Restoration had removed the danger from Puritanism and the Revolution of 1688 had reduced the pressure of Rome, those who had stood side by side in the battle with these two powerful adversaries themselves became divided. One party stressed the paramount claims of reason more and more, while the other turned with an increasingly blind affection toward history and tradition. Political events favoured the Latitudinarians. The High Church party lost a great part of its strength when some of the saintliest, and most learned, of its members went into exile from the national Church rather than take the oath of allegiance to William and Mary. Those who remained and their successors were suspect for generations, since they clung with a stubborn loyalty to the Stuart cause long after all hope of its success had disappeared. But this parting of the ways was only a possibility in Taylor's day. Chillingworth and Laud both wished the Church of England to be truly Catholic and at the same time to be unhampered both in thought and in learning. Suspicion and a lost cause had not yet made the High Church men obscurantist, and the spiritual depth and fervour of the Latitudinarians had not yet been rationalized away. Chillingworth, More, and their friends lived austere lives and pursued a high aim. They were engaged in the search for truth rather than in the pursuit of happiness, which seemed such a satisfying occupation to their spiritual descendants. What was in the early Latitudinarians only a leaning toward Socinianism—and Taylor himself has been accused of that fault[1]—became a cold Deism which took all life and reality out of religion. Jeremy Taylor could never have developed along those lines. He would have parted company with any system of thought which chilled the souls of its adherents, however neat might be the intellectual basis on which it rested. Spiritual beauty, delight in and wonder at the love of God, and a life of ordered holiness which reflected such a state was what he valued most, and he dedicated his greatest gifts to bringing men and women to that condition.

---

[1] That he was called a Socinian by the Ulster Presbyterians may perhaps be considered only as proof that his theology differed from theirs, but S. T. Coleridge, who admired Taylor greatly, placing him with Bacon, Shakespeare, and Milton as one of the four great geniuses of the English language, thought him "half a Socinian in heart". *Table Talk*, 4 June 1830.

Nature had equipped him admirably for such a task. His grace of style, the imaginative faculty and the depth if restricted range of that sympathy which underlay his literary gifts, helped to place him among the most valued of confessors, and the greatest of devotional writers. It was in these spheres that he gave the Church of England his most valuable service. Theology and theologians abounded, it was devotion that was needed, and devotion which should be as catholic and reformed as the Church itself. Not everyone who wishes to do so can produce devotional literature that is both adequate and original; it needs great art, as well as great and infectious holiness. The writer who has these gifts together has genius. Taylor's drawbacks as a theologian, his too great elaboration of an argument, and a certain amount of inconsistency could not operate to the injury of his devotional work. There argument was not so much needed as manifold illustration and vivid restatement of a few simple truths. One who teaches devotion will do no harm to his subject, no matter how long he may dwell upon it, if he can continue to show it in a new light. In one case the aim is to convince, the other to attract. Since the facts which underlie the pursuit of holiness are not many, consistency is not put to a severe test.

When Anthony Wood said that Taylor was esteemed the perfect artist he said as much about him as could be put into so few words. The artist in Taylor was always greater than the theologian. It might be interesting to speculate what kind of literature he would have produced if, when he took his degree at Cambridge, he had gone to Court in some minor post and associated with the London wits, instead of taking Holy Orders and associating with the Oxford clergy. But immediately that line of thought is checked by the conviction that Taylor could never have done anything else but take Orders. He was a born Christian, a born priest, and a born preacher. There is not one story, or hint of a story, in the brief accounts which survive of him which suggests that he was anything but holy in character from beginning to end. The marvel is that one so good, and so artistic, should have been so robust. He was neither self-righteous nor a prig, nor did his love of beauty in any way degenerate into affectation.

When we say that he had a love of beauty it is necessary to limit the meaning of the word to some extent, for not all beauty found him immediately responsive. The broad face of nature, the grandeur of mountains, the awe to be found in a great storm, or in the aroused sea, did not appeal to him much. It was in all the minutiae of creation that he had such a loving delight. A blossoming rose, the tendrils of a vine, the flashing of light from the ruffled surface of water, a lark in flight, the sheen on the breast of a dove, or the little wavy marks which the tide makes on the sand; these were all things which he was capable of describing with an inspired rapture because he had observed them with the most sympathetic attention. He could play with such things with the most delicate fancy, and ennoble them with striking and musical language.

Linguistically it was an age of borrowing. The intellect of the day was demanding forms of expression which the language itself could not furnish. A son of his time, Taylor borrowed, and to some extent coined the words he needed. But the years have dealt very well with his vocabulary on the whole. Certainly his language is not so obsolete as Milton's, even if it is not so free from dead words and phrases as Baxter's. No one need be excessively puzzled by Taylor. Anyone who reads more than a page or two soon becomes familiar with the meaning of such words as "deturpated" for deformed, "immorigerous" for disobedient, "intenerate", to soften, "paranymph", a bridesmaid or lady's maid, "stultiloquy" for foolish talking. It is a little more confusing when he uses a fairly common English word according to its Latin or Greek etymology, and contrary to its normal development; as, for instance, "insolent", meaning unusual, "extant figures", meaning figures in relief, or speaks of "an excellent pain" when he means a pain which is very severe. A habit of Taylor's which draws attention to itself is his peculiar fondness for giving a plural form to an abstract noun; such as "strengths", "tolerations", "prudencies". He also used the comparative degree to express a state just short of the superlative; as, for example, "the Libyan lion drawn from his wilder foragings". When we have added to these idiosyncrasies a love of pairs of adjectives almost as great as that which animated the compilers of the Book of Common Prayer, and a knack of sometimes compressing his similes to the point where they are so concentrated as to be almost ridiculous, Taylor's worst tricks of style have been mentioned.[1]

The type of wit in which Andrewes indulged, consisting in torturing words until they yielded up as many different meanings as possible, is comparatively rare in Taylor; but he had, what

[1] E.g. *Works*, Vol. 3, p. 315: "And what can we complain of the weakness of our strengths", etc.

was often considered a part of wit, the capacity to seize on, and bring out, the affinities of things.[1] It is this gift which, in De Quincey's opinion, placed him with Burke among the greatest of rhetoricians.[2] Taylor is never willing to leave his subject alone. He plays with it, presents it first in this light, and then in that, ornaments it with all his gifts of thought and fancy; and it is not until it has had lavished upon it all that he considers arresting, interesting, or beautiful, that he is willing to pass on. It is this habit of mind which dictates his style and makes his sentences one impetuous, "thought-agglomerating flood".[3] Long as are the sentences into which this way of thinking betrayed him, their length in no way obscures their meaning. This is chiefly because they consist of a series of short statements about the same subject strung together by the word "and". It would be quite possible to repunctuate Taylor's works and, without altering a single word, reduce his sentences to a modern brevity.

Taylor belonged to the last, fine flowering of the Elizabethan genius, before Puritanism had given restraint and order to English prose at the cost of splendour. His place is with Robert Burton, and Sir Thomas Browne; though when he published the defence of episcopacy, which was his first important book, the *Anatomy of Melancholy* had already been through five editions and its author had been dead three years. It was six years since Browne had issued his *Religio Medici*. But though he was the last of these three to form, he surpassed the other two—Browne in many respects, Burton immeasurably. They were all stored with learning and poured it out lavishly, but Burton was content for his subject-matter to take care of itself; he set it down in a good sound fashion, trusting to the rich and quaint texture of his thought to gain him his effects. Taylor was not content with the thought by itself, the presentation of it must be as lovely as he can make it, and it is all done with an appearance of consummate ease. His language comes with a rush, and the effect upon the reader is to hurry him forward as if he were borne upon wings. The style swoops and soars with the freedom of a bird. There is in Taylor's sentences everywhere, but most of all in the sermons, a joy which often rises to ecstasy. Hazlitt spoke of "the glad prose of Jeremy Taylor" and as usual he had chosen the right adjective.[4]

[1] Dr Johnson defines wit as "A combination of dissimilar images, or the discovery of occult resemblances in things apparently unlike". *Dictionary.*
[2] De Quincey, *Essay on Rhetoric.*
[3] S. T. Coleridge, *Miscellanies*, London, 1892, p. 181.
[4] Hazlitt, *Spirit of the Age*, Oxford, 1928, p. 41.

T

The loveliest fancies, the most musical cadencies, are joined to produce the happiest of effects. It is this joyous prodigality of beauty which is the chief attraction of Taylor's decorated style. No one else ever came quite near it. Browne preferred to construct his sentences on the Latin model; Taylor hardly troubled to construct his at all. He seemed to write with speaking in view and trusted to the tone, and inflection of voice, to carry off a change of tense and to link the proper noun to the proper verb. Both were masters of rhythm and both lavished all the power of their imaginations on the ornamentation of their themes. But Taylor had a spontaneity and freedom which Browne had not. Browne's sentences are like a solemn procession following a magistrate or a bier, Taylor's like a wedding train.

Richly ornamented as his style is, the ornamentation is never superfluous. The images which he elaborates as well as those which he is content to leave undeveloped do in fact, bring the reader a little nearer the heart of Taylor's thought. That this thought, when apprehended, is in reality very weak, is an old charge against him. Coleridge referred to it in his famous description of Taylor's prose as "a ghost in marble".[1] While it is true that, apart from the concept and style, nothing in itself very original is to be found in Taylor's works, it is also to be remembered that we are nowhere promised any such thing by the author himself. His mission, as he saw it, was to teach men the plain way of holiness, not to engage in any deep philosophical discussions, or to propound any startling theme. Taylor may have been without the ability to do either of these things; certainly in *The Liberty of Prophesying* and in the discussion on original sin provoked by *Unum Necessarium* he showed no such gifts; but it must be continually borne in mind that Taylor's style was admirably suited for the purpose to which he put it, the inculcating, and encouraging people to the practice of, the ordinary teachings of the Christian religion. For this object, argument, appeal, the compelling phrase, the arresting word, are all brought into operation.

Keble drew an interesting comparison between Burke's famous description of the Queen of France at Versailles and the sentence in which Taylor speaks of "the strange evenness and untroubled passage" of Lady Carbery's death, to illustrate the difference between the rhetorical and the poetic mind; he preferred to class Taylor with the poets rather than the rhetoricians. Burke

[1] S. T. Coleridge, *Letters*, 3 November 1814.

deliberately speaks for a certain premeditated effect. Taylor says
what he has in his mind as the poet writes his verses—in the way
most natural to the speaker and the subject—and he would
probably have clothed his thought in much the same fashion if
he had never been called upon to give it public utterance.[1]
This is no doubt true to some extent. Taylor did produce beautiful
prose with extraordinary facility, but that does not mean that
he paid no attention to what he had to say. The parallel between
the image and the idea which he wished to present is generally
too sustained to be entirely spontaneous. The poet's lyric may in
its first form spring unbidden from the heart, but he will submit
it to many a revision before he lets it go to take its chance in the
world. It was no doubt the same with Taylor. The happy inspiration had to take on a good deal of polish. In the case of the
famous passage on the death of Lady Carbery, as in many other
of Taylor's loveliest paragraphs, the basis is one simple, observed
fact—in this case the flowing of a river; the stream merging itself
in the ocean, the ocean blending with the infinite. It illustrates
excellently the strength and weakness of Taylor's mind. The idea
was one which nine out of ten preachers walking on the banks
of a river on a calm evening and meditating upon life and death
would be likely to hit upon, but for those nine the temptation to
spin out the parallel and moralize upon it would be too great.
Taylor describes what he sees in language which is both exact
and stimulating, and compresses the image to the point where it
seems one with the idea suggested. This fusion of thought and
symbol is undoubtedly a poetic characteristic.

The habit of constant enrichment has brought down upon
Taylor's style the condemnation of being over gaudy. South
began the attack in the generation which succeeded Taylor's
own, and in all the confident superiority with which each age
writes down its predecessor.[2] But no criticism could be more
blundering. Style to be good must achieve its purpose and will
to some extent resemble its purpose. It would be absurd to
embellish the directions on a fire alarm; but the prose which is
designed to appeal to all the complex body of thoughts and
emotions, which are bound up in religion, will probably be none
the less effective if it employs a variety of presentment, and
decoration. Taylor's feeling for words was very much akin to
his feeling for concrete loveliness; they were things beautiful in

---

[1] Keble, *Praelectiones Annis MDCCCXXXII*, the third lecture, *passim*.
[2] South, *Works*, Oxford, 1823, Vol. 4, p. 153.

themselves not merely for what they represented. An arresting phrase presented itself to his mind as a miniature picture, and an old word of this kind was no more to be despised because of its age and rareness than an old painting. For us, with less imagination and less knowledge, the effect is not the same; but Taylor's prose is so rich in fancy, so full of light and colour, that it is beyond the power of a few obsolete phrases to clog it. In general the most admired of Taylor's effects are gained by carefully selected, carefully wrought images, by language both striking and musical, in which alliteration is not disdained, and by an underlying vivacity of mind.

It was for artistry and gifts like these that Coleridge classed Taylor with Bacon, Shakespeare, and Milton; his poor opinion of Taylor's thought we have already noticed. Mason in one of his later letters to Gray called Taylor "the Shakespeare of English prose", and this flattering comparison has since been repeated with all the frequency which such an attractive piece of adulation would be sure to win. Yet beyond what we have just said there is very little justification for it. Shakespeare is the greatest of English poets because both in mind and heart he was greater than all others, not merely because he had greater gifts of expression, and loved some kinds of beauty. Taylor lacked completely all the things which made the real Shakespeare: love for humanity only because it is human, the ability to understand and reproduce a vast diversity of men and women, a universality of mind to which no part of creation was alien or antagonistic. These were not Taylor's gifts, and we do him no service in attempting to claim them for him. Certain characters he not only failed to understand but was quite out of sympathy with—sinners, for instance. Many preachers of righteousness have regarded them with that stricken love which thinks no sacrifice too great for the redemption of men fallen through ignorance and the craft of the devil. Taylor could speak in the conventional way about the fascination of sin, while all the time he found it hard to understand how anyone could find it fascinating. An evil liver was either deplorably weak or deliberately wicked. Good men were, of course, trapped by temptation now and then or puzzled in their consciences, just as they were often slack and needed to be roused. It was to fulfil these purposes that he wrote and preached. But Taylor does not often seem to have found the individual himself interesting. It was what he might be rather than what he was which was dominant in the mind. This is not the fault of all preachers.

Anyone who reads a page of Taylor, and then a page of Donne, feels himself in two totally different intellectual countries. The two have entirely dissimilar conceptions of man and his Saviour. Taylor is not, like Donne, perpetually awed by the immensities of God, Heaven and Hell. His aim is manifest and his subject well within his grasp. There is no mystery, and only a limited if clear vision. They differed both in genius and in experience. Taylor's life had always been well approved and godly. Donne had been a gross sinner, and realized the awfulness and narrowness of his escape—if indeed he had escaped. He knew, and could sympathize with all the distortion of purpose with which the strong desires of the flesh could harass the soul. Taylor understood best those who like himself were Christian by inheritance, but who felt the need to lay a firmer hold on what they had received. Unbelief had attracted him as little as the sins of the flesh, neither did he, for the sake of the intellectual certainty to be gained by it, start from the position of the atheist and think his way up as Baxter deliberately did.[1] The famous moral demonstration, beautiful though it be, is such a thing as faith would devise to strengthen itself rather than reason create for its own conviction. Taylor never understood the doubts and fears which may attack even the best-intentioned, or that with perfect honesty a certain type of mind finds it hard to believe.

Very frequently a comparison is made between the genius of Taylor and that of Milton, possibly with the feeling that as they both belonged to the same age and were on opposite sides each may fitly represent his party. They are by no means the best persons for that purpose and the comparison is more interesting for the dissimilarities than otherwise. In a long and eloquent passage, Coleridge placed these two side by side, but after some paragraphs of differences the only likenesses that he could discern were that both were good men, both wrote in favour of intellectual liberty, both had learning and genius and wrote hymns, both endeavoured to help forward education by the production of a Latin Accidence.[2] Such similarities, it is readily seen, are not important.

Yet the comparison does serve to draw attention to Taylor's real originality, a point which few of his biographers seem to appreciate sufficiently. He was an innovator in both the concept

[1] *Autobiography of Richard Baxter*, ed. Lloyd Thomas (Everyman), p. 26.
[2] S. T. Coleridge, *Apologetic Preface to Fire, Famine and Slaughter*.

and style of his books. It does not injure his claim in this respect that he used rhetorical images which were common property, for he remade them in a way which converted them into his own. He was one of the first to write a whole treatise on religious liberty, a Life of Christ in English, and the first to write in English, and on his own plan, a complete manual of casuistry. But what is greater still he brought to theology a sweetness of mind to which that science had long been a stranger. Place him side by side with Baxter and see the difference. Page after page of that noble book, *The Saint's Everlasting Rest*, is defiled by a calm assumption of fiendishness on the part of God and an equally calm assumption of the right of the "saints" to delight in the contemplation of that fiendishness and its results. In these facts there is sufficient proof of his originality. In style no one ever wrote like Taylor before, and though Rust afterwards produced one creditable imitation, no one else has written like him since. Possibly his isolation helped to bring this about, for apart from the Matchless Orinda, Taylor seems to have been outside contemporary literary influences of a secular nature until he became the friend of Evelyn. It is noteworthy that from that time onward he tended more and more to avoid his characteristic exuberance, and to bring his prose more into line with the growing fashion for plainness.

There were many in his time who shared the same sincerity that possessed Taylor, and had a similar high purpose. There were some who, like him, consciously sought to make their prose beautiful, but none who had such loveliness of thought, or who if they had possessed it, could have clothed it with such a prodigality of noble language. The nature of Taylor's prose and the usefulness of his devotional writings have together insured his survival. *Holy Living and Holy Dying* and the *Sermons*, supposing that they had been written in another manner, could not for their intrinsic qualities have perpetuated Taylor's fame except among a small circle; but they kept it alive and secured him an audience when the style by itself was unpopular. Together they have spared Taylor's reputation the vicissitudes which the names of many of his great contemporaries have undergone. Yet it is sometimes said that Taylor has been neglected, and in some ways perhaps he has. As a devotional writer his popularity has remained steady, not beginning to wane seriously until perhaps a generation or so ago. Even as pure literature, in spite of ups and downs, his writing has never been subjected to that peculiar, and apparently wilful, misunderstanding which Milton has had to endure. Throughout the eighteenth century, when the dominant literary ideals were anything but the same as Taylor's, Warburton, Gray, Dr Johnson, and John Wesley, to name adverse types, were not sparing in their praise. With the appearance of the romantic school the chorus of Taylor's admirers rises more loudly still. Coleridge, Southey, De Quincey, Christopher North, Hazlitt, and Thackeray were all enthusiastic in their praise. It would be hard to find any, except perhaps two or three of the very greatest, who have found a more continuous understanding among the discerning. But as a theologian he has indeed met with neglect, and in quarters where such neglect seems almost unaccountable. Canon Ollard has pointed out how extraordinary it is that the bishops in the eighteenth century should have been so little influenced by Taylor's great book on confirmation.[1] But the episcopal ideal had changed. The Georgian churchmen were not of the kind for whom Taylor wrote. Yet even here the neglect was not so complete as it might seem. In 1825, a time when Church life is generally held to have been at zero, Bishop Howley then at London is said to have recommended *Ductor Dubitantium*, of all books, to his clergy.[2] Joshua Watson, a friend of the bishop's and the leading layman of his day, was an enthusiastic admirer of Taylor, so possibly the suggestion came from him.

At no other time has the Anglican Church produced so much great writing as she did in the seventeenth century. Traherne and George Herbert both expressed the purest devotion in the most exquisite of silver-toned prose. Isaac Walton, Fuller, Chillingworth, Bramhall, and Laud could all write more than competent English. Nor are Taylor and his contemporaries now without a message. Indeed, the desire to turn toward them for intellectual inspiration is growing stronger among a certain school of theologians as the fashion to admire their writing grows among one group of literary men. Our times are sufficiently similar for us to understand these particular forefathers of ours, and for their approach to problems not unlike our own to interest us. They fought passionately for freedom, in thought as well as in life, and if they disagreed it was in their ideas of what was the

---

[1] S. L. Ollard, "Confirmation in the Anglican Communion", *Confirmation*, S.P.C.K., Vol. 1, p. 162.

[2] McColl, *Reformation Settlement*, p. 289. In 1822, Heber published his complete edition of the works of Taylor and must have anticipated considerable support for so bulky and expensive a publication.

best safeguard for that freedom. On the Continent the protagonists in a similar struggle were losing their fight. Slowly a despotism which sought to regulate every phase of men's lives was tightening its grip. Physical science and a changing social structure were presenting the Church with hitherto unsolved problems in thought and life. All this is not unlike the situation which we ourselves are facing to-day. Those who seek a solution to these difficulties will do well to remember the respect for authority, and at the same time the honesty of mind which tried all authority, rejecting that which was spurious or useless, with which the Carolines undertook their task.

Some parts of their theology are of less practical use to us now than they were, for the progress of learning has invalidated them to a great extent. But we may suppose that if the knowledge of this has come to Taylor and his friends, in the places wheresoever they are, they accept it with equanimity since they would rejoice in its cause. We may admire the style in which they dressed their thoughts as we admire the clothes in which they dressed their bodies, but both are a little too elaborate for use in our day. It is their spirit which we need to imitate. Among them Jeremy Taylor was an acknowledged leader, and it was right for him to be so since he embodies their ideals in a peculiar degree. It is because he was one of the noblest products of a very noble age, because he was a man more than ordinarily rich in knowledge and imagination and a pre-eminent master of lovely prose, that he is likely to endure.

LAUS DEO

APPENDICES

A

TAYLOR'S WORKS

In a few cases, where the title is excessively long, its short form only is given.

1. *A Sermon Preached upon the Anniversary of Gunpowder Treason.* Oxford, 1638. 4to.
2. *Of the Sacred Order and Offices of Episcopacy.* Oxford, 1642. 4to. The London issue of 1647 is the same edition with a new title-page.
3. *A Discourse concerning Prayer Extemporary.* Anon. London, 1646. 4to.
4. Θεολογία Ἐκλεκτική, or, *A Discourse of the Liberty of Prophesying.* London, 1647. 4to.
5. *An Apology for Authorized and Set Forms of Liturgie.* London, 1649. 4to. This is an expanded edition of item 3 and bore Taylor's name.
6. *The Great Exemplar of Sanctity and Holy Life according to the Christian Institution; described in the History of the Life and Death of the Ever-blessed Jesus Christ, The Saviour of the World.* London, 1649. 4to. The second edition, London, 1653. Fol., has some additions to the text, a fine portrait of Taylor by Lombart, many fine large engravings by Faithorne, and the title printed in red and black.
7. *Prayers before and after Sermon*, in "Choice Forms of Prayer, by several Reverend and Godly Divines, used by them before and after Sermon". London, 1651. 4to.
8. *The Rule and Exercises of Holy Living.* London, 1650. 12mo. This edition contains "Prayers for Our Rulers", which was altered in subsequent editions into "Prayers for the King".
9. *A Funeral Sermon Preached at the Obsequies of the Right Honourable and Most Virtuous Lady, The Lady Frances, Countess of Carbery.* London, 1650. 4to. 1651. Fol.

10. *The Rule and Exercises of Holy Dying.* London, 1651. 12mo. Has a folding plate by Peter Lombart.

11. *Clerus Domini, or, A Discourse of the Divine Institution, Necessity, Sacredness, and Separation of the Office Ministerial.* London, 1651. fol.

12. *A Short Catechism for the institution of Young Persons in the Christian Religion: to which is added an explication of the Apostles Creed, composed for the use of schools in South Wales.* London, 1652. 12mo.

13. *A Discourse of Baptism.* London, 1652. 4to.

14. *Two Discourses, One, Of Baptism; Two, Of Prayer.* London, 1653. 4to.

15. *Twenty-seven Sermons Preached at Golden Grove; Being for the Summer Half-year, Beginning on Whitsunday and ending on the Twenty-fifth Sunday after Trinity.* London, 1651. Fol.

16. *Twenty-five Sermons Preached at Golden Grove; Being for the Winter Half-year, Beginning on Advent Sunday, until Whitsunday.* London, 1653. fol. Items 15 and 16 were published together in 1653, two volumes folio, London. The title page, 'Ενιαυτός, *A Course of Sermons for All the Sundays of the Year.* There was a second edition in 1667. London. Two volumes in one. Fol.

17. *The Real Presence and Spiritual of Christ in the Blessed Sacrament proved against the doctrine of Transubstantiation.* London, 1654. 8vo.

18. *The Golden Grove; or a Manual of Daily Prayers and Litanies. Also Festival Hymns, according to the manner of the ancient Church, composed for the use of the devout, especially of younger persons.* By the author of *The Great Exemplar.* London, 1655. 8vo. This book incorporates item 12. It has a folding frontispiece by Hollar, showing Lord Carbery's seat, Golden Grove.

19. *Unum Necessarium, or The Doctrine and Practice of Repentance.* London, 1655. 8vo. Has a portrait by Lombart.

20. *Deus Justificatus, or a Vindication of the Glory of the Divine Attributes in the question of Original Sin, against the presbyterian way of understanding it.* (On the next page) To the Right Honourable and Religious Lady Christian [sic], Countess Dowager of Devonshire. London, 1656. 12mo. The first edition bears "The Stationer's Postscript to the Reader", signed R. Royston, and was published without Taylor's permission. He published it himself with other works a year later.

21. *Correspondence between John Warner, Bishop of Rochester, and Doctor Taylor, concerning the chapter of Original Sin in the Unum Necessarium.* London, 1656. 12mo.

22. Σύμβολον 'Ηθικο-πολεμικὸν, *or a Collection of Polemical and Moral Discourses.* London, 1657. Fol. Has a fine portrait by Lombart. This is a reissue in one volume of items 2, 4, 5, 17, 18, 20. "The former impressions of these books having been spent, and the world being willing enough to receive more of them, it was thought fit to draw into one volume all these

lesser books which at several times were made public, and which by some collateral improvements they were to receive now from me might do some more advantages to each other, and better struggle with such prejudices with which any of them hath been at any time troubled", *Works*, Vol. 5, p. 2.

23. *A Discourse of the Nature and Offices of Friendship. In a letter to the Most Ingenious and Excellent M. K. P.* London, 1657. 12mo.

24. *Two Letters to Persons Changed in their Religion.* London, 1657. 12mo.

25. *A Collection of Offices, or Forms of Prayer in cases ordinary and extraordinary, taken out of the scriptures and the ancient liturgies of several churches, especially the Greek. Together with a large preface in vindication of the liturgy of the Church of England.* Anon. London, 1658. 8vo. Has a frontispiece showing Christ in an attitude of prayer, which is said to have caused Taylor's imprisonment.

26. *A Latin Letter in John Stearne's* Θανατολογία. Dublin, 1659. 8vo.

27. *Ductor Dubitantium, or The Rule of Conscience in all her general measures; serving as a great instrument for the determination of Cases of Conscience.* London, 1660, two vols. Fol. Has a portrait by Lombart.

28. *The Worthy Communicant, or A Discourse of the Nature, Effects and Blessings consequent to the worthy receiving of The Lord's Supper.* London, 1660. 8vo.

29. *Certain Letters concerning Original Sin, in A Second Part of a Mixture of Scholastical Divinity,* by Henry Jeanes. Oxford, 1660. 4to.

30. Letter (on Prayer) prefixed to Henry Leslie's *Discourse of Praying with the Spirit and with the Understanding.* London, 1660. 4to.

31. *A Sermon Preached at the Consecration of Two Archbishops and Ten Bishops.* London, 1661. 4to.

32. *A Sermon Preached at the Opening of the Parliament of Ireland.* London, 1661. 4to.

33. *Rules and Advices to The Clergy of the Diocese of Down and Connor.* Dublin, 1661. 8vo.

34. *Via Intelligentiae.* A Sermon Preached to the University of Dublin. London, 1662. 4to.

35. *A Sermon Preached in Christ's Church, Dublin, July 16 1663. At the Funeral of the Most Reverend Father in God, John, late Lord Archbishop of Armagh, and Primate of All Ireland. With a Succinct narrative of his whole life.* London, 1663. 4to. The first edition was printed for John Crooke at the Sign of the Ship in St Paul's Churchyard. Royston's edition was the third, though printed only a month later.

36. Ἑβδομάς Ἐμβολιμαῖος, a supplement to the Ἐνιαυτός. London, 4to. 1663.

37. *The Righteousness Evangelical Described. The Christian's Conquest over the Body of Sin. Fides Formata, or Faith working by Love.* In three Sermons Preached at Christ's Church, Dublin. Dublin, 1663. 12mo.

38. *A Dissuasive from Popery*. London, 1664. 4to.

39. Χρίσις Τελειωτική, *A Discourse of Confirmation*. London, 1664. 8vo. Has a portrait.

40. *The Second Part of the Dissuasive from Popery*. London, 1667. 4to.

41. *Three Letters to one Tempted to the Communion of the Church of Rome*. London, 1673. Fol.

42. *Christ's Yoke and Easy Yoke, and yet the Gate to Heaven a Strait Gate in two excellent Sermons*. By a learned and reverend divine. London, 1675. 12mo.

43. Δεκὰς Ἐμβολιμαῖος, *A Supplement to the* Ἐνιαυτὸς. London, 1667. Fol. This is a reissue in one volume of items 1, 9, 31, 32, 34, 35, 36, with two sermons on The Minister's Duty in Life and Doctrine.

44. *A Sermon Preached at the Funeral of that worthy knight, Sir George Dalston*. London, 1683. 8vo.

45. *On the Reverence Due to the Altar*. Edited from the Original MS. by J. Barrow. Oxford (Parker), 1848. 4to.

A Form of Consecration or Dedication of Churches and Chapels according to the use of the Church of Ireland was printed at Dublin by John Crook in 1666 and was added to the quarto edition of the Prayer Book issued by the same printer in 1700. The authorship of the form, and the authority by which it was added to the Prayer Book, are both unknown. The Revd F. R. Bolton, Vicar of East Markham, Nottinghamshire, has made an exhaustive examination of the Rite and is of the opinion, on stylistic and theological grounds, that it is the work of Jeremy Taylor.

From time to time portions of Taylor's works have been republished by editors and given fresh titles. These added to Taylor's Bibliography merely cause confusion.

B

PSEUDO-TAYLORIANA

BOTH during and after Taylor's lifetime his name was attached to books of which he was not the author. The first of these, *A New and Easy Institution of Grammar*, was published in 1647. The facts about it were never really obscure. It was generally reckoned to be Wyatt's, and Taylor's share limited to writing a preface, possible revision of the whole, and lending his name.

The Psalter, or the Psalms of David, by the Rt. Honourable Christopher Hatton (Oxford, 1644), offers greater difficulties. The title page went unchallenged until, in his *Athenae Oxoniensis*, Wood made public his opinion that the Psalter was the work of Taylor. On the title page of the eighth edition (1672) Taylor's name was substituted for

Hatton's; both were then dead. The preface deals with the causes which led the author to undertake his work, historical proofs of the value of the psalms, and a reference to previous editions of the Psalter which had been put out on a similar plan. This is followed by the psalms themselves as set in the Prayer Book, with a collect prefixed to each in which the sentiment of the succeeding psalm is gathered up.

Hatton can hardly be expected to have had the knowledge of early Church history, the lives of the Fathers, and liturgiology, which the preface claims, but of course Taylor was well acquainted with them all. On the other hand, the tone in which the writer speaks of joining the King is that of a person whose coming was of consequence, more certainly, than that of a chaplain would be. Previous to this the writer has always fortified himself against discontent abroad with his books and retirement, circumstances which a priest, whose ordinary life might be expected to lie in those pursuits, would hardly think it necessary to mention. The writer intended his book for "an instrument of public charity to Christians of different confessions", a sentiment which would fit either Taylor or Hatton, who, according to *The Liberty of Prophesying*, was thinking a good deal about Christian unity at this time.

In style the preface is flatter, and the sentences shorter, than either the Gunpowder Treason sermon or *Episcopacy Asserted*, the two publications of Taylor's which came nearest to this period, and there is a striking absence of Taylor's characteristic words. This is noteworthy, since apart from this work Taylor's style shows a continuous development. There is a touch or two here and there reminiscent of his manner, but they are few.[1] In the prayers the same stylistic evidence weighs against his authorship. They are generally shorter than the prayers found in Taylor's undoubted work; they express a steady, but not impassioned, devotion; they rarely embroider the theme, a habit which Taylor elsewhere seems unable to resist. All the evidence points to this edition of the Psalter having been the work of Hatton, but that Taylor supplied the learning and touched up the whole. A story to that effect would be enough to make Wood set Taylor down as the author.

A Discourse of Auxiliary Beauty provides a still more curious puzzle. It was issued by Royston in 1656, the author's name not being given. In 1662 it came to a second edition, this time it was said to be the work of J. T. D. D. Taylor had signed his *Discourse of Friendship* in just that way. The third edition claimed it as the work of a "late learned bishop". Wood included it in his list of Taylor's works, and White Kennet also said it was Taylor's. This is the evidence. It would not be overwhelming if the contents of the book gave it a little support, but they give it none. Both Wood and Kennet need the help of

[1] *Works*, London, 1862, Vol. 2, p. 749. Hatton's Psalter was not included in Heber's edition of Taylor.

someone stronger than the other if their evidence in a doubtful point is to be believed. Undoubtedly the initials, appearing as they did in Taylor's lifetime and going unchallenged, offer some difficulty, but they were only initials; other people in England no doubt had a right to them, their very ambiguity made it possible for an unscrupulous person to hint at Taylor's authorship in a way it would be difficult to deny. But oddly enough the publisher did his best to upset the legend which the title page was fostering, for he says that the MS. was brought to him anonymously and both the occasion and the writer of it was a woman.

The book is a dialogue between two women, one an Anglican, the other a Puritan, on the sinfulness or otherwise of painting the face. It is brightly written with some attempt at imitating Taylor's style, which was, of course, well known. There is a little theology in it, but no more than anyone in that theological age would be likely to possess. Downham's *Christian Warfare* and Perkins' *Cases of Conscience* are both mentioned, but this is not remarkable, since they were both very popular. Contents and style are both against Taylor's authorship. It would be tempting to suppose that Mrs Taylor herself wrote it if there were any real evidence to support such a piece of guesswork. It could have been done at some time just after their marriage. The initials were hers as much as her husband's, though of course she laid no claim to the D.D. unless possibly as a family joke, and in that case to put it on the title page of her book would be quite in accordance with the spirit of that little *jeu d'esprit*. It would explain better than any other hypothesis Taylor's not repudiating the book, and it is quite possible that the wife of such a well-known literary figure as Jeremy Taylor should attempt some writing and imitate her husband's style. This theory would also bear out the statement made by the publisher. However, there is no evidence on which a conclusive statement could be based.[1] Heber suggests Mrs Katherine Philips, but admits that he has no reason for doing so. Sir Edmund Gosse puts forward Christiana, Countess of Devonshire, for the honour, on the slight grounds that she was a blue-stocking and a friend of Taylor. But in that case she would be almost certain to want the glory of authorship and her name would appear without ambiguity on the title page. There remains the possibility that it was the work of some catchpenny author who deliberately tried to suggest Taylor's authorship. This is not unlikely because there is another case in which it was certainly done.

In 1684 a book called *Contemplations on the State of Man* was published and at once became very popular. In the next fifty years it went through ten editions. Prefixed to it were two short addresses to the reader.

[1] Bliss, *Sale Catalogue*, pt. 1, p. 116, describes the book as by Dr Gauden, but also says that it is often ascribed to Jeremy Taylor and sometimes to Obadiah Walker. In his note to *Ath. Ox.*, Vol. 3, col. 790, Bliss suggested that Walker was the author.

One, signed B. Hale, D.D., says nothing about the author but commends the work to the "courteous reader". The other says:

"CANDID READER,
        "The most learned and pious Jeremy Taylor, D.D. late Lord Bishop of Down and Connor, in Ireland, having left these holy Contemplations in the hands of a worthy friend of his, with a full purpose to have printed them, if he had lived; but since it hath pleased God to take that devout and holy person to himself—the better to advance devotion and sanctity of life, and to make men less in love with this frail life, and more with that which is eternal, it is thought fit to make them public.
        "I beseech God to conduct us all, by the many helps and assistances which he hath been graciously pleased to afford us, to further us in piety and holiness of life, is the prayer of
                                "Thy friend,
                                        ROBERT HARRIS."[1]

Harris it will be noticed does not say who the friend was to whom Taylor left his MS. or explain why this friend passed it on to him. Neither Harris nor Hale are the names of any known acquaintances of Taylor. Hale may possibly be Dr Bernard Hale, Archdeacon of Ely; but as he died in 1663 he could only have seen the *Contemplations* in MS. But most likely he had no connexion with the book whatever; he had been a person of importance and had been dead long enough to make it safe to use his name. What happened was this. In 1672 there appeared, without place or publisher's name, a book called *A Treatise of the difference between the Temporal and the Eternal, composed in Spanish by Eusebius Nieremberg S.J. translated into English by Sir Vivien Mullineaux. Knt, since reviewed according to* (i.e. compared with) *the tenth and last Spanish edition.* It was prefixed by an address to Catherine of Portugal, signed J. W. Someone discovered this book, reduced it to about a third of its original size by picking out sentences here and there and stringing them together. The result of this ingenious piece of book-making was published in 1684 as *Contemplations on the State of Man*, with the two addresses which have been described. It was a bold thing to do only twelve years after the subject of the piracy had itself appeared.

Juan Eusebio Nieremberg (1595–1658) was a Spanish Jesuit of German extraction. He was born, lived and died in Madrid. In spite of a reputed tinge of Molinism, his devotional works were very popular, his *Diferencia de lo Temporal y Eterno* (1640) being among the most successful of them all. It has gone through fifty-four editions in Spanish and has been translated into Latin, Arabic, Italian, French, German, and Flemish as well as English. It is quite possible that Taylor saw it

[1] *Works*, London, 1862, Vol. 1, p. 350.

in one of these editions, but if he did that is the only connexion he can possibly have had with it, since the truncated edition is beyond doubt made from Mullineaux' translation.[1]

One more important book was unwarrantably connected with Taylor. When Heber, in 1822, published his splendid edition of Taylor's writings, he included in it a work called *Christian Consolations*. He went to some trouble to do so for he had it "transcribed for the printer's use from the single copy extant in the Bodlean Library".[2] But as soon as it was published Alexander Knox saw that it could not have been written by Taylor, and gave his reasons in a letter to his lifelong correspondent, Bishop Jebb.[3] Heber supposed that the book was written at some time when Taylor was in retirement at Portmore, to comfort Lady Conway, who was somewhat subject to fits of religious depression. The author examines the five means of a Christian's comfort: faith, hope, the graces of the Holy Ghost, prayer, and the two Sacraments. Whoever the author was, his theology was Calvinistic, and he had a habit, which Taylor never had, of considering a text sufficient comfort for the most complicated state of mind. The style is far more sober and restrained than anything Taylor ever wrote, even in his least exuberant moments. But even if Pope's aphorism that "there is nothing so foolish as to be sure of knowing a great writer by his style" holds good here, the strongest argument still remains. It is the theology which offers the really conclusive evidence. While it is admitted on all sides that Taylor was inconsistent; Calvinism, especially its teaching on predestination, and its consequent attitude to minor sins, he uncompromisingly repudiated at all times in his life. The writer of this tract both accepts predestination, and holds views on the inevitability of sin which would make Taylor shudder. It has been suggested that Bishop Hacket was the author, and some passages of it proved to be identical with his sermons. Yet here again the resemblance may prove nothing more than the fact that some industrious compiler has been at work. Halkett and Laing (*Dictionary of Anonymous and Pseudonymous Literature*) continue to class this as Taylor's, but until the theology has been satisfactorily explained such an attribution is hard to accept.

A number of books of less importance than these we have just described, have also been attributed to Taylor. In no case is his authorship reasonably likely; they may therefore be briefly listed here:

1. *The Martyrdom of King Charles, or his conformity with Christ in his sufferings*. Hage, 1649. 4to. Halkett and Laing, *D.A.P.L.*, say that this is by Henry Leslie, Bishop of Down and Connor.

---

[1] The real authorship was proved by Churton in *A Letter to Joshua Watson, Esq.*, London, 1848.

[2] *Works*, Vol. 1, p. vi.

[3] *Correspondence between Bishop Jebb and A. Knox, Esq.*, ed. Forster, London, 1826, Vol. 2, p. 514.

2. *Christ or Antichrist, or the celebrated Ludolf's true and easy way to Union among christians*. London, 1658. 8vo. Authorship unknown.
3. *The Church of England Defended*. London, 1674. Fol. Authorship unknown.

      Lowndes (*Bibliographer's Manual*) mistakenly gives all three as the work of Taylor.
4. *The Ephesian and Cimmerian Matrons*. London, 1668. 8vo. By Walter Charleton, M.D. "*The Ephesian Matron* is sometimes wrongly attributed to Jeremy Taylor", Halkett and Laing, ibid.

C

JEREMY TAYLOR'S CHILDREN

Sons

William, buried at Uppingham, 28 May 1642.

A boy, unnamed. His death is mentioned on 19 July 1656, as having taken place recently.

Two boys, unnamed. Their deaths are mentioned in a letter of 22 February 1657, as having taken place recently. Taylor has now "but one son left".

A boy, unnamed. Born and died, between 9 April and 27 April 1658.

Edward, buried at Lisburn, probably an infant, 10 March 1661. In all probability he was the child whose birth was expected in August 1659.

Charles, buried at St Margaret's, Westminster, 2 August 1667. He was about twenty-four years old. Lady Wray is supposed to have stated that he took his M.A. at Dublin and was intended for the Church, but his name does not occur in the College books and there is no support for the statement in either of its parts.

Daughters

Phoebe, no marriage traceable.

Mary, married Francis Marsh, who was successively Dean of Connor, Bishop of Limerick, and Archbishop of Dublin. Evelyn met them in London on one occasion and thought Mrs Marsh a lady of unusual ability (*Diary*, 26 February 1680).

Joanna, married Edward Harrison, M.P. for Lisburn. Her daughter married Sir Cecil Wray, and is the reputed originator of some long accepted myths about Jeremy Taylor.

Lady Wray is said to have mentioned a son, Edward, who was a captain of horse in the King's service and was killed in a duel with a fellow officer named Vane, who died of his wounds. If she said so, it would seem that her imagination had been embroidering the career of Edward, who was buried, most probably as an infant, at Lisburn.

U

D

RELICS OF TAYLOR

THERE are a number of things in existence which are said to have belonged to Taylor. At Uppingham is a pulpit and patten said to have been used by him. The watch said to have been given to Taylor by Charles I was in 1909 in the possession of Colonel Jeremy Marsh, R.E., of London, a descendant of Taylor. Bonney (*Life of Jeremy Taylor*, London, 1815, p. 368) describes the watch as "Plain, and having only a single case, with a gold dial-plate, the figures of which are raised. The hands are of steel, and the maker's name is Jacobus Markwich, Londini. Originally it had no chain and went by means of catgut. Bishop Taylor caused a second case of copper to be made for it, covered with green velvet, and studded with gold. At the bottom the studs are so arranged as to represent a mitre, surrounded by this motto, '*Nescitis Horam*'." The gems taken from the King's Bible, which he is said to have given to Taylor at the same time, were in the possession of Mr J. T. Roberts of New York, who claimed to have inherited them. In a letter of 6 July 1897 (*D.N.B.*), he describes them as "Two diamonds and a ruby set in a ring, bearing the date 1649".

Dromore Cathedral has a chalice and patten presented by a member of Taylor's family, possibly his daughter, more probably his wife. It bears the inscription: "*In ministerium ss. mysteriorum in ecclesia Christi redemptoris de Dromore Deo dedit humillima ancilla D. Joanna Taylor.*" The date mark is obscure, but would seem to be 1796. Taylor's church at Ballinderry contains a Prayer Book said to have been used by him, and a pulpit from which he is supposed to have preached. A silver teapot, the property of the Diocese of Down and Connor, in the possession of the Bishop, is said to have belonged to Taylor.

One more interesting relic of Taylor remains to be discussed. It is a small box, three and five-eighths of an inch by one and five-eighths, made of dark shell handsomely spotted with white, with a silver lid and a large agate forming a boss. It is said to have contained formerly a small glass vessel for holding the species of wine, though this is now missing. It bears the inscription: "*Haec pyxis quondam erat usui Jer. Taylor. Episcopo.*" In 1898 the box was in the possession of the Rev P. E. George of Bath, who restored it to a lineal descendant of Taylor. From the existence and supposed use of this box, it was conjectured that at some time in his life Taylor was in the habit of communicating sick persons with the reserved Sacrament (*Hierurgia Anglicana*, 1903, Vol. 2, p. 164). The Communion of the sick is mentioned twice in the works of Taylor, *Holy Living* (*Works*, Vol. 3, pp. 214 ff.) and *Holy Dying* (ibid., pp. 416 ff.), but there is nothing in either of these places to suggest that the consecrated elements were carried to the sick person. Canon Christopher Wordsworth has shown that the likelihood of the box being a true pyx is not very great, though it may have been a receptacle for eucharistic bread or wafers. There is not room in it for a glass vessel, however small. The inscription, though in old lettering, is of no value, for it was composed within living memory by a clergyman named May, and executed by Mr Vokes, a Bath jeweller. Until May suggested an ecclesiastical use, the box had always been known to its possessors as Jeremy Taylor's snuff-box. See *Transactions of the St Paul's Ecclesiological Society*, Vol. 8, pt. 2; also Vernon Staley, *The Ceremonial of the English Church*, 2nd ed., 1900, p. 223.

There are original portraits of Jeremy Taylor at All Souls College, Oxford, and at Trinity College, Dublin. A copy of that at All Souls is at Gonville and Caius College, Cambridge. Many excellent contemporary engravings of him were published with early editions of his works. Bonney published, with his *Life of Taylor* in 1815, an engraving taken from an original portrait of Taylor which had been destroyed. Heber was of the opinion that this portrait had been tampered with, since the face was too young to be contemporary with the episcopal robes.

E

EXTRACT FROM THE ADMISSION BOOK OF GONVILLE AND CAIUS COLLEGE, CAMBRIDGE

Tailor *Jeremias Tailor filius Nathanaelis Tonsoris Catabrigae natus et*
postea *ibidem literis instructus in Schola publica Sub.Mro. Lovering*
Episc. D. *p' decennium anno a'tatis suae 15° admisus est in Collegium Nostrum Augusti 18° 1626 pauper scholaris Fidejussore Mro. Bachcro t. Solvit pro ingressu.*

Sic est Tho Bachcroft.

F

TAYLOR'S USE OF THE WORD "REASON"

HE ought not to assume that Taylor and his contemporaries, certainly those connected with the Cambridge Platonists, used "reason" entirely in its modern sense of a narrow ratiocinative faculty only. Taylor is never quite so careful about terms as he should be, but by comparison of some of the outstanding passages in his works where the word "reason" occurs, it is possible to arrive at some idea of what he wished it to convey: "It is not guided by natural arguments only but by revelation and all other good means."[1] "It is a transcendent that runs through all topics."[2] "When revelation, and philosophy, and public experience, and all other grounds of

[1] *Works*, Vol. 5, p. 495.   [2] *Ibid.*, p. 498.

probability or demonstration have supplied us with matter then reason does but make use of them."[1] It can be prejudiced by birth and education, etc.[2] It may err and be inculpable.[3] It is clear that he means by this something more than an intellectual faculty only. He seems to mean by "reason", the exercise in judgement of all a man's powers, both spiritual and mental. Perhaps Bishop Butler's phrase "A superior principle of reflection, or conscience",[4] would best describe it.

G

THE BOOKS TAYLOR RECOMMENDED TO HIS CLERGY

THE books which Taylor recommended to his clergy for their study are of interest, as they show what were expected to be the main preoccupations of the minister in the seventeenth century. They also emphasize how international his outlook was; Latin made the works of all ages and countries accessible to him, without either the labour of learning languages or reliance on the inadequate medium of translation:

"There are many who have by great skill, and great experience, taught us many good rules for the interpretation of scripture; amongst which those that I shall principally recommend to you, are the books of St. Austin, *De Utilitate Credendi*, and his iii. *lib. de doctrina christiana*; the *Synopsis* of Athanasius, *The Prooems* of Isidore, *The Prologues* of St. Hierome; I might well add the *scholia* of Oecumenius, the *catenae* of the Greek fathers; and of later times the ordinary and interlineary glosses; the excellent book of Hugo de S. Victoire, *De eruditione didascalica*; *Ars interpretandi scripturas*, by Sixtus Senensis; Serarius his *prolegomena*; Tena his *Introduction to the Scriptures*; together with Laurentius e Villa-Vincentio, Andreas Hyperius *De ratione studii philosophici*, and the *Hypotyposes* of Martinus Cantapratensis; Arias Montanus his *Joseph*, or *De arcano sermone*, is of another nature, and more fit for preachers, and so is Sanctes Pagiune his *Isagoge*; but Ambrosius Catharinus his book *Duarum clavium ad sacram scripturam*, is useful to many good purposes: but more particularly, and I think more usefully, are those seven rules for interpreting scriptures written by Ticonius, and first made famous by St. Austin's commendation of them, and inserted into the fifth tome of the *Biblioth ss. pp.* Sebastian Perez wrote thirty-five rules for the interpretation of scripture: Francis Ruiz drew from the ancient fathers two hundred and thirty-four rules: besides those many learned persons who have writ Vocabularies, Tropologies, and expositions of words and phrases; such as are Flacius Illyricus,

---

[1] *Works*, Vol. 5, p. 495.   [2] Ibid., p. 503.   [3] Ibid., p. 499.
[4] *Butler's Works*, Oxford, 1874, Vol. 2, p. 23.

Junius, Hierome Lauretus, and many others, not infrequent in all public libraries."[1]

It will be seen that the priest's main attentions are to be directed toward Bible study and preaching. St Augustine's *De Doctrina*, for instance, is occupied with both these subjects. Isidore of Seville's *Prooemia in Libros Vet. et Nov. Test* were brief introductions to the books of the Old and New Testaments and some parts of the Apocrypha. Oecumenius, Bishop of Trikkala in Thessaly about A.D. 990 was the reputed author of commentaries on the Apocalypse, Acts, Catholic and Pauline Epistles. Hugh of St Victor's *Eruditionis Didascaliae* was a compendium of general knowledge which included an introduction to the Bible. The Dominican Sixtus of Siena published at Venice in 1566 a book called *Bibliotheca sancta ex praecipuis Catholicae Ecclesiae auctoribus collecta*, which deals with Bible study as a whole, and gives a valuable list of authorities on the Bible. The *Proloquia* of Serarius (Antwerp, 1625) Migne rated so highly that he used it as the introduction to his *Sacrae Scripturae Cursus Completus*. Laurentius e Villa Vincentio published in 1565 his work, *De Formandis Sacris Concionibus*, a book dealing with sacred oratory. Arias Montanus (1527–1598) was one of the most outstanding scholars and theologians of his time. He was an Orientalist, an Exegetist, and gained considerable distinction at the Council of Trent. He published at Antwerp in 1572 a polyglot Bible to which his *Prolegomena* was a most valuable introduction.

If Taylor's clergy were capable of reading and making use of books such as these, the standard in Northern Ireland must at least have been as good as the average in England.

H

ARCHBISHOP BRAMHALL AND THE PRESBYTERIANS

BRAMHALL'S dealings with the Presbyterians in his diocese have often been compared favourably with those of Jeremy Taylor. As the following extract shows the circumstances were not the same. Bramhall had to deal with men who were willing to meet him and listen to suggestions of compromise, Taylor with total irreconcilables.

"When the benefices were called over at the visitation, several appeared, and exhibited only such titles as they had received from the late powers. He (Bramhall) told them, 'they were no legal titles, but in regard he heard well of them, he was willing to make such to them by institution and induction'; which they thankfully accepted of,—But when he desired to see their letters of orders, some had no other but their certificates of ordination by some

[1] *Works*, Vol. 8, p. 520.

Presbyterian classes, which, he told them, did not qualify them for any preferment in the Church. Upon this, the question arose. 'Are we not ministers of the Gospel?' To which his Grace answered, 'that was not the question'; at least, he desired for peace sake, that might not be the question for that time. 'I dispute not' he said, 'the value of your ordination, nor those acts you have exercised by virtue of it; what you are, or might be, here when there was no law, or in other Churches abroad. But we are now to consider ourselves as a national Church limited by law, which among other things takes chief care to prescribe about ordination; and I do not know how you could receive the means of the Church, if any should refuse to pay you your tithes, if you are not ordained as the law of this Church requireth; and I am desirous that she may have your labours, and you such portions of her revenue as shall be allotted to you, in a legal and assured way'. By this means he gained such as were learned and sober."[1]

I

SELECT BIBLIOGRAPHY

Books to which only one or two references have been made are not included here, but will be found fully described in the notes on the passages where they occur.

ADAIR, PATRICK. *True Narrative of the rise and progress of the Presbyterian Church in Ireland*. Ed. Killen. Belfast, 1866.

ANDREWES, BISHOP LANCELOT. *Works*. 11 vols. Oxford. (L.A.C.T.)

AUBREY, JOHN. *Brief Lives chiefly of Contemporaries*. Ed. Clark. 2 vols. Oxford, 1898.

BAGWELL, RICHARD. *Ireland under the Stuarts*. 3 vols. London, 1909–16.

Baker MSS. c. 2. 24, fol. 109. Cambridge University Library.

Baxter, Richard, Autobiography of. Ed. Lloyd Thomas. London.

BONNEY, H. K. *The Life of Jeremy Taylor*. London, 1815.

BRAMHALL, ARCHBISHOP JOHN. *Works*. 5 vols. Oxford. (L.A.C.T.)

BROWN, W. J. *Jeremy Taylor*. London, 1925.

BRYANT, A. *The England of Charles the Second*. London, 1934.

BUCHAN, JOHN. *Oliver Cromwell*. London, 1934.

BUNYAN, JOHN. *Grace Abounding to the Chief of Sinners*. London, 1891.

BURNETT, BISHOP GILBERT. *History of His own Times*. 3 vols. London, 1753.

BURTON, ROBERT. *The Anatomy of Melancholy*. 3 vols. London, 1932.

Calendar of State Papers Relating to Ireland (1603–1670). 13 vols.

Cambridge Bibliography of English Literature, vol. 2. C.U.P., 1940.

Cambridge History of English Literature, Vols. 3–7. Cambridge, 1932.

---

[1] "Athanasius Hibernicus, or The Life of John, Lord Archbishop of Armagh" (prefixed to his *Works*, ed. 1677) by John (Vesey), Bishop of Limerick, p. 35.

Cambridge Modern History, Vols. 2–3. Cambridge, 1935.

CARMODY, W. F. *Lisburn Cathedral and Its Past Rectors*. Belfast, 1926.

CARTE, THOMAS. *An History of James, Duke of Ormonde*. 3 vols. Fol. London, 1753.

CASTELLIO, SEBASTIAN. *Concerning Heretics*. An anonymous work attributed to Sebastian Castellio. Now first done into English, together with excerpts from other works, of Sebastian Castellio and David Joris on religious liberty. By Roland Bainton. London, 1936.

Carte MSS. Bodleian Library, Oxford.

CHILLINGWORTH, WILLIAM. *The Religion of Protestants a Safe Way to Salvation*. 2 vols. London, 1839.

CHURTON, EDWARD. *A Letter to Joshua Watson, Esqr., D.C.L., giving an account of a singular literary fraud practised on the memory of Bishop Jeremy Taylor*. London, 1848.

CLARENDON, EDWARD, EARL OF. *History of the Rebellion and Civil Wars in England*. 8 vols. Oxford, 1816–17.

COLERIDGE, S. T. *Notes on the Anglican Divines*. Ed. Derwent Coleridge. 2 vols. London, 1853.

—— *Aids to Reflection*. London, 1890.

—— *Table Talk and Omniana*. London, 1888.

—— *Miscellanies*. London, 1892.

Confirmation. 2 vols. S.P.C.K., London, 1934.

Conway Letters. Ed. Marjorie Hope Nicholson. Oxford, 1930.

COOPER, C. H. *Annals of Cambridge*. 4 vols. Cambridge, 1842.

COTTON, H. *Fasti Ecclesiae Hibernicae*. London, 1845–78.

CROSS, F. L. *The Oxford Movement and the Seventeenth Century*. London, 1933.

DE QUINCEY, THOMAS. "Essay on Rhetoric", *Collected Works*. Vol. 10. Ed. Masson. London, 1897. See also Vol. 13, p. 427, note, for an interesting comment on Taylor's style.

Dictionary of National Biography.

DIXON. *Trinity College, Dublin*. London, 1902.

DONNE, JOHN. *Sermons, Selected Passages*. Ed. Pearsall Smith. Oxford, 1919.

DOWDEN, E. *Puritan and Anglican*. London, 1900.

DOYLE, PHILLIS. "Church and State. The *Jure Divino* Theory of Episcopacy in the English Church", *Church Quarterly Review*, January 1930.

DUYCHINCK, G. L. *Life of Bishop Jeremy Taylor*. New York, 1860.

ELRINGTON, C. R. *Archbishop Ussher's Complete Works with Life*. 17 vols. Dublin, 1847–64. The first fourteen volumes only are edited by Elrington, the remainder by J. H. Todd.

Encyclopedia, The Catholic. Ed. Herbermann. 15 vols. New York, 1913.

Encyclopedia of Religion and Ethics. Ed. Hastings. 13 vols. Edinburgh, 1908.

Evelyn, John, Diary of. Ed. W. Bray. New Edition with Life of the Author and Preface, by H. B. Wheatley. 3 vols. London, 1906.

EWART. *Handbook to the Diocese of Down.* Belfast, 1886.

FRERE, BISHOP W. H. *History of the English Church in the Reigns of Elizabeth and James I.* London, 1924.

FULLER, THOMAS. *The Church History of Britain.* 3 vols. London, 1868.

GARDINER, S. R. *History of England, 1603–1642.* 10 vols. London, 1883–4.

—— *History of the Great Civil War.* 4 vols. London, 1893.

—— *History of the Commonwealth and Protectorate.* 4 vols. London, 1903.

—— "A Note on the Authorship of Liberty of Conscience, or The Sole Means to obtain Peace and Truth", *English Historical Review,* Vol. 1, p. 144.

—— "The Clergy's Paper tendered concerning Religion", ibid., Vol. 2, p. 341.

—— "The Transplantation to Connaught", ibid., Vol. 14, p. 700.

GEE and HARDY. *Documents Illustrative of English Church History.* London, 1921.

Gentleman's Magazine, 1783, p. 144; 1790, p. 301; 1791, pp. 515, 720; 1792, p. 109; 1855, p. 376. This last, "A Caius Man's comments on Eden's edition of Heber's Taylor", is the most useful of these contributions.

GLANVIL, JOSEPH. *Sadducismus Triumphatus.* 2nd Edit. Ed. More. London, 1682.

GOOCH, G. P. *English Democratic Ideas in the Seventeenth Century.* London, 1898.

GOSSE, SIR EDMUND. *Jeremy Taylor.* London, 1903.

GRANGER, J. *Biographical History of England,* Vol. 3, p. 254. 4 vols. London, 1779.

HALKETT and LAING. *Dictionary of Anonymous and Pseudonymous Literature.* 6 vols. London, 1932.

HALLAM, HENRY. *Constitutional History of England.* 3 vols. London, 1930.

—— *Introduction to the Literature of Europe in the fifteenth, sixteenth and seventeenth Centuries.* 2 vols. London, 1837–9.

HAMPER, WILLIAM. *Life, Diary and Correspondence of Sir W. Dugdale.* London, 1827.

Harleian Miscellany, The. 10 vols. London, 1808–13.

HARRISON, WILLIAM. *Elizabethan England.* Ed. Furnivall. New edition by L. W. Walter Scott Publishing Company, London. No date. This is Books 2 and 3 with a small portion of Book 1 of *The Description of Britaine* from Hollinshed, with Furnivall's and L. W.'s notes.

HEBER, BISHOP REGINALD. *The Whole Works of the Right Reverend Jeremy Taylor, D.D., with a Life of the Author.* Revised and corrected by the Rev. Charles Eden. 10 vols. London, 1847–52.

HERBERT, GEORGE. *Works.* 2 vols. London, 1859.

HEYLYN, PETER. *Aerius Redivivus, or The History of the Presbyterians.* Oxford, 1670.

HOOKER, RICHARD. *Of the Laws of Ecclesiastical Polity.* 2 vols. London, 1907.

HUGHES, T. S. *Selections from Taylor's Works. With Life.* London, 1831.

HUNT, J. *Religious Thought in England from the Reformation to the End of the Last Century,* Vol. 1. 3 vols. London, 1873.

HUTCHINSON. *Memoirs of the Life of Colonel Huchinson.* London, 1848.

HUTTON, W. H. *A History of the Church of England from the Accession of Charles I to the Death of Anne.* London, 1903.

—— *A Life of Laud.* London, 1895.

JULIAN. *Dictionary of Hymnology,* p. 1,118. London, 1907.

KENNET, BISHOP WHITE. *A Register and Chronical Ecclesiastical and Civil. From the Restoration of King Charles II.* Fol. London, 1727.

KIRK, BISHOP K. E. *Some Principles of Moral Theology.* London, 1921.

—— *Conscience and Its Problems.* London, 1927.

LAUD, ARCHBISHOP WILLIAM. *Works,* 7 vols. in 9. Oxford. (L.A.C.T.)

LEWIS, GEORGE. *Robert Sanderson.* London, 1924.

LLOYD. *Memoirs of the Lives, Actions, Sufferings and Deaths of those that suffered for the Protestant Religion in our late Intestine Wars.* Fol. London, 1668.

LOWNDES. *The Bibliographer's Manual.* Ed. Bohn. 5 vols. and an appendix. 11 parts. London, 1857–66.

McADOO, H. R. *The Structure of Caroline Moral Theology.* London, 1949.

MAITLAND, F. W. *The Constitutional History of England.* Cambridge, 1920.

MANT, RICHARD. *A History of the Church of Ireland.* 2 vols. London, 1839–41.

MASON, A. J. *The Church of England and Episcopacy.* Cambridge, 1914.

MASSON, D. Life of Milton. 6 vols. Cambridge, 1881.

MATHEWS, LEMUEL. *A Pandarique [sic] Elegie upon the death of the R.R. Father in God, Jeremy, late Lord Bishop of Doune Connor and Dromore.* By Le Mathews, A.M. a sacr. domest. Dublin, 1667.

MAXWELL, CONSTANTIA. *A History of Trinity College, Dublin.* Dublin, 1946.

MAY, E. H. *A Dissertation on the Life, Theology and Times of Dr. Jeremy Taylor.* London, 1892.

Milton, John, Prose Works of. With an Introductory Review by Robert Fletcher. London, 1836.

MITCHELL, W. F. *English Pulpit Oratory from Andrews to Tillotson.* London, 1932.

MORE and CROSS. *Anglicanism.* London, 1935.

MULLINGER, J. B. *A History of the University of Cambridge.* London, 1888.

NEAL, DANIEL. *A History of the Puritans.* 5 vols. London, 1822.

OLLARD and CROSSE, Eds. *A Dictionary of English Church History.* Oxford, 1912.

PATTISON, MARK. *Isaac Casaubon.* Oxford, 1892.

PHILLIPS, J. R. *Memoirs of the Civil War in Wales and the Marches.* 2 vols. London, 1874.

PHILLIPS, W. A., Ed. *A History of the Church of Ireland.* 3 vols. Oxford, 1934.

PORTER, CLASSON. *Ulster Biographical Sketches.* Second Series. Belfast, 1884.

RANKE, LEOPOLD VON. *A History of England Principally in the Seventeenth Century.* 6 vols. Oxford, 1875.

Rawdon Papers. Ed. Berwick. London, 1819.

REID, J. S. *A History of the Presbyterian Church in Ireland.* Ed. Killen. 3 vols. Belfast, 1867.

Review, Quarterly. Vol. 131, July–October 1871. Article on Jeremy Taylor.

RUST, BISHOP GEORGE. "A Funeral Sermon Preached at the Obsequies of the Right Reverend Father in God, Jeremy, Lord Bishop of Down." Printed in Heber's edition of Taylor's *Works,* Vol. 1, p. cccxi.

SANDERSON, ROBERT. *Lectures on Conscience and Human Law.* Ed. Ch. Wordsworth. London, 1877.

SCOTT. "Bishop Jeremy Taylor at his Visitation", *Irish Church News.* September 1894.

SELDEN, JOHN. "Table Talk." Published in *Table Talk from Ben Jonson to Leigh Hunt.* London, 1934.

SHAW, W. A. *History of the English Church during the Civil Wars and the Commonwealth.* London, 1900.

SLATER, T. A. *Manual of Moral Theology.* 2 vols. London, 1925.

Sloan MSS. British Museum.

SMITH, PEARSALL. *The Golden Grove. Selections from Jeremy Taylor.* With introduction. Oxford, 1930.

STONE, DARWELL. *A History of the Doctrine of the Holy Eucharist.* 2 vols. London, 1909.

SWANZY, H. B. *Biographical Succession Lists of Dromore Diocese.* Belfast, 1933.

Tanner MSS. Bodleian Library, Oxford.

TAYLOR, JEREMY. Manuscript Letters of, in the possession of Sir John Murray.

Tracts on Liberty of Conscience, 1614–1661. Ed. Underhill. London, 1864.

TREVELYAN, G. M. *England under the Stuarts.* London, 1930.

TULLOCH, JOHN. *Rational Theology and Christian Philosophy in England in the Seventeenth Century.* 2 vols. Edinburgh, 1872.

Ulster Journal of Archaeology. October 1896, pp. 13 ff.; January 1897, p. 105; July 1897, p. 277.

VENN, JOHN and J. A. *Alumni Cantabrigienses, Part 1, covering the period up to 1751.* Cambridge, 1922–7.

VINCENT, EDGAR. "Some Aspects of the English Reformation, 1550–1660", *Church Quarterly Review*, October 1929.

WAKEMAN, H. O. *The Church and the Puritans, 1570–1660.* London, 1897.

WALKER, JOHN. *An Attempt towards Recovering an Account of the Numbers and Sufferings of the Clergy of the Church of Enggland in the late Grand Rebellion.* Fol. London, 1714.

WARE, SIR JAMES. *Works.* Ed. Harris. Vol. 1, *Irish Bishops.* 3 vols. in 2. Fol. Dublin, 1739–46.

WATSON, FOSTER. *The English Grammar Schools to 1660.* Cambridge, 1908.

WHEELDON, J. *The Life of Bishop Taylor, and the Pure Spirit of his Writings, Extracted and Exhibited for General Benefit.* London, 1793.

WHITE, NEWPORT J. D. *Four Good Men.* Dublin, 1927.

WHITING, C. E. *Studies in English Puritanism from the Restoration to the Revolution, 1660–1688.* London, 1931.

WILLIAMS, ETHYN MORGAN. "Erastianism in the Great Rebellion", *Church Quarterly Review*, April, 1930.

WILLMOTT, ROBERT ARIS. *Bishop Jeremy Taylor, His Predecessors, Contemporaries, and Successors.* London, 1864.

WOOD, ANTHONY. *Athenae Oxoniensis.* With additions by Philip Bliss. 4 vols. London, 1813–20.

WORDSWORTH, CHRISTOPHER, Ed. *Ecclesiastical Biography.* 6 vols. London, 1810.

WORSLEY, E. *Truth Will Out or a Discovery of some Untruths smoothly told by Dr. Jeremy Taylor in his Dissuasive from Popery.* Liege, 1665.

INDEX